An Introduction to Early Childhood Education: An Interactive Text
Debra Dyer

D1616752

Table of Contents

Chapter 1
An Introduction to Early Childhood Education and Care

What is Early Childhood Education?

Thinking Ahead

1. What is early childhood education?
2. What role do teachers play in children's lives? In the lives of families?
3. What is a philosophy of education and how can you use it in your professional practice?
4. What are the standards of professional development which underpin most early childhood educational programs?

"Early Childhood Education"

Teaching and working with young children is a challenging, fulfilling, and exhausting profession. It requires physical stamina, energy, patience and specific knowledge and skill sets. Yet it is one of the most rewarding life pathways adults may choose - the reward of witnessing an infant's first giggle, a toddler's first step, and a Kindergartner's first "written" story.

This is an exciting time to be teaching children from birth to age eight. Early childhood education has been enjoying an era of transformation in the past few decades. This extraordinary reform in early childhood has been influenced by: 1) an increased knowledge of child development and learning, 2) research-based, intentional curricula that provides learning opportunities for even the infant, 3) the increasing prevalence of preschool programs, and 4) research that corroborates the notion that high-quality early childhood education has a positive and lifelong effect on children (Morrison, 2012).

Early childhood education also benefits from increased public recognition and the funding that flowed from the growing respect for the field. In 2009, despite a serious economic recession, the American Recovery and Reinvestment Act set aside billions of dollars for early childhood education. This public recognition that early childhood education gives all children an advantage, but especially at risk children, was validated in a 2008 poll which found that 7 in 10 voters  wanted state and local governments to provide prekindergarten for all American children (Wilson, 2008). Groups such as the respected Committee for Economic Development, deems early childhood education as a necessary investment in the future of the United States (Galinsky, 2006). Research suggests expanding early learning initiatives would provide benefits to society of roughly $8.60 for every $1 spent (U.S. Department of Education, 2016).

However, the history of early childhood education funding follows a bumpy road. The drastic budgetary cuts as a result of the 2013 federal government budget sequestration ($85 billion in overall federal funds and $403 million to the Head Start program) were problematic because we know that early childhood education is a sound long-term investment that pays for itself and prepares our nation's future workforce for success. In Head Start alone, 57,000 children were cut from the program in 2013 (Office of Head Start, 2014). Sequestration's impact on Head Start directly harmed economic recovery by eliminating jobs and services to children and families that help them move into the middle class.

In December 2014, President Obama convened state and local policymakers, mayors, school superintendents, corporate and community leaders, and advocates for the White House Summit on Early Education, highlighting collective leadership in support of early education for America's children. These leaders shared best practices in building the public-private partnerships that would expand early education in communities across the country. Participants discussed effective strategies and programs that support and elevate high-quality early childhood education.

This Summit resulted in a 1 billion dollar commitment to early childhood education:

1. Over $330 million in new actions from corporate and philanthropic leaders to expand the reach and enhance the quality of early education for thousands of additional children.

2. Up to $750 million in new federal grant awards announced by Secretaries Duncan and Burwell, to support early learning for over 63,000 additional children across the country. These investments will expand high-quality preschool or grow the supply of early care and education for infants and toddlers beginning in 2015.

3. The launch of **Invest in US**, a new initiative created by the First Five Years Fund, a bipartisan non-profit organization, in partnership with private philanthropic leaders, in response to the President's call for action.

4. New private and philanthropic resources and support for *Early Learning Communities*, an initiative of *Invest in US*. *Invest in US* will connect communities and states interested in expanding early learning programs and opportunities with 10 leading partners that have committed to helping connect leaders with resources, planning grants, technical assistance, and other support for their youngest learners (White House Press Secretary, 2014).

Additionally, President Obama's 2017 budget request expands access to high-quality early learning while investing in innovation and evaluation to promote the implementation of evidence-based practices for our youngest learners and improve educational outcomes in the early grades. The budget:

1. **Supports voluntary, universal preschool.**
   The mandatory Preschool for All initiative would invest $75 billion over 10 years in a federal-state partnership aimed at providing all 4-year-olds from low- and moderate-income families with access to high-quality preschool, while encouraging states to expand those programs to reach additional children from middle-class families and establish full-day kindergarten policies.

2. **Builds on the success of the Preschool Development Grants program to help jumpstart Preschool for All.**
   Consistent with the requirements of the *Every Student Succeeds Act*, the budget provides $350 million for Preschool Development Grants in the Department of Health and Human Services intended to better coordinate and expand early learning services for children and families.

3. **Supports special education services to children ages 3 through 5.**
   The request provides an increase of $35 million over the fiscal year 2016 level for the *Individuals with Disabilities Education Act* (*IDEA*) Part B, Section 619 Preschool Grants, as well as additional flexibility for schools and districts to provide coordinated early intervention services for preschool-age children

4. **Provides additional funds for early intervention services for infants and toddlers.**
   The request for *IDEA* Part C Grants for Infants and Families is an increase of $45 million over the 2016 level and would allow the Department to reserve $15 million to make new competitive grants to public-private partnerships to support community-based model demonstration projects that increase screening and delivery of evidence-based services. (U.S. Department of Education, 2016)

These dramatic changes in the early childhood field are reforming the professional role and responsibilities of early childhood educators. As early childhood educators we take on many roles in the course of a day: teacher, researcher, playmate, caregiver, advocate and family liaison. No matter what role one assumes, the high-quality professional must possess the knowledge, skills, dispositions necessary to teach, design and implement programs, and inform families and communities about early childhood issues. Early childhood **professionals** must possess the disposition of reflectiveness on their teaching and collaborations and continually improve and broaden their skills and knowledge. High-quality educators also endorse high standards for themselves and their students.

Developing the abilities to successfully and intentionally teach young children requires that early childhood educators be thoroughly and sensitively prepared. They need to be knowledgeable about child growth and development, program planning and implementation, and effective interaction and communication with children and parents. Developing a sensitive understanding of diversity to respect and honor all members of a group is vitally important. In any setting, relationship-building is at the core of education. It becomes even more important in early childhood education as teachers and families unite to create common goals for children. To be successful requires that an early childhood educator possesses a strong foundation of knowledge and skills, as well as dedication, commitment and reflectiveness.

The opportunity to make a difference in the exciting field of early childhood education has never been greater or better supported. The National Association for the Education of Young Children (NAEYC) is widely regarded as best representing the present and future in the field of early childhood education. Headquartered in Washington, D.C. and founded in 1926, NAEYC is the world's largest and most widely recognized professional organization of early childhood educators. Its major objective is to serve as a voice and advocate for the needs, rights, and welfare of young children from birth through age 8.

"Week of the Young Child, Invest in the Early Years"

To achieve its stated mission "to serve and act on behalf of the needs, rights and well-being of all young children with primary focus on the provision of educational and developmental services and resources (NAEYC Bylaws, Article I., Section 1.1)" NAEYC has established standards for teacher preparation at the associate, baccalaureate, and graduate-degree levels (NAEYC, 2009). NAEYC (2005) also directs an accreditation system for high-quality children's programs and offers resources – conferences, peer-reviewed journals and position papers – to support continuous professional development for educators.

Utilizing NAEYC's definition of early childhood as being birth through age eight, we will use the following age groupings:

1. *Infants and toddlers:* birth to 36 months
2. *Preschoolers:* 3- and 4-year olds
3. *Kindergartners:* 5- and 6-year olds
4. *Primary grades 1, 2 and 3:* 6-, 7-, and 8-year olds

The early childhood field is comprised of child care centers and home-based care, preschools, kindergartens, and primary grade schools. Young children are continuously learning; at the same time they require love and care. Families expect programs to provide education and enrichment experiences beyond basic caregiving (Smith, 2000). Consequently, it is important to *not* differentiate between child care and early education, but instead, guarantee children's access to programs that are both caring and educational.

Research confirms that high-quality programs providing education and care promote children's cognitive development (including language and emergent literacy), foster children's social skills (interactions with other children and self-regulation), and encourage holistic growth across all developmental domains (Burchinal, 1999). All children benefit from quality education and care, yet children from families with low incomes suffer most from poor quality care while having the most to gain from higher quality care (Carnegie Task Force, 1994). Sadly ironic, young children who live in poverty are less likely to attend preschool than children from middle- and high-income families (Bredekamp, 2011).

Why the Investment in Quality Early Childhood Education Pays Off

James Heckman, the Henry Schultz Distinguished Service Professor of Economics at the University of Chicago, a Nobel Laureate in Economics, and an expert in the economics of human development has developed what he has termed as the "Heckman Equation". After a lifetime of research into the benefits of quality early childhood education, Heckman's equation estimates a $7 return on every $1 of investment in early childhood care and education (heckmanequation.org). His calculation is based on the following factors:

- Investment in early childhood development directly influences economics, health and social outcomes for individuals and society.

- Quality early childhood education from birth to age 5, when brain development is at its most rapid rate, fosters cognitive skills in addition to attentiveness, motivation, self-control and sociability.

- At-risk children from disadvantaged environments are less likely to get effective early childhood supports, but are in need of them most.

- Poor health, dropout rates, special education rates, poverty and crime can be addressed and substantially reduced by investment in quality early childhood education and societal supports.

How can this investment in quality early childhood education be best facilitated? Heckman's suggestions include:

- Invest in early childhood education as a long-term, cost-effective budgetary strategy even in tight economic times.

- Prioritize investment in quality early childhood education for at-risk children.

- Develop cognitive and character skills early by investing in the "whole child".

- Provide developmental resources to children and their families.

- Invest, develop and sustain to produce the gains children make in quality early childhood settings (heckmanequation.org).

We now turn our attention to the various types of early childhood settings servicing children from birth to age eight.

Child Care

The term *child care* has traditionally referred to the education and care delivered to young children in various settings outside their homes less than 24 hours a day. Child care is typically provided in either *child care centers* or *family child care homes.* Child care centers usually include children from infancy through pre-school-age and may offer before- and after- school "wrap around" care for children in half-day programs and primary grade children.

The family child care home caregiver provides in-home care for a small group of various aged children. Both types of settings operate under state-mandated group size and adult-to-child ratio regulations. Funding is from parent tuition or public subsidies for children in low-income families.

Preschool

"How Important is Preschool?"

Preschool programs typically operate to care for and educate 3- and 4-year old children. These programs may be supported by community organizations, faith-based organizations such as churches and temples, and by universities and colleges in the form of onsite care and/or laboratory schools. Funding for preschool programs is derived primarily from public funds and parent tuition. Public prekindergarten and Head Start are two noteworthy types of preschool intended for children in low-income families.

"Why Preschool is So Important"

Public Prekindergarten

Prekindergarten (Pre-K) refers to state- and locally-funded preschools serving primarily children from low-income families and children deemed "at-risk" due to factors such as the home language being one other than English. The principal purpose of

prekindergarten is to prepare children for kindergarten entrance. Its intent is to give children "a leg up" on formal education, and to equalize the learning opportunities between the children in these programs and children from middle- and upper-class homes.

"What Does 'High Quality' Preschool Look Like?"

Head Start

Head Start is a federally funded program which was initiated by the U.S. government in 1965. Head Start was conceived for disadvantaged children as part of President Lyndon Johnson's War on Poverty. The intent was to give children a "head start" on later school performance. Proponents of Head Start argued that an earlier start in formal education would decrease both the numbers of later school dropouts and the numbers of children identified for special education. Head Start serves not only the educational needs of 3- and 4-year old children, but additionally provides access to health screenings, referrals and follow-up, parenting resources, and social services. Head Start has flourished to include services for infants and toddlers (Early Head Start) and their families. The program served 943,534 children in 2014, reaching only slightly more than half of the eligible preschool children (Children's Defense Fund, 2014).

"Hanging in the Balance: A Head Start for Low-Income Kids"

Quality is critical in Head Start, principally because it serves the most vulnerable children in our country. The national Head Start Program Performance Standards (Head Start, 1998) provide the monitoring system to ensure compliance. Due to its broad reach, the Head Start Program Performance Standards address a comprehensive list of services such as: child development, health and safety, specific special education disability categories, and nutrition standards.

Research shows that Head Start has a positive effect on children's overall development, health care, and preparation for school, including improved literacy skills and social-emotional development (Barnett, 2008). Although the goal of closing the achievement gap between poor and middle-class students has not yet been achieved, Head Start has had a great influence on narrowing the gap (Zill, Sorongon, Kim, Clark, & Woolverton, 2006).

Early Intervention and Early Childhood Special Education

Early intervention refers to services for children ages birth to three with, or at risk for, developmental delays or disabilities. Eligibility is determined on a state-to-state basis. The services – including speech therapy, occupational therapy, and physical therapy - are provided under Part C of IDEA (Individuals with Disabilities Education Act). The expectation for these services is that by addressing developmental delays early in a child's life, the child may not need services later on.

Early Childhood Special Education provides services organized and delivered to children age 3 through 8 with disabilities and special needs. With increased likelihood, these services will be delivered in a typical early childhood program (Division for Early Childhood & NAEYC, 2009). The Division for Early Childhood of the Council for Exceptional Children and NAEYC (2009) developed a joint statement defining early childhood inclusion:

> Early childhood inclusion embodies the values, policies, and practices that support the right of every infant and young child and his or her family, regardless of ability, to participate in a broad range of activities and contexts as full members of families, communities, and society. The desired results of inclusive experiences for children with and without disabilities and their families include a sense of belonging and membership, positive social relationships and friendships, and development and learning to reach their full potential.

High-quality, full inclusive programs include the facets of access, participation and supports. Access provides children with a continuum of learning opportunities, activities, and environments. Participation is the engagement of all children and supports are the educational and legal framework of inclusion.

"Early Childhood Special Education for Future Teachers"

Kindergarten and Primary Grades

In the United States, Kindergarten is designed for five- and six-year old children as the preparatory year before first grade. Entrance age for kindergarten differs from state to state. For example, New York State allows children who are five on or before December 1, to enter public kindergarten, while Florida accepts children who are 5 on or before September 1. The national trend is toward an older admission age, with many parents and professionals supporting an older rather than a younger kindergarten age.

The primary grades include first, second and third grades (6 through 8 years of age). The curriculum brings a heavier emphasis on specific content areas such as literacy, math, science, and social studies. Many of these areas are integrated within the basic curriculum and organized around literacy-building skills. Primary grade children are learning to read so that in later grades they can read to learn.

"Daily Routines in Kindergarten Classes"

Why Become an Early Childhood Educator?

Teaching young children is a truly rewarding experience, with everyday being uniquely challenging and gratifying. However, when one chooses to teach young children, one must weigh all the factors in this career decision. Future educators need to become familiar with what the work necessitates, possible career options, and whether their career choice is a good match with their own strengths, dispositions and personal goals (Colker, 2008). It is also important that the prospective

educator understand the development of young children, help young children connect with the changing world of their families, and promote developmentally appropriate practice in curriculum and environments. Becoming a reflective practitioner is of prime importance in the evolution of an early childhood educator. The effective early childhood educator brings to the profession specific attitudes, attributes, and abilities and assumes many complex and interrelated roles.

"Occupational Video – Early Childhood Educator"

"Early Childhood Teaching"

Role of the Teacher

The early childhood professional needs to have a clear understanding of the attributes, attitudes, and abilities of effectiveness in their chosen profession. Educators need to understand the numerous facets of their complex and interconnected roles. Additionally, educators need to develop evaluation and judgment skills, and make efficacious decisions in classroom situations.

Teacher as Instructional Leader

The role of the teacher in instruction has never been as prominent and vital as it currently is. An instructional leader plans, guides, teaches and assesses learning. Formalized learning standards which are federally and state mandated provide the framework for curriculum and assessment. Assuming the instructional leader role compels the early childhood professional to be intentional in the planning-teaching-assessment cycle. Being intentional means being purposeful and clear about what to teach, teaching so that children learn and obtain specific knowledge and skills, and pointedly assessing the meeting of the learning objectives. The instructional leader engages children in interesting learning activities and spends copious amounts of time in planning the learning.

In the changing landscape of early childhood education, inclusive classrooms are becoming more prevalent. The fields of early childhood general education and early childhood special education meld together, creating the need for educators who have the skills and knowledge necessary to teach all children. The instructional leader builds collaborative relationships to support the learning of inclusive populations of children.

Teacher as Nurturer

Early childhood educators are encouraged to nurture children with touch and physical affection (Allen, 1986). Hugging, holding, and genuinely encouraging a child are all necessary for children's psychological and cognitive growth. Teachers who exchange handshakes, hugs, and affectionate touch model safe touch. This provides the opportunity for children to learn and utilize appropriate, safe touch and helps them to discern it from inappropriate and unsafe touch.

Building strong attachments is another way to facilitate nurturance. Bowlby's (1982) concept of attachment in early development includes both an exploratory system and an attachment system. The exploratory system propels the child's goal of learning about the world. The attachment system impels the child to stay close to an adult so that the child feels a sense of safety and security. These two systems operate as a balance to one another, providing young children with a secure base from which to explore and learn. Children who develop an emotional attachment to their teachers are more competent learners, as they feel more confident responding to new materials and activities.

Early childhood professionals who nurture children assist them in establishing affectionate, caring relationships. Forming strong, supportive attachments sets the stage for the multitude of future relationships as children move into the wider world beyond their immediate family. Educators help children learn that the people in their lives matter the most.

"Building Positive Relationships with Young Children"

Teacher as Communicator

Responsive teachers employ both verbal and nonverbal interactions which clearly display respect and affection for children (NAEYC, 1991). Teacher-initiated verbal interactions include asking open-ended questions, giving directions, direct instruction, and conversations. Nonverbal interaction is critical for building communication skills with

young children. Smiling, hugging, holding, using eye contact, and kneeling at the child's level are all models of respectful and warm nonverbal interactions.

Carefully listening to children's concerns and conversations as well as comforting and reassuring them, establishes trusting relationships. Engaging in this daily type of reassurance promotes children's trust and confidence in the teacher. The self-assurance that is built extends into the meaningful activities in which teachers and children engage.

Initiating conversation with young children should begin with direct eye contact and saying the child's name. Clear communication that children can understand based on their developmental and intellectual levels reduces misperceptions. Supportive interactions are typified by sincere and specific praise, encouragement, and welcoming words. These all strengthen teacher-children relationships and motivate children to learn (Smith, 1982).

Teacher as Facilitator

Young children learn through multiple opportunities for self-expression, problem-posing and problem-solving, exploration, imaginative play, testing hypotheses, and inventing. Teachers support the child's learning by providing engaging and motivating environments that hold rich resources and an abundance of intentional activities, large blocks of time to explore, and a balance of teacher-initiated and child-initiated learning.

Self-expression is fostered through individual exploration and consolidation of learning. Opportunities for fantasy, story-telling and role-playing enfolded in imaginative play also promotes self-expression. Curiosity, risk-taking, and divergent-thinking flourish in an environment where teachers encourage children to problem-solve, explore a wide range of possibilities, and self-select activities. Risk is a vital component of play. It allows children to be challenged, to problem-solve and to think outside the box. Teachers most skillfully facilitate children's creative thought in well-planned and organized environments using intentionally created lessons based on teacher and student curriculum ideas. Creativity, not chaos, is the hallmark of the environment created by the facilitative teacher.

Teacher as Planner

Children's needs include motivation for learning, activity, attention, and success. Teachers plan for these needs through curricular activities in a balanced and integrated instructional format. To avoid chaos, inappropriate behavior and frustration for both children and adults, daily routines and transitions must also be planned for. The many routines and transitions, with proper planning, can become valuable learning opportunities. Wait time during transitions and routines should be minimal and filled with songs, finger plays, stories, poems and learning games. Teacher flexibility is paramount as plans are always subject to change in the event of schedule changes, unforeseen weather events and children's body rhythms.

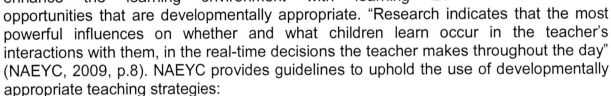

Another aspect of the role of teacher as planner is to enhance the learning environment with learning opportunities that are developmentally appropriate. "Research indicates that the most powerful influences on whether and what children learn occur in the teacher's interactions with them, in the real-time decisions the teacher makes throughout the day" (NAEYC, 2009, p.8). NAEYC provides guidelines to uphold the use of developmentally appropriate teaching strategies:

- Teachers create a caring community of learners that supports all children to develop and learn.
- Teachers teach to enhance the development and learning of all children by providing a balance of adult-guided and child-guided experiences.
- Teachers plan curriculum to achieve important learning goals through learning experiences that include play, small group, large group, interest centers and routines.
- Teachers assess children's development and learning in order to plan, implement and evaluate the effectiveness of the classroom activities as well as children's progress and achievement.
- Teachers establish reciprocal relationships with families which embody mutual respect, cooperation, shared responsibility, and negotiation of conflicts toward achievement of shared goals. (Copple & Bredekamp, 2009, pp. 16-23)

"Early Childhood Literacy Lesson Planning Video"

Teacher as Lifelong Learner

All children deserve teachers who are committed to continual learning and professional development, developing into effective early childhood educators. Throughout their careers, teachers, like children, progress through developmental stages needing opportunities for professional development, networking, support and training to hone their teaching skills, avoiding burn out and maturing into professionals (Katz, 1977).

Lilian Katz (1977) has identified four stages of professional growth and development in educators: *survival, consolidation, renewal,* and *maturity*. The first developmental stage, *survival* is evidenced by educators' awareness of the realities of teaching. Katz distinguishes teachers at this stage as needing support, guidance and training to develop a reference point of teacher knowledge and skill. In the second stage, *consolidation,* teachers' knowledge and skills coalesce and they begin to focus in on individual needs, strengths, and so on. Professional development includes broadening teacher knowledge base and awareness of resources. In the third stage, *renewal,* teachers often experience a level of diminishing enthusiasm, commitment, and creativity. Renewal includes new experiences such as visiting other programs, reading an assortment of professional materials, attending conferences, and networking with other professionals. The last developmental stage, *maturity,* provides the opportunity for teachers who have integrated their knowledge and skills into their personal philosophy to experience deeper insight into their profession. Teachers at this stage write and publish articles, engage in consultation with other professionals, and present at workshops and conferences.

Teacher as Reflective Practitioner

Teacher as reflective practitioner is a role that should be developed from the first to the last day of a teaching career. Reflective practice "is taking the time to rethink and rework teaching plans, strategies, words, and actions – and scrutinizing them through the lens of ethical decision-making, all the while considering the effects of your behavior on self and others" (Jalongo & Isenburg, 2012, p.6) Insightful reflectiveness increases self-perception, teaching skill, and greater sensitivity for young children. Reflectiveness often elevates a teacher's consciousness to greater commitment to the betterment of the lives of young children and their families.

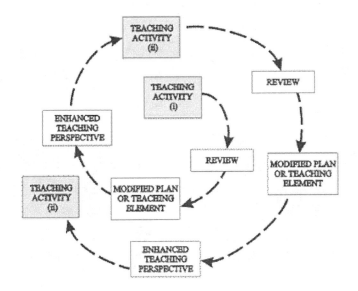

The art of becoming a reflective practitioner is refined throughout a lifetime of dedication to the profession as an early childhood educator. Research suggests that a professional's reflections often begin with a focus on themselves, then moves to a focus on the task of teaching, and finally focuses on the impact of their teaching on students (Taggart & Wilson, 2005). This progression of attention begins with the novice who has a limited repertoire of teaching strategies to the in-service teacher who is focused on the "how to" of teaching to the experienced teacher who is focused on the enduring consequences of teaching and learning on children.

Eby, Herrell and Jordan (2006) have outlined the characteristics of a reflective practitioner:

- Reflective practitioners are **active**. They search out information that enhances the quality of their teaching and curriculum, enriches their classroom environment and allows them to better meet the needs of all their children.
- Reflective practitioners are **persistent**. They think through difficult issues and persist regardless of the time and energy that may need to be expended.
- Reflective practitioners are **caring**. They have sincere concern for other humans, respect their students as individuals, and endeavor to create nurturing classrooms.
- Reflective practitioners are **skeptical**. They are critical thinkers who realize there are few unequivocal truths – that every precept must be investigated and analyzed.
- Reflective practitioners are **rational**. They do not follow the latest educational fad, but instead, gather data to make a well-informed

decision. They do not do what is often impulsive and most expedient, but instead, use thoughtfulness to proceed with intentionality in all aspects of their teaching.

- Reflective practitioners are **proactive**. They anticipate questions and address issues before problems present themselves.

The reflective practitioner contemplates on academic concerns, teaching effectiveness, and learners' needs before, during, and after teaching.

Teacher as Advocate

In the field of early childhood education, child advocacy is defined as taking action for the well-being and betterment of children, supporting families, and appealing for the cause of high-quality programs. Becoming an advocate for children and for the profession is central to the role of teacher of young children. However, this role is often ignored when considering the many "hats" an early childhood educator wears. Yet, there is no lack of issues to effectively advocate for in the lives of children and their families.

Advocacy takes place at many different levels – from families who approach their child's teacher or program director to ask for an arts program, to teachers who approach the school board to request additional funds for books to help their students meet rigorous academic standards, to groups of business leaders who form coalitions with early childhood caregivers, to professional associations who create opportunities to educate policymakers about a particular problem that young children face. At all levels of advocacy, caring adults take a stand on behalf of children. (Robinson & Stark, 2002)

"Child Advocates"

Becoming informed is key for early childhood professionals. To make a tangible difference in the lives of children and families, early childhood professionals have the obligation of becoming knowledgeable advocates for children and the profession (NAEYC, 2009). Powerful advocates draw on their real-life experience as well as scientifically-based research to further early childhood causes. Informed advocacy necessitates both sensitivity to the stories of children and their families and expertise in

both understanding and communicating the central issues of the field. These central issues include but are not limited to meeting the needs of children with disabilities and providing exemplary environments and resources.

Teachers advocate for the children in their classrooms with disabilities. With more than 13 percent of the nation's children receiving special services (US Department of Education, 2016), the role of the teacher becomes key in shaping the quality of inclusion, in creating an atmosphere of acceptance, and in supporting skill and knowledge acquisition. Children with special needs absolutely require the services and program that will maximize their potential. The early childhood teacher is part of the process of advocating for children with disabilities and ensuring children receive appropriate services.

Teachers advocate for the best possible environment and resources for each child in their programs. All children deserve and flourish in rich learning environments that are replete with appropriate resources to engage them in learning. However, children from poverty and ethnically diverse backgrounds are especially at risk for lagging behind their peers, requiring enriched environments and responsive teaching. American children from families living in poverty or in households in which parent education is low characteristically enter school with lower levels of foundational skills such as math, reading, and language (Copple & Bredekamp, 2009). Early childhood education which offers dynamic and motivating environments with intentional teaching can go far in closing the achievement gap which now exists.

Teachers also advocate for the highest quality care and education. High quality care and education promote healthy development and learning. "To ensure that teachers are able to provide care and education of high quality, they must be well prepared, participate in ongoing professional development, and receive sufficient support and compensation" (Copple & Bredekamp, 2009, p.xiii). Raising teacher qualifications and fairly compensating highly qualified teachers are two ways to improve the educational quality for children. . In addition, early childhood professionals have an obligation to keep up to date with the latest research development in the field and to engage in continuous collaboration with other professionals.

Becoming a Professional

A profession is an occupation that necessitates comprehensive education and/or specialized training. Professions usually mandate qualifications for entry and standards for practice in the profession. A framework which details a focused body of knowledge and expertise supports the decision-making and behavior of the professional.

The Six Standards of Professional Development

Becoming a professional is not an automatic transition occurring upon the attainment of academic degrees. Professionalism evolves with experience, advocacy, reflectiveness as well as formal education. The NAEYC (2009) has formalized the standards under which early childhood educators implement policy and program:

> These standards describe what early childhood professionals are expected to know and do, defining essential learning outcomes in professional preparation programs and presenting a shared vision of excellence. These standards offer practitioners a framework for applying new knowledge to critical issues. They support important *early learning* goals across settings serving children from birth through age 8. They support critical *early childhood policy* structures including professional credentialing, accreditation of professional preparation programs, state approval of teacher education programs, and state professional development systems.

Standard 1: Promoting Child Development and Learning

The early childhood educator needs to know the fundamentals of how children develop and learn. This entails awareness and understanding of young children's characteristics, developmental milestones, needs and the various influences on children's development and learning. This knowledge enables the early childhood professional to create purposeful experiences and enriching environments.

Knowledge of child development supports developmentally appropriate practice with young children. The foundation of developmentally appropriate practice (DAP) is built upon three major planks – knowledge of child growth and development, knowledge of the individual child, and knowledge of the social and cultural contexts in which children reside. Childhood professionals "use their understanding of young children's characteristics and needs, and of multiple interacting influences on children's development and learning, to create environments that are healthy, respectful, supportive, and challenging" (NAEYC, 2009). Developmentally appropriate practice will be addressed in greater detail later in this book.

Developmentally appropriate practice also includes culturally appropriate practice – sensitivity and intentionality when responding to children's cultural backgrounds and needs. Children in early childhood settings will, in all likelihood, reflect the diversity of the United States. Children bring with them the settings in which they have been enculturated – class, gender, ethnicity, language, and disability are all factors molding each unique individual. Responsive teaching requires early childhood educators to teach children of all cultures.

In addition to addressing the individual needs of children, early childhood educators concentrate on creating enriched environments that are challenging, respectful and supportive. Challenging environments are those in which educators provide a variety of purposeful learning opportunities that are neither too easy nor too frustrating. Providing support through careful scaffolding of learning constitutes one of many skills in the early childhood educator's toolbox. Respectfulness is shown for each child's abilities or disabilities as well as his/her culture, home language, and community context. Supportive environments create individualized experiences based on children's strengths, interests and meaning-making.

Standard 2: Building Family and Community Relationships

Partnering with children's families and communities creates positive relationships that support successful early childhood education. Early childhood professionals "understand and value the importance and complex characteristics of children's families and communities" (NAEYC, 2009). In order to facilitate this professional growth, early childhood educators need to familiarize themselves with the community in which

children live and understand the lives of the families. Supporting families in their quest for a better life for their children requires the professional to support, empower and be respectful of them. Strong, positive home-school collaboration makes families partners in all phases of children's development and learning.

Respectfulness for families is better demonstrated than only espoused. Exhibiting respect for families and the communities in which they live include: validating children's home languages and integrating them in the classroom, maintaining an open-door school and classroom policy with families, and setting clear classroom expectations that are communicated to families. Partnering with parents and building respectful, reciprocal relationships can only empower families in the educational pursuits for their children.

Standard 3: Observing, Documenting, and Assessing

One of the most important jobs as an early childhood professional is to observe, document and assess the learning of each child. Assessment data is utilized in decision-making concerning individual children's educational and developmental strengths and needs. Assessment results are also communicated to parents and families in a meaningful and understandable way. Early childhood professionals "know about and use systematic observations, documentation, and other effective assessment strategies in a responsible way, in partnership with families and other professionals, to positively influence the development of every child" (NAEYC, 2009).

Observation skills can be sharpened with daily practice. By systematically observing and documenting children's behaviors, the early childhood professional gathers data about young children's development and learning. The data can then be used to create individual, small group and large group lessons that meet the needs of all the students in the classroom. Accommodations for children with disabilities can also be provided.

Standard 4: Using Developmentally Effective Approaches to Connect with Children and Families

The early childhood professional understands that "teaching and learning with young children is a complex enterprise, and its details vary depending on children's ages, characteristics, and the settings within which teaching and learning occur" (NAEYC, 2009). The early childhood professional has the skill and knowledge to integrate understanding of relationships with families and children; understanding of developmentally effective methods of teaching and learning; and knowledge of developmentally appropriate curriculum design and implementation (Morrison, 2012). An entire chapter in this book will be devoted to developmentally appropriate and responsive practice.

Standard 5: Using Content Knowledge to Build Meaningful Curriculum

Developmentally appropriate practice compels the early childhood professional to not only understand the developmental domains of the child but also to be knowledgeable in the academic (content) disciplines of the curricula and the pedagogical knowledge of how to effectively teach the content knowledge. The content areas in early childhood education include: language, literacy, and reading; music and the arts; mathematics; science; health and physical education; and social studies. Appropriate pedagogy involves incidental teaching, tactical teaching, and direct instruction (Hatch, 2005). The daily framework of pedagogy includes large group, small group, center-based, and cooperative learning.

Standard 6: Becoming a Professional

There is a common misconception in early childhood education that the professional only has to care and be concerned about young children – that working with young children is merely a "natural" extension of maternal or paternal instincts. Early childhood education is often dismissed as "easy" due to the comparative lack of complexity in the content. In reality, the early childhood educator must possess extensive knowledge to create opportunities and environments that produce quality outcomes. Early childhood educators are expected to be knowledgeable in play and development; curriculum planning and educational programming; health, safety and nutrition; working with parents and agencies; interventions; classroom management and guidance; assessment and evaluation; and diversity and inclusion (Jalongo & Isenburg, 2010).

"They (students prepared in early childhood degree programs) are continuous, collaborative learners who demonstrate knowledgeable, reflective, and critical perspectives on their work, making informed decisions that integrate knowledge from a variety of sources" (NAEYC, 2009). In order to put knowledge into practice, teachers need to adopt the disposition of reflectiveness. A **disposition** refers to one's internally motivated habits and characteristic ways of approaching a situation. A professional disposition is an obligation to act in consistently accountable and ethical ways. Becoming a reflective practitioner involves internalizing and daily practicing the disposition of reflection.

Reflective practice includes taking time to think about and rethink teaching plans, strategies, and scheduling. It also involves ethical decision-making that considers the effects of those decisions on children, families and the society as a whole. Reflective practice also includes deliberate careful consideration about your students, their families, the theories upon which teaching is based, the pedagogy you use and the content that is taught (Morrison, 2012). The reflective teacher is an introspective teacher who considers all aspects of a child's life.

Teachers who are reflective practitioners regard their career path as a journey to greater perceptiveness in, and understanding of how to facilitate learning as well as a greater sensitivity to children and their families. Reflectiveness is a challenging commitment to professional and personal excellence to make a difference in the lives of children. For responsive early childhood educators, teaching is certainly "a passionate profession that can challenge both our hearts and minds" (Smith, 1982, p. 54).

Developing a Philosophy of Early Childhood Education

A professional philosophy is a concise statement regarding the values, dispositions, beliefs and attitudes that influence a professional's behavior and decisions. An early childhood professional's philosophy, as in other professions, evolves with time and experience in the profession. The professional philosophy provides the touchstone of one's belief in how children learn and develop; what they should learn; and best practice in teaching.

"The Science of Early Childhood Development"

One's teaching philosophy is shaped by history – personal history, one's experience in the field, the history of the field of early childhood education, and the events and issues influencing the field. Your teaching philosophy guides and focuses your teaching; makes your intentions clear and acknowledged; and encourages you to continuously reflect on the principles of your teaching. What are the foundational elements of your professional philosophy? The following serve as prompts for your thinking:

- Your view of children. How do young children learn? What is their role in their own learning?
- Your view of the teacher. What is the teacher's role in the child's learning? How does that view affect your teaching?
- The role of the environment. What type of environment do you want to create for your students? How does your belief system support the creation of rich environments for learning?
- The role of assessment. What kind of assessment will you use to evaluate the children's meeting of objectives? How will you use assessment data to design learning experiences to meet individual needs?
- The learning. What do you want children to learn, achieve, accomplish, and enjoy?
- The theorists. What approach or approaches provide the framework for your classroom curriculum, environment, and practice? (Jalongo & Isenburg, 2012)

Formulating a philosophy of early childhood education additionally warrants reflection on the culture of early childhood education. **Culture** can be defined as the rules and expectations of behavior for a group member and these rules are passed on from generation to generation. These rules denote what group members regard as important, and determine what values shape their decisions and behavior. The culture is transmitted explicitly through various channels such as formal education, experience, mentoring and implicitly through shared vocabulary, shared identity, shared beliefs, and shared values (Bredekamp, 2011,).

Shared vocabulary expedites communication and minimizes misunderstandings within cultural groups. The meanings of terms such as *play, integration, developmentally appropriate,* and *intentional teaching* are idiosyncratic to the professional culture and are not always defined the same way in broader society. A fundamental skill in joining a profession is learning the shared vocabulary.

Shared identity engenders a sense of belonging to a cultural group; it provides an identity as a member of a profession. There are a multitude of roles in early childhood education – caregiver, childcare provider, and teacher. *Educator* is a more professional, broader term which depicts the overall responsibility of the early childhood professional.

Shared beliefs are those which guide the profession. A few of those beliefs in early childhood education include:

- The belief in **developmentally appropriate practice** as the foundation for effective and responsive teaching.
- The belief that all children have potential, regardless of their social contexts, abilities, and disabilities.
- The belief that early childhood professionals can make a difference in the lives of children, their families and their communities.
- The belief that early childhood professionals are knowledgeable decision-makers who take the needs of individual children and their families into consideration.

Shared values have their roots in developmentally appropriate practice and NAEYC's ethical code (2005):

- Appreciate childhood as a unique and valuable stage of the human life cycle
- Base our work in knowledge of how children develop and learn
- Appreciate and support the bond between the child and family
- Recognize that children are best understood and supported in the context of family, culture (including ethnicity), community, and society
- Respect the dignity, worth, and uniqueness of each individual (child, family member, and colleague)
- Respect diversity in children, families, and colleagues
- Recognize that children and adults achieve their full potential in the context of relationships that are based on trust and respect.

These values endure throughout a changing economic and political landscape that does not always respect and value the importance of early childhood education.

Morrison (2012) suggests that there are steps an early childhood professional needs to take in crafting one's professional philosophy: read widely to get ideas and points of view; reflect on the purposes of education, curriculum, learning and teaching; discuss with successful educators their philosophy and practices; and write and evaluate a draft of one's philosophy. The final step is to finalize the draft into a polished piece that will "be like a compass throughout your career" (p. 27).

Importance of Quality in Early Childhood Education

In the past few decades one of the most significant changes in families around the world has been the increasing dependence on child care, pre-schools and wrap-around care for school-age children. Parents are concerned about finding high-quality care for their children to prepare them for school entry. Research repeatedly demonstrates the effectiveness of quality care in improving outcomes for children. Children who participate in high quality programs display better language and mathematics ability and fewer behavior problems than children in lower quality settings (NICHD Early Child Care Research Network, 2002). The power of high quality programs is most evident in the lives of children from low-income families.

"The Importance of High-Quality Early Childhood Education"

Setting Standards for Quality Child Care through Licensing

Both center-based care and family-based child care are regulated by each state's child care licensing standards. Regulations set minimum requirements for a program to officially operate. These guidelines establish teacher/child ratios, health and safety requirements, site requirements, and teacher qualifications.

"Quality Early Childhood Teachers"

These standards are set to protect children and to ensure their development, yet these standards vary dramatically from state to state. While setting the minimum requirements for quality care and education, many programs far exceed these standards, providing exemplary settings for children. Still other programs barely meet the minimum standards (NACCRRA, 2009). Many states make the child care decision easier for parents by operating quality rating and improvement systems (QRIS). These rating systems award stars to programs that exceed the minimum benchmarks of licensing, such as having better child/adult ratios, more credentialed teachers and greater numbers of learning resources. Centers with a higher number of stars may receive higher reimbursement rates and often are preferred by parents who are more than willing to pay higher tuition.

Setting Standards for Quality Child Care through Accreditation

To ensure the overall quality of early childhood education, NAEYC has provided the leadership and commitment to high-quality standards by administering a voluntary accreditation system. Early childhood centers and schools providing care and education to children from birth to kindergarten may elect to go through the process to gain this highly regarded accreditation. Since 1985, NAEYC has offered the system of accrediting with the goal being to raise the level of early childhood education by ensuring the quality  of children's daily experiences and promoting positive child outcomes. Presently, there are nearly 7,000 programs nationally that have NAEYC accreditation (NAEYC, 2016).

The NAEYC accreditation framework includes ten program standards with specific criteria focused on best practices in the early childhood field and the benefits to stakeholders in early childhood education. There are four groups of early childhood education stakeholders: children, teachers, family and community partners, and the program administration. The first five standards focus on children – the most important stakeholders. Standard six focuses on teachers, while standards seven and eight are directed at families and community partners and standards nine and ten address program administration. These standards were conceived to universalize the characteristics of high quality (NAEYC, 2005):

Standard 1: Relationships – The program promotes positive relationships among all children and adults to encourage each child's sense of individual worth and belonging as a part of a community and to foster each child's ability to contribute as a responsible community member.

Standard 2: Curriculum – The program implements a curriculum that is consistent with its goals for children and promotes learning and development in each of the following areas: social, emotional, physical, language, and cognitive.

Standard 3: Teaching – The program uses developmentally, culturally, and linguistically appropriate and effective teaching approaches that enhance each child's learning and development in the context of the program's curriculum goals. Teachers purposefully use multiple instructional approaches to optimize children's opportunities for learning.

Standard 4: Assessment of children's progress – The program is informed by ongoing systematic, formal, and informal assessment approaches to provide information on children's learning and development. These assessments occur within the context of reciprocal communications with families and with sensitivity to the cultural contexts in which children develop. Assessment results are used to benefit children by informing sound decisions about children, teaching, and program improvement.

Standard 5: Health – The program promotes the nutrition and health of children and protects children and staff from illness and injury.

Standard 6: Teachers – The program employs and supports a teaching staff that has the educational qualifications, knowledge, and professional commitment necessary to promote children's learning and development and to support families' diverse needs and interests.

Standard 7: Families – The program establishes and maintains collaborative relationships with each child's family to foster children's development in all settings. These relationships are sensitive to family composition, language, and culture.

Standard 8: Community relationships – The program establishes relationships with and uses resources of the children's communities to support the achievement of program goals.

Standard 9: Physical environment – The program has a safe and healthful environment that provides appropriate and well-maintained indoor and outdoor physical environments. The environment includes facilities, equipment, and materials to facilitate child and staff learning and development.

Standard 10: Leadership and management – The program effectively implements policies, procedures, and systems that support stable staff and strong personnel, fiscal, and program management so all children, families, and staff have high-quality experiences. (Includes teacher/child ratios and group sizes.)

Pathways to Professional Development

Developmentally appropriate practice calls for excellent early childhood professionals who possess a knowledge base about how children learn and develop:

> This knowledge is the starting place for teachers in the many decisions they make – the long-term ones as well as the minute-by-minute ones: how to organize the environment to help children do their best, how to plan curriculum that engages children and helps them reach important goals, how to adapt teaching strategies for the group and for individual children. (Copple & Bredekamp, 2009, p.33)

Becoming an early childhood professional encompasses this knowledge as well as knowledge of the profession and its ethical code, and the current public issues that influence the profession and the professional.

Knowledge and demonstration of the skills needed to be an early childhood professional proceed as a result of certification and credentialing. Certification requirements vary from state to state, yet the trend is toward stricter professional standards and higher levels of formal education.

"Developing Teachers Pathways and T.E.A.C.H."

The CDA Program

The Child Development Associate (CDA) is a national credentialing program that provides early childhood professionals working with infants to 5-year olds the opportunity to develop in a competency-based assessment system. An important part of the CDA is demonstrated competencies relating to the nurturance of children's physical, social, and emotional, and intellectual growth. The CDA was begun in 1975 and has served as a nationally recognized system of criteria for early childhood training and education. Only the Council for Professional Recognition in Washington, DC can award a CDA credential. Over 370,000 educators have received their CDA credentials to date, and there are now nearly 15,000 professionals applying for the CDA credential annually (CDA Council, 2016). There are four types of CDA credentials:

- Center-based Preschool
- Center-based Infant/Toddler
- Family Child Care
- Home Visitor

The CDA Competency Standards, composed of Goals and Functional Areas, form the basis of the CDA program. The six Competency Goals establish the framework for the early childhood professional's performance, with the thirteen Functional Areas describing the major tasks that need to be completed in order to carry out the Competency Goals. The goals areas and functional areas are the same for each credential, but the content varies for each type of credential. The Competency Goals are:

- **Goal I** – To establish and maintain a safe, healthy learning environment
- **Goal II** – To advance physical and emotional competence
- **Goal III** – To support social and emotional development and to provide positive guidance
- **Goal IV** – To establish positive and productive relationships with families
- **Goal V** – To ensure a well-run, purposeful program responsive to participant needs
- **Goal VI** – To maintain a commitment to professionalism

If a professional does not have a degree in early childhood education or early intervention, earning a CDA credential is vitally important. The requirements of the CDA include:

- 120 clock hours of formal training/CDA coursework within the past 5 years
- 480 hours of experience working with children within the past 5 years
- Documents that verify competence in early care and education, including:
  - A professional resource file
  - Parent opinion questionnaires
  - The CDA Assessment Observation Instrument
  - An oral interview
  - A written assessment

A state may demand a specific infant and toddler credential as well. For instance, in New York, the NYSAEYC (New York State Association for the Education of Young Children) offers the Infant Toddler Care and Education credential which formally acknowledges the specialized skills and knowledge base an Infant/Toddler specialist must possess. A professional holding this credential can be head of a group in a center program.

"Earning a CDA Credential Makes Me a Better Teacher"

Associate Degree Programs

Increasingly, community colleges offer two year degrees in early childhood education. These associate degrees provide foundational knowledge in child growth, development and learning as well as working with children, families and agencies. Child care aides, child care providers, directors of franchised/corporate centers and director-owners of family child care can all advance in their professions by securing an associate degree. Often, early childhood professionals use an associate degree to propel them forward into a 4-year degree

Baccalaureate Degree Programs

Four-year programs provide deeper and broader comprehensive knowledge of early childhood education organized around the six professional preparation competencies. The initial certification categories vary state to state. For instance, New York certifies its professionals in either birth-2nd Grade or 1st -6th grades, while its neighboring state,  Pennsylvania, certifies in Pre-K – 4th grade and 4th-8th with a content specialty. A four year degree with certification enables a professional to teach in a school, move into administration, or become a public policy advocate.

Master's Degree Programs

Many colleges and universities offer graduates with a 4-year degree an advance degree that leads to initial certification (pre-professional) or permanent certification for an undergraduate holding initial certification (in-service). Graduates of master's degree programs are also qualified to be program directors and assistant directors. Many master degree recipients, with years of practical experience in education, may be eligible to teach in community colleges and serve as adjunct faculty in 4-year degree programs.

Summary

- Early childhood education is an exciting field that covers the expansive age range of birth to 8 years old. Professionals work in a variety of settings: child care centers, family based care, early intervention, preschools, kindergartens, primary grades, public schools and private schools.

- Becoming an early childhood professional necessitates an understanding and assumption of many roles. The many "hats" the professional wears involves a complex repertoire of skills, knowledge, and dispositions that are developed initially through formal education and refined with experience.

- The early childhood profession sets standards for high-quality programs for children.

- Early childhood professionals are part of a cultural group which shares a common vocabulary, identity, values, and beliefs. From these commonalities, the professional can craft her/his uniquely personal professional philosophy of how children learn and develop.

- There are various entry points into the early childhood professional development and varied terminal points where professionals merge formal education with practical experience.

Key Terms

accreditation system
alignment
child care centers
child care licensing standards
Child Development Associate Credential (CDA)
culture
Developmentally Appropriate Practice (DAP)
disposition
early childhood education
early childhood special education
Early Head Start
early intervention
family child care
Head Start
Head Start Program Performance Standards
Individuals with Disabilities Act (IDEA)
kindergarten
National Association for the Education of Young Children (NAEYC)
Prekindergarten (pre-K)
preschool

primary grade
professionals
quality rating systems (QRS)

Suggested Readings

Brazelton, T.B. & Greenspan, S.I. (2000). *The irreducible needs of children: What every child must have to grow, learn, and flourish.* New York: Perseus Books.

Feeney, S. (2011) *Professionalism in early childhood education: Doing our best for young children.* Washington, DC: NAEYC.

Hyson, M. (Ed.). (2003). *Preparing early childhood professionals: NAEYC's standards for programs* Washington, DC: NAEYC.

Suggested Websites

Council for Early Childhood Professional Recognition
www.cdacouncil.org

National Association for the Education of Young Children (NAEYC)
www.naeyc.org

National Institute for Early Education Research (NIEER)
www.nieer.org

Reflections

- If you have not already done so, develop a professional resource portfolio or computer folder. Your professional portfolio should house your philosophy of education, activity ideas, literature lists, site observation reflections, professional journals, ethical dilemma responses, DVD's, lists of websites, and any other resources that will help you as a novice teacher. Organize your portfolio around the six NAEYC Standards for Professional Preparation Programs, to confirm your meeting of all six standards.

- Review the NAEYC accreditation standards and your state's licensing standards. Reflect on how both set of standards are influenced by the shared values of the profession. Is either set missing any major principles of the other?

- Design a strategic plan for your own personal development as a teacher. What experiences will you use at this stage of your development to continue to grow as a professional?

- Research one of the current issues for which strong advocates are needed: children in poverty, homeless children, children who lack medical insurance for example. How can you effectively advocate in your local community and at the state level for these children?

References

Allen, J. (1986). Safe touch: Reassurances for child care workers. *Day Care and Early Education, 14*(3), 14-16.

Barnett, W.S. (2008). *Preschool education and its lasting effects: Research and policy Implications.* Boulder, CO: Education and the Public Interest Center & Education Policy Research Unit. Retrieved March 30, 2012 from http://epicpolicy.org

Bowlby, J. (1982). *Attachment and loss. Vol. 1: Attachment* (2nd Ed.). New York: Basic Books.

Bredekamp, S. (2011). *Effective practices in early childhood education: Building a foundation.* Upper Saddle River, NJ: Pearson Education.

Burchinal, M. R. (1999). Child care experiences and developmental outcomes. *Annals of the American Academy of Political and Social Science, 563*(1), 73-97.

Carnegie Corporation. (1994). *Starting points: Meeting the needs of our youngest children.* New York: Author.

Children's Defense Fund. (2014). *The state of America's children.* Washington, DC: Children's Defense Fund.

Colker, L. (2008). Twelve characteristics of effective early childhood teachers. *Young Children (63)*2, 68-73.

Copple, C. & Bredekamp, S. (2009). *Developmentally appropriate practice in early childhood programs* (3rd Ed.). Washington, DC: National Association for the Education of Young Children.

Council for Professional Recognition. (2016). *Assessment system and competency standards for infant/toddler caregivers.* Washington, DC: Author.

Division for Early Childhood (DEC) and National Association for the Education of Young Children (NAEYC). (2009). *Early childhood inclusion: A joint position of the Division for Early Childhood of the Council for Exceptional Children and the National Association for the Education of Young Children.* Chapel Hill, NC: Author.

Galinsky, E. (2006). *The economic benefits of high-quality early childhood programs: What makes the difference?* Washington, DC: Committee for Economic Development.

Hatch, T. (2005). Improving schools in turbulent times. *The New Educator, 2,* 267-276.

Heckman, James. www.heckmanegation.com.

Head Start. (1998). *Head Start program performance standards.* Washington, DC: U.S. Department of Health and Human Services.

Jalongo, M. R. & Isenberg, J. P. (2012). *Exploring your role in early childhood education.* Upper Saddle River, NJ: Pearson Education.

Katz, L. (1977). *Talks with teachers.* Washington, DC: National Association for the Education of Young Children.

Morrison, G. S., (2012). *Early childhood education today.* Upper Saddle River, NJ: Pearson Education.

National Association for the Education of Young Children. (1991). Guidelines for appropriate curriculum content and assessment in programs serving children ages 3 through 8. *Young Children, 46* (3), 21-38.

National Association for the Education of Young Children. (2005). *NAEYC Early Childhood Program Standards and Accreditation Criteria: The mark of quality in early childhood education.* Washington, DC: Author.

National Association for the Education of Young Children. (2016). *NAEYC Standards for Early Childhood Professional Preparation Programs.* Washington DC: NAEYC.

National Association of Child Care Resources and Referral Agencies (NACCRRA). (2009). Available online at www.naccrra.org

National Institute of Child Health and Human Development, Early Child Care Research Network. (2002). The relation of first grade classroom environment to structural classroom features, teacher, and student behaviors. *The Elementary School Journal 102,* 367-387.

Robinson, A. & Stark, D. R. (2002). *Advocates in action: Making a difference for young children.* Washington, DC: NAEYC.

Smith, A. F. (2000). Reflective Portfolios. *Childhood Education, 76* (4), 204-208.

Smith, C. A. (1982). *Promoting the social development of young children: Strategies and activities.* Palo Alto, CA: Mayfield.

Taggart. G. L. & Wilson, A. P. (2005). *Promoting reflective thinking in teachers: 50 action strategies* (2nd ed.). Thousand Oaks, CA: Corwin.

United States Department of Education. (2013). *Effects of preschool curriculum programs on school readiness: Report from the preschool curriculum evaluation research initiative.* Washington, DC: US Department of Education.

Wilson, D. M. (2008). A huge opportunity for middle-income children: An interview with Libby Doggett. *Harvard Education Letter 24*(6).

Zill, N., Sorongon, A., Kim, K., Clark, C. & Woolverton, M. (2006). *Children's outcomes and program quality in Head Start* (FACES 2003 Research Brief). Washington, DC: Head Start Bureau.

Chapter 2
Early Childhood Foundations: History and Current Issues

A Historical Glance at Early Childhood Education

Thinking Ahead

1. Why is it important to learn from the past?
2. Which people throughout history have had the greatest influence on early childhood education?
3. How has the view of children changed through history? How has this changing view influenced early childhood programs and services?
4. What are some of the current trends affecting early childhood education and what has been their impact?

The field of childhood development and education has its roots in a very long past history, is presently experiencing a resurgence of attention, and is forward-looking in the impetuses that will shape education for the 21st century. The beliefs of many philosophers, psychologists, and educators dating back to the 17th century have influenced early childhood education as it is understood in the 21st century. To know where early childhood education is going, it is important to know from where it has come.

Education in the 16th and 17th Centuries

During the Colonial Period in America, children were generally viewed and treated as miniature adults, dressing like adults and doing adult work (Spodek, 1985). Children were believed to be inherently evil and it was desirable to curb children's sinful nature early in life. In 1647, Massachusetts required the establishment of schools for young children. The schools were places to care for children, to instill piety and moral character through the reading of the Bible, to teach children the value of hard work and to learn skills for adulthood (Hacsi, 1995).

During the early part of the 1600's philosophers, psychologists, and educators were focusing their attention on early childhood as its own unique and distinctive stage of life. The Eastern European religious leader, **Johann Amos Comenius (1592-1670)** was one of the educational reformers who wrote about his vision for a modern system of education for all children. Comenius saw nature as the primary method of fostering children's growth, implying a timetable for development and learning that should prevent pushing children too hard. He believed in three key ideas (Wolfe, 2000): 1) Learning should be pleasurable and not punitive, 2) Teachers should follow children's lead in learning, 3) Children should learn in their home language.

Comenius' ideas were radical for his time, yet many of his ideas are fundamentals in modern early childhood education: children need to be active, they learn through their senses, and their interests should be used as a vehicle for learning. His book, *Orbis Pictus* is regarded as the first known picture book.

"Jan Amos Komensky (John Amos Comenius)"

Around 1690, the English doctor and philosopher **John Locke (1632-1704)** was one of the first to emphasize the importance of early childhood experience, the importance of education, and the importance of play. Locke believed that children are born with a *tabula rasa*, a blank slate. The experiences children have and the environments in which they live shape what is written on the slate. This view persists today in the way that education is promoted as compensatory for children of poverty and disadvantaged environments. The belief is that if all children are born with the same general capacity for cognitive development, the difference in learning and achievement are attributable to the quality of the child's environment.

Locke viewed parents as children's first teachers, but cautioned that academic instruction should be playful (Beatty, 1995). He encouraged parents to use children's internal need for approval to manipulate them into acceptable behavior – reasoning with children instead of physically punishing them.

The beliefs of Comenius and Locke went far in countering the adverse view of children in the 17th century. The belief that children are innately evil was beginning to shift to the belief that children are inherently good. The foundation built by philosophers such as Comenius and Locke smoothed the way for others to direct their focus on education as more humanistic.

Education in the 18th and 19th Centuries

During this era, children were being forced to work long hours under adverse conditions. The philosopher and author, **Jean-Jacques Rousseau (1712-1778)** emerged with a romantic belief of the child as innocent. Rousseau suggested that society has a corrupting influence on children and that children should be treated with sympathy and benevolence. He is best remembered for his book, *Emile*, about a fictitious child who is raised by Rousseau 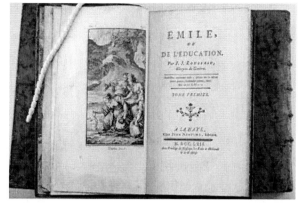 from birth to adolescence. In his classic work, Rousseau addressed the rights of children by posing the radical idea that children are innately perfect and optimal development unfolds naturally from birth, thus confirming the importance of early education. He validated the importance of individual freedom and learning through interaction with the environment.

"Rousseau, or on Education"

Although *Emile* was fictional, it served as a guide for manipulating and directing children's actions and thoughts implicitly (Procher, 1998). He advocated for a prolonged childhood reserved for activities that interest the child, without direct adult instruction. Rousseau believed that the medium of sensory-based play was necessary for children's learning. In an essential departure from thought which had preceded him, Rousseau believed that mothers were incapable of being children's primary teachers. Instead, he advocated turning the children over to male tutors to teach and rear children (Beatty, 1995).

Rousseau was one of the first to propose the concept of stages of development which children traverse, each in a unique way. He believed that children should not be rushed through the stages, but instead they should be allowed a natural maturation according to their innate developmental timetable. Here we see the first shift of thought from home-based to school-based education. Many of his beliefs persist today in the works of Jean Piaget's cognitive developmental stages and the maturationists' belief in development being biological.

Rousseau presented a way of thinking about young children that was then carried on by Pestalozzi and Froebel in their writings.

The Swiss educator, **Johann Heinrich Pestalozzi (1746-1827)**, declared that all persons have the right to an education to learn the skills and knowledge that would make them successful in life. The purpose of education, according to Pestalozzi, was to develop children's moral, physical, and intellectual powers (Williams, 1999). Focusing on the welfare of poor children, he was concerned about a growing industrialized society that was generating an increasing gap between rich and poor, resulting in children being raised in urban environments.

"John Heinrich Pestalozzi Theory and Impact on Education"

Influenced by Rousseau's writings and belief in naturalism, Pestalozzi purchased a farm and began a school called Neuhof where he developed and implemented many of his ideas about teaching the whole child. Unlike earlier theorists, he worked directly with children, experimenting new methods. Pestalozzi followed many of Rousseau's ideas of schools and curriculum based on a holistic approach to teaching children across all their learning domains – cognitively, physically, socially, morally and emotionally (Henson, 2003).

Pestalozzi, like Rousseau, believed that children build knowledge through hands-on discovery – a precursor of Piaget's theory of constructivism – and he strove to build a community-minded consciousness in students. Pestalozzi designed an innovative method of teaching children living in poverty that centered on the key beliefs (Null, 2004):

- All children are capable of learning
- Learning begins with parents as the first teachers
- Teacher-student discourse and activities should focus on hands-on manipulation of real objects
- Natural experiences in the course of daily living are the source of learning
- Arts and physical education are essential components of a comprehensive education

Pestalozzi deviated from Rousseau's belief about mother-teachers, and instead, validated the importance of mothers teaching their children at home. In his fictional work, *How Gertrude Teaches Her Children* Pestalozzi advocated that the child learn at "the school of the mother's knee" until six years of age, and that this learning should be through playful, firsthand experiences around a child's interests. One of Pestalozzi's enduring contributions is that of "object lessons" – activities using manipulatives to measure, count, build, feel and touch. Center-based learning incorporating this idea is a common, daily pursuit in early childhood classrooms.

Robert Owen (1771-1858) was both a British educator and political and social activist who shared Pestalozzi's concern for children in poverty. He believed that the environment in which children live is the major influence on their achievement, beliefs and behavior, and that a benevolent society must act in its own best interest by providing an environment which will positively shape children into responsible people. Owen strongly rejected harsh, punitive practices of the day as ways to control children's behavior. Instead, he sanctioned more humane treatment of children.

In 1816, Owen campaigned against child labor, establishing the first factory day nursery for children 18 months to 10 years old so that children could be cared for and supervised while their parents worked in the mill. Owen fueled the British infant school movement, which concentrated children's social and cognitive learning in cooperative, exploratory settings. The first infant school was opened in London in 1818, creating an enduring legacy that still exists today. Owen's example has seen resurgence in burgeoning corporate-subsidized child care that many companies today offer their employees.

"Robert Owen & the Cooperative Movement"

One of Pestalozzi's students, **Friedrich Froebel (1782-1852)**, built on Pestalozzi's ideas, extending them into a program. He took Pestalozzi's ideas of teaching and transformed them into a curriculum and educational methodology. Froebel earned the title of *Father of Kindergarten.* He envisioned a "garden of children" being educated through a curriculum using play as both a structured, more teacher-directed activity and as a freer creative self-expression.

Froebel continued Rousseau's theory of the natural unfolding of a child's growth and learning. The teacher's role is to carefully observe the child's unfolding, and to then provide activities that will facilitate the child's learning in accordance with his development and interest. The role of the teacher is a "guide on the side" and designer of experiences and activities.

Froebel believed that unstructured play was not the optimal learning environment and that teachers were responsible for preparing the environment and then guiding and directing the learning. The foundation of modern, intentional teaching was laid during this era. Froebel designed a systematic, planned curriculum in which there were gifts, occupations, songs and games.

**"Froebel Kindergarten Gifts Early Childhood
Education History of Toys"**

The *gifts* Froebel designed were educational toys children could manipulate, explore and learn from under the guidance of the teacher. It was through directed play with these gifts that Froebel sought to maintain children's interest in learning. These gifts offered children the opportunity to work through prescribed tasks to acquire the knowledge that was inherent in the materials and activities. The first gift was a box of six wooden balls in the colors of the spectrum – red, orange, yellow, green, blue, and violet – with attached corresponding colored strings. Froebel and his teachers identified more than 100 games that could be played with this one game and accompanying songs and rhymes (Wolfe, 2000).

The Gifts

Presently, there are ten gifts designed to help children learn through directed play and manipulation. The first six gifts represent solid geometry, gift seven allows exploration of surfaces, gift eight represents line, gift nine represents the point, and gift ten merges the use of point and line (Morrison, 2012). Froebel's gifts are still used throughout modern day preschools and kindergartens around the world. They have also inspired the creation of modern toys such as large building blocks, Lincoln Logs and Legos, and 3-dimensional puzzles.

In addition to his gifts, Froebel conceived what he called *occupations* – craft activities such as drawing, paper weaving, modeling with clay, paper folding, lacing cards, and sewing. These activities encouraged children to be creative and to explore different materials as well as to train children's eye-hand coordination and mental activity. Froebel believed that the use of gifts and occupations engrossed children in symbolic representation of events and objects in the real world – such as designing the architecture of a building.

Froebel was the first to advocate education outside of the home that served as extensions of the home. This provided a new venue and a new role for women – many upper- and middle-class women passionately promoted kindergartens across Europe and the United States. To ensure that these kindergarten teachers were trained properly, Froebel created a training program for mothers and teachers (Beatty, 1995).

The Kindergarten Movement

Spreading the Froebelian message of the value of a kindergarten education steeped in harmonious, natural learning, the first kindergarten in the United States was established by **Margarethe Schurz (1832-1876)** in Wisconsin in 1856. Schurz had been a student of Froebel in Germany and after emigrating to the United States, introduced a German-speaking kindergarten to teach her and her neighbors' children.

Elizabeth Peabody (1804-1894), inspired by Margarethe Schurz, organized the first English-speaking kindergarten in Boston in 1860, and subsequently wrote the first American kindergarten textbook for teachers (Snyder, 1972). Peabody traveled to Germany, studied Froebelian methods, and returned to the United States with her new knowledge. She adapted the Froebel's "children's garden" to include individualized instruction to suit children's particular needs, and careful teacher guidance to allow children to develop fully (Follari, 2011). Peabody created the American Froebel Society to regulate the distinction and authenticity of kindergarten programs and is recognized as the first champion of the American kindergarten movement.

Susan Blow (1843-1916), devoted her life to expanding the kindergarten movement as well as remaining true to Froebel's theory and practice. Blow was specifically concerned about inferior teacher-training programs because she believed that qualified, high quality teachers were essential for the perpetuation of the Froebelian kindergarten movement (Blow, 1900). Teachers worked directly with children in the mornings and attended lectures in the afternoons, blending theory and practice. Blow found the first public kindergarten in St. Louis, Missouri in 1873, assisted by the St. Louis superintendent of schools, William Harris, who was concerned that children did not go to school until age 7.

"KETC | Living St. Louis | Susan Blow Kindergarten"

In 1892, Blow brought together a group of Americans passionately devoted to the kindergarten movement, forming the International Kindergarten Union (IKU). Much later the IKU became the Association for Childhood Education International, a group which advocates for the education and well-being of children around the globe, and which is still active today.

Over time, Froebel's method became increasingly inflexible and unyielding due to its teacher-directed practice. Undirected play as Froebel envisioned it was wasteful and trivial, thus leading to an academic kindergarten. The Progressive Movement lead by John Dewey (1859-1952) began the 20th century with a call for a redirection in American education.

John Dewey (1859-1952), through his positions as professor of philosophy at the University of Chicago and Columbia University and his writing, attempted to further his theory of schooling called **progressivism**. Dewey believed that the purpose of education is to further the functioning of a democratic society by producing thoughtful, problem-solving citizens. He valued children's unfolding development and interests as the core of education. Dewey emphasized three key components of education (Dewey, 1938): experience with authentic materials, meaningful to the individual child, and based on real life problem-solving.

"Progressive Education in the 1940s"

"Education is the process of living and not preparation for future living" (Dewey, 1929, p.7) was one premise that formed the framework of Dewey's theory. Curriculum should contain daily encounters with activities in which children learn about life and the skills required for living. In addition to acquiring life skills, Dewey believed in building a love of learning through collaborative, critical inquiry in an environment that supports the learner as a co-learner with the teacher. The role of the teacher is to discover the children's interests, thoughts, and feelings and build engaging educational activities – emergent curriculum-based on them (Hyun & Marshall, 2003). Dewey also believed in the school as a social institution with the students, teachers, and parents making up the community.

"John Dewey Experience and Education: A Brief Summary"

Dewey attempted to seek a balance between too much teacher-directed instruction in the Froebelian tradition and the backlash of too much unguided, unfocused classroom time (Beatty, 1995). He advocated a balance of open, unstructured play and purposeful guidance in developmentally appropriate practice.

G. Stanley Hall (1844-1924), the first American to receive a doctorate in psychology, created the **child study movement** – understanding individual differences in children by directly observing them in their daily lives. Hall initiated the effort to promote education as a respected science because of the utilization of a scientific approach to observing children (Null, 2004). He believed in aligning the educational curriculum with the developmental stages of children. Hall was a vigorous critic of Froebelian theory, claiming that its rigidity had little scientific basis.

Patty Smith Hill (1868-1946), a kindergarten teacher from Louisville, Kentucky emerged during the height of the convergence of Froebelian thought, the child study movement and Dewey's progressivism. Hill studied under Hall and developed a new kindergarten curriculum based on purposeful play. She was deeply committed to the "whole child" approach which valued the input of physicians, artists, social workers and other diverse areas. Hill was influential in the Louisville kindergartens becoming part of the public schools in 1903.

Patty Hill's conception of kindergarten rests on three purposes (Hill 1926/1987, p.12):

- The most imperative function is "to minister to the nature and needs of children from 4 to 6 years of age."
- The kindergarten teacher's second duty is to see the relation of her work to the first-grade curriculum and lay the foundation that children need "without sacrificing the right of the kindergarten child to free, full development on his own level."
- The third function is to connect kindergarten to the home, to reduce the gap between the two, and to build on the learning that takes place there.

In 1905, Hill became a teacher educator at Teachers College, Columbia University and remained there for thirty years. In 1929 she helped establish the National Association for Nursery Education, which changed its name to the National Association for the Education of Young Children in 1964, and today this association boasts over 100,000 members. More than anyone else in the kindergarten movement, Patty Smith Hill is responsible for kindergarten as we know it today.

Education in the 20th Century

Maria Montessori (1870-1952) initially chose medicine as her career and became the first woman in Italy to earn a medical degree. She was given a job working with poor children in the slums of Rome – children who were judged to be mentally deficient. Montessori believed that these children were not lacking in mental ability due to biology, but because of the lack of mental stimulation and opportunities for learning in their environment. She reasoned that children need order and structure and that the senses are the source of intellectual growth, thus the senses need to be trained.

Montessori developed a set of physical materials that were self-correcting, to be used in a prescribed manner.

In 1907, Montessori opened a school called *Casa dei Bambini* (Children's House) for children ages 4 to 7. The curriculum taught academic skills, manners and cleanliness in a carefully prepared environment with the teacher offering highly detailed instructions. Self- discipline and autonomy were also key elements in her philosophy. She deviated from the others in her field then and today, in her opinion of play. Montessori rejected play as a waste of children's time (Snyder, 1972). Montessori's major contributions are child-sized furniture and materials, materials that appeal to the senses such as sandpaper alphabets, and the intentional organization of the learning environment. There has been a resurgence of interest in the Montessori method since the reintroduction of her work in the 1950's and 1960's (Rambusch, 1962).

"Maria Montessori: Her Life and Legacy (Davidson Films, Inc.)"

The Nursery School Movement

At the beginning of the 20th century, several forces influenced early childhood education in the United States. Following World War I (1914-1918), there was an increased concern for the well-being and education of young children. At the same time, Dewey's laboratory school with its emphasis on child observation signified an understanding of the need to ground educational theory and practice in the study of children. Consequently, universities established laboratory schools for the purposes of child study and teacher training. These schools, called **nursery schools,** provided nurturing education and care for middle- and upper-class children younger than kindergarten age and a site for teachers to study children and hone their teaching practice. At the same time, the leaders in the progressive education movement believed that education could transform the lives of poor children specifically and society generally.

Sisters **Margaret McMillan (1860-1931)** and **Rachel McMillan (1859-1917)** were working to improve the lives of young children in London. The McMillans had backgrounds in social welfare and great interest in easing the plight of children living in poverty. The sisters created open-air nursery schools which emphasized outdoor play, nutrition and health care, and active, hands-on learning (Beatty, 1995). Margaret was ahead of her time in that she believed that nursery schools and well-trained teachers have a great effect on the brain development of young children during the brain's most formative period (McMillan, 1912).

Caroline Pratt (1867-1954), a contemporary of Patty Smith Hill also attended the kindergarten education program at Teachers College, and like Hill, believed that children need a much less structured curriculum than Froebel's philosophy allowed. Pratt developed her own materials – blocks and toys - and stocked classrooms with these plus crayons and paper. She believed fervently in children's self-directed play in which they could hypothesize, answer their own questions, and learn how to think.

Demonstrating her commitment to open-ended play as the most powerful force in a young child's learning, in 1913 Pratt opened the Play School (later called the City and Country School) in the Greenwich Village area of New York City. The curriculum of the school focused on children's creativity in the arts and expansive first-hand experiences through frequent field trips (Wolfe, 2000).

Caroline Pratt is well known for her design of wooden unit blocks. These wooden blocks that are used in modern early childhood classrooms are various three-dimensional shapes and mathematically precise so that they can be used to teach the concept of fractions. Pratt crafted wooden people to signify families and community helpers, giving children a way to use pretend when extending the block play.

Lucy Sprague Mitchell (1878-1967) was a close associate of Pratt, establishing a long and productive collaboration. Mitchell studied at Teachers College with Dewey, where her progressive philosophy focused on improving children's lives through education, was molded. In 1916, Mitchell initiated the formation of the Bureau of Educational Experiments (B.E.E.), a teacher-education and research institution. The goals of the Bureau were to focus on child development instead of curriculum, observe how development is influenced by experiences and activities, establish norms of stages of development, and to develop reflective teacher-researchers (Wolfe, 2000).

The Bureau's relocation to 69 Bank Street caused a change of name to the Bank Street College of Education. In this new location, a teacher education facility with a lab school and research center was established. At Bank Street, the seeds of a rich history of early childhood educational philosophy were planted. Mitchell brought the principles of open-ended play and the value of firsthand experiences that had been inculcated during her time at the City and Country School. These tenets formed what is now called the **Bank Street Approach**, a hands-on curriculum based on individual children's development which is intentionally scaffolded by well-trained teachers. The influence of the Bank Street conception moved into the New York City public schools by the 1940's. The once revolutionary ideas of the progressive schools became widely accepted mainstream elements in education (Sullivan, 1996).

"Bank Street College of Education Empowers New Teachers"

Other Historical Contributors to Early Childhood Education

Arnold Gesell (1880-1961), a physician at the Yale University Clinic for Child Development and a student of G. Stanley Hall, studied the process of maturation. Gesell was the first to provide systematic, normative descriptions of children's development across all domains from birth through age 10 (Jalongo & Isenberg, 2012). Gesell's research is often referred to as "ages and stages" due to its structure of typical characteristics of children categorized by ages, representing the predictable stages of development for all children. Although Gesell studied children representing mostly the upper-middle class, he promoted the **maturationist theory** which believes that the sequence of changes in abilities and behavior is predominantly influenced by children's biological growth process rather than by culture, experience and learning.

Erikson's Stage Theory in its Final Version			
Age	*Conflict*	*Resolution or "Virtue"*	*Culmination in old age*
Infancy (0-1 year)	Basic trust vs. mistrust	Hope	Appreciation of interdependence and relatedness
Early childhood (1-3 years)	Autonomy vs. shame	Will	Acceptance of the cycle of life, from integration to disintegration
Play age (3-6 years)	Initiative vs. guilt	Purpose	Humor; empathy; resilience
School age (6-12 years)	Industry vs. Inferiority	Competence	Humility; acceptance of the course of one's life and unfulfilled hopes
Adolescence (12-19 years)	Identity vs. Confusion	Fidelity	Sense of complexity of life; merging of sensory, logical and aesthetic perception
Early adulthood (20-25 years)	Intimacy vs. Isolation	Love	Sense of the complexity of relationships; value of tenderness and loving freely
Adulthood (26-64 years)	Generativity vs. stagnation	Care	Caritas, caring for others, and agape, empathy and concern
Old age (65-death)	Integrity vs. Despair	Wisdom	Existential identity; a sense of integrity strong enough to withstand physical disintegration

Erik Erikson (1902-1994), a psychologist who was greatly influenced by cultural anthropologists, developed theory that addressed the unique considerations for children's emotional needs. His developmental stage theory of social and emotional development endures today as a foundation of belief about children's personality evolvement. The socioemotional development of children, according to Erikson, results from the consequences of a series of conflicts, each of which addresses an essential concern of the human mind (Eliason & Jenkins, 2008). His seminal book, *Childhood and Society* (1950/1963) proposes an eight-stage theory of personal and social development wherein at each stage of life a person confronts a major crisis which requires successful negotiation between two thresholds on a continuum. One example is Autonomy versus Doubt. If there is not a successful resolution of these major challenges along the life span, Erikson hypothesized that later difficulties in personality development would result. With the knowledge that young children are highly sensitive to the impact of relationships with the adults in their lives, Erikson's theory has been used to guide interactions with infants and young children. He proposes that early childhood professionals must foster close, secure attachments with children.

**"Erik Erikson's Psychosocial Stage
of Autonomy vs. Shame and Doubt"**

Jean Piaget (1896-1980), a Swiss psychologist, is the most universally known theorist in the area of cognitive development. Piaget's work and writings have created greater interest and research in education and developmental psychology in the last over 50 years than those of any other person, except for Lev Vygotsky. He spent his life studying children's cognitive development, primarily through observation and evaluation of children's problem-solving techniques. Piaget observed that children think in countless different ways at different ages, generating his stage theory (Piaget, 1961). "Children don't think like adults" is a simplistic way of understanding Piaget's theory. Piaget believed that children learn through experimentation, using their initiative to construct their own knowledge and understanding through adaptation to their environment.

"Jean Piaget: How a Child Thinks"

Piaget described children as moving through four stages of intellectual development – sensorimotor, preoperational, concrete operational, and formal operational. He proposed that children strive for **equilibrium**, or balance, in their beliefs and understandings of the events they experience. New information is dealt with either by **assimilation** – fitting it into a child's existing belief or by **accommodation** – the child changing his/her ideas to accept the new information (Piaget, 1969). Through their interaction with the world, children test their theories causing them to be strengthened, amended, or discarded. The theory that supports the belief that children construct their own knowledge is called constructivism.

"Piaget's Developmental Theory: An Overview"

Piaget concluded that time and experiences were needed to expedite maturation. He believed that both nature (biological growth) and nurture (people, experiences, and occurrences) influenced development (Piaget, 1975). There are many modern criticisms of Piaget's work (which are discussed in Chapter 4), yet his tremendous contributions endure at all levels of early childhood education.

Piaget lived a long life researching, writing and promoting the theory of constructivism, while his contemporary, Lev Vygotsky, lived a relatively short life. Despite living only 38 years, Vygotsky's prolific writing has taken us beyond the theories of Piaget and in the past thirty years has become more influential in the field of learning and teaching than Piaget.

Lev Vygotsky (1896-1934), a Russian psychologist whose theory emphasized the importance of language in cognitive development, was a relative unknown in Western theory until the early 1960's. His work remained obscure during the first half of the 20th century due to the Stalinist government's suppression. Vygotsky's work was not translated into English until 1962.

Vygotsky's **sociocultural theory** is based on the belief that children learn from social interaction, utilizing language within a cultural context. Unlike Piaget who believed that development precedes learning and is dependent on an internal schedule of maturation, Vygotsky posited that learning and development were influenced by the social occurrence of language and occur simultaneously; learning is a social construction with adults and peers in the child's culture molding what children learn and know. Using scaffolding and support from adults and "expert peers", a child can move through increasingly difficult levels of understanding and accomplishment. Vygotsky called this area of cognitive potential the zone of proximal development (ZPD). The ZPD is the distance between the independent level of problem-solving (the actual developmental level) and the level of potential development the child could achieve with adult guidance or peer collaboration. Lending a contrast to Piaget's theory, the role of the adult is of major importance in Vygotsky's view.

"Vygotsky's Developmental Theory: An Introduction"

For Vygotsky, "Learning awakens a variety of developmental processes that are able to operate only when the child is interacting with people in his environment and in collaboration with his peers. Once these processes are internalized, they become part of the child's individual developmental achievement" (Vygotsky, 1978, p. 244). It is safe to say that Vygotskian theory has been the leading influence on learning and teaching in the past thirty years.

B.F. Skinner (1904-1990), was the primary creator of the **behaviorist theory,** a theory that emphasizes the jobs of environmental conditions (stimuli) and overt behaviors (responses) in learning. The basic conjecture of this theory is that children learn through the results of their own purposeful responses and that consequences determine whether a child will continue a particular behavior that resulted in the consequences. Skinner theorized that positive behaviors can be increased through the use of reinforcers such as praise and smiles, and negative behaviors can be decreased through punishment, such as the withdrawal of privileges and materials. The teacher's structuring of the environment for learning is of prime importance.

"Reinforcement Theory"

"Behaviorism: Pavlov, Watson and Skinner"

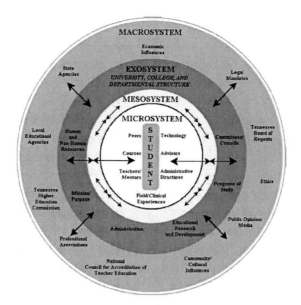

Urie Bronfenbrenner (1917-2005), an American developmental psychologist, is best known for his **ecological theory** which addresses children's development within the context of a system of relationships that shape their environment. Though Bronfenbrenner acknowledges the importance of biological influences on development, his theory underscores the social and cultural world in which children live and the way that children shape their worlds and the people residing in those worlds (Jalongo & Isenberg, 2012). These **bi-directional social and cultural contexts** which are intertwined include the immediate family, extended family, educational setting, community, and broader society. These contexts are analogous to a set of nesting dolls – each embedded within the other, acting autonomously but operating as a unit when put together. Bronfenbrenner's theory includes five nested dolls – five different social systems – the **microsystem**, **mesosystem**, **exosystem**, **macrosystem**, and **chronosystem**. The microsystem is where the child lives and experiences most of his/her life – the home, school, neighborhood, and with friends. The mesosystem includes the interactions across microsystems, exemplified by the way the school supports home literacy. The exosystem links social systems in which children do not have direct interaction, but that indirectly influences children. One example would be the parents' workplace and the educational system that places great stress on the parent in different ways – one may demand overtime work and the other may demand parental support of children in after-school homework. The macrosystem includes the values, culture, beliefs, laws, and customs of the society in which the child lives. The chronosystem includes the environmental dimensions over time – divorce, death, and technology advancement are examples.

"Urie Bronfenbrenner's Ecological Theory"

 **Albert Bandura (1925-)**, a contemporary psychologist, is the leading **social learning theorist,** who broadened the principles of behaviorism and combined them with cognitive theory to develop the theory of social learning. Bandura believes that children learn much of their social behavior from watching, and imitating others. Social learning theory emphasizes the importance of modeling to explicitly demonstrate expected behavior and learning. Identification with key family members in influencing language development, responses to stress and anger, developing moral sense, and learning socially acceptable behavior is a core tenet of social learning theory (Bandura, 1997). Learning by modeling and by vicarious learning – observing the consequences of other's behavior – are basic principles of Bandura's theory.

"Bobo Doll Experiment (Bandura)"

Jerome Bruner (1915-2016), a contemporary constructivist theorist was influenced by the work of Piaget. Yet unlike Piaget, Bruner did not propose stages of cognitive development. Instead, he suggested that learning is much like a computer, combining external factors and internal factors; the mind codes and organizes information as it is taken in. Bruner promoted the idea of **discovery learning** as the most important process for learning, emphasizing children's need for freedom and autonomy to explore their interests (Bruner, 1991). Bruner was also credited with helping found the Head Start early childcare program. Bruner was deeply impressed by his 1995 visit to the preschools of Reggio Emilia and established a collaborative relationship with them to improve educational systems internationally.

"Jerome Bruner"

Many of these theories and theorists and their influences on early childhood education will be discussed in depth in Chapter 4.

Modern Movements and Influences

Education and the Political Scene

As World War II ended in 1945, the Cold War began – a period of United States and Soviet Union frenzied competition for world dominance of nuclear power and space exploration. This hostility created a social and political atmosphere and a re-thinking of the purpose of education. The Cold War created a national consciousness which has sparked educational trends that persist to the present day.

In 1957, the Soviet Union was the first nation to successfully launch a satellite, *Sputnik.* National fear of Soviet domination ensued; *Sputnik* was an event that almost singlehandedly created a massive educational policy response. In 1958, Congress passed the National Defense Education Act (NDEA), providing federal funding for math, science, technology and foreign language education. This was only the beginning of decades of increasing federal government funding and 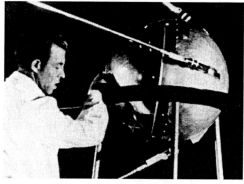 involvement in educational policy. Quality education still is thought to be the singularly most important variable in maintaining dominance in the world.

The 1950's was a decade of awakening interest in the Civil Rights of Americans. Although much of the legislation was not passed until the 1960's, American consciousness-raising began with landmark cases such as *Brown v. Board of Education.* In 1896, the case of *Plessy v. Ferguson* had confirmed the legality of "separate but equal" public places including schools. The law assumed that the opportunities and facilities were equal for all races when in fact they were not. The 1954 case *Brown v. Board of Education* overturned the *Plessy v. Ferguson* legislation, sowing the seeds of the Civil Rights Movement:

> Segregation of children in public schools solely on the basis of race deprives children of the minority group of equal opportunities, even though the physical facilities and other "tangible" factors may be equal. The "separate but equal" doctrine adopted in *Plessy v. Ferguson* has no place in the field of public education. (FindLaw)

"Brown v. Board of Education"

But legislation hammered in the halls of Congress and adjudicated in our highest court does not ensure reality in the daily lives of American students.

More than fifty years since *Brown v. Board of Education,* the education of much of the nation's minorities remains unequal. Classes of predominantly minority students are more likely to have less competent and experienced teachers in schools with fewer materials and less challenging curriculum, receiving less state and local funding (Morrison, 2012). As a result, the wide achievement gap between white students and minorities persists. Minority children who have experienced unequal educational opportunities, poverty, and test bias to name a few factors have lower reading and mathematics achievement test scores (National Center for Education Statistics, 2015).

In the 1960's the Civil Rights Movement flourished as the American consciousness was forced to admit the inequity in the lives of citizens who were members of minorities and people with disabilities. Public education was one of the institutions where discrimination existed. **The Civil Rights Act of 1964** protected the rights of individuals in public arenas such as public schools. This bill was later amended in 1972 and the name of the education amendment was renamed **The Equal Opportunity Act of 1964.**

One provision in the 1972 amendment was **Title IX** which provided for gender equity in public schools: No person in the United States shall, on the basis of sex, be excluded from participating in, be denied the benefits of, or be subjected to discrimination under any program or activity receiving federal financial assistance (FindLaw). Females were now guaranteed equal access in both academics and sports in public education.

Another piece of legislation passed during this era of ground-breaking lawmaking was the **Economic Opportunity Act of 1964 (EOA).** This was part of President Lyndon B. Johnson's War on Poverty initiative. Several social programs addressing the health, general welfare, and education of Americans living in poverty were launched. A few of these programs – Head Start and Early Head Start - are in existence today. These programs will be discussed at length in Chapter 5.

In 1965, Congress passed the **Elementary and Secondary Education Act (ESEA)** with the intent of more fully funding elementary and secondary public education. The ESEA, through Title I, provided funds to educate children from high-needs American families. High-needs is based on a family's eligibility for their children to receive free and reduced-lunches. School districts utilize Title I monies to provide academic support to children in academic content areas during the school year and in summer school programs. More than 59,000 schools, serving more than 21 million children receive Title I funds (U.S. Department of Education).

A Nation at Risk, a report published in 1983, criticized the quality of the educational system in the United States and its preparation of a workforce. The report compared the educational system with other advanced nations and found the quality of teaching and learning in the United States wanting. The memorable and incendiary language: "The educational foundations of our society are presently being eroded by a rising tide of mediocrity that threatens our very future as a Nation and a people" and "If an unfriendly foreign power had attempted to impose on America the mediocre educational performance that exists today, we might well have viewed it as an act of war" (A Nation at Risk) precipitated a national reaction emphasizing achievement testing and comparisons of American students with children in other industrialized nations. So began the standards movement – a commitment calling for "back to basics" and holding educators accountable for students' performance on tests.

In 1989, President George H.W. Bush met with the governors of the states at their annual Governor's Conference. At this meeting, a list of learning goals – **Goals 2000** - for all American children was established:

By the Year 2000:

- All children in America will start school ready to learn.
- The high school graduation rate will increase to at least 90 percent.
- All students will leave grades 4, 8, and 12 having demonstrated competency over challenging subject matter including English, mathematics, science, foreign languages, civics and government, economics, the arts, history, and geography, and every school in America will ensure that all students learn to use their minds well, so they may be prepared for responsible citizenship, further learning, and productive employment in our nation's modern economy.
- United States students will be first in the world in mathematics and science achievement.
- Every adult American will be literate and will possess the knowledge and skills necessary to compete in a global economy and exercise the rights and responsibilities of citizenship.
- Every school in the United States will be free of drugs, violence, and the unauthorized presence of firearms and alcohol and will offer a disciplined environment conducive to learning.
- The nation's teaching force will have access to programs for the continued improvement of their professional skills and the

opportunity to acquire the knowledge and skills needed to instruct and prepare all American students for the next century.

- Every school will promote partnerships that will increase parental involvement and participation in promoting the social, emotional, and academic growth of children.

The first goal most directly affects early childhood education. The Goals 2000: Educate America Act (P.L.103-227) was signed into law on March 31, 1994 by President Bill Clinton.

The **No Child Left Behind Act of 2001** (NCLB) is a United States act of Congress that came about as a result of wide public concern about the state of American education. First proposed by the administration of George W. Bush immediately after he took office, the bill passed in the United States Congress with bipartisan support.

"ESSA Explained: Inside the New Federal K-12 Law"

NCLB is a reauthorization of the Elementary and Secondary Education Act which included Title I, the government's educational aid program for disadvantaged students. – NCLB supports standards-based educational reform based on the belief that setting high standards and establishing measurable goals can improve individual outcomes in education. According to the tenets of NCLB, the emphasis in education should be on scientifically-based practice. Scientifically-based practice is based on cognitive science which studies how people learn, the science of child development, and effective instructional strategies and environments. The Act requires states to develop assessments in basic skills. States must give these assessments to all students at select grade levels in order to receive federal school funding. NCLB expanded the federal role in public education through annual testing, annual academic progress, report cards, teacher qualifications, and funding channels. The Act does not assert a national achievement standard; standards are set by each individual state.

However, the **Common Core State Standards** – a set of learning standards co-authored by the National Governors Association Center for Best Practices and the Council of Chief State School Officers – initially were adopted in 45 of the states. Common Core Sate Standards arose from a simple idea: that creating one set of challenging academic expectations for all students would improve achievement and college readiness. The drive for common learning goals in English/language arts and mathematics produced an extraordinary response. The Common Core State Standards provide a consistent, clear understanding of what students are expected to learn, so teachers and parents know what they need to do to help them. The standards are designed to be robust and relevant to the real world, reflecting the knowledge and skills that our young people need for success in college and careers. With American students fully prepared for the future, our communities will be best positioned to compete successfully in the global economy (Common Core State Standards).

But there was also an extraordinary backlash against the Common Core Standards. Critics argued that the standards were not developmentally appropriate for K-3rd grade students, that many of the skills erroneously expect students to learn in the same way and at the same rate, that early childhood educators did not participate in the standards' creation, there is a lack of research that the early childhood standards are supported by research, that play and the teacher facilitation of the play is not considered, and that mastery the standards will not necessarily narrow the poverty gap (Washington Post, 2014). By 2016, several states reversed their adoptions of the standards, and nearly half backed out of their initial promise to use assessments designed to measure mastery of the standards. Presently, 42 states utilize both the ELA and Math Common Core Standards, with Minnesota using only the ELA Standards. Despite the controversy surrounding the Common Core Standards, they provide teachers a consistent roadmap of the skills and knowledge children need to be successful in today's world.

Race to the Top was a $4.35 billion United States Department of Education competitive grant created to spur and reward innovation and reforms in state and local district K-12 education. It was funded as part of the American Recovery and Reinvestment Act of 2009 and was announced by President Barack Obama and Secretary of Education Arne Duncan on July 25, 2009. States were awarded points for embracing certain educational policies: performance-based evaluations for teachers and principals based on multiple measures of educator effectiveness (and are tied to targeted professional development and feedback), adopting common standards (although adoption of the Common Core State Standards was not required), adoption of policies that do not prohibit (or effectively prohibit) the expansion of high-quality charter schools, turning around the lowest-performing schools, and building and using data systems. States were eligible for different funding awards based on their share of the federal population of children between the ages of 5-17. One of the most controversial provisions require that in order to be eligible, states couldn't have laws prohibiting the use of measures of student achievement growth in teacher evaluations (U.S. Department of Education, 2014).

The Round 1 winners were announced on March 2010 with Delaware receiving 100 million and Tennessee receiving 500 million. Round 2 winners were awarded their grants on August 2010: District of Columbia (75 million), Florida (700 million), Georgia (400 million), Hawaii (75 million), Maryland (250 million), Massachusetts (250 million), New York (700 million), North Carolina (400 million), Ohio (400 million), and Rhode Island (75 million). Round 3 winners were announced in December 2011: Arizona (25 million), Colorado (18 million), Illinois (43 million), Kentucky (17 million), Louisiana (17 million), New Jersey (38 million), and Pennsylvania (41 million).

The U.S. Department of Education put out Annual Performance Reports (APR), cataloguing the grantees' progress in implementing reform plans and meeting goals for student outcomes. The APR also includes reports and updates on laws, statutes, regulations, and/or guidelines that impact reform plans, as well as updates on progress in meeting the invitation priorities in the approved plans (innovations for improving early learning outcomes; expansion and adaptation of statewide longitudinal data systems; P-20 coordination, vertical and horizontal alignment; and school-level conditions for reform, innovation, and learning).

Was there educational progress made as a result of the Race to the Top funding, which ended in mid-2015?

According to the Center for American Progress (www.americanprogress.org/issues/education, 2014) three overarching findings emerged in the review of the data from Race to the Top:

- Many of the lowest-performing schools in RTT states have achieved impressive results in a short period of time. Over the past few years, states reported on the progress of implementing reform models in their lowest-performing schools. Many states described schools where educators and students had improved performance to such an extent that their schools could move out of the ranks of the "lowest-performing." RTT states also showed their willingness to take action by intervening in low-performing schools that failed to improve.

- Four RTT states are at or near full implementation of their educator evaluation systems, and all other states are in the process of implementing their systems. Implementing new, more rigorous educator evaluation systems is technical and arduous work. It is a time-consuming effort that requires significant collaboration from state and district leaders, school administrators, and teachers. It is noteworthy that six states have evaluation systems in full implementation at the four-year mark.

- All RTT states have adopted college- and career-ready standards and are making progress toward implementation of assessments aligned with those standards. States provided educators with professional development opportunities and training on new, more rigorous standards. Although states have made progress, a few are struggling with implementation of the new standards (2014).

This report shows concrete data of increased student outcomes, as well as greater accountability measures being instituted, as a result of the 4.35 billion dollar investment.

Concurrently, the Departments of Education and Health and Human Services designed a grant-funded program for Early Childhood Education, titled Race to the Top-Early Learning Challenge fund. The purpose of the 500 million dollar grant was to support States' efforts to: (1) increase the number and percentage of low-income and disadvantaged children in each age group of infants, toddlers, and preschoolers who are enrolled in high-quality early learning programs; (2) design and implement an integrated system of high-quality early learning programs and services; and (3) ensure that any use of assessments conforms with the recommendations of the National Research Council's reports on early childhood ((§1832(b)(1), title VIII, Division B of P.L. 112-10, the Department of Defense and Full-Year Continuing Appropriations Act, 2011). The First Phase amount of 500 million dollars in the grant was awarded in varying amounts to nine states – California, Delaware, Maryland, Massachusetts, Minnesota, North Carolina, Ohio, Rhode Island and Washington. Eleven more states – Colorado, Illinois, New Mexico, Oregon, Wisconsin, Georgia, Kentucky, Michigan, New Jersey, Pennsylvania, and Vermont – received a total of 500 million more.

ESSA (Every Student Succeeds Act), the latest reauthorization of the fifty-year old Elementary and Secondary Education Act, was signed into law on December 10, 2015 by President Obama. In many ways ESSA is a reverse from the No Child Left Behind Act in that states have significant leeway in a wide range of areas, and the role and power of the U.S. Department of Education is diminished. The major tenets of the law are:

- States are required to adopt academic content standards in reading, mathematics, and science. Standards in other content areas are optional. These standards do not have to be the Common Core State Standards.

- Annual testing in reading and mathematics is still required for all students in grades 3 through 8, and once in high school. However, states can opt to administer shorter, frequent assessments throughout the school year that result in a single score rather than administering one comprehensive test.

- Schools must continue to report student achievement by subgroup and to issue an annual state report. States may substitute the SAT or ACT for the high school state achievement test. States must continue to administer a science test once in grades 3 through 5, once in grades 6 through 8, and once in high school.

- Schools must use at least three academic indicators such as student proficiency on state tests, student growth on state tests, and English Language Proficiency. At the high school level, schools must also include graduation rates. There is no longer the requirement for 100 percent proficiency and adequate yearly progress has been eliminated.

- Once every three years, states are to identify schools for comprehensive district support. These schools include those at the lowest 5 percent of Title 1 schools, high schools with graduation rates of less than 67 percent, and schools with one or more low-performing subgroups among the lowest 5 percent of all title 1 schools. If the district is unable to help underperforming schools meet the state's improvement criteria within four years, states are required to implement "more rigorous actions". States can include factors such as student engagement, faculty engagement school climate/safety, or whatever else the state feels is significant. Schools will no longer be labeled as failing if they miss a single target for a single group of students.

- The term "highly qualified teachers" has been replaced with a provision that all teachers working in programs supported by Title 1 funds must meet their state's certification and licensure requirements. This provision stipulates that teacher evaluation based on student growth measured on a standardized test will cease to exist, but states may elect to make it part of their individual teacher evaluation process. (www.ed.gov/essa).

The ESSA provisions give the states greater decision-making in how proficiency is measured, however the aim of ESSA is the same as NCLB– to ensure that all students, particularly special populations and historically disadvantaged students, are well-served by new policies and approaches.

Education for Diverse Learners

Education for All Handicapped Children Act (sometimes referred to using the acronyms EAHCA or EHA, or Public Law (PL) 94-142) was enacted by the United States Congress in 1975. This act required all public schools accepting federal funds to provide equal access to education and one free meal a day for children with physical and mental disabilities. Public schools were required to evaluate handicapped children and create an educational plan with parent input that would emulate as closely as possible the educational experience of non-disabled students. The act also required that school districts provide administrative procedures so that parents of disabled children could dispute decisions made about their children's education. Once the administrative efforts were exhausted, parents were then authorized to seek judicial review of the administration's decision.

PL 94-142 also contains a provision that disabled students should be placed in the least restrictive environment - one that allows the maximum possible opportunity to interact with non-impaired students. Separate schooling may only occur when the nature or severity of the disability is such that instructional goals cannot be achieved in the regular classroom. Finally, the law contains a due process clause that guarantees an impartial hearing to resolve conflicts between the parents of disabled children to the school system.

The law was passed to meet four major goals: to ensure that special education services are available to children who need them, to guarantee that decisions about services to disabled students are fair and appropriate, to establish specific management and auditing requirements for special education, and to provide federal funds to help the states educate disabled students.

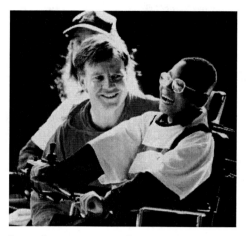 In 1990, the Education of All Handicapped Children Act was reauthorized and renamed the **Individuals with Disabilities Education Act (IDEA)**. The law governs how states and public agencies provide early intervention, special education, and related services to children with disabilities. It addresses the educational needs of children with disabilities from birth to age 18 or 21 in cases that involve 11 specified categories: intellectual disabilities, hearing impairments (including deafness), speech or language impairment, visual impairment (including blindness), serious emotional disturbance, orthopedic impairments, autism, traumatic brain injuries, other health impairments, or specific learning disabilities, and multiple disabilities and who, because of the condition needs special education and related services. In 2004, further revisions included legislation governing how states provide early intervention services for infants, young children, and school-age children with disabilities. Provisions call for increased improvement in access to free appropriate public education for children with disabilities including (Follari, 2011, p.135):

- Children to be educated in the least restrictive environment
- Teachers and parents to jointly create individualized plans for children
- School-wide support and aid to guarantee optimal success for children with disabilities
- High expectations for all children
- Accountability of professionals to children and families
- Equitable educational decisions for all children
- High-quality pre-service teacher education designed to prepare teachers to best meet students' distinctive and diverse needs with research-based teaching approaches

"IDEA: Individuals with Disabilities Education Act - History and Summary"

Approximately 10 to 12 percent of the nation's students have some type of disability (Morrison, 2012). IDEA applies to infants and toddlers (age birth to 36 months) and students (age 3 through 21). IDEA consists of four parts, but the parts of most interest to educators are Part B and Part C.

IDEA, Part B provides the underpinning of all special education and related services. Part B provides guidelines for children ages three to twenty-one. Part B defines free and appropriate public education, least restrictive environment, state and local education agency eligibility for funding, evaluations, procedural safeguards to protect children and families' rights, conflict resolution, enforcement and use of funds, grants for preschool programs, and individual education programs (Morrison, 2012)

IDEA, Part C provides early intervention for children thirty-six months and younger who require services due to developmental delays. Part C gives states the option whether to serve infants and toddlers in programs and whether to serve at-risk toddlers.

The Seven Principles of IDEA:

1. *Zero reject:* No child can be excluded from an education.
2. *Nondiscriminatory evaluation:* A fair evaluation is necessitated to determine if the child has a disability and if so, the education the student should receive.
3. *Multidisciplinary assessment:* A group of people – the team – utilize multiple means of evaluation to design a child's educational program.
4. *Appropriate education:* All students between the ages of three and twenty-one receive a free and appropriate education suited to their ages, maturity, achievements, disability, and parental goals.
5. *Least restrictive environment:* If possible, students with disabilities must be educated with students who do not have disabilities.
6. *Procedural due process:* IDEA provides mediation and impartial hearings if disagreements arise.
7. *Parent and student participation:* IDEA makes provisions for shared decision-making involving parents, students, and educators.

In order to receive individually designed instruction which meet the unique needs of a child with a disability and at no cost to the parents, children must meet eligibility standards, determined on a state-to-state basis. Additionally, some states provide early intervention services for infants and toddlers as well as their families deemed at risk of developmental delay. The purpose of early intervention is to prevent a potential problem rather than treating an already existing one.

The **Individuals with Disabilities Education Improvement Act (IDEIA)** was signed into law in December 2007. Section 619 of Part B (also known as Early Childhood Special Education) applies expressly to preschoolers with a disability. In order to meet the individualized needs, the law necessitates a team of educators and family members create an individualized education plan for each student.

The **Individualized Education Plan (IEP)** is designed and implemented by the school district team to meet the distinct needs of the child, after confirmation that the child meets the disability requirements. The written IEP must contain the following information (Bredekamp, 2011, pp.151-152):

1. A statement of the child's present levels of academic achievement and functional performance.
2. A statement of measurable annual goals, including academic and functional goals designed to:
    *   Meet the child's needs that result from the child's disability to enable the child to be involved in and make progress in the general education curriculum, and
    *   Meet each of the child's other educational needs that result from the child's disability.
3. A description of benchmarks or short-term objectives.
4. A description of:
    *   How the child's progress toward meeting the annual goals will be measured; and
    *   When periodic reports on the progress the child is making toward meeting the annual goals (such as through the use of quarterly or other periodic reports, concurrent with the issuance of report cards) will be provided.
5. A statement of the special education and related services and supplementary aids and services, based on peer-reviewed research to the extent feasible, to be provided to the child, or on behalf of the child.
6. A statement of any individually appropriate accommodations that are necessary to measure the academic achievement and

functional performance of the child on state- and district-wide assessments.

The **IEP Team**, by law, must include:

- The child's early childhood teacher
- The child's early childhood special education teacher
- The child's parents or guardians
- A representative of the community who has certain specific knowledge and qualifications
- An individual who can translate the instructional implications of assessments data (this may be one of the other members of the team such as one of service providers)
- Other individuals, chosen by the parents or the agency, who have special knowledge about the child, including related services providers such as the occupational therapist or speech pathologist.

 **Early Intervention Services (EI)** are provided under Part C of IDEA to children from birth to thirty-six months with developmental delays, a diagnosed disability, or as provided by some states, at risk for developing a developmental delay. Instead of an IEP, children in this age range have an **Individualized Family Service Plan (IFSP)**. The IFSP provides the guidance for the early intervention process for children identified as eligible for services. The family is an integral part of the IFSP process in both the development of it and the facilitation of their child's services.

Following diagnostic testing or a developmental evaluation, the child receives EI services from a team of specialists. The child's family and team of specialists collaborate to plan, implement and assess services that the family and team have designed for the unique needs of the child.

The IFSP, like the IEP, is a written plan in which specific information must be included (Morrison, 2012, pp.152-153):

1. The child's present levels of physical, cognitive, language, social or emotional, and adaptive development
2. The family's resources, priorities, and concerns relating to enhancing the development of the child with a disability
3. The major outcomes to be achieved for the child and family; the criteria, procedures, and timelines used to determine progress; and whether modifications or revisions of the outcomes or services are necessary

4. Specific early intervention services necessary to meet the unique needs of the child and the family, including the frequency, intensity, and the method of delivery
5. The environments in which services will be provided, including justification of the extent, if any, to which the services will not be provided in a natural environment
6. The projected dates for initiation of services and their anticipated duration
7. The name of the service provider who will be responsible for implementing the plan and coordinating with other agencies and persons
8. Steps to support the child's transition to preschool or other appropriate services

The IFSP focuses on the family as the center of the child's life, includes outcomes for the family, integrates the services of multiple agencies into one coherent plan, appoints a service coordinator, and recognizes the value of natural environments as the venue for intervention services. Natural environments are the everyday activities, routines, and places where children and their families would spend their time if the child had no disability. Natural learning environments are important for young children because the learning takes place in the contexts where children will use the new skill (Dunst, 2001).

Inclusion provides many of the same benefits of natural environments, most notably that children with disabilities grow and learn with typically developing peers. These environments include schools, homes, religious settings, parks, and recreational venues. Inclusive settings provide the opportunity for all children to participate, learn and succeed.

Early childhood inclusion embodies the values, policies, and practices that support the right of every infant and young child and his or her family, regardless of ability, to participate in a broad range of activities and contexts as full members of families, communities, and society. The desired results of inclusive experiences for children with and without disabilities and their families include a sense of belonging and membership, positive social relationships and friendships, and development and learning to reach their full potential. The defining features of inclusions that can be used to identify high quality early childhood programs and services are access, participation, and supports. (DEC/NAEYC, 2009)

Access may include *structural modifications* such as doorways wide enough for a wheelchair, *instructional modifications* such as extra time, and *technological* *modifications* such as a large computer screen. **Participation** may require a range of approaches from routines-based teaching to explicit interventions such as scaffolding. **Supports** form a system that sustains the efforts of the educational team. These supports include ongoing professional development for the families, teachers, and administrators so that the inclusive practices will be effective.

Universal Design for Learning (UDL) is a teaching and learning approach that helps to ensure that high quality learning experiences are multi-modal, multi-dimensional, meaningful, intentional, and exciting for every child. Universal Design for Learning began as an architectural principle that plans the environment for optimal accessibility and usage. Recently UDL has been extended into the design of learner-centered classrooms that are carefully planned for optimal use of space, materials, technology and curriculum. "Universal Design is the design on products and environments to be usable by all people, to the greatest extent possible, without the need for adaptation or specialized design" (Mace, 1996).

UDL calls for the creation of curriculum that provides for:

- Multiple means of representation – various ways of acquiring knowledge and information

- Multiple means of expression and assessment – alternatives for demonstrating the knowledge and information acquired

- Multiple means of engagement – intentionally utilizing student interest and motivation (Palley, 2001).

UDL can be used in the support of students with disabilities as well as those who learn in a variety of ways. The emphasis of UDL is on equal access to curriculum, and is supported by the reauthorization of IDEA (2004), as well as the provisions of NCLB (2002) and ESSA (2014).

Education and Cultural Awareness

Few countries have the richness of diversity enjoyed by the citizens of the United States. Projections are that by 2050, minorities will comprise more than 47 percent of the American population (Morrison, 2012). School populations are representative of this shift in demographics. For decades, the American school has been the place for "Americanizing" children from diverse ethnic backgrounds, however schools have moved to an increased embrace of culturally responsive practices.

Culturally responsive practice means acknowledging and honoring diversity by supporting all students' unique cultures, including (Follari, 2011):

- Religious diversity
- Linguistic diversity
- Ethnic and racial diversity
- Diversity in beliefs and traditions
- Diversity in developmental abilities

Guidelines for quality practice include the following research-based suggestions (NAEYC, 1995):

- Foster home-school connections, using translation software or community services when needed
- Maintain children's home language (which assists, not hinders, in learning English)
- Invite families to participate in class activities whenever possible
- Seek out resources and information that will help you understand and value individual cultures
- Include a child's home language in your classroom whenever possible (label shelves, incorporate numbers and simple words into the class vocabulary)
- Give all children opportunities to represent their knowledge and experiences in a variety of ways (verbal, visual, kinesthetic, etc.)

It is important that early childhood educators keep children and their family culture, special needs, and language in mind when selecting materials and resources for their classroom practice.

Summary

- The history of early childhood education includes many adults who went against established thought about children, generally accepted social and disciplinary practices, and traditional ways of educating young children.

- The field of early childhood education represents a rich tradition of care, education, and advocacy for very young children. Theorists, researchers, and educators in the field have advanced their research and beliefs about young children's growth and development. This corpus of research underpins contemporary ideas.

- Cultural awareness allows us to work and communicate effectively, both verbally and nonverbally, with members of diverse cultural groups. Knowledge of culture is important so that we can better understand our students and the contexts in which they live and develop.

- Throughout the history of the United States legislation has been passed that supports the education of a diverse population. Diversity is a broad term which refers to the many ways in which one person is distinctive from another. An important associated concept to diversity is inclusion.

Key Terms

accommodation
assimilation
Bank Street Approach
behaviorist theory
child study movement
Common Core State Standards
culturally responsive practice
Early Intervention Services (EI)
ecological theory
Education for All Handicapped Children Act (EAHCA)
Elementary and Secondary Education Act (ESEA)
equilibrium
Every Student Succeeds Act (ESSA)
Froebel's gifts
Inclusion
Individualized Education Plan (IEP)
Individualized Family Service Plan (IFSP)
maturationist theory
No Child Left Behind Act (NCLB)
nursery schools
progressivism
social learning theory
sociocultural theory
stages of development
Universal Design for Learning (UDL)

Suggested Readings

Mintz, S. (2004). *Huck's raft: A history of American childhood.* Cambridge, MA: Belknap Press.

Roopnarine, J.L. & Johnson, J.E. (Eds.). (2009). *Approaches to early childhood education.* Upper Saddle River, NJ: Merrill/Pearson.

Wellhousen, K. & Kieff, J. (2002). *A constructivist approach to block play in early childhood.* NY: Delmar.

Suggested Websites

A History of American Education Web Project
www.ux1.eiu.edu

American Montessori Society
www.amshq.org

Association for Childhood International
www.acei.org

Office of Head Start
http://eclkc.ohs.acf.hhs.gov

Reflections

1. Throughout history, there have been swings in beliefs and practice related to many issues. In your portfolio, write a brief statement for each bulleted issue, in which you state your beliefs and the influences that shaped your beliefs:
   - The views of children and how they develop and learn
   - The role of families at home and in society
   - Early childhood settings as care or education, or both; the goals and purpose of the programming
   - International educators and philosophers and their influence on American schooling

2. Visit an area child-care center or school, and arrange an interview with the director or school administrator:
   - Find out the program's mission and vision
   - Find out the school's philosophy and the theory that the program is grounded by
   - Find out the role and beliefs of the families
   - Make notes about your impressions of how the environment supports the data you have collected from the interview
   - What visible signs do you see of the mission, vision, philosophy and view of children and families?

3. Observe the environment and teaching practices in public school prekindergarten and kindergarten classrooms. Reflect on what the founders of kindergarten might have thought about present-day early childhood programs in public schools. What is aligned with the traditional views and what is contrary?

References

Bandura, A. (1997). *Self-efficacy: The exercise of control.* New York: Freeman.

Beatty, B. (1995). *Preschool education in America: The culture of young children from the colonial era to the present.* New Haven, CT: Yale University Press.

Blow, S. (1900/1999). Kindergarten education. In K. M. Paciorek & J. H. Munro (Eds.). Guilford, CT: Dushkin/ McGraw-Hill.

Bredekamp, S. (2011). *Effective practices in early childhood education: Building a foundation.* Upper Saddle River, NJ: Pearson Education.

Bruner, J. (1991). The narrative construction of reality. *Critical inquiry, 18*(1), 1-21.

Dewey, J. (1929). *My pedagogic creed.* Washington, DC: Progressive Education Association.

Dewey, J. (1938). *Experience and education.* New York: Touchstone.

Division for Early Childhood (DEC) and National Association for the Education of Young Children (NAEYC). *Early childhood inclusion: A joint position statement of the Division for Early Childhood of the Council and the National Association for the Education of Young Children.* Chapel Hill, NC: Authors.

Dunst, C. (2001). Participation of young children with disabilities in community learning Baltimore: Paul H. Brookes.

Eliason, C. & Jenkins, L. (2008). *A practical guide to early childhood curriculum.* (8th Ed.). Upper Saddle River, NJ: Pearson Education.

Erikson, E. (1950/1963). *Childhood and society* (2nd Ed.). New York: Norton.

Every Student Succeeds Act (ESSA) www.ed.gov/essa.

FindLaw. U. S. Supreme Court. *Brown v. Board of Education (1954) 347 U.S. 483 (1954);* accessed April 11, 2012, from http:/caselaw.lpfindlaw.com.

Follari, L. M. (2011). *Foundations and best practices in early childhood education.* (2nd Ed.). Upper Saddle River, NJ: Pearson Education.

Hacsi, T. (1995). From indenture to family foster care: A brief history of child placing. *Child Welfare, 74*(1), 162-181.

Henson, K. (2003). Foundations for learner-centered education: A knowledge base. *Education, 124,* 5-16.

Hill, P. S. (1926/1987). The function of the kindergarten. *Young Children, 42*(5), 12-19.

Hyun, E., & Marshall, J. (2003). Teachable-moment-oriented curriculum practice in early childhood education. *Journal of Curriculum Studies, 35* (1), 111-127.

Mace, R.L. (1996). *Accessible environments: Toward universal design. Raleigh, NC: North Carolina University.*

McMillan, M. (1912). The nursery school. In K. M. Paciorek & J. H. Munro (Eds.). *Sources: Notable selections in early childhood education.* (2nd Ed.). Guilford, CT: Dushkin/McGraw-Hill.

Morrison, G. S., (2012). *Early childhood education today.* Upper Saddle River, NJ: Pearson Education.

National Center for Education Statistics (NCES). (2012). Available online at http://nces.ed.gov/programs.

Null, J. W. (2004). Is constructivism traditional? Historical and practical perspectives on a popular advocacy. *Educational Forum, 68,* 180-188.

Piaget, J. (1961). The stages of the intellectual development of the child. In K. M. Paciorek & J. H. Munro (Eds.). *Sources: Notable selections in early childhood education.* (2nd Ed.). Guilford, CT: Dushkin/McGraw-Hill.

Piaget, J. (1969). *The psychology of the child.* New York: Basic Books.

Piaget, J. (1975). *The development of thought.* New York: Viking Press.

Procher, L. (1998). Missing pieces: A review of history chapters in introductory early childhood education textbooks. *Journal of Early Childhood Teacher Education, 19*(1), 31-42.

Rambusch, N. M. (1962). *Learning how to learn: An American approach to Montessori.* Baltimore, MD: Helicon.

Sullivan, K. (1996). Progressive education: Where are you now that we need you? *Oxford Review of Education, 22*(3), 349-356.

U.S. Department of Education. Office of Elementary and Secondary Education, Office of State Support. (2015). *Improving Basic Programs Operated by Local Educational Agencies (Title I, Part A).*

Vygotsky, L. S. (1978). *Mind in society.* Cambridge, MA: Harvard University Press.

Wolfe, J. (2000). *Learning from the past: Historical voices in early childhood education.* Mayerthorpe, Alberta: Piney Branch Press.

www.washingtonpost.com/news/answer-sheet/wp/2014/05/02/6-reasons-to-reject-common-core-k-3-standards-and-6-axioms-to-guide-policy/

Chapter 3
Developmentally Appropriate Practice

The Meaning of Developmentally Appropriate Practice

Thinking Ahead

1. What is developmentally appropriate practice?
2. What does research say about developmentally appropriate practice?
3. What are the varied roles of an early childhood teacher?
4. What is a Code of Ethical Conduct, how is it used, and what is its importance?
5. What is the importance of play in the multiple domains of development?

Throughout the early childhood educator's studies and career, the term developmentally appropriate practice (DAP) will become part of his or her daily language and practice. This chapter addresses the definition of developmentally appropriate practice, the research-based foundation of developmentally appropriate practice, developmentally appropriate practice guidelines, and the teacher's decision-making and role in developmentally appropriate practice. The latest NAEYC position statement (2009) reflects both the enduring legacy and evolution in the early childhood education field. The commitment to  excellence and equity underpins the legacy of developmentally appropriate practice while new knowledge of how children develop and learn elicits the evolution in developmentally appropriate practice.

"Developmentally Appropriate Early Childhood Education"

Developmentally appropriate practice (DAP) is teaching that is consonant with the age, abilities, experience, and interests of young children. It requires the teacher knowing each child individually in order to *meet children where they are*. Concurrently, the teacher is responsible for *setting challenging goals while making them achievable* by scaffolding and intentionality. Developmentally appropriate practice is not about making things easier for children. Rather, it is about striking a balance between goals and experiences suited to young children's learning *and* challenging enough to foster children's progress and learning. Best practice is based on a solid research base

grounded in major principles in human development and learning. Developmentally appropriate practice requires the teachers *draw on a wide repertoire of teaching strategies* to help each child continue to make learning and developmental progress.

DAP requires core consideration of three factors in all teaching practice that is based on how children develop and learn optimally: 1) What is known about child development and learning; 2) What is known about each child as an individual; and 3) What is known about the social and cultural contexts in which children live (Copple & Bredekamp, 2009).

Considering What is Known about Child Development and Learning

During early childhood, teachers who are knowledgeable about child development make relatively accurate predictions about children's expertise based on their chronological age ranges. Well-informed, expert educators can "make broad predictions about what children of a particular age group typically will be like, what they typically will and will not be capable of, and what strategies and approaches will most likely promote their optimal learning and development" (Copple & Bredekamp, 2009, p.9). Knowing age-related attributes helps guide teachers' expectations of children's performance and capabilities, the organization of the learning environment, intentional interactions and activities, and materials. At the same time, teacher's knowledge of child development tells them that the individual children in any group will have some developmental similarities.

Considering What is Known about Each Child as an Individual

Children demonstrate a broad range of inconsistency across every domain of development – physical, cognitive, social, and emotional – while being consistent within the range of "typical" development. To be an effective early childhood educator, one must get to know each child individually. Getting to know the individual abilities, needs, and interests of each child enables the educator to adapt and respond to individual variations. The educator uses a variety of data collection – observation, artifacts of student work, individual child assessments, clinical interviews, and family surveys – to make plans to promote each child's optimal individual development and learning. Children will differ across many domains, contexts, and age. They also differ in their interests, strengths, personalities and approaches to learning.

The term **individually appropriate** denotes teaching practice which considers the interests, strengths, personality and approaches to learning of each individual child and being responsive to these distinctions. Developmentally and individually appropriate practice demands that teachers do not have universal expectations for all the children in the groups, but instead accept that children will learn in varying ways and at varying times. Consequently, to support and nurture children's progress, teachers must continuously assess individual strengths, areas in which children are struggling, what interests children, and what meets their unique needs.

Children may also have special learning needs – sometimes diagnosed, but often not. These children fall outside of the range that is considered "typical" and whether they are children with developmental delays or disabilities or children who are gifted, they add another layer of diversity to the group. In addition, living in poverty or a home where English is not the primary language and being homeless or transient, presents challenges that need sensitive and intentional responsiveness from the teacher. Developmentally appropriate practice is necessary for children with special learning needs to make meaningful progress.

Considering Children's Social and Cultural Contexts

Learning and development occur in and are shaped by social and cultural settings (Bronfenbrenner, 1979). Culture refers to the values, behaviors, beliefs and traditions that a group shares and conveys from one generation to the next. Bronfenbrenner has suggested that children live within a system of influences at many levels, commencing with the family. The interrelationships among children, family members, neighborhoods, family friends, schools, and peers influence children's growth most directly and deeply. He also has suggested that broader systems such as educational systems, the government, and media, wield important but less direct influence on children (Bronfenbrenner, 1986).

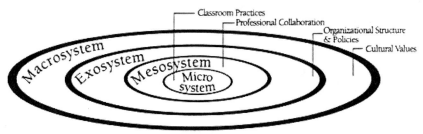

FIGURE 1. Bronfenbrenner's ecological system framework and factors affecting the implementation of inclusion

"Talking About Practice Especially Social Cultural Theory in Childhood Education"

Children learn the values, behaviors, beliefs and traditions as well as daily habits and enduring expectations of their social and cultural contexts. This learning begins early in a child's life and is embedded so deeply, the child's responses are automatic and without conscious awareness. This learning comes through both explicit teaching by family members and implicit observation of the surroundings. These understandings include the "rules" of behavior, interaction style, how we regard time and personal space, dress codes, and many other attitudes and behaviors (Copple & Bredekamp, 2009).

Young children respond to and make sense of new experiences through the lenses of the social and cultural contexts to which they have become accustomed to. For experiences to be **culturally appropriate** – meaningful, respectful, and germane – teachers must be knowledgeable of the social and cultural contexts in which children and families thrive. Using this knowledge, teachers may then design activities built on children's prior experience, interests, and specific social and cultural understandings.

All children must adjust to the social and cultural context of formal schooling; often early childhood programs differ greatly from the security of the home culture. This transition can be both confusing and unsettling for young children, making them feel uncertain and inexperienced. To make this a smoother transition, responsive teachers need to probe their own cultural experiences and biases. In doing this, teachers must investigate their power in the classroom culture as well as their level of respect toward those whose cultural backgrounds are different. Most imperatively, teachers need to be careful to not set their own culture as the "norm" by which they judge the cultures and social contexts of the children in their groups.

Putting it All Together in Decision-making

All three factors – what is known about child development and learning, what is known about each child's individual development, and what is known about the social and cultural contexts in which children live – are intertwined, influencing each other in the molding of the individual child. For example, children all over the world follow a comparable developmental blueprint when acquiring fine motor skills – moving from a palmar grasp and bringing the object to their face, to a scissor grasp and a mouthing of the object, to transferring a toy from hand to hand, to using a pincer grasp use of the hands as tools for feeding, to manipulation of small objects such as drawing tools and small toys. However, there is great individual variation due to the tools, toys, and experiences children are exposed to as well as the cultural traditions and occupations. Barbara Rogoff (2003) poignantly represents this in *The Cultural Nature of Human Development* in a picture of a 9 month old Efe tribe child brandishing a machete to cut a fruit that has been gathered by his cultural group. All three factors have influenced the child's fine motor development at a very young age.

In making decisions regarding a child's educational needs an effective teacher first considers the child's age and developmental level in relation to a "typically developing" child. "This knowledge provides a general idea of the activities, routines, interactions, and curriculum that will be effective with that group (Copple & Bredekamp, 2009, p. 10). The teacher looks at the individual development of the child situated within the setting of the family, culture, community, history and prior experiences. In this way, the teacher can optimally meet the child *where he/she are.*

The History of Developmentally Appropriate Practice

The field of early childhood education has a long history of reflection on developing practice. Evidence has emerged throughout this history which underscores the importance of appropriate experiences that foster learning and development. Well-defined and coherent professional standards articulated by professional associations provide the framework for developmentally appropriate practice. The framework typically includes facets such as  curriculum planning, teacher preparation, inclusion, ethical practice and learning standards. One of these professional associations, the National Association for the Education of Young Children (NAEYC), provides the conduit through which to produce and disseminate information, position papers and guiding practice serving children from birth to age 8 and their families.

Thirty years ago, NAEYC addressed the need for standards of practice for young children by writing the Developmentally Appropriate Practice (DAP) and Code of Ethical Conduct statements. The NAEYC marshaled its forces "...in an effort to stave off the increasing demands for academic instruction in early childhood programs" (Marsh, 2003, p. 26). In addition to pushdown curriculum, DAP evolved to address two other significant early childhood issues: lack of universal high-quality early education programs and growing concerns over lags in achievement among certain groups of children, particularly children living in poverty.

"Developmentally Appropriate Practice (Introduction)"

Pushdown curriculum is a response to political and societal demands for more academics and a belief in "back to basics". This has led to high-pressure practices such as long periods of whole group instruction, workbooks and a disappearance of play in kindergartens and preschools as well as standardized testing and pervasive grade retention in the first and second grades. In the era that began with *A Nation at Risk* (1983) and proceeded to *No Child Left Behind* (2001), and is presently under ESSA (2014) rules, the debate has turned to what is appropriate instruction and subject content for young children. Child advocates became alarmed at what they described as the erosion of childhood and the "miseducation" (Elkind, 2007) of young children. Experts in child development warned that children are being hurried into performing and functioning in ways that do not match up to their modes of learning.

Program quality is a crucial factor in how much children benefit from early education programs. Developmentally appropriate programs of high quality benefit and enhance children's learning and development while poor quality programs do not. Despite the broad knowledge of developmentally appropriate practice NAEYC has distributed, there still exists many poor quality programs in which children's needs are not optimally met.

Closing the achievement gap has been a major tenet throughout NAEYC's history. Nearly one of three children coming to kindergarten lack the basic abilities needed to succeed and most often these children come from families living close to or below the poverty line (Douglas-Hall & Chau, 2007). Although living in a low-income family does not assure school failure, children from poverty are more likely to experience low achievement than children from more financially secure homes. Families living in poverty have a more difficult time meeting their child's social, physical, and cognitive needs. This contributes to an achievement gap between children living in poverty and their more financially fortunate peers.

The NAEYC's response to these three issues is embedded in its DAP positions. In regards to pushdown curriculum, the NAEYC has established practices which are best for young children and practices that diminish the success children will experience in school and in life. In a response to program quality, the NAEYC has identified and defined practices that exemplify high quality as an important step in creating and broadening the availability of such programs to young children. Because the early years are vital and contributory to closing the achievement gap, NAEYC has been influential in identifying effective early learning strategies which address the needs of all children and especially those at greatest risk for school failure.

The NAEYC, after collecting information from early childhood educators all over the country, published a position paper in 1986 defining the concept of developmentally appropriate practice and a set of guidelines for programs serving children from birth to age 8. This was followed by an NAEYC book summarizing the support in the literature for DAP as well as describing exemplars of appropriate and inappropriate practices for  programs serving young children (Bredekamp, 1987). The first iteration delineated between practice that is right and practice that is wrong. With a theoretical lens relying heavily on the work of Jean Piaget, the original DAP statement promoted the use of a play-based, child-initiated, integrated curriculum that reflected both age and individual appropriateness. Age appropriateness is the awareness of universal milestones of normal development across all domains expected in all children. Individual appropriateness recognizes that not all children develop in exactly the same way and within the same timeframe.

What was missing in the first DAP set of guidelines was the consideration of social and cultural contexts. The assumption was that all children learn in much the same way, with contextual and historical differences contributing very little variation to the pathway of learning. Consequently, the preponderance of belief in much of the early childhood community during this era was that all children would benefit from a child-centered approach (Marsh, 2003) that was grounded in white, middle class values of schooling (Mallory & New, 1994). Mallory and New argued that the type of culturally specific standards advocated in the 1987 DAP guidelines maintain social inequities by discouraging the development of alternative methods of teaching which may better meet the needs of non-dominant groups of children.

The 1997 DAP revised document incorporated the work of theorists who place greater emphasis on the social and cultural aspects of a child's life. Lev Vygotsky's work asserts that children assume historically, socially, and culturally ways of thinking, speaking, and interacting from the contexts in which they live. From this perspective, learning and development are both social and individual. The role of the teacher became much more significant than in the child-initiated model. The teacher supports and expands the cognitive functions that are developing, provides experiences that are challenging yet can be accomplished with adult or more capable peer guidance and works both individually and collaboratively with children (Marsh, 2003). NAEYC members and a revision committee had considered the debate, criticism, and reflection offered after the release of the 1987 edition and several key changes were made to the 1997 document (Bredekamp & Copple, 1997).

The 1997 version of DAP also began to challenge the *either/or thinking* of the 1987 edition – the dichotomized belief of educational practice being either appropriate or

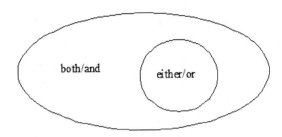

inappropriate. Should preschool emphasize cognitive growth or social-emotional development? Should there be only child-initiated or teacher-planned activities? Either/or thinking assumes there is only one right way and ignores the complexity of learning and development. The 1997 and 2009 editions address the research that shows children are

better served with a *both/and* thinking which rejects oversimplified explanations of complex processes of learning and requires diverse perspectives and multiple answers and strategies to be valued. The 1997 revision also incorporated evidence of exemplary educational practice from national and international settings. These included Reggio Emilia, the Project Approach, Montessori, and Head Start/Early Head Start (Follari, 2011).

The 2009 DAP was generated less by critique as was the 1997 version, and more by the significant amount of new knowledge and rapidly changing contexts of both children and early childhood settings. The dramatic increase in children attending center programs, the contributions of research on development and learning, and the changing demographics of young children, necessitated the evolution of professional practice - thus, the roughly 10-year intervals of the NAEYC revision process of developmentally appropriate practice. In addition to the continuation of *both/and* thinking, the following instructional strategies form the framework of the 2009 DAP goals (Copple & Bredekamp, 2009):

- Skillful balance of child-initiated activities and direct instruction
- Providing routines, boundaries, and limits, and allowing student choice
- Recognizing universality and individuality in child development
- Fostering the foundational skills, attitudes, and engagement that prepare children for successful lifelong learning in school and beyond
- Supporting children's need to collaborate in group work and to work on individual tasks
- The need for children to develop self-regulation

The major shift from the 1987 to 2009 versions of DAP is the emphasis on the diverse cultural contexts of children (Copple & Bredekamp, 2009). The emphasis on sensitive response to the economic, cultural, and linguistic differences of children and their families became the focus of the revised DAP statement. This shift transpired in response to changing demographics in both schools and communities emphasizing the need to be prepared to teach all children from all contexts. Guidelines from NAEYC's Developmentally Appropriate Practice (DAP) in Early Childhood Programs address a child's culture as part of appropriate practice. The guidelines make it clear to teachers "to pay attention to the social and cultural contexts in which their children live and to take these into account when shaping the learning environment and their interactions with children and families" (Copple & Bredekamp, 2009, p.331).

Recent research on early brain development, early intervention, and the correlation of economic diversity to school readiness has raised awareness of the importance of home culture in children's development. Three of NAEYC's (2005) program accreditation criteria include standards that address: 1) nurturing relationships that treat all children with respect, 2) providing materials that reflect the diversity in the classroom and the community, and 3) using teaching strategies that attend to the diversity of children. In addition, the 2009 revision highlights the increase in the number of English language learner children and families. This iteration of DAP also calls for stronger collaboration and articulated alignment between early care and education programs and elementary schools.

The 2009 edition of Developmentally Appropriate Practice builds on the most recent research. It emphasizes excellence and equity to close the achievement gap, intentionality and effectiveness in producing positive short- and long-term learning and developmental outcomes, and joy in purposeful learning. In addition, the most recent version preserves the enduring values of the early childhood education field – commitment to the whole child, respect for individual and cultural diversity, partnering with families, and the value of play. The NAEYC continues to advocate for high quality and appropriate programs for children; high standards in preparation and continual professional development for teachers; and awareness, validation and respect for the richness and influence of diversity in children's familial and community settings.

The Research Base of Developmentally Appropriate Practice

It is not enough for early childhood educators to base their programs on what they think is true about how young children learn or what we want to believe about young children's development. Developmentally appropriate practice has its roots in the theory and studies of programs and practices that produce successful outcomes for all children. Developmentally Appropriate Practice is based on twelve interconnected principles that are research-based, forming a solid framework for decision-making needed by teachers, families, and programs (Copple & Bredekamp, 2009, pp.11-15):

Principle 1 – All the domains of development and learning – physical, social and emotional, and cognitive – are important, and they are closely interrelated. Children's development and learning in one domain influence and are influenced by what takes place in other domains.

To teach children in an effective manner, all domains must be considered, planned for, and assessed. In addition, the interconnectedness of the domains must be recognized. For example, young children's language not only influences their ability to communicate, but also their social interactions and cognitive development in phonemic awareness. Research verifies the importance of a wide-ranging curriculum that includes all the developmental domains of children.

Principle 2 – Many aspects of children's learning and development follow well documented sequences, with later abilities, skills, and knowledge building on those already acquired.

Research submits that children traverse a relatively predictable progression of development during the first nine years of life . Variations in how the development is demonstrated and the meaning attached to the change may be dependent on the cultural and linguistic context of the child. This knowledge of developmental stages enables the teacher to prepare the learning environment, the curriculum and the learning activities.

Principle 3 – Development and learning proceed at varying rates from child to child, as well as at uneven rates across different areas of a child's individual functioning.

Within "typical" development there exists a wide range of variability. In addition, each child represents a unique mixture of temperament, aptitude, and personality shaped within her/his social and cultural contexts. Children who have special needs or abilities may bring additional demands which will require additional resources and actions. Given the wide range of development, decisions about curriculum, placement and teaching should be individualized and tailored to each child's needs as much as possible.

Principle 4 – Development and learning result from a dynamic and continuous interaction of biological maturation and experience.

The intersection of genetics, physical world, typical development and social world produce the uniqueness of individual children. It is paramount that the early childhood educator first, gets to know each child in her/his group and then employs the knowledge, persistence and intentionality to ensure the success of each of those children.

Principle 5 – Early experiences have profound effects, both cumulative and delayed, on a child's development and learning; and optimal periods exist for certain types of development and learning to occur.

Children's early experiences have a collective effect on their development and learning; the result may be positive or negative. For example, supportive, cognitively stimulating environments in the early years promote brain development and the formation of neural pathways. But if the environment is barren of stimulation and rich language experiences, the brain "prunes out" the brain synapses that are not invigorated. Sensitive periods exist in a child's development in which learning of certain skills occurs optimally. It is crucial that children receive the consistent environmental inputs and supports for learning as early as possible.

Principle 6 – Development proceeds toward greater complexity, self-regulation, and symbolic or representational capacities.

A universal characteristic of development is that children's learning and performance becomes increasingly complex across all domains. Young children think concretely and move to more abstract thinking with maturity and experience. Additionally, young children with time and supports in development, move from total dependence on others to competence and internal control. Adults play a sizeable role in supporting children as they learn to self-regulate. Children also move from utilizing concrete objects – such as using a play telephone – to more abstract, symbolic thought – using a block to represent a telephone. Symbolic representation plays a vital role when children begin to learn about written language and numeracy.

Principle 7 – Children develop best when they have secure, consistent relationships with responsive adults and opportunities for positive relationships with peers.

From the beginning of a child's life, nurturing relationships with responsive adults are necessary to form secure attachments that will support the child's development across all domains. Through these first relationships with parents or other primary caregivers, the stage is set for the child's future relationships. As the child's world expands, the opportunities to develop trusting relationships with other adults and peers expand. Positive teacher-child relationships are vital in supporting a child's cognitive, social and emotional growth.

Principle 8 – Development and learning occur in and are influenced by multiple social and cultural concepts.

Bronfenbrenner developed the ecological theory which posits that there are many direct and indirect influences that impact children. These include the family, neighborhood, community, schools, and cultural values. The influences are interrelated and bi-directional – they shape the context of children's lives and are also impacted by the child. Culture refers to the beliefs and patterns of behavior taught by a society to its members. Early childhood educators need to understand and respect the sociocultural contexts in which children learn and develop and at the same time prepare the child to function in the larger global society by giving them the skills, rules and linguistic ability of the dominant society (Delpit, 1995).

Principle 9 – Always mentally active in seeking to understand the world around them, children learn in a variety of ways; a wide range of teaching strategies and interactions are effective in supporting all these kinds of learning.

The constructivist theory of cognitive development hypothesizes that young children construct their knowledge and understanding of the world through their experiences, social interactions, media and cultural tools. Children take the input and create their own hypotheses of the world. After constructing new knowledge, children take this deep understanding and apply it to new situations and settings. To sustain this learning, teachers must have a repertoire of teaching strategies and the professional awareness of best practice that will maximize the context, learning goals, and needs of each child.

Principle 10 – Play is an important vehicle for developing self-regulation as well as for promoting language, cognition, and social competence.

Play is a pursuit common to young children across the countries of the world. It gives children the opportunity to develop competencies across all domains – cognitive, physical, social, and emotional. Research shows a link between play and basic capabilities such as memory, self-regulation, and social skills and school success

(Johnson, Christie & Wardle, 2005). From infancy, children are learning about the world around them through the use of their senses in playful acts. As children grow, they engage in physical play, object play, dramatic play, constructive play and games with rules. Within the realm of play, children learn to assume and maintain roles, develop self-regulation, play by the rules of the group and plan the play scenario. Children also advance in cognitive, emotional, social, and linguistic development utilizing the vehicle of play.

> **Principle 11 – Development and learning advance when children are challenged to achieve at a level just beyond their current mastery, and also when they have many opportunities to practice newly acquired skills.**

Much of Vygotsky's work is built around the concept of the **ZPD** – zone of proximal development – which states that a child has an actual and a potential level of learning. The distance between what a child can do independently (actual level) and what the child can do with assistance (potential level) is the ZPD. When children work at their potential level, they experience what can be done independently before they can actually do it independently. Once the child reaches the skill level that she/he can accomplish independently, a new ZPD is formed.

The role of the teacher becomes paramount in that he/she must create a rich learning environment that promotes motivation and engagement and the teacher must make use of scaffolding and strategies to sustain the mastery of new skills and challenges. By creating tasks just beyond the child's independent level, adults and "expert peers" provide the assistance that enables the child to be successful. However, the teacher must keep in mind of a delicate balance that must be struck – the tasks cannot be too easy that boredom results, nor can the tasks be too difficult so that frustration and withdrawal result.

> **Principle 12 – Children's experiences shape their motivation and approaches to learning, such as persistence, initiative, and flexibility; in turn, these dispositions and behaviors affect their learning and development.**

Approaches to learning focus on *how* children learn as opposed to the content they learn. Approaches to learning include children's emotions about learning as well as their behavior during learning. Temperament, self-regulation, language skills, family dynamics, early education programs and social skills all contribute to a child's approach to learning, which then influences a child's readiness for school.

NAEYC Position Statements The governing board of the NAEYC has generated position statements to state the Associations' position on certain early childhood policy, practice and professional development issues. In developing and disseminating position statements, NAEYC aims to:

- take informed positions on significant, controversial issues affecting young children's education and development

- promote broad-based dialogue on these issues, within and beyond the early childhood field

- create a shared language and evidence-based frame of reference so that practitioners, decision makers, and families may talk together about key issues in early childhood education

- influence public policies

- stimulate investments needed to create accessible, affordable, high-quality learning environments and professional development

- build more satisfying experiences and better educational and developmental outcomes for all young children. (NAEYC, 2009)

Some examples of position papers are those stating NAEYC's principles on the topics of Curriculum, Assessment and Program Evaluation; Screening and Assessment of Young English Language Learners; and Respecting and Responding to Diversity. The detailed position papers may be found on NAEYC's website (www.naeyc.org).

Understanding the Role of the Teacher

"So You Want to be an Early Childhood Educator"

According to the NAEYC (2009) guidelines for developmentally appropriate practice, the role of early childhood educators has five interrelated elements: 1) creating a caring community of learners, 2) teaching to enhance learning and development, 3) planning curriculum to achieve important goals, 4) assessing children's learning and development, and 5) establishing reciprocal relationships with families. What happens in the classroom is a complex mélange of decision-making in all five of these important components. Teachers' roles include questioner, planner, assessor, instructor, scaffolder, nurturer, partner and advocate.

"Early Childhood Educator"

Intentionality is also imperative in both long-term decisions and minute-by-minute ones. Intentional teaching includes creating the environment, taking into consideration the curriculum, tailoring it to the individual child, planning learning activities, and interacting with children (Copple & Bredekamp, 2009). The intentional teacher "acts with knowledge and purpose to ensure that young children acquire the knowledge and skills (content) they need to succeed in school and in life" (Epstein, 2007, p.1). This commitment to purposeful and thoughtful planning and implementation occurs even when "teachable moments" arise. The intentional teacher is guided by the learning outcomes of the program as well as his/her knowledge of child development and learning. Effective early childhood educators must also know each of their children individually in order to intentionally place them on the developmental continuum in relation to the learning goals.

"Intentional Teaching"

Creating a Caring Community of Learners

Early childhood settings are usually the first environment outside of the home in which young children experience care and education. The concept of a **caring community of learners** integrates several early childhood education ideas: the importance of both care and education, the need for positive relationships between children and adults, the significance of the learning environment – both indoor and outdoor, the organization of the learning context and the materials and equipment (Bredekamp, 2011).

"Reimagining Classrooms: Teachers as Learners and Students as Leaders"

Children learn most effectively when they feel safe, cared for and respected. Safety in a setting is dependent on external forces such as teacher supervision, monitoring and setting limits, as well as internal forces such as children's self-regulation, sense of responsibility and socially acceptable expression of emotions. Children feel cared for when their interactions with adults are secure and comfortable, when teachers foster engagement in learning, and the environment and schedule are organized, orderly, and healthy. The intentional, exemplary early childhood educator also provides guidance for children as they learn to self-regulate, and become socially and emotionally competent.

Children feel respected when each child's unique strengths, interests and perspectives are recognized as valuable contributions, and when children hear and see their home language and culture reflected in the classroom activities and interactions. Teachers plan ways for children to work and play collaboratively, and make a point of including children with special needs in the classroom culture. Inclusion of children with disabilities benefits both the children with special needs as they feel respected and included in the classroom culture, and children following a typical course of development as they gain an understanding of the similarities and differences of their peers.

It is the responsibility of all the stakeholders in the learning community to create and contribute to the community of learners. The skills young children learn as a caring community of learners are lifelong skills that will aid them in their lives after school.

Teaching to Enhance Development and Learning

It seems to be a given that teaching is the primary role of the teacher, however it is not quite that simple. Early childhood teachers engage in practice that partners and guides children as they learn. Teachers carefully prepare the environment to assure that it provides engaging and intentional learning in a setting respectful of children's diverse backgrounds and learning styles. Developmentally appropriate teaching practice balances adult-guided and child-guided experiences. However, even during child-guided experiences, the teacher is responsible for directing and supporting the experiences the child needs to learn and develop. Teachers often do this by asking questions which draw out children's ideas, interests and hypotheses. They make flexible plans and standards-based learning activities.

In order to be optimally successful, teachers must make it their priority to get to know each child and his/her individual strengths and needs. Effective early childhood educators thoughtfully plan the learning experiences with both the students and the learning goals in mind. Thorough knowledge of the curriculum and the standards of the program are necessary. Teachers use a variety of strategies so that children attain benchmarks across all the domains (physical, social, cognitive, and emotional).

"How to Know Each Individual Child in a Preschool Classroom: Preschool Teacher Tips"

Teachers maintain an extensive compendium of skills and strategies – in curriculum, activities, and materials – to effectively stimulate each child's learning and development. Effective early childhood educators know how and when to use the various strategies in their repertoire most strategically. Teachers adapt their strategies, experiences, materials, and equipment to meet the needs of a wide range of children's abilities and they are prepared to meet the special needs of individual children.

Teachers also use various groupings and contexts such as teacher-led group work, whole group direct instruction, child-initiated play, and small group center work. Developmentally appropriate goals are both challenging and achievable. In all the settings, teachers scaffold the learning through the use of the Gradual Release of Responsibility Model – direct instruction/modeling leading to guided practice leading to independent practice ending in independent application. Children also need plenty of opportunity to practice newly acquired skills.

Daily routines offer opportunities for valuable learning – diapering and toileting, transitions, clean up, meals, arrival and departure for example. During the routines, intentional teachers engage in purposeful, engaging interactions with children. Through these routines, content area knowledge and skills can be taught – clean up songs that teach phonological skills, mealtime jobs that teach math.

"Clean Up Song - by ELF Learning (classroom)"

Planning Curriculum to Achieve Important Goals

Curriculum is the *what* – the content that children are expected to learn; the curriculum includes the knowledge, skills, understandings and competencies children are expected to attain and the plans for the learning activities that serve as the vehicle for reaching the learning goals. The desired goals must be identified and clearly conveyed, must be across all domains of development and learning, and understood by all the stakeholders – children, teachers, administrators, and families. The goals of the curriculum must be clearly defined and the curriculum must be constructed so the goals are addressed in a sequential, coherent way. The learning goals are derived from a knowledge base that programs and states have adopted in creating standards for what children should know and be able to do.

"Linking Curriculum and Assessment:
Using Assessment Information to Individualize Children's Learning"

For curriculum to be effective it must be implemented with great consideration of individual differences and cultural variation among young children. Curriculum must also offer flexibility and ways of adapting the activities and the materials. Teachers need to be familiar with the key learning goals and expected outcomes as they plan the daily classroom learning activities.

Effective early childhood educators make meaningful connections of new learning to the vocabulary, concepts, and skills children already know and in which they have interest. Much of this interconnected work is done through projects and inquiry-based, hands-on learning where learning is integrated and purposeful. Sequence is also important as many areas of learning and development contain a logical order of concept and skill building. Effective and intentional educators must have knowledge of these progressions to plan for logical, sequential activities and materials.

Assessing Children's Development and Learning

It is not enough for early childhood teachers to plan and implement effective learning experiences; teachers must also evaluate children's progress toward the learning goals  embedded in the classroom activities. Intentional teaching is aligned to the learning outcomes and subsequent assessment which will evaluate children's progress. The focus is on children's progress toward educationally and developmentally significant goals. Assessment is also essential for guiding teacher planning and decision-making about curriculum and individual students. Assessment aids in identifying children who might benefit from special services or supports, and provides a means to communicate with all stakeholders (McAfee, Leong & Bodrova, 2004).

In order to be developmentally appropriate, assessment needs to be ongoing, strategic and purposeful, while taking into consideration the unique strengths and needs of each child. The means of assessment must be appropriate for young children and contain multiple methods including teacher observation, work samples, and authentic activities. There needs to be a well thought out system for data collection and analysis and utilization of the data in planning. Vygotsky's theory of the zone of proximal development reminds teachers that children can demonstrate competency when assisted. Therefore, it is necessary to assess children both at their independent level and at the level with which they can be successful with assistance.

Assessing children in developmentally appropriate ways requires responsiveness to assessment that is appropriate for the child's age or developmental level, is individually appropriate to get the best information about each child, and is culturally appropriate in terms of a child's linguistic, social and cultural background.

Establishing Reciprocal Relationships with Families

The NAEYC (2009) guidelines emphasize the importance of reciprocal relationships among teachers, administrators and families of young children. This two-way relationship which shares power in decision-making encompasses mutual respect, shared responsibility, cooperation, and negotiation of conflicts toward the achievement of shared goals. The effective early childhood teacher acknowledges the family as a vital source of information regarding their child; the teacher strives to respect and include the family's

knowledge and perception of their child. This relationship is created through regular and frequent two-way communication, using the home language.

Establishing this important partnership has as its goal the formation of an optimal support system for children. Family choice, goals, and decision-making are acknowledged and respected. The teacher shares valuable knowledge of and experience with children in general and individual children in particular. Both sides of the partnership share their knowledge of the child and their understanding of child development and learning through day-to-day communication and planned conferences.

Excellent teachers of young children make intentional efforts to build partnerships with families by (Copple & Bredekamp, 2009):

- Making family members feel welcome in the classroom
- Inviting family participation in the child's program
- Allowing for open dialogue
- Maintaining frequent, positive two-way communication
- Acknowledging parents' choices and goals for their child
- Responding with sensitivity and respect to parents' preferences and concerns
- Keeping an open mind about different perspectives where cultural diversity exists

Sensitive educators also link families with a range of services based on family resources, need, and priorities.

The Role of Children

Children are active participants in their own learning. They love to explore their own world to find out more about it and to gain competence. Effective teachers of young children allow their children choice in where they go in the classroom, what they work on, and how they demonstrate competency. Children are given the opportunity to participate in many activities – ongoing projects, activities, play, group games, storytelling, reading, outdoor play and socialization. In developmentally appropriate programs children become part of a close group, working and playing together and expressing friendship and affection for each other.

Code of Ethical Conduct

Each of us embraces values and behaviors that we prize in ourselves and others – compassion, loyalty, and hard work, for example. These personal beliefs affect our behavior and decision-making in our daily lives. Values define our idea of what is good and ethics refers to the way we apply our values to our daily behavior and decision-making. Occasionally, one has to make a choice between two or more competing values.

Although useful in guiding us individually and in our family lives, a personal moral code is inadequate to oversee professional behavior. What may be common sense to one professional may not appear that way to another; our initial reactions are colored by family, community, religion, culture, etc. Professional ethics are "the kinds of actions that are right or wrong in the workplace and are a public matter" (Feeney & Freeman, 2004, p.6).

A **Code of Ethics** that has been formally adopted in a profession is necessary to reaffirm a commitment to high standards and to making equitable decisions. Codes of ethics contain guidelines for regulating acceptable and unacceptable conduct in the job. Although the details of ethical codes may vary from profession to profession, there are some universal elements such as confidentiality and treating people with respect regardless of sex, race, ability, ethnicity, and ability. An ethical code also defines the core values of a particular field and provides direction for professionals when they are grappling with conflicts and **ethical dilemmas**. An ethical dilemma is a complex situation for which there may be more than one solution and for which the law does not provide strict guidelines. An ethical dilemma requires deciding the correct thing to do when two or more values conflict.

The *NAEYC Code of Ethical Conduct* (2005) directs early childhood educators as they build relationships with children, families, colleagues and society. The NAEYC Code also provides addenda for program administrators, principals, professional development, and teacher educators.

"NAEYC Code of Ethical Conduct"

A Code of Ethics is built upon a commitment to certain core values that buttress a profession and are rooted in the professional culture. The *NAEYC Code of Ethical Conduct* (2005) in its Core Values articulates a commitment to:

- Appreciate childhood as a unique and valuable stage of the human life cycle
- Base our work on knowledge of how children develop and learn
- Appreciate and support the bond between the child and family

- Recognize that children are best understood and supported in the context of family, culture, community , and society
- Respect the dignity, worth, and uniqueness of each individual (child, family member, and colleague)
- Respect the diversity in children, families, and colleagues
- Recognize that children and adults achieve their full potential in the context of relationships that are based on trust and respect

The Code is divided into segments directed toward professionals' ethical responsibilities to children, families, colleagues and community and society. Each section contains an introduction to the major responsibilities of the early childhood educator in each setting. Following the introduction are stated Ideals – statements that reflect best professional practice – and Principles – statements describing practices that are mandatory, prohibited, or allowed in each context.

The first principle is the most important and supersedes all others: "Above all, we shall not harm children. We shall not participate in practices that are emotionally damaging, physically harmful, disrespectful, degrading, dangerous, exploitative, or intimidating to children" (NAEYC, 2005, p.3). The Code does not explicitly tell the professional what to do in an ethical dilemma. Rather, the Code provides direction on what comprises ethical and unethical practices much like the Developmentally Appropriate Practice outlines standards of practice that are considered appropriate and inappropriate.

Ethical Responsibilities to Children

Young children are the most vulnerable human beings and are dependent on the benevolence of the adults around them. Adults hold an inordinate amount of power over young children in terms of authority, size, and strength. Keeping this in mind, the Principles compel early childhood educators to:

- Care for and educate young children in positive and stimulating emotional and social environments, and to assess children's learning in developmentally appropriate ways
- Build individual relationships with each child, adapting teaching strategies, learning environments and curricula

- Not participate in practices that discriminate against children on the basis of sex, race, national origin, religious beliefs, medical condition, disability or family structure
- Keep children safe and healthy
- Include families and staff in decision-making

As stated before, the principle that achieves these ideals, above all the others, is that early childhood educators "shall do no harm" to children. The responsibility to do no harm includes recognizing the signs of abuse, documenting and reporting suspicions of abuse, and assisting families in accessing needed resources.

Ethical Responsibilities to Families

The DAP's statement confirms the importance of family involvement in children's care and education. In turn, the Code of Ethics includes ideals and principles related to responsibility to families, appealing to early childhood educators to:

- Share knowledge of development and information about their child in ways families can understand and in their home language
- Respect the child's family values and cultures
- Include families in decisions concerning program and assessment
- Help families build valuable resource support networks

Maintaining confidentiality as well as hammering out solutions for conflicts are included in the early childhood educator's responsibilities to families. Despite a busy teaching day and scheduling conflicts with parents, it is imperative that educators tirelessly work to extend a welcome to the families of young children.

Ethical Responsibilities to Colleagues and Employees

The ideals of ethical practice must be applied to the profession itself when collaborating with colleagues. This includes maintaining relationships of respect, trust, confidentiality, collaboration, and cooperation; sharing resources; collaborating in professional development; and respecting one another as professionals. The Code of Ethics includes ideals and principles related to responsibility to colleagues, reminding early childhood educators to:

- Maintain the highest respect for colleagues by respecting their work and reputations

- Maintain the dignity of colleagues as we attempt to resolve conflicts
- Not participate in practices that discriminate against a co-worker because of sex, race, national origin, religious beliefs or other affiliations, age, family structure, disability, or sexual orientation

As an employer, the Code provides guidance for working with employees. Ideally, as professionals, we endeavor to promote safe and healthy conditions, maintain a climate of trust, secure adequate and equitable compensation and support professional development. The Code of Ethics reminds early childhood educators to:

- Maintain high quality program standards, including performance improvement and dismissal guidelines
- Maintain confidentiality in dealing with issues that are associated to an employee's job performance
- Not making hiring, retention, or termination decisions based on an individual's sex, race, national origin, religious beliefs or other affiliations, age, family structure, disability, or sexual orientation

Ethical Responsibilities to Community and Society

The nature of early childhood educational settings involves the immediate community and the larger society outside of the school or center. Our ethical responsibilities to the community are to:

> Provide programs that meet the diverse needs of families, to cooperate with agencies and professions that share the responsibility for children, to assist families in gaining access to those agencies and allied professionals, and to assist in the development of community programs that are needed but not currently available. (NAEYC, 2005, p.6)

The nature of early childhood education also calls the larger society to share responsibility for the welfare and security of young children. This obligation includes advocating for the best interests of children in early childhood programs and in society and to serve as a spokesperson for the rights and needs of young children globally. The Code of Ethics reminds early childhood educators to:

- Communicate openly about the nature and scope of services provided
- Hire persons whose competence, qualifications and character make them suited for the position
- Be familiar with laws and regulations which serve and protect children and be vigilant in enforcing those laws and regulations
- Report programs that are violating laws or regulations to the appropriate authorities
- Protect the health, safety, and well-being of our children and inform parents when children have been endangered

The Importance of Play

Much has been written about the benefits and purposes of play. As academics and technology invade the early childhood classroom, child-initiated play is becoming less valued and disappearing from the lives of children (Hirsh-Pasek, Golinkoff, Berk & Singer, 2008). Early childhood educators have long known the benefits of play across all domains of a child's development and have respected play as the primary way young children learn. The NAEYC's 2009 position statement on developmentally appropriate practice (Copple & Bredekamp, 2009) states that "play is an important vehicle for developing self-regulation as well as for promoting language, cognition, and social competence" (p. 14) across all ages. Vygotsky (1978) believed that play leads development; Piaget (1980) believed that play "fosters the social life and constructive activity of the child" (p. viii).

"Importance of Play"

"Kathy Hirsch-Pasek – Importance of Play"

The information in this section will aid educators in responding to parents' queries such as "Does my child only play during the day? When are they learning?" Administrators who are not well-versed in developmentally appropriate practice may also question your teaching strategies that are play-based. We need to help parents and administrators understand the benefits and purposes of play in a curriculum that promotes learning and development. But first, we need to explore the kinds of play in which children engage.

Kinds of Play

Social play occurs when children play with each other in small groups. Mildred Parten (1932), a children's play researcher, suggested dividing play by the social interaction among children demonstrated in the play. These classifications are:

- *Unoccupied play* – The child does not play with anything or anyone else; the child stands or sits doing nothing observable.
- *Solitary play* – The child plays alone, unaware of other children. Even as children mature, they may intermittently seek solitary play as a means of getting away from the group or because they have a task or project that they want to accomplish.
- *Onlooker play* – The child spends a great deal of time watching others play. This allows the child to comprehend *how* to play.
- *Parallel play* – The child plays individually with toys or other materials similar to those children playing nearby. Its purpose is often to allow children to become acquainted with one another, to gain social acceptance, or to provide a secure transition from solitary play to cooperative play.
- *Associative play* – Children engage in the same activity and may interact with one another, but no attempt is made to organize the play or to assign roles.
- *Cooperative play* – Children organize the play with give-and-take interaction, sharing ideas, goals, roles, materials, and equipment.

"Types of Play"

Play experiences provide children with the opportunity to interact, learn social skills, try out social behaviors, resolve conflicts, learn self-regulation, and learn about themselves. Additionally, play provides the vehicle for developing cognitive, motor, language, literacy and emotional skills.

Play Promotes Significant Cognitive Skills

Play gives the child vast opportunity to express thoughts and ideas. Children are given occasions to hypothesize, test the hypotheses, plan and organize the experiments, create, explore and try out new skills. According to Piaget (1952) play allows children to create new knowledge through assimilation and to acquire information through hands-on experiences and accommodation of old schema. Play allows a child to use all her/his senses to learn about the world. Play is active and allows a child to learn "by doing". Vygotsky (1978) believed that through play the child develops abstract meaning separate from the objects in the world, which is a critical feature in the development of higher mental functions. Play allows rigorous academic learning attainment without the tension or strain often associated with structured learning experiences. Through open-ended play, children are allowed to explore their creativity, expanding their imaginations, and inventing new ideas and solutions to problems.

Play Promotes Motor Development and Good Health

Play is active and is a natural activity of mentally and physically doing something. In active play, children are never passive, but instead they are refining large muscle dexterity and coordination through running, jumping, hopping, skipping, climbing and throwing.

Active play promotes good health. The CDC reports huge increases in childhood obesity in the past 30 years. From 1976 to 2010, the percentage of obese 2- to 5-year olds increased from 5% to 8.4%. In 2011-2012, 8.4% of 2- to 5-year-olds had obesity compared with 17.7% of 6- to 11-year-olds and 20.5% of 12- to 19-year-olds (CDC 2016).

The causes of obesity are numerous and complicated genetics, poor nutrition, and inactivity are among these causes. The CDC (2016) makes the following recommendations to offset the obesity dilemma in our country:

- Children need to engage in 60 minutes or more of daily, moderate activity.
- Preschoolers should have at least 60 minutes of structured play (in 15-minute increments) where children are increasing endurance, flexibility and coordination. In addition, preschoolers need a minimum of 60 minutes daily in unstructured play inside and/or outdoors.

"Child Motor Skills"

Play Supports Language and Literacy Development

Communication skills are partially developed through play with peers and the need to communicate with each other in their play (Morrow, 2001). Play expands vocabulary and increases language development through the opportunities for conversation with playmates, by listening to their peers, and by having correct syntax modeled in their conversations. Play provides rich language events because children must organize and plan the play and subsequently maintain the play roles. Literacy development is fostered in play through children's need to read and write throughout the play. A great example of this is "playing school" with a "teacher" and "students".

Play Permits Children to Develop Socially

Play episodes provide openings for children to learn how to be leaders (directing the play) as well as followers (following the leader's directions). Children are able to try out and expand different roles, learn to give and take, empathize with the feelings of others, share, play by the rules, resolve problems, and cope with disappointment (Stegelin, 2005). Play provides the practice in the social skills that the child's culture expects for success. Play encourages a child to be a contributing part of a group by being collaborative, cooperative and flexible.

Play Supports Positive Emotional Development

Play is pleasurable and enjoyable (Elkind, 2003). Play allows children the opportunity to express their thoughts and emotions, test ways of feeling and behaving, learn self-regulation through the support of their playmates, and discover one's self. Play allows children to be in control and powerful when they are the play leaders and then allows children to explore frustrations, fears and anxieties when they are the play followers. One of the most important outcomes of play is the sense of ownership through control of one's choices to experiment in play scenarios, and with materials, feelings and ideas.

Early childhood educators are acutely aware of the inherent value of play for its own rewards and for the behaviors it guides. Teachers need to be vigilant about protecting large blocks of time daily for unstructured and structured play. These blocks of time devoted to play may be the most critical times of the day for children.

Summary

- Developmentally appropriate practice is teaching that is aligned with children's ages, abilities, interests, and experiences, and supports children's attainment of challenging but achievable goals.

- Decisions about developmentally appropriate practice are based on knowledge of child development and learning, knowledge about children as individuals, and knowledge of the social, cultural, and familial contexts in which children live.

- The role of the early childhood educator has five interconnected facets: 1) creating a caring community of learners, 2) teaching to enhance learning and development, 3) planning curriculum to meet important goals, 4) assessing children's learning and development, and 5) establishing reciprocal relationships with families.

- Well-grounded research about development and learning provides the framework for NAEYC's position statements on developmentally appropriate practice. The NAEYC's position statements provide sound substantiation for early childhood educators' practice.

- Research confirms that play contributes to self-regulation, attention, problem solving, social and emotional skills, good health, language development, creativity, and literacy and numeracy skills.

Key Terms

achievement gap
age appropriate
caring community of learners
Code of Ethics
culturally appropriate
curriculum
developmentally appropriate practice
ethical dilemma
individually appropriate
position statement
reciprocal relationships
social play

Suggested Readings

Copple, C. & Bredekamp, S. (2006). *Basics of developmentally appropriate practice: An introduction for teachers of children 3 to 6.* Washington, DC: National Association for the Education of Young Children.

Kostelnick, M.J., Soderman, A.K. & Whiren, A.P. (2011). *Developmentally appropriate curriculum: Best practices in early childhood curriculum* (5th ed.). Upper Saddle River, NJ: Pearson.

Wassermann, S. (1990). *Serious players in the primary classroom.* NY: Teachers College Press.

Suggested Websites

ASCD Whole Child Initiative
www.wholechildeducation.org

National Institute for Early Education Research
www.nieer.org

Scholastic, Inc.
www.scholastic.com/teachers/article/why-children-need-play

Reflections

1. Reflect on your own school experiences as a first or second grader. Can you remember specific events in which you felt your teacher understood your individual needs and interests? How did you know this? How did you feel?

2. Observe a group of toddlers or 4-year olds in an early childhood classroom. Reflect on whether the materials and environment are age appropriate. Then reflect on how well you think the teacher meets the individual needs of young children in a group.

3. Why do you think play is important? Visit an early childhood classroom and evaluate the kinds of play, opportunities for play, and materials for play.

4. How will use the NAEYC Code of Ethics in your daily interactions with children? Colleagues? Community?

References

Bredekamp, S. (Ed.). (1987). *Developmentally appropriate practice in early childhood programs serving children from birth through age 8.* Washington, DC: NAEYC.

Bredekamp, S. (2011). *Effective practices in early childhood education: Building a foundation.* Upper Saddle River, NJ: Pearson Education.

Bredekamp, S. & Copple, C. (Eds.). (1997). *Developmentally appropriate practice in early childhood programs serving children from birth through age 8.* Washington, DC: NAEYC.

Bronfenbrenner, U. (1979). *The ecology of human development: Experiments by nature and design.* Cambridge, MA: Harvard University Press.

Center for Disease Control and Prevention. (2016). Childhood overweight and obesity. Retrieved August 8, 2016, from http://www.cdc.gov/obesity/childhood

Copple, C. & Bredekamp, S. (Eds.). (2009). *Developmentally appropriate practice in early childhood programs serving children from birth through age 8.* Washington, DC: NAEYC.

Delpit, L. (1995). *Other people's children: Conflict in the classroom.* New York: New Press.

Douglas-Hall, A. & Chau, M. (2007). *Basic facts and low-income children birth to age 6.* New York: National Center for Children in Poverty, Columbia University.

Elkind, D. (2003). Thanks for the memory: The lasting value of true play. *Young Children. 58*(3), 46-51.

Elkind, D. (2007). *The power of play: Doing what comes naturally.* Cambridge, MA: DeCapo Press.

Epstein, A. S. (2007). *The intentional teacher: Choosing the best strategies for young children.* Washington, DC: NAEYC.

Feeney, S. & Freeman, N. K. (2004). *Ethics and the early childhood educator: Using the NAEYC code.* Washington, DC: NAEYC.

Follari, L. M. (2011). *Foundations and best practices in early childhood education* (2nd Ed.). Upper Saddle River, NJ: Pearson Education.

Hirsh-Pasek, K., Golinkoff, R. M., Berk, L. E. & Singer, D. (2008). *A mandate for playful learning in preschool: Applying the scientific evidence.* New York: Oxford University Press.

Marsh, M. (2003). *The social fashioning of teacher identities.* New York: Peter Lang.

McAfee, O., Leong, D. J. & Bodrova, E. (2004). *Basics of assessment: A primer for early childhood educators.* Washington, DC: NAEYC.

Morrow, L. M. (2001). *Literacy development in the early years: Helping children read and write* (4th Ed.). Boston, MA: Allyn & Bacon.

National Association for the Education of Young Children. (2005). *NAEYC early childhood program standards and accreditation criteria: The mark of quality in early childhood education.* Washington, DC: NAEYC.

National Association for the Education of Young Children. (2005). *Code of ethical conduct and statement of commitment.* Retrieved May 15, 2012, from http://naeyc.org/files/codeofethicalconduct

National Association for the Education of Young Children. (2009). Position papers. Retrieved August 9, 2016 from htpp://naeyc.org/files/positionpapers

Piaget, J. (1952). *The origins of intelligence in children.* New York: International Universities Press.

Piaget, J. (1980). In C. Kamii and R. Devries (Eds.). *Group games in early education* (p.vii). Washington, DC: NAEYC.

Parten, M. B. (1932). Social participation among preschool children. *Journal of Abnormal and Social Psychology, 27,* 243-269.

Rogoff , B. (2003). *The cultural nature of human development.* New York: Oxford University Press.

Stegelin, D. A. (2005). Making the case for play policy: Research-based reasons to support play-based environments. *Young Children, 60*(2), 76-85.

Vygotsky, L. S. (1978). *Mind in society.* Cambridge, MA: Harvard University Press.

Chapter 4
Theories of Learning and Development and their Application in the Classroom

Development and Learning

Thinking Ahead

1. What is development? What is learning? How are these processes related?
2. What is a theory? What is the relationship of theory, research, and practice?
3. What are the key components of the major theories of development? Who are the theorists identified with each theory?
4. What are the key components of the major theories of learning? Who are the theorists identified with each theory?

Effective, developmentally appropriate teaching requires that teachers understand how children think and learn and how to most effectively support children's healthy development across all domains – cognitive, physical, social, and emotional. Because children's development is foundational to teaching and learning, it is necessary for educators to examine the theories of children's development and learning. First, we need to define development and learning.

"CompSAT Child Development and Learning"

What is Development?

Development is the complex and dynamic cognitive, language, physical, motor, social, emotional, and moral processes that change over one's lifetime (Berk, 2016). Development depends on the important interaction between biological maturation and physical and/or social experiences, often referred to as nature and nurture factors. The domains of learning develop both independently of each other and are interwoven with one another, thus producing the "whole child"

view of child development. Development occurs as children grow, adapt, and transform in response to varied experiences. For instance, biologically, most children around the world develop language at about the same age. However, the social interaction with adults and siblings, as well as a child's temperament and cultural background influence the rate and type of language development individual children enjoy. Knowing some basic principles of development helps us to understand patterns of development in children and provides a framework for working with children in early childhood settings. Jalongo and Isenberg (2012) offer an outline of five important principles of development (pp. 94-95):

1. **Development in each domain – physical, motor, social, emotional, and cognitive – influences and is influenced by development in other domains.**

2. **Physical development occurs in an orderly and predictable sequence.** Development occurs from the top of the body to the bottom (**cephalocaudal**) – from the head to the neck, trunk, and so forth – and from the center of the body outwards (**proximodistal**) – beginning with the large trunk and arm muscles, working its way out to the smaller muscles in children's hands and fingers.

3. **Development proceeds at different rates in each individual and in each developmental area.** There is a wide range of individual variation in the timing of developmental changes that are influenced by biological, environmental, and **sociocultural factors** such as family, temperament (emotional responses such as shyness or distractibility), learning style, and experience. Only when children deviate considerably from the average ages for these developmental milestones is there cause to consider their development exceptional, either delayed or advanced.

4. **Development is greatly affected by the kinds of experiences children have.** Experiences are cumulative; therefore, they can either positively or negatively affect children's developing

knowledge, skills, and attitudes. Experiences that occur regularly have more powerful, lasting effects than those that occur rarely.

5. **Development results from the interaction of each child's biological, environmental, and cultural influences.** Today, it is accepted that three major factors – biological, environmental, and cultural – are tightly interconnected, making each person unique. **Biological factors** begin internally in the genetic make-up, which determines traits such as weight and height; **environmental factors** are external and include experiences such as language, poverty and health care; and **cultural factors** come from family, community, and the media.

What is Learning?

Learning is a change in the level of knowledge or facility in a skill that results from experience and/or instruction. Learning is different than development, although they each influence the other. Children's development can provide the opportunity to learn. Piaget (1952) believed that development leads learning. For instance, when a baby develops the ability to crawl, she will have a wider range of environment in which to explore and learn through her senses. Other theorists believe that learning can also drive development or occur in tandem with development (Vygotsky, 1978).

As children encounter more experiences in the world, they begin to understand more complex concepts, affecting their cognitive growth. The experiences that make up the curriculum are the core of this learning process. Therefore, the curricular experiences one provides for children need to be based on the theories of how children learn.

"Baby and Toddler Milestones, Dr. Lisa Shulman"

"Development of Pre-Primary Children from 2-6 Years"

Influences on Children's Development

The first five years of a human's life is a time of a child's most rapid development. During this stage of maturation all the domains – physical, cognitive, social, and emotional – are acquiring foundational knowledge and skills. Additionally, children are forming their personalities, morals, attitudes, and behaviors. Exemplary educators need to be well-informed about the influences which shape their students. Being well-informed allows an educator to make sound decisions for their students.

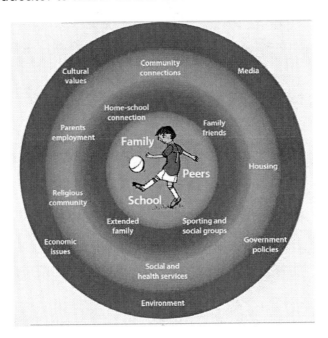

The Brain and Children's Development

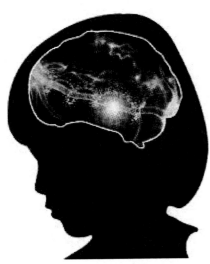

During the last 25 years, the most thrilling discoveries about brain and child development have been possible due in large part to advanced technology. **Magnetic resonance imagery (MRI)** and **positron emission tomography (PET)** scans allow us to view the brain functioning and allow us to compare the brains of adults and children (Johnson, 2005).

Brain development is profoundly affected and shaped by its experiences, and brain growth affects learning. During childhood – particularly in the first three years of life – the brain is most receptive to experience. These **windows of opportunity** are the primary times for learning – times when the brain is most open to various experiences. In the past, researchers believed that the first few years were such a critical period that after age 5 the window for learning began to close. We now know that the brain remains somewhat flexible throughout life.

"Brain Development"

The newborn's brain is comprised of billions of neurons, or nerve cells. The interactions, language, manipulations, and play babies engage in with adults develop brain connections that allow learning to happen. With repeated use, these brain connections that carry information – **synapses** – become permanent. If synapses are not used, they will be pruned away. This **pruning**, also known as **neural shearing** is analogous to pruning tree branches to strengthen those that remain on the tree. Neural shearing occurs throughout life, with new synapses being formed and unused ones being pruned away. Consequently, children who do not have the benefit of a parent or caregiver talking or reading to them may have difficulty with literacy and language in later life. Pruning produces more brain efficiency which aids in learning and memory. Pruning also increases the brain's flexibility – **plasticity** – the brain's ability to alter and change in response to experiences.

Results of brain research lead us to several conclusions (Bredekamp, 2011, p. 101):

- The brain's most significant development occurs before birth, placing great importance on prenatal care
- Early experiences change and organize the physical structure of the brain
- Different parts of the brain are more responsive to experiences at different times. There are windows of opportunity for particular types of learning
- Neglect, abuse, and stress pose serious threats to healthy brain development. Preventions and early intervention become even more important in light of the potentially negative consequences for brain development
- Brains develop best when children experience loving relationships, play, opportunities to explore their world, interesting and engaging things to learn about, and healthy, safe environments
- Brain development is integrated; as children get older, the areas within the brain become better connected

Brain research tells us that young children's brains are more likely to develop typically and achieve optimal learning when they are exposed to enriching and meaningful experiences and environments. Conversely, young children's brains are vulnerable to atypical development if they grow up in impoverished, unhealthy environments.

Social and Cultural Influences

While we agree that there are universal development characteristics of most children, the cultural and social settings in which children grow, appreciably shape their development. The **cultural setting** includes the language, dialect, behaviors, values and beliefs of the group to which the child belongs. The **social setting** includes the influential people in children's lives, including families, peers, teachers, and community
members. Being aware of the diverse backgrounds of children empowers both educators and children in being accepted for who they are. This helps children learn to care for, respect, and be tolerant of one another and the world around them.

NAEYC's position statements on linguistic and cultural diversity (2009) and developmentally appropriate practice (Copple & Bredekamp, 2009) powerfully assert that children's linguistic and cultural diversity are important factors in development and learning. It is necessary for the early childhood educator to create a classroom atmosphere that honors the child's home language and culture while supporting the child's acquisition of English as a second language.

"What Is the Most Important Development / Tom Weisner"

Developmental Exceptionalities

Every classroom holds a community of learners who embody varying abilities that need to be recognized and nurtured, as well as needs that need to be supported and given services to develop and learn. **Children with special needs** is a term that describes children who may have health issues such as asthma, severe allergies, mental and/or emotional health issues, and physical and/or cognitive disabilities. **Children with disabilities** is a more exact term that refers to children who have been identified with a specific category of disability such as blindness or autism. In the city of Reggio Emilia, Italy – a center of decades of early childhood education innovation (which will be discussed at length in a later chapter) – the term **Children with Special rights** is used to describe these children.

The term **exceptional learner**, although less frequently used, refers to either children with disabilities or children with giftedness and talents. This term is reflected in the name of the professional association for special educators – the **Council for Exceptional Children (CEC).** Early childhood special educators belong to the **Division for Early Childhood (DEC)** of the CEC.

"Walking the Path with Twice Exceptional Learners"

Special educators and advocates for children with special needs also advocate for the use of **person-first language.** This is language that recognizes that the child is first, regardless if the child has a disability or not. The child is of primary importance and the disability is only a part of his/her identity. For this very reason, we say "a child with down syndrome", not "a down's child". The use of person-first language may feel clumsy at first, however, one of the tenets of inclusion is the value and respect accorded children regardless of disability.

Theories of Development and Learning

A **theory** is an affirmation of principles and ideals explaining how things happen; theories explain how children learn and develop. Noted expert on children's development, Laura Berk, posits that theories "guide and give meaning to what we see and…theories that are verified by research often serve as a sound basis for practical action" (2008). Theories of learning and development affect how people treat children, how they teach children, and how they construct classroom learning environments.

LEARNING THEORY
The Core of what we do.

Understanding child learning and development aids teachers in many ways, such as:

- Enabling one to explain to others, particularly families, the intricate process of learning and expectations of the child the teacher and the family may have, and correctly interpreting children's behavior as appropriate for their age or in need of intervention
- Knowing predictable sequences of development and learning to effectively plan curriculum and differentiate instruction to meet the learning needs of all children
- Establishing and assessing goals that are achievable, yet challenging for children within a certain age range
- Predicting themes and activities that will be engaging and meaningful to children
- Using information to identify and diagnose potential disabilities or developmental delays in children

Effective early childhood professionals use their knowledge of child development and learning in their daily practice. The theories we discuss in this chapter are often used to explain how children learn and develop. For each theory, we will describe development from that theoretical perspective and identify how each theorist has most influenced our views on development, and then we will apply it to best practices.

Modern Theories of Development

Erik Erikson's Psychosocial Theory (1902-1994)

Erik Erikson, a psychologist who taught at both Harvard and Yale, became interested in the influence of culture and society on child development. His book, *Childhood and Society*, which was first published in 1950, is a seminal piece of research used by educators, sociologists, and psychologists.

Stages of Psychosocial Development

Infant
Toddler
Pre-schooler
Grade-schooler
Teenager
Young Adult
Middle-age Adult
Older Adult

Integrity vs Despair
Generativity vs Stagnation
Intimacy vs Isolation
Identity vs Role Confusion
Industry vs Inferiority
Initiative vs Guilt
Autonomy vs Shame & Doubt
Trust vs Mistrust

Increases in Complexity

Proposed by Erik Erikson

Erikson suggested an eight-stage theory of development in which at each stage of a person's life an individual encounters a major "crisis" that influences one's social and personal development and reflects the particular culture unique to each individual (Erikson, 1993). Healthy social interactions come from successfully resolving the unique social conflicts at each stage, and these resolutions influence the individual's attitudes and skills. Erikson believed that in the earliest years of life, behavior patterns develop that influence and regulate a person's interactions and decisions for the rest of his or her life.

However, Erikson also believed that it was possible for a person to return to earlier stages and settle issues from a previous stage of development. He also proposed that the dilemmas at each stage continue to reappear in our relationships and work life throughout our lives.

"Erickson's Psychosocial Development / Individuals and Society"

Three of the stages are crucial to development in the years between birth and 6 years old:

Stage 1 – Trust versus Mistrust (birth to 18 months).
At this stage of development, the major task of infants and caregivers is to develop the child's trust in their own abilities, in the people around them, and in their world. Adults provide the social and emotional models that allow infants and toddlers to develop trust as well as autonomy. This is the stage in which strong **attachment** is established. This is the special bond that is established between a baby and the important adults in his or her life. With a strong bond, the child develops a sense of security and well-being. The baby uses this sense of reassurance as a safe base to go out and explore the world. Dixon (2003) calls this the "invisible bungee-cord" – a link between the child and the caregiver.

The caregiver serves as the "home base", positioning himself or herself in proximity near the child. The child wanders away, exploring and learning about his or her world, when the invisible bungee cord of anxiety and fear springs the child back toward the mother or other secure attachment figure. This sense of security and consistency provided by the trusting relationship allows the child to develop cognitively as well as socially and emotionally.

Babies' trust develops through the establishment of responsive relationships with their caregivers. Adults need to ensure that infants have caregivers who consistently meet their needs, whose response to the child is consistent, and who nurture the child's feelings of trust. By providing these things, infants develop a sense of safety, security, and predictability in the consistency of the people in their world.

When children's needs are not met, they find it almost impossible to develop trust and confidence in themselves or those around them. The world poses threats and insecurity to these children and often they have difficulty developing emotional attachments in their adult lives. Children who are not given the opportunity to establish strong, consistent attachments with primary caregivers often lack the virtue of **empathy** – the ability to put one's self in another person's place and understand their feelings and perspectives.

Stage 2 – Autonomy versus Shame and Doubt (18 months to 3 years old). At this stage of development, the child's task is to acquire a sense of independence without being made to feel shamed or doubtful. Becoming an autonomous human is a large undertaking in growing up. A truly autonomous child will have a strong sense of self, will be able to separate confidently from primary caregivers for short periods of time, and will attempt to do things on his own. This is a period of development when children are fiercely independent one moment and clingy and fearful the next.

This burgeoning self-confidence is nurtured by providing opportunities for toddlers to engage in self-help habits such as feeding and dressing. Giving children simple choices – such as selection of activities and materials – helps children gain a sense of independence in making choices. It is also important in this stage of development to set clear limits so that children can work on **self-regulation** – the inner control of actions and decision-making. Caregivers and teachers must also remain flexible as the toddler runs the gamut of emotions from independence to dependence. When teachers are understanding and sensitive to this fluctuation of behavior and emotions, it is easier to cope with toddlers and successfully support their growth in confidence and self-assuredness.

Stage 3 – Initiative versus Guilt (3 to 5 years old). At this stage of development, the child's task is to acquire a sense of purpose and to show initiative in his work and play. At this age, children enjoy tackling new tasks, playing with other children and adults, taking on the responsibility for their materials and themselves, and discovering new things. At this stage, children are more focused and generally exhibit greater self-regulation. If children have successfully navigated the second stage, their autonomy is established and they are more  interested in accomplishing tasks than acting out for their own individual control of a situation. During this stage, children's increasing abilities are particularly evident in an explosion of language and improved motor skills. Upon successfully negotiating this stage, a child will emerge competent and confident. She will be able to plan and complete a task as well as view mistakes as learning opportunities.

According to Erikson, this is a developmental stage where children's development can go in either of two directions: positively toward confidence or negatively toward guilt and discouragement. If a child's initiatives are continually punished or thwarted or if adults do for children what they can do for themselves, they may begin to feel guilt, discouragement, and withdrawal. Educators support children's development in this stage by balancing the child's need to explore and take risks with their safety.

Children's use of pretend play allows them one way to make choices and decisions and to take risks that increase their sense of autonomy and competence. Educators are encouraged to:

- Focus on children's gains as they learn new skills, not on the mistakes they make as they learn
- Encourage independence through daily tasks
- Provide children with many opportunities to select and use materials during long, uninterrupted periods of play
- Set expectations that are within the ZPD (Zone of Proximal Development) of individual children, focusing the curriculum on real problems and things, and on doing

Erikson's theory recognizes that development continues throughout the life span. The other stages include: industry versus inferiority, identity versus role confusion, intimacy versus isolation, generativity versus stagnation, and ego integration versus despair. Understanding the effort needed to reconcile each "crisis" in later stages enables early childhood educators in their diligent support of children's negotiation through the earliest stages.

Urie Bronfenbrenner's Ecological Systems Theory (1917-2005)

Urie Bronfenbrenner, an American psychologist developed the **Ecological Systems Theory** which emphasizes the significance of social and cultural influences on development (1979). Although Bronfenbrenner recognizes the biological influences on human development, his theory acknowledges the diverse cognitive and social influences on development. His theory, which recognizes the importance of the contexts and people that shape children's worlds, provided the framework of the **Head Start** program's comprehensive services.

"Ecological Systems Theory"

Bronfenbrenner believed that the most direct impact comes from children's proximate environments – the things and people children make direct contact with such as their homes, families, schools and communities. The wider contexts are those that the child may not have direct contact with, but which have a marked effect on the child's world such as the parents' workplace policies and public school systems. The broadest contexts include values, laws, and life events that influence a human's development across a lifetime.

These bi-directional social and cultural contexts are interrelated, influencing each other and impacting the developing child. This model is best represented as nested circles, much like the nested Russian matryoshka dolls. Each block, embedded in the others, acts independently but operates dependently when put together. There are five different social systems influencing each other and the development of the child:

1. The **microsystem** is the context closest to the individual and is where the child experiences most of her relationships and activities. This includes the home, family, schools, neighborhood, child care programs, friends, and religious institutions. In each context the child plays a particular role such as the daughter, the playmate, or the student; there are specific tools and people in each context with which the child interacts.

2. The **mesosystem** connects two or more of the child's microsystems, such as the connection between home and school. The concept here is that influences that take place in one setting spill over into other settings. Parent-teacher conferences are a good example of a linking in the mesosystem.

3. The **exosystem** consists of society's greater systems and policies that influence the individual such as the educational system, the media, health, law, and politics. The exosystem connects two or more social settings that may or may not directly influence the child – for example, the parents' workplace and the educational system. If the parents' workplace deducts part of their salary for time spent in a parent-teacher conference, the parent may not be able to afford the time necessary to address the child's educational needs.

4. The **macrosystem** is the largest, most global, and most remote influence on children's development. This circle of influence includes the values, beliefs and customs that influence the larger society as well as the individual living in that society. In any society there are some cultural values that are central to the structure of that society – the value of education is a prime example.

5. The **chronosystem** is the pattern of transitions and environmental events over the life course of an individual's life. Divorce and its effects on a child's development is an example of the chronosystem.

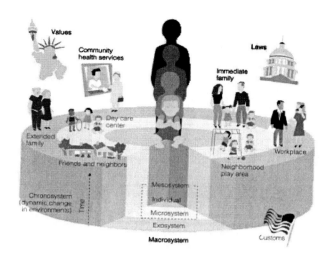

Educators use Bronfenbrenner's theory to direct their interactions with children and their families. Best practice encourages us to observe children in diverse social settings and to get to know the families and communities that influence the development of each child. Welcoming families' perspective and knowledge about the child as well as their involvement in the classroom is essential. Maintaining a bi-directional line of communication between home and school is crucial in promoting student success.

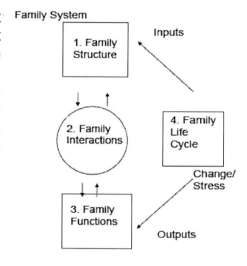

Family Systems Theory views family members as interconnected parts with each member influencing the others in predictable and recurring ways (Welch, 2007). Individual family member dynamics and the influence of the family members on one another, affects the behavior of each person in the family. Understanding the systematic functioning of the family – family boundaries, roles, rules, hierarchy – enables educators to more effectively support diverse children and their families.

Bronfenbrenner's goal in the formulation of his ecological systems theory is to get psychologists and educators to think more intentionally about the multidimensional influences of children's contexts on their development and to consider how children at the same time influence their own environments.

Jean Piaget's Cognitive-Developmental Theory (1896-1980)

Jean Piaget's **Cognitive-Developmental Theory** is a stage theory of intellectual development that has had immeasurable impact on the field of early childhood education. Piaget's work – though criticized in recent years for limitations that have been challenged by current research – still remains a primary influence in early childhood education. While others of his time asked *what* or *when* a child learns something, Piaget was most interested in *how* a child learns something.

"Piaget's Stages of Cognitive Development / Processing the Environment"

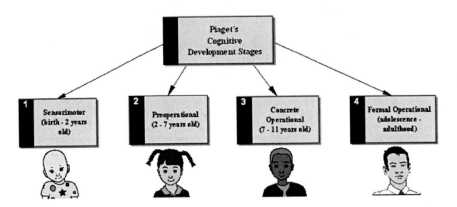

Piaget was born in Switzerland and began his career as a biologist, but turned to the field of psychology. In 1919 Piaget took a job at the Alfred Binet Laboratory School in Paris, standardizing the French version of a British intelligence test. While doing his work, Piaget began to question the answers children gave on the test at different stages of their development and sought the answers to his questions. He began by collecting detailed minute-by-minute observational data of his own three children beginning at each of their births. Piaget focused on how children's thinking, reasoning, and perception differ from those of adults, and how children ponder their world.

Piaget rejected both the idea that learning is solely intrinsic (emanated from the child) or solely extrinsic (imposed by the environment), and instead posited that a child's interaction with his environment allowed the child to construct his own knowledge. Children construct their knowledge by giving their own meaning to the places, people, and objects in their world, and that this knowledge construction is only possible by giving children every opportunity to do things for themselves. Piaget's theory of how children learn is called **constructivism**. Piaget stressed the importance of children's curiosity to propel the learning and play as an avenue of learning.

Piaget believed that through continuous interaction with their environment children construct their knowledge and organize it into inborn structures called **schema** – organizing structures that people use for cognition or to guide behavior. As a child gains experience and accumulates knowledge, the schemas develop and change. For example, a toddler has a dog, Priscilla. When the toddler goes to the zoo, she sees a zebra and calls it "Doggie" because it has four legs. With increased experience and through the mediation of language, the toddler creates an accurate schema file for dogs and another for zebras. **Adaptation** is the procedure of changing schema in response to experience. Adaptation happens in one of two ways: through assimilation and accommodation. **Assimilation** happens when new information is understood in the context of existing schema. The toddler assimilates her new schema for dogs into her existing schema file labeled "dogs" when she meets different types and sizes of dogs other than her own pet dog. **Accommodation** occurs when new information can't fit into an existing schema; the child must modify the existing schema or create a new one. The zebra could not be assimilated into the dog schema, so a new schema for zebras had to be constructed.

Two-year-old Gabriella has learned the schema for "cow" from her picture books.

Gabriella sees a moose and calls it a "cow." She is trying to assimilate this new animal into an existing schema. Her mother tells her, "No, it's a moose."

Gabriella accommodates her schema for large, shaggy animals and continues to modify that schema to include "mommy moose," "baby moose," and so forth.

Disequilibrium is an imbalance in cognition that follows the introduction of new information or experience that cannot be understood. Piaget believed that humans strive for equilibrium to make our world make sense. **Equilibration** is that process of creating new schema or adapting existing ones with the intent of reestablishing balance in a child's cognition. Learning depends on the progression of adapting schema through the process of either assimilation or accommodation until equilibrium is achieved.

Piaget believed that children all pass through the same four stages when developing their cognitive skills. The age and rate at which children accomplish these stages of development may vary from individual to individual, yet each stage has characteristics unique to that particular stage. The first three stages occur during the early childhood years: the **sensorimotor stage** (birth to 2 years) during which the child relies on his senses and reflexes to manipulate materials and learn about his world, the

preoperational stage (2 to 7 years) during which the child begins to form ideas based on his perceptions and shows an increased ability to think symbolically and conceptually as evidenced in his increased use of imaginative play and language, and the **concrete operational stage** (7 to 12 years) during which the child uses logical thinking to solve concrete problems and form ideas based on reasoning. The fourth stage – the **formal operation stage** (12 years and older) – is characterized by higher order conceptual and hypothetical thinking. We will look in depth at each of the first three stages.

The Sensorimotor Stage (birth to 2 years) begins with a baby's first reflexes and then progresses to purposeful reactions to a child's environment through the use of his sensory capabilities – sight, hearing, taste, touch, smell – and his expanding motor skills. Toward the end of this stage, **object/person permanence** occurs. Object permanence is the realization that something exists even when the child cannot see it. This important milestone allows the child to hold objects, people, and events in his memory. This is also the stage at which children experience **separation anxiety**. They cry when their caregiver leaves them because they understand that the adult continues to exist somewhere else other than where the child is. The child's cry is an effort to bring the important adult back into view. In addition, this is the stage at which children see things only from their own cognitive or emotional viewpoint; Piaget called this **egocentrism**. The child's experiences assure him that he stands at the center of his world and controls the events that occur.

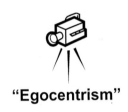

"Egocentrism"

Caregivers need to provide stimulating, safe, and colorful objects for infants and toddlers to reach for, grasp, manipulate, and explore. They also need to encourage sounds and response to stimuli – clapping, singing, and finger plays. When children are beginning to experience object/person permanence and separation anxiety, it is important to make as few changes in their lives as possible. **Continuity of care** is an important policy that caregivers need to adopt, especially for infants and toddlers in the sensorimotor stage of development.

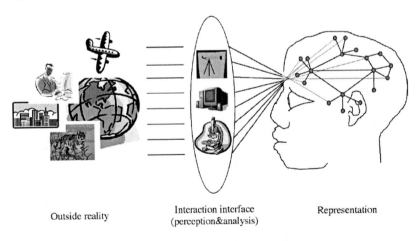

Outside reality   Interaction interface (perception&analysis)   Representation

The Preoperational Stage (2 to 7 years) is the stage in which children experience major cognitive developments. Due to the explosion of language in this stage, children develop **symbolic representation** – the ability to mentally represent an object that is not present such as pretending to talk on a "telephone" represented by a wooden block. The child continues to display egocentrism, and projects **animism** – giving life to inanimate objects such as thinking that animals talk. During this stage of development children also show **centration** in thinking – the focus on one characteristic of an object or event, such as color, size, or shape, to the exclusion of others. Because preoperational children believe what they see and tend to make incorrect generalizations, they do not have a strong sense of qualities belonging to objects. For example, they misconstrue "large" with "heavy". Piaget conducted a classic experiment to demonstrate this level of thinking in children. He put two sets of coins on a table in two lines, each line with the same number of coins, but with the coins in one line spread farther apart. When asked which line had more coins, children almost always responded that the line which had the coins spread farther apart had more coins.

"Piaget's Theory of Cognitive Development"

Educators and caregivers need to prepare classrooms that encourage exploration and discovery, with interesting experiences and materials as well as large blocks of uninterrupted time to explore the materials. Preoperational stage children think concretely so cognition should include using concrete materials and experiences such as math manipulatives, picture schedules, and field trips.

The Concrete Operation Stage (7 to 11 years) is the stage in which children's thinking becomes more analytical and logical. Children possess the characteristic of **reversibility** – the ability to think through a series of steps and then mentally reverse the steps, returning to the starting point. The child in this stage begins to notice more precise difference in classes of objects – for example, the schema of dogs can hold many different varieties of dogs such as poodles and retrievers. The concrete operational child displays flexibility of thought by holding several classifications and qualities in his mind – a car can be large, blue and a van all at the same time.

"Concrete Operational Stage – Deductive Reasoning"

"Piaget – Stage 3 - Concrete Reversibility"

Educators need to guide the continued concrete thinking of children in this stage with the use of more advanced concrete materials and visual aids – diagrams, graphs, graphic organizers, informational text structures – and real problems to solve.

Although Piaget's theory was widely accepted during the 1970's impacting teaching strategies and environments, critics in recent years have challenged many of the fundamental precepts of Piagetian theory. Piaget's work has been criticized for limitations that have been challenged by recent research. For example, researchers have found that with clearer directions and in certain contexts, young children can accomplish tasks Piaget thought impossible (Case & Okamoto,1996) such as taking the perspective of another person, and the ability to conserve quantities. In addition, many educators believe that Piaget emphasized thought processes and neglected children's feelings and social relationships. Because much of his observation was done on his own three children – white, Swiss, middle class – critics claim his work is not scientific research. When Vygotskian theory began to pervade educational settings, Piagetian theory was criticized for causing educators to focus on skills and knowledge children had not yet developed instead of what children could do with assistance.

Despite the criticism of Piaget, his stages of cognitive development have produced our overall view of how children think in their early years and provide a framework for the creation of curriculum that challenges young children's thinking.

Lev Vygotsky's Sociocultural Theory (1896-1934)

Lev Vygotsky, a Russian psychologist, studied the works of Sigmund Freud, Maria Montessori and Jean Piaget, searching for answers about children's learning and cognitive processes. Vygotsky was a prolific writer, writing or publishing over 180 scientific works before his untimely death of tuberculosis at the age of 37. Although he was a contemporary of Piaget, Vygotsky's work did not enter the field of education until the 1980's. This was due to the fact that many of his writings were hidden from the English-speaking public by the repressive Stalin communist regime (Dixon, 2003). Prior to the publication of a multi-volume series of Vygostsky's writings, Piagetian theory dominated the field of child psychology. After the publication of *Mind in Society* (1978), Vygotsky's theory of learning and development became more influential than Piaget's.

Putting Vygotsky's Theories Into Classroom Practice

Combining Thought and Language With Socialization – A Dynamic Process

Vygotsky claimed that culture and social interactions shape what children learn about the world. For years, educators believed that children's knowledge was constructed from personal experience. While Vygotsky believed that concept, he thought that personal and social experience – shaped by families, communities, education, socioeconomic status, and culture – cannot be separated (Mooney, 2000).

Children learn primarily through their relationships with other people, chiefly in their dialogue with each other and with a more knowledgeable "expert" – adult or peer. Vygotsky emphasized the importance of social interaction with peers and adults, the influence of family and culture, play as a primary vehicle for learning and that learning occurs first at the social level and then on an individual level (Jalongo & Isenburg, 2012).

"Lev Vygotsky's Theory of Cognitive Development Exam Prep Videos"

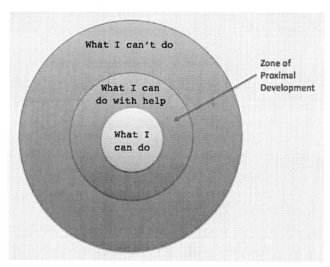

Whereas Piaget believed that development had to precede learning – children must be functioning in a certain stage of development in order to be able to learn certain conceptual knowledge – Vygotsky stated that development is a continuous process propelled by learning. This was a revolutionary stance in that it dramatically changed the role of the teacher and the foundations of curriculum building. Three major concepts pervade Vygotsky's theory: the zone of proximal development (ZPD), scaffolding, and the role of the adult.

The **zone of proximal development** is the distance between the most difficult task a child can do independently (actual level of learning) and the most difficult task a child can do with assistance (potential level of learning). When children work at their potential level of learning, they are exposed to learning that is potentially at an independent level before they can actually do it. Vygotsky believed that a child at this potential level of learning a new concept or skill can benefit from interaction with an "expert peer" (children who already possess a desired skill or conceptual knowledge) or adult.

"ZPD Zone of Proximal Development"

This assistance that an "expert peer" or adult provides a child is known as **scaffolding**. In the same way as a house builder uses a scaffold to reach heights of the house that are out of reach, adults and expert peers can assist a child in reaching a new concept or skill by providing supportive information. In order to provide effective scaffolding, the teacher's role becomes very important.

The **role of the adult** in Vygotskian theory becomes primary in the learning of children. The adult has to perceptively observe children, effectively plan curriculum and provide a learning environment which encourages conversations, social interaction, and collaborative learning. Adults need to use their observations to determine where children are in the independent learning process, what they are capable of doing with assistance, their individual needs, and the social context in which they live.

Effective and intentional curriculum planning relies on these keen observations. Unlike Piagetian theory which posits that stages of development are tied to physical development and that curriculum should support children at their current level of development without stretching those limits, Vygotsky held the view that children's cognitive development encompasses the skills and concepts that children can do independently and which they can acquire from the examples, modeling, and scaffolding of peers and adults. Vygotskian theory supports curriculum planning that extends children's learning by stretching and challenging their competence.

Vygotsky believed that language is the mediator allowing shared experiences which build cognitive development. He asserted that conversation is necessary to ask questions, get clarification, pose hypotheses, as well as to develop more complex communication skills. According to Vygotsky, verbalizing an idea leads to greater understanding. Educators need to question children and encourage peer interactions which support children's learning and development.

Vygotsky explained the relationship between language and thought as a process moving from interpersonal (between people) to intrapersonal (within the person) – conversation becomes an individual's thinking. Interpersonal knowledge construction (socially constructed knowledge) is turned into intrapersonal thought through **private speech** (Vygotsky, 1962). In young children as well as adults, private speech often presents itself as "thinking out loud". Children utilize private speech to talk to themselves to embed thought and as a tool for self-regulation to manage their behavior.

"Vygotsky has helped teachers to see that children learn not only by doing but also by talking, working with friends, and persisting at a task until they 'get it' (Mooney, 2000, p. 92)". Strategies such as **cooperative learning** activities (center-based learning, think-pair-share, cooperative learning groups) that contain mixed ability levels provide valuable opportunities for children to learn. Center-based learning, group project-based learning, imaginative play, and mixed-age grouping all allow children possibilities for problem-solving through negotiation and conversation. The teacher also acts as a collaborator with children as they construct knowledge.

Despite living a very short life, Vygotsky made a significant impact on the field of child development and learning. His emphasis on the influence of the social and cultural contexts on the unique, individual development of children revolutionized the science of psychology which had previously theorized that development occurred in universal and uniform stages. Probably, Vygotsky's primary contribution to the field of child development is his awareness of the importance of interaction with teachers and peers in promoting children's knowledge.

Abraham Maslow's Hierarchy of Needs Theory (1908-1970)

Abraham Maslow, a humanistic psychologist, originated a theory of human development based upon a hierarchy of universal basic needs for healthy personality development. Basic needs including physiological needs such as food, water and shelter, and safety and survival needs such as psychological safety and security form the base of the hierarchy. Growth needs – love and belonging, self-esteem and respect for others comprise the upper levels of the hierarchy. **Self-actualization** – the desire to use one's talents and competence to their fullest with the intent of making life meaningful and fulfilled – sits at the top of the hierarchy.

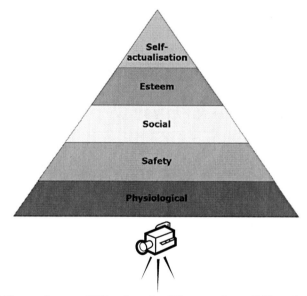

"Overview of Maslow's Hierarchy of Needs"

Maslow believed that his theory provides a framework for understanding people's motivation. His theory provides a lens through which we can view the holistic development of the child – the interrelatedness of the cognitive, emotional, physical, and social needs. Unless the basic needs are met, a person cannot proceed up the hierarchy to achieve the growth needs, and ultimately self-actualization. If children are hungry, emotionally insecure, and/or housing insecure, healthy development and learning cannot effectively occur. Meeting children's basic needs should be the heart of public policy and early childhood practice.

Early childhood educators need to go beyond meeting children's basic needs – ensuring adequate health, safety, nutrition, as well as access to health and dental services and social services. Effective early childhood programs must also have as their goal establishing positive, nurturing relationships with and among children and adults while building children's self-esteem by building their competencies. Helping children feel like

part of a learning community can satisfy the need for belonging and love. Providing predictable, daily routines help children feel secure while encouraging problem-solving and independence fulfills the need for self-esteem. Young children will not reach what Maslow called self-actualization, yet quality early childhood programs and educators can build the foundation.

We have described the developmental theories of Erikson, Bronfenbrenner, Piaget, Vygotsky, and Maslow. While developmental theories are connected to age of children, learning theories apply regardless of age. In the next section, descriptions of the most influential theories of learning are presented.

Modern Theories of Learning

B.F. Skinner's Behaviorism Theory (1904-1980)

Behaviorism or **behavioral theory** is one of the most influential learning theories of the 20th century. This theory categorizes all learning by the behavior that can be observed and measured. Behaviorists view the environment as the most influential component of learning and learning comes from a change in behavior. By controlling the consequences in the environment either positively or negatively, behavior and ultimately learning can be fostered. For behaviorists, learning is a compilation of knowledge and responses through exacting reinforcement. Using pleasant and unpleasant consequences to modify behavior is called **operant conditioning**.

"B. F. Skinner – Introduction to Operant Conditioning and Free Will"

Psychologist B.F. Skinner developed the idea of operant conditioning through years of research and experimentation. Skinner experimented with training rats to press a lever that would reward them with food. As a result of experimenting with animals and people, he theorized that all human behavior can be modified by the use of **reinforcers** or consequences, both positive and negative. Positive reinforcers strengthen the regularity of desired behaviors, while negative reinforcers decrease the occurrence of undesired behaviors and increase the occurrence of the desired behaviors.

"Positive and Negative Reinforcement"

Positive reinforcement follows a behavior and can be expressed as either a reward or in the form of praise, initiating a pattern of the positive behavior being repeated. Negative reinforcers are unpleasant consequences to be avoided, therefore modifying the behavior to conform to the hoped-for response. Negative reinforcement is not punishment which is a temporary solution; the purpose of using consistent reinforcers is to permanently embed the positive behavior so that when reinforcers are slowly removed, the negative behavior disappears.

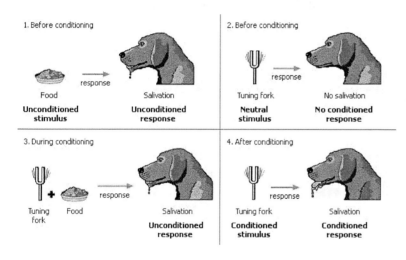

Behaviorist theory believes that learners are passive receivers of environmental stimuli, therefore making the adult the controller of the environment and the shaper of children's behavior. Skinner reasoned that this shaping of children's behavior is done by using a reinforcement and cueing system, rewarded at every small step, in a carefully designed environment.

There is a large body of research supporting the use of behaviorism, particularly with children with disabilities (Sandall, Hemmeter, Smith, & McLean, 2005). Often behavioral strategies are used to teach children with physical disabilities functional behaviors such as dressing, and to address challenging behavior in children with emotional disorders. Early childhood educators employ behavioral theory in their practice by using praise specifically and intentionally, acknowledging children's even smallest progress toward goals, and encouraging positive behavior by providing positive consequences.

Arnold Gesell's Maturationist Theory (1890-1961)

Maturation theory considers development as a biologically pre-determined progression unfolding in predictable sequences under appropriate conditions. Even though all children progress through universal stages of development, they proceed at varying rates. Consequently, maturationists assume that if a child is not "ready" to learn

a skill, intervention will be futile. According to this theory, as outlined by Arnold Gesell, development is an internal, genetic plan and assumes that attempting to teach concepts, skills or behaviors before they occur in the genetic plan is at best, fruitless and at worst, harmful to children's learning (Gesell, 1933).

Arnold Gesell was a physician who studied the theory of maturation at the Yale University Clinic for Child Development. He was the first theorist to provide standardized descriptions of children across all domains of learning. His research is frequently referred to as "ages and stages" because it provides characteristic descriptions of children from birth to ten that represent a predictable series of development that transcends culture, race, economic status, and experience.

Maturationist theory pervaded much of early childhood education during the early 20th century into the 1980's and 1990's. This theoretical perspective led educators to believe that schools needed to wait on formal instruction until children were "ready" for certain experiences – particularly literacy – to be learned efficiently and effectively. Subsequent research asserts that children's development of skills and concepts is heavily influenced by their cultural contexts and experiences (Rogoff, 2003), negating much of maturationist theory. Maturationist theory has been largely replaced by other theories of learning and development, but vestiges of it influences early childhood practice in many schools. Kindergarten "redshirting" – holding children who are deemed "at risk" out of kindergarten and delaying entry until they are more "ready" for the academic rigor – remains a common maturationist practice in many areas of the US.

The idea of developmental readiness has its origins in maturation theory. Although more recent theory has supplanted much of maturationist theory, there remains best practice that has its roots in this theory. Gesell's theory has assisted parents and educators in defining expected behaviors for children at certain ages so that age-appropriate experiences can be planned. Assessment of children's developmental levels is necessary to plan what children can perform independently and what children will be able to accomplish next with support.

Albert Bandura's Social Learning Theory (1925-)

Social learning theory was built on behaviorist theory, but differs in that instead of emphasizing direct reinforcement of a person's behavior to modify it, social learning theory suggests that people learn from observing the consequences of another person's behavior. By directly observing, the observer can then imitate the behavior. This theory holds significance in the field of education.

"Albert Bandura's Social Learning Theory"

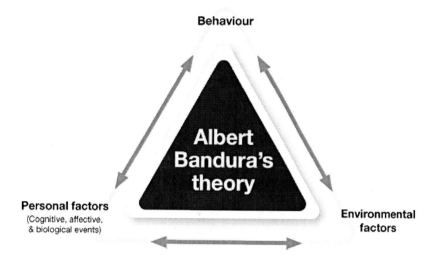

Behaviour

Albert Bandura's theory

Personal factors
(Cognitive, affective,
& biological events)

Environmental
factors

Albert Bandura, a contemporary psychologist and behaviorist, believed that children watch a behavior, develop it into a mental image that requires memory to hold it in their mind, and then model the behavior they observed. As a result, modeling is an important learning strategy that parents and educators use to demonstrate expected behaviors. Bandura also postulated that children learn vicariously by observing the consequences of other's behaviors in the form of reward or punishment, without having to experience the reward or punishment themselves.

Social learning theory acknowledges the importance of a child identifying with primary family members in influencing their language acquisition, developing a moral compass, learning socially acceptable behavior, and dealing with aggression (Bandura, 2001). The key family members which the child emulates provide the model that the child imitates. Social learning beliefs bridge behavioral theories with cognitive theories by acknowledging the active role children play in their own learning and the cognitive effects on learning (Bandura, 2001).

Social learning theory supports best practice in the classroom: direct modeling of appropriate behaviors, promoting student independence and self-efficacy, providing opportunities for students to practice self-regulation, and children as active learners.

Howard Gardner's Multiple Intelligences Theory (1943-)

Prior to Howard Gardner's work, intelligence was believed to be a single ability that can be enhanced, taught, changed and measured by one score on an intelligence test. However, Gardner, a psychologist at Harvard University, chose to study and define intelligence in a more realistic, broader view of learning and thinking. He addressed the concept of intelligence not by asking "What do you know?", but instead asking "How do you know?" From his research, he formulated eight different "frames of mind" or multiple intelligences (MI): verbal/linguistic, logical/mathematical, musical, visual/spatial, bodily/kinesthetic, interpersonal, intrapersonal, and naturalistic.

1. Verbal/linguistic – using language to express ideas and understand ideas
2. Logical/mathematical – ability to analyze, reason, solve logical problems (often termed as scientific thinking)
3. Musical – ability to produce and appreciate music; sensitivity to rhythm and tempo
4. Visual/spatial – forming images in the mind
5. Bodily/kinesthetic – controlling and using body movements
6. Interpersonal – understanding, working, and getting along with others; sensitivity to their feelings
7. Intrapersonal – awareness of one's own feelings, personal strengths and challenges
8. Naturalistic – sensitivity to the natural world, animals, and plants

"Howard Gardner of the Multiple Intelligence Theory"

Each intelligence encompasses unique cognitive skills that can be used to solve problems, create new problems, and create new products that are culturally valuable (Torrance, 2003). In Gardner's view, the fundamental requirements of any intelligence are that it must be comprised of a set of problem-solving skills, and potential to create new things. The emphasis on creative-problem solving of real-life problems is an important tenet in Gardner's work because it allows the learner to discover how to reach a goal, and through created products, how to exhibit his understanding.

Gardner suggests we all have intelligences which stand out, however our more dominate intelligence works in concert with the weaker intelligences to assist in problem-solving and creativity. Knowing each student's capabilities and utilizing Gardner's theory of Multiple Intelligences helps educators to reach all learners when both teaching and assessing conceptual learning. Evaluating students through the lens of multiple intelligences does not mean that each child should be taught differently; it allows the teacher to differentiate teaching and assessment practice.

Best teaching practice incorporates the use of the theory of Multiple Intelligences when curriculum approaches that tap all intelligences are used, teaching is designed to solve real-life problems and meets children's cultural and learning needs, and assessment strategies allow children to demonstrate learning in multiple ways across multiple intelligences. In addition to using these best teaching practices in an explicit way, it is equally important that teachers reflect on their own intelligences and how they are reflected in teaching styles and preferences. By balancing learning activities, materials, and teaching strategies, teachers ensure that every student is using their strengths and engaging in activities that strengthen their less developed intelligences.

Information Processing

With the advent of computers in the 1970's, researchers, in their quest to explain the development of children's thinking, used the computer as an analogy of the human mind. Information Processing (Munakata, 2006) views the mind as a symbol manipulating system through which information flows. Information enters the mind as input introduced through the senses, is coded, translated, and organized. Flowcharts map the precise sequence of thinking children use to solve problems and complete tasks. By analyzing the steps children take in their skill building, interventions may be put in place to promote more efficient learning and development.

In the same vein as Piaget's theory, Information Processing theory respects children as active constructors of knowledge who attempt to make sense of their world. But Information Processing rejects the idea of developmental stages; it views development as a continuous change. Thought processes such as perception, attention, memory, schema building, planning, problem solving, and comprehension are similar at all ages but present to a greater or lesser degree (Berk, 2016).

In Conclusion

Anthropologist Margaret Mead said: "If one cannot state a matter clearly enough so that an intelligent twelve year old can understand it, one should remain within the cloistered walls of the University and laboratory until one gets a better grasp of one's subject matter" Educational theory has suffered from the overuse of cryptic jargon, marginalizing those who need to understand it most – classroom practitioners and early childhood educare providers. Knowing the theoretical foundation of early childhood education is crucial to providing quality care and education. We need educators that both enjoy being with children and understand how children learn and grow. Theory needs to be real, valued, used and tested daily by educators in the classroom. This is the bridge from theory to practice that effective, knowledgeable and intentional educators bring to early childhood education.

Summary

- Development is the complex and dynamic cognitive, language, physical, motor, social, emotional, and moral processes that change over one's lifetime.

- Learning is a change in the level of knowledge or facility in a skill that results from experience and/or instruction.

- Brain development, social and cultural influences, and disabilities all influence the development and learning of young children.

- A theory is an affirmation of principles and ideals explaining how things happen; theories explain how children learn and develop. Educational theories are important because they influence teachers' beliefs about how children learn and ways teachers structure the curriculum and learning environment.

- The most influential theories of social-emotional development are Erikson's psychosocial theory, Bronfenbrenner's ecological systems theory, and Maslow's hierarchy of needs. The foremost theories of cognitive development are Piaget's constructivism theory and Vygotsky's sociocultural theory.

- The most renowned learning theories are Skinner's theory of behaviorism, Gesell's maturationist theory, Bandura's social learning theory, and Gardner's theory of Multiple Intelligences, and Information-Processing.

Key Terms

accommodation
adaptation
animism
attachment
assimilation
behaviorism
biological factors
centration
cognitive developmental theory
constructivism
cultural factors
cultural setting
development
disequilibrium
ecological systems theory
egocentrism

empathy
environmental factors
equilibration
exceptional learner
exosystem
family systems theory
information processing
learning
macrosystem
maturationist theory
mesosystem
microsystem
neural shearing
object/person permanence
operant conditioning
person first language
plasticity
pruning
psychosocial theory
reinforcers
reversibility
scaffolding
schema
self-actualization
self-regulation
social learning theory
social setting
sociocultural factors
sociocultural theory
symbolic representation
synapses
theory
windows of opportunity
zone of proximal development

Suggested Readings

Baker, A.C. & Manfredi/Petitt, L.A. (2004). *Relationships, the heart of quality care: Creating community among adults in early care settings.* Washington, D.C.: NAEYC.

Mooney, C. G. (2000). *Theories of childhood: An introduction to Dewey, Montessori, Erikson, Piaget, and Vygotsky.* St. Paul, MN: Redleaf Press.

Roopnarine, J.L. & Johnson, J.E. (Eds.). (2009). *Approaches to early childhood education* (5th Ed.). Upper Saddle River, NJ: Pearson.

Suggested Websites

Constructivist Teaching and Learning Models:
www.ncrel.org/sdrs/areas/issues

Jean Piaget Society for the Study of Knowledge and Development:
www.piaget.org

Project Zero Website:
www.pzweb.harvard.edu

Reflections

1. Reflect on your own experiences as a student in elementary school as well as middle and high schools. What theory of learning seemed to be predominant? What evidence do you have of this? Can you remember specific occurrences of positive reinforcement? Modeling? Collaboration for co-construction of knowledge? Scaffolding?

2. Observe in an early childhood setting. Reflect on the complexity of dramatic play and block-building. How does this type of interaction support co-construction of knowledge and self-regulation?

3. Reflect on Maslow's hierarchy of needs. Do you know families who are struggling to meet basic needs? If so, how does this affect their lives and choices? Now, project yourself at the self-actualization stage. Describe who you will be as a person and what you will be doing.

References

Bandura, A. (2001). Social cognitive theory. *Annual Review of Psychology. 52.* Palo Alto, CA: Annual Review.

Berk, L. E. (2016). *Infants and children* (8th ed.). Boston, MA: Allyn & Bacon.

Bredekamp, S. (2011). *Effective practices in early childhood education: Building a foundation.* Upper Saddle River, NJ: Pearson Education.

Bronfenbrenner, U. (1979). *The ecology of human development: Experiments by nature and design.* Cambridge, MA: Harvard University Press.

Case, R. & Okamoto, Y. (1996). *The role of central conceptual structures in the development of children's thought.* Chicago, IL: University of Chicago Press.

Copple, C. & Bredekamp, S. (2009). *Developmentally appropriate practice in early childhood programs.* (3rd ed.). Washington, DC: NAEYC.

Dixon, W. E. (2003). *Twenty studies that revolutionized child psychology.* Upper Saddle River, NJ: Pearson.

Erikson, E. H. (1993). *Childhood and society.* New York: Norton. (Original work published 1963).

Gesell, A. (1933). Maturation and patterning of behavior. In C. Murchison (Ed.). *A handbook of child psychology.* Worchester, MA: Clark University Press.

Jalongo, M. R. & Isenberg, J. P. (2012). *Exploring your role in early childhood education.* Upper Saddle River, NJ: Pearson Education.

Johnson, M. H. (2005). *Developmental cognitive neuroscience.* (2nd Ed.). Oxford, UK: Blackwell.

Mooney, C. G. (2000). *Theories of childhood: An introduction to Dewey, Montessori, Erikson, Piaget, and Vygotsky.* St. Paul, MN: Redleaf Press.

Munakata, Y. (2006). Information processing approaches to development. In D. Kuhn & R. S. Siegler (Eds.) *Handbook of child psychology: Vol.2. Cognition, perception, and Language* (6th ed., pp. 426-463). Hoboken, NJ: Wiley.

National Association for the Education of Young Children. (2009). *NAEYC Standards for Early Childhood Professional Preparation Programs.* Washington DC: NAEYC

Piaget, J. (1952). *The origins of intelligence in children.* New York: International Universities Press.

Rogoff , B. (2003). *The cultural nature of human development.* New York: Oxford University Press.

Sandall, S., Hemmeter, M. L., Smith, B. J., & McLean, M. E. (Eds). (2005). *DEC recommended practices: A comprehensive guide for practical application in early intervention/early childhood special education.* Longmont, CO: Sopris West, and Missoula, MT: Division for Early Childhood, Council for Exceptional Children.

Torrance, E. P. (2003). The millennium: A time for looking forward and looking back. *Journal of Secondary Gifted Education. 15*(1), 6-13.

Vygotsky, L. S. (1962). *Thought and language.* Cambridge, MA: MIT Press.

Vygotsky, L. S. (1978). *Mind in society.* Cambridge, MA: Harvard University Press.

Welch, K. J. (2007). *Family life now: Conversation about marriages, families, and relationships.* Boston, MA: Allyn & Bacon.

Chapter 5
Early Childhood Programs and Models

An Introduction to High-Quality
Early Childhood Programs

Thinking Ahead

1. Why is there an increasing demand for quality early childhood education programs?
2. How does the Montessori approach provide for the needs of young children?
3. How does the Reggio Emilia approach provide for the needs of young children?
4. How does the Waldorf approach provide for the needs of young children?
5. How does the Head Start program provide for the needs of young children?
6. How does the High/Scope program provide for the needs of young children?
7. How does the Creative Curriculum program provide for the needs of young children?
8. How does the Project Approach provide for the needs of young children?

An early childhood program provides a structure of care and education for children ages birth to 8 years old. For many years, the topics of early childhood education and care were regarded as separate entities. However, in recent years the early childhood community has attempted to offer a more holistic definition of appropriate early childhood settings. The term "educare" has emerged, its definition melding the components of education and care into an inextricable relationship. "Adequate care involves providing quality cognitive stimulation, rich language environments, and the facilitation of social, emotional, and motor development. Likewise, adequate education for young children can occur only in the context of good physical care and of warm affective relationships" (Bowman, Donovan, & Burns, 2001, p. 25).

Across the spectrum of high-quality educare programs is the commonality of developmentally appropriate practice, yet these programs often differ greatly in their approach to education and curriculum. This is due in part to the reality that DAP is a philosophy and approach to working with children; it is not a curriculum (Copple & Bredekamp, 2009). While all programs share a collective allegiance to the core principles of developmentally appropriate practice, the actual programs vary across curriculum models.

Some of these early childhood programs may be federally funded free programs, with Head Start being an example, or may be funded by nonprofit or for-profit agencies who charge tuition. Early childhood programs may be located in public school systems or may be housed in childcare centers, agencies, places of worship, etc. Unlike many other countries such as Sweden, Australia, and France where educare programs for preschoolers are offered free and universally to all children, the United States' model has no true uniformity. The U.S. programs vary in availability, eligibility requirements, program structure, curriculum, and quality.

Quality in early childhood care and education refers to the excellence of the program. Excellence is often predicated on the program exceeding minimum standards and offering more than just ordinary care. High-quality programs benefit children and their families, while poor-quality programs are disadvantageous to children's development and learning. Poor-quality programs often suffer from lack of resources, sub-standard conditions, under-prepared professionals, and insufficient staffing. High-quality programs, on the other hand, offer children a variety of benefits which lead to "higher levels of language development, greater social competence, a better ability to regulate their behavior, and better academic performance than do their peers in poor-quality programs" (Kostelnick, Soderman, & Whiren, 2011, p.11).

So what are some of the components of high-quality programs? The National Institute for Early Education Research (NIEER, 2015) publishes an annual report analyzing eight indicators of quality in early childhood programs:

- The teacher holds a Bachelor's Degree and focused training in early childhood education
- The teacher assistant has a Child Development Associate (CDA) credential or higher

- The staff receives at least 15 hours of in-service training each year
- The curriculum is aligned to the early learning standards set by each state
- Class size is capped at 20 with a teacher-to-child ratio of 1:10 or better
- Screenings and referrals are made for intervention programs
- Children receive at least one meal daily
- Frequent on-site visits are used to evaluate the program

Other research (Biddle & Berliner, 2002) adds to the list of factors which make early childhood programs high-quality:

- Educators are well prepared and well compensated
- Staffing is stable
- Warm, attentive relationships are established between adults and children
- Environments are safe and healthy
- Environments are stimulating
- Family engagement is evident
- There are connections to comprehensive community services

The National Association for the Education of Young Children (NAEYC), the nation's largest organization of early childhood educators, began accrediting programs in 1985, with the goal of raising early childhood program quality. Today, NAEYC accredits over 7,000 early childhood programs serving over 623,000 children from birth through

National Association for the Education of Young Children

kindergarten (NAEYC, 2012). This voluntary accreditation system is based on ten standards that programs must achieve: relationships with children, curriculum, teaching, assessment of children's progress, health, teaching staff, family collaboration, community relationships, physical environment, and leadership and management. Meeting and maintaining these standards makes it possible to attain quality of care and education for young children.

"NAEYC Accreditation – The Right Choice for Kids"

Any excellent program clearly articulates the goals of the program, the early childhood principles and practice that sustain the program's purpose, and the explicit roles of those working in the program. The program's philosophy will be visibly apparent in the structure, materials, activities, and relationships that make up the daily lives of the children, their families, and the educators. Throughout history, beginning with Froebel's kindergarten, early childhood educators have developed high-quality programs for young children. In this chapter, we will examine some of the most noteworthy programs designed to meet the needs of children and their families. We will review each program's purposes, curriculum, teacher role and how the program meets the needs of children and their families. While no one program can meet the needs of all children, these programs – Montessori, Reggio Emilia, Waldorf, Head Start, High/Scope, Creative Curriculum and the Project Approach – are widely used in the United States and around the world. Two of the programs, Montessori and Reggio Emilia originated in Italy while Waldorf began in Germany. High/Scope, Head Start, Creative Curriculum and the Project Approach all have their roots in the United States.

Montessori

Montessori early childhood education continues to be a common household phrase in the United States and around the world, enjoying great popularity with parents and professionals and having a significant impact on early childhood educare. Maria Montessori originally designed her educational program to meet the needs of developmentally delayed and impoverished Italian children who she believed would never fully develop their intellectual capabilities without an appropriate, structured education. Montessori later went on to create a curriculum which would meet the needs of all children. Today, there are approximately 20,000 Montessori schools found all over the globe serving children from birth to 18 years old, with more than 5000 schools in the United States.

**"Nurturing the Love of Learning:
Montessori Education for the Preschool Years"**

According to the Montessori Method, the four most important aspects in understanding how children learn include:

1. The **absorbent mind** speaks to children's natural curiosity which enables them to interact directly with their environment through their senses and to learn before being formally taught
2. The **prepared environment** is carefully structured by the teacher to support children's exploration and to nurture children's independence

3. **Sensitive periods** are phases of time when a child is ready to master specific skills or concepts that cannot be fully or efficiently mastered at other times

4. **Autoeducation** is the idea that children are capable of educating themselves if given large blocks of time to work with self-correcting materials

"The Montessori Method"

The Absorbent Mind

Montessori believed that children learn through purposeful work by using their senses to understand their world. She believed that children, particularly from age 4 to 7 are internally motivated to learn and do not need external rewards. This inspired her to be concerned with the environment that children work in, both in the materials and design.

In order for children to learn by doing and through repetition, Montessori believed that it was the teacher's responsibility to set up the environment for learning, provide the appropriate materials and then to step away while children had plenty of time and space in which to explore and experiment. Unlike most of the early childhood educators before and after her, Montessori dismissed free play as a waste of valuable learning time and she minimized the value of social interaction for children's learning (Wolfe, 2000). Children are supplied with individual mats to work on so as not to be bothered by their peers.

The Prepared Environment

Montessori believed that a prepared environment best prepares children to do things independently. Before Montessori, making materials and furnishings accessible and child-sized was not a widely accepted idea; educational spaces up to that point were adult-oriented. The prepared environment provides learning experiences and materials in an organized and systematic format. Spaces are neat, orderly and free of clutter, making them aesthetically pleasing, and meeting children's need for orderliness in their environment.

The furniture in a Montessori classroom is lightweight and scaled down so that it can be easily moved, and from which children can take and return materials without difficulty (Mooney, 2000). Montessori did not believe in cluttering up the walls with bright colors and wall adornment that could be distracting and over-stimulating. Instead, she advocated clean, white spaces where children could hang their work in an aesthetically pleasing way. Materials are to be clean, in good condition and neatly stored on shelves that are not overflowing with items.

"Calm, Order & Preparing the Environment"

These truly child-centered spaces allow for children's freedom to explore materials created for three different purposes: practical life and motor development, sensory materials to train the senses, and academic materials to teach literacy and math (Morrison, 2012). All of these activities are taught in a specified and exacting way. Montessori designed self-correcting materials, emphasizing that there was only one right way to use each of the materials.

The practical life activities are life skills which include: greeting a visitor, writing a thank you note, washing and caring for possessions, and self-care skills such as buttoning, zipping and tying. The sensory materials develop children's observational skills to build readiness for reading, build cognitive skills such as sorting and classifying, and encourage readiness for math. The academic materials are exercises in writing that lead to reading, including sandpaper letters and numbers.

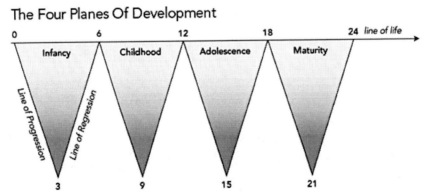

The **Line of Progression** illustrates the progression and peak of sensitive periods.
The **Line of Regression** indicates the passage into the acquisitive stage when assimilation, refinement and acquisition of skills occur.
Maturation implies a finality in the system of rebirths although individuals continue to grow throughout their lives.

Sensitive Periods

Montessori thought that the sensitive periods begin in infancy allowing the child to absorb the stimuli and cues which when internalized result in development and learning. Children have absorbent minds eager to take in, model, and imitate the stimulation to which they are exposed (Montessori, 1966). This emphasizes the need for accurate and appropriate modeling by caregivers and educators. Emphasis should also be placed on the importance of the first three years particularly in the development of language and motor coordination. Development in these two areas enables the consolidation of later social, physical, cognitive, and emotional growth. Therefore, the early years provide sensitive periods for optimal learning which provides the framework for future learning.

"Infant Toddler Sensitive Periods"

Autoeducation

Montessori believed that children need to care for themselves and their environment. Montessori warned teachers that children who are not allowed the independence to take care of themselves will not learn how to. It is sometimes easier to do things for children, but that short-term thinking does not help children learn and develop skills for the long-term. In order for a child's unique developmental pathway to be realized, Montessori felt the child needed to be able to function independently.

Building this self-sufficiency gives children the liberty to self-select activities, materials and exploration. This self-direction in the prepared environment maximizes a child's development while she is in the sensitive periods of her learning. Montessori believed that children who are actively engaged in a prepared environment with freedom of choice in activities will naturally educate themselves.

The Teacher's Roles and Functions

Teachers in Montessori programs are carefully trained in accredited teacher-training programs intentionally designed around Montessori's principles. The teacher, or *directress*, is the major educational influence in the child's life and the teacher must maintain great respect for the rights and abilities of each child (Follari, 2011). Not interfering with children's natural exploration is an important aspect of the teacher's role: "It is necessary for the teacher to guide the child without letting him feel her presence too much, so that she may be always ready to supply the desired help, but may never be the obstacle between the child and his experience" (Montessori, 1967, p.25). The teacher needs to make children the center of learning.

"Trevor Eissler 'Montessori Madness!' – 321 FastDraw"

Montessori believed that the teacher's major roles are to prepare the environment, demonstrate materials, and observe children. Preparation of the environment includes ensuring the learning materials and activities provide an appropriate learning experience for each child and the freedom of choice and time to explore. Demonstration of the materials should be done in an orderly and sequential manner with plenty of teacher support. Usually, this demonstration is done through individual instruction using brief, simple directions. Observation of each child takes place initially and is ongoing, providing valuable information so the teacher can prepare the best environment for each child. Through teacher observation and insight, teachers become familiar with each child's readiness level.

The Montessori method lost favor after the 1920's due in part to Montessori's view on play and her refusal to change any part of the method. There was a revival of the Montessori method in the United States during the 1950's. In recent years, thousands of Montessori schools have been created, however, the name "Montessori" is not copyrighted so any school can make the claim they follow the method. The best way to ensure that a school is a true Montessori school is to check its accreditation. Two Montessori accrediting organizations, the American Montessori Society (AMS) and the Association Montessori Internationale (AMI), provide teacher preparation, information, and accreditation certification.

Reggio Emilia

Reggio Emilia, a city in northern Italy, is a community where its early care and education centers epitomize exceptional teaching practice in early childhood education. The globally recognized schools of Reggio Emilia, Italy, have been called "the place theory and practice touch like the magic moment when night becomes day" (Bredekamp, 2008, p.49). Countless books, articles, and exhibits have been published about this approach in the past 20 years. The international educational community has been drawn to this aesthetically beautiful, community-school collaborative program.

"Introduction to Reggio Emilia"

Following the destruction of World War II, a community group of educators, parents, and children, led by Loris Malaguzzi (1920-1994), shared a vision for rebuilding the educational system of early childhood care and education. The destruction of the war  brought new hopefulness for a society dedicated to improving the lives and futures of children. Both war and Fascism had demonstrated that obedient people are dangerous people. As a result, the Reggio Emilia citizens' of vision and hope for the future was to raise a generation of critical thinkers who could take responsibility for themselves and their community (Instituzione of the Municipality of Reggio Emilia, 2012). Malaguzzi oversaw until his death in 1994 the evolution of this previously volunteer parent cooperative group into a world-renowned municipality-run system of preschools and infant/toddler centers serving children from birth to 6 years old. The schools are publicly funded and inclusive: children with disabilities and/or in need of social services are given first priority.

Since the mid-1970's, international organizations have pointed to Italian education for children with disabilities as the most inclusive of all countries of Europe (Begeny & Martens, 2007). In 1971, the Italian Parliament passed the first law concerning education for children with disabilities and established the right to a desegregated education of children in public schools. Many special education experts who have been outside observers are amazed by the atmosphere of welcoming and respect in the Reggio Emilia infant and toddler programs and preschools for the developmental and social needs of children across the full range of abilities (Palsha, 2002). Children with disabilities or special needs are referred to as "children with special rights", emphasizing children's rights as full citizens as opposed to children being deficient in some way.

The program philosophy is that "things about children and for children are only learned from children" (Malaguzzi, 1995, pp.43-44). Reggio is neither a curriculum nor a model – it is an approach that draws on several theories in an integrated manner. The Reggio Emilia approach draws on the theories of Vygotsky, Piaget, and Dewey in its approach to learning, yet the guiding framework is profoundly influenced by the sociocultural theory which is embodied in the belief that learning is based on relationships (Edwards, 2003).

The core values of Reggio Emilia affirm an abiding respect for children's capabilities, the importance of families, and attention to aesthetics and detail. Children learn to engage in constructive dialogues and problem-solving while utilizing their own learning styles. Reggio is based on the belief that children are much more capable than expected in an ages and stages philosophy of development; given the right opportunities for learning and appropriate adult support, children can engage with their world in a creative way.

"ReggioWEB"

Malaguzzi defined the elements of the Reggio Emilia approach using the imagery of "the hundred languages of children". Malaguzzi's poem (1998) entitled "The Hundred Languages of Children" begins:

> *The child is made of one hundred.*
> *The child has a hundred languages, a hundred hands, a hundred thoughts.*
> *A hundred ways of thinking, of playing, of speaking.*

These "hundred languages" represent the processes and products of children's learning and understanding. The languages include drawing, writing, sculpture, building, photography, inventing, music, words, numbers, and much more. Teachers are trained to create environments in which children are given the opportunity to use all the hundred languages in their learning.

"The Hundred Languages of Children"

The principles and features that guide the Reggio Emilia approach include an emergent curriculum; collaboration among home, school, and community; strong educator roles; beautiful, enriching spaces for learning; and documentation of learning.

Emergent Curriculum

The emergent curriculum emerges from the interests of children rather than teachers' pre-planned curriculum and lessons. The curriculum is developed around what children are engaged in, not solely on what adults believe children should learn. The children determine the topics that they are interested in and from which long term

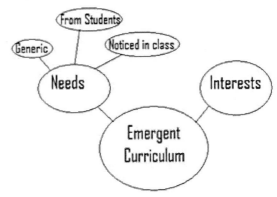

projects can emerge. Because the learning is deeply personal, the understanding becomes much deeper and enriched. The themes of study can last for months at a time, continuing as long as it takes for children to feel they have explored all they need to and are satisfied that they have a real understanding of it (Seefeldt, 1995).

"Emergent Curriculum"

Children are viewed as competent, resourceful individuals who are capable of constructing complex, meaningful ideas. Teachers have a presence in the decision-making; in advance they establish general goals and plans for possible directions for the learning. Teachers utilize their observational skills to collect data from children's conversations with the purpose of synthesizing children's interest in specific topics. After an analysis of children's discussions, teachers use the data to plan trips or introduce materials that will capture the imagination and curiosity of the children. Large blocks of time and beautiful spaces with access to materials provide the environment for solitary work, small group collaboration, and community building. Teachers meet almost daily to discuss the project, children's learning, and ways to deepen the understanding. Families and communities are invited to join this collaborative spirit, and are considered valuable resources and partners in learning.

Teaching and learning occur in short- and long-term projects facilitated by the teachers and families, and often initiated by the community.

> A project which we view as a sort of adventure and research, can start through a suggestion from an adult, a child's idea, or from an event such as a snowfall or something else unexpected. But every project is based on the attention of the educators to what the children say and do, as well as what they do not say and do not do. The adults must allow enough time for the thinking and actions of children to develop. (Edwards, Gandini, & Forman, 1998)

An example of a short-term project is one at the Diana School in Reggio Emilia where the children explored a puddle after a rainstorm. The children got to run through the puddle, investigate their reflections in the water, and then to use a mirror and artwork to replicate the reflections of objects in water. An offshoot of the initial experience in the puddle was a study of reflections in shadows. An example of a long-term project is a 4-month project about dinosaurs that a group of 5- and 6-year old children undertook with the support of their teachers and parents. The impetus for this project came from children's interest in and play, around the topic of dinosaurs.

Collaboration

Collaboration among school, home, and the community at large is fundamental to the Reggio Emilia philosophy. Malaguzzi (1998) called the approach "an education based on relationships". Family and community members are included frequently in the children's pursuit of specific topics and activities, and to provide the support of their expertise. Each school is constructed as a system in which the families, teachers, children, community, and environment are interconnected. The Reggio approach is a reflection of Vygotsky's sociocultural theory that believes children learn through social interaction.

Teachers emphasize and respect the role of parents as a child's first teacher. Parents are believed to have rights as do their children; these rights include participating actively and freely in their children's educational lives. In addition, many of the projects children engage in revolve around the life of their community. The surrounding city often serves as a catalyst of interest for a project. The connection between the internal learning environment and external life outside of the classroom is used by the Reggio teachers to sustain relationships that foster learning.

Teacher Role

In addition to the classroom teachers, each school has a specialist called an *atelierista*, an expert in the visual arts who works closely with the teachers and children to support the demonstration of learning through media and symbolic representation. The *pedagogista* is a specialist in teacher education who participates in problem solving with the teachers in the planning and implementation of the projects. The *pedagogista* visits each center for one day a week, establishing a relationship with the teachers, children, and families. Her role is to bridge theory and practice by offering expertise in the content and teaching practice as well as addressing the practical problems that arise.

Teachers assume multiple roles in the Reggio Emilia approach – that of researcher, facilitator, and partner in learning. Teachers carefully observe and document children's conversations to know how to plan the projects. Teachers also provoke children's thought by asking open-ended questions, displaying materials to extend children's thinking, and documenting the learning (Caldwell, 1997). Teachers are involved and ready to support and guide but are dedicated to interfering as little as possible as the children work. This demonstrates respect for the children's power and capabilities in their own learning.

Another role of the teacher is to thoughtfully observe and document the emergent learning. As the project progresses, the teachers work with the *atelierista* to collect, arrange, and display artifacts that document children's thinking and learning. These artifacts include photographs of children at work, transcripts of children's discussions, as well as children's drawings, construction, sculpture, etc.

In addition to the interactions that teachers have with children and supportive professionals, teachers also meet with parents informally during the day and formally in scheduled meetings to discuss projects, children's ideas, pedagogy, and community matters. In the Reggio spirit of collaboration and reflection and the dedication to providing the best experience for children, teachers are committed to open, collaborative, and mutually supportive relationships with parents as well as children and other professionals (Gandini, 2002).

Environment

Reggio teachers recognize the power of the learning environment, viewing the environment as the "third teacher" after the parents and teachers (Gandini, 1997). The learning spaces are designed with two predominant goals (Edwards, 2003):

- To encourage children to experience their world through new perspectives (see things differently, think about familiar things in unique ways, etc.)

- To provoke children's thinking, questioning, representing, and sharing

The layout of the physical space is welcoming and pleasing, with plenty of space for objects and activities which inspire discovery in the pursuit of learning. There is attention to detail in the color of the walls, the arrangement of furniture, and the placement of windows and doors which allow light to pour into the spaces. Everywhere there is children's work displayed: paintings, sculpture, mobiles, drawings, collages, etc. Children's work is treated with care and respect since it is not only decoration, but also documentation of the children's complex thinking skills and learning processes.

The *atelier* is a studio used by the *atelierista*, the children, parents, and teachers in the school. The *atelier* is equipped with tools and materials for new projects as well as past projects and experiences. This is also the workshop where teachers and the *atelierista* construct *documentation panels*. Each classroom contains a mini- atelier which provides the space to continue construction and exploration. The children's work in a variety of media is not viewed in the Reggio approach as just artwork, but is instead the symbolic representation documenting the learning process.

Documentation

The process of documentation, which is done collaboratively through observation, collecting a variety of documents, and interpreting them gives teachers the opportunity to make informed curricular and pedagogical choices in the assessment of the process and product of children's project work. Documentation is a formative assessment tool, used during the process of the experience or project. Unlike summative evaluation – data collected and evaluated at the end of a learning experience with the purpose of grading and comparing children's progress – documentation is a naturally integrated part of the everyday teaching-learning process. Documentation is a tool for teachers, parents, and children to reflect on the learning process and outcomes of groups of children as well as individuals. By making learning visible in the documentation of student artifacts, words, and actions, teachers have the opportunity to analyze the thinking and potential of children.

Transcripts of the children's discussions, photographs of the children's endeavors, and products of their thinking using media are captured and arranged by the *atelierista* and teachers to record the learning process. Documentation allows what occurs in children's minds and cannot be seen to be made visible. The functions of documentation are (Morrison, 2012, p. 166):

- To make parents aware of children's learning and to maintain parental involvement
- To allow teachers to understand children better and to evaluate their own work as a means of self-evaluation to promote professional growth
- To facilitate communication and exchange of ideas among educators
- To make children aware that their effort is valued
- To create an archive that traces the history of the school and the pleasure of learning by many children and their teachers

"Documentation: Transforming Our Perspective"

The Reggio Emilia approach which blends the theories of Piaget, Vygotsky, and Dewey, flourishes in the context of northern Italy due in large part to the universal view of early childhood education as a human right. This belief is supported by large amounts of governmental financial support as well as a genuine philosophical commitment. U.S. educators have incorporated pieces of the Reggio Emilia approach into their early education, calling themselves "Reggio-inspired". Although the Reggio Emilia approach cannot in its entirety be transported to other countries, the goal of partnerships in learning and the commitment to children's rights can be successfully infused in any program.

Waldorf

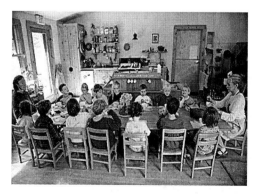

Waldorf education was founded by Rudolph Steiner, an Austrian philosopher in 1919, in the wake of destruction that followed World War I. Steiner devoted his life to the exploration of spirituality and human potential. He believed that there is no limit to human potential for growth and development and that potential is only maximized when the three major components of self – mind, body, and spirit – are fully developed.

Steiner conceived a philosophy called *anthroposophy,* the study of human wisdom and belief that a human's intellectual faculties can be utilized to gain spirituality. Although Waldorf education strives to educate the whole child – the heart, the hands, and the head – this philosophy is not taught explicitly in Waldorf schools (Nicholson, 2000). Instead, Waldorf education strives to instill a love of learning in children, to ensure that children develop as a whole person with all three developmental elements addressed, and to support a child's evolution into a free and creative thinker.

"Why Waldorf"

The first Waldorf school was founded in 1919 to serve the children of employees at the Waldorf-Astoria cigarette factory in Stuttgart, Germany. The first American Waldorf school was opened in New York City in 1928. The Waldorf schools operated under four conditions (Follari, 2011, p. 243):

- The school was open to all children regardless of race, class, ethnicity, ability level
- The school was coeducational
- The K-12 curriculum was viewed as a unified, complete program
- The teachers bore the primary responsibility for control of the administration of the school, with minimal outside interference

The Waldorf school movement has spread throughout the world and is one of the largest independent school organizations in the world. As of 2016, there were over 1,000 independent schools and 2,000 kindergartens worldwide in over 60 countries. There are countless public schools, homeschooling environments, and charter schools who use methods that are foundational to Waldorf education.

Steiner believed that children develop through 3 distinct stages:

- Early childhood (birth to 7 years old)
- Middle childhood (7-14 years old)
- Adolescence (14-21 years old)

For the purpose of this text, we will look at the early childhood and middle childhood stages.

Early Childhood

This stage of development ranges from infancy to the time when the child has all of his adult teeth. Steiner believed that during this stage the environment of children and the people in it hold the

greatest influence on children's development. The relationships the child builds with others during this stage provide the protection and attachment the child needs as well as the opportunity for cognitive, social-emotional, motor, and language development.

"Waldorf Early Childhood"

Steiner believed that during this stage children need to build their physical bodies and imaginations. Children are provided with daily, long periods of outdoor play to exercise both their bodies and curiosities and to develop spiritually in concert with nature. Foods that children consume are nutritious, organic and often grown in the school garden. Children use natural materials such as wood, cloth, and plants.

Unlike Montessori, Steiner believed that creative and fantasy play should occupy a large part of the child's school day. Appropriate play is self-initiated with open-ended materials made out of natural materials – wood blocks, yarns, scarves, household items, sculpting materials, and dress up clothes. There are long, uninterrupted blocks of time and plentiful open-ended materials to engage children in play. Construction, pretend play, knitting, cooking, sculpting, and gardening, are among the self-initiated activities in the Waldorf school day.

"Denver Waldorf School Early Childhood Curriculum"

Steiner resisted pushing children into early academic instruction, as he believed that learning is a lifelong process and building a strong, healthy body and creative mind provides the firm foundation for later learning (Follari, 2011). There is no formal academic instruction in the early childhood classrooms; early literacy experiences include oral storytelling by teachers and children and fine motor development through painting and sculpting. In Waldorf education, formal reading and writing instruction does not begin until late in second grade or third grade.

Middle Childhood

Steiner believed that the middle childhood is a time of deepening imagination and through the use of the realm of imagination more complex cognitive tasks are learned.

 Literacy and numeracy skills are learned in a fully integrated curriculum that includes art, music, woodworking, knitting and sewing, and dance. Students engage in hands-on activities that make abstract concepts understandable (Nicholson, 2000). Children engage in a special form of dance called **eurythmy**, a form of dance in which body movements parallel musical tones and words.

"Eurythmy and Waldorf Education Excerpt from Eurythmy DVD"

The middle childhood years offer a time for exploration of academic areas using language, imagination, and emotions. Teachers offer opportunities for students to use multiple ways of representing their learning – music, visual art, drama, dance, storytelling, writing, and graphic organizers (Nicholson, 2000).

Teacher Role

The role of the teacher is viewed as particularly important because the teacher serves as a model for children to imitate. The teacher plays four major roles (Follari, 2011 p. 249):

- Storyteller
- Personification of the parent figures
- Protector of the child's inherent drives and creativity
- Nurturer of children's play

"Waldorf: Be a Teacher"

The teacher prepares the classroom environment to make it home-like with functional furniture, soft lighting and aesthetically pleasing artwork. Materials from nature are collected and teachers learn how to knit, weave, sew, and create pictures using pieces of fluffy colored wools – a handcraft called *felting* (Waldorf Kindergarten Association, 1993). In assuming the role of teacher as storyteller, the teacher has to learn many poems, songs and stories to tell and sing.

Another role the teacher must assume is that of precise and purposeful observer. In order to meet the needs of individual children, knowing each child's interests, abilities, and needs is of prime importance. Through careful observation, the teacher gets to know each child individually and is better able to support each child's growth and development.

The teacher is the personification of the model parental role – supportive, nurturing, loving, and vigilant. Daily activities in the Waldorf school imitate daily home life: gardening, woodworking, baking, and caring for the classroom space (Fenner & Rivers, 1995). The teacher purposefully teaches each of these skills by first modeling the action by drawing the students in with a song or poem (Follari, 2011). Teachers model the ideal parental approach in maintaining a gentle, peaceful tone of voice and being a model of care and thoughtfulness.

Waldorf education contains many beliefs that impact all of early childhood education. Addressing all domains of the child's development is respected throughout all of early childhood education as is careful preparation and maintenance of the environment. Additionally, integrated curriculum and hands-on learning is a foundational early childhood education belief. Early childhood education has enjoyed the benefits of the Waldorf education movement envisioned by Rudolf Steiner.

Head Start

In the 1960's research emerged that supported the notion that early environments have a profound influence on young children's development. The concept of **early intervention** to negate many of the effects of poverty received support throughout the civil rights, educational, and sociology communities (Kagan, 2002). As part of President Lyndon B. Johnson's "War on Poverty", the Head Start Program was conceived and piloted in 1965. Head Start's purpose was to serve children from low-income households by providing extensive early childhood education, nutrition and health services, and parent programs. The main purpose of an entitlement program such as Head Start is to offer an enriched program to children from lower incomes – the "head start" that could reverse the cycle of poverty, and ensure children's readiness for kindergarten.

HEAD START

The 2015 statistics on poverty show an alarming number of American children under the age of 5 – 4,704,000 – live in poverty. The term poverty is defined by income thresholds. One of those designations is *low income* which is used to denote families whose income is at or below twice the federal poverty level (NCCP, 2016). For instance, the 2015 National Poverty Guidelines indicate that a family of three with an income of $20,090 is at the *poverty level* and that a family of three making twice that amount or less would be considered at the *low income* level. Children from homes that experience low income or poverty are more likely to suffer from inadequate nutrition, insecure housing, abuse and/or neglect, and lack of adequate health care. Affordable, high-quality childcare is a scarcity for children coming from these homes. Often, the adults in these children's lives are working several part-time jobs to make ends meet and are unable to give their children consistent, nurturing environments which encourage positive social and coping skills. Increasing children's social competence is emphasized in Head Start programs.

As public schools entered the prekindergarten arena in the 1990's, offering many 4-year-olds pre-school education, Early Head Start Programs serving children prenatal to three years old were begun. The increased awareness of the importance of early education and care the original Head Start generated led to the awareness that quality early educare must begin with our youngest and most vulnerable. Today, Early Head Start serves over 105,000 children birth to three years old (NHSA, 2012). In addition, to Head Start and Early Head Start, programs include Family and Community Partnerships, Migrant and Seasonal Head Start, and American Indian/Alaska Native Head Start.

In 2015-2016 Head Start and Early Head Start served approximately 1,097,049 children and pregnant women in over 2,800 programs across the United States. This number included 133,829 children with disabilities and 52,699 children who experienced homelessness during their year in Head Start. More than 830,000 families received Family Services such as mental health care, dental health care, housing assistance, parenting education, smoking cessation, job education and more (NHSA, 2016).

In 2015, Head Start had a paid staff of 243,000 people and 1.1 million volunteers, of which approximately 782,000 are parents (NHSA, 2016). The total 2015 federal funding for Head Start was $8,285,544,370. Ludwig and Phillips (2007) estimate that for every $1 invested in Head Start, there is a 7-9% annual return on investment (ROI) in the reduced cost of pre-school education, decreased number of children in special education and remediation programs, fewer grade retentions from Pre-K to grade 12, etc.

Head Start is administered by the Administration for Children and Families (ACF) in the Department of Health and Human Services. The Department of Education collaborates with the Department of Health and Human Services to lend support for the expansion and enrichment of Head Start programs. At the local level, any local public or private nonprofit or local for-profit agency or organization qualifies for funding to establish a Head Start program (Morrison, 2012).

The American Recovery and Reinvestment Act of 2009 (ARRA), or as it is more commonly referred to – the "stimulus package" – increased funding to early childhood education in the hope of positively impacting children's lives at the earliest opportunity. Head Start received an additional $2.1 billion to be divided between Head Start ($1 billion) and Early Head Start ($1.1 billion). However, the Federal Sequestration in 2013 slashed Head Start funding by $405,000,000, causing the loss of programming to 57,265 at-risk and the loss of 18,000 staff members (NHSA, 2016). Funding levels have begun to be reinstated yet the majority of the children living in poverty in the United States still do not receive Head Start services.

"Head Start Education"

Programs

To be eligible for Head Start and Early Head Start services, children must meet age requirements and families must meet income guidelines. Early Head Start enrolls children birth to three years of age, while Head Start includes children from three to five years old. Income criterion is based on the poverty guidelines established annually by the Department of Health and Human Services (US Department of Health and Human Services, 2012). Eligibility is determined by whether a family income falls below the sanctioned poverty line. Ninety percent of the children must meet the income eligibility benchmarks, while the other ten percent of the enrolled children may be from families that earn above the established poverty level.

2015 Poverty Guidelines for the 48 Contiguous States and the District of Columbia	
Persons in family/household	Poverty guideline
1	$11,770
2	15,930
3	20,090
4	24,250
5	28,410
6	32,570
7	36,730
8	40,890
For families/households with more than 8 persons, add $4160 for each additional person.	

SOURCE: Federal Register, Health and Human Services January 22, 2015

In 1972, the Head Start program was expanded to include comprehensive educational, health, and family services for children with disabilities. By law, at least ten percent of the enrollment in Head Start must include children with disabilities. In actuality, local programs may have more than ten percent of its enrollment children with disabilities. Research continues to support the positive outcomes for children with disabilities who gain access to intervention before age 5 and who are included in classrooms with typically developing peers (Hume, Bellini, & Pratt, 2005).

Migrant and Seasonal Head Start provides services that meet the unique needs of migrant and seasonal families. **Migrant families** are those who move from one geographic location to another to work in agricultural work. **Seasonal families** are those who have had a permanent residence for two years but who travel seasonally to engage in agricultural work. Migrant and Seasonal Head Start programs serve infants, toddlers, and pre-school age children by providing quality educare while their parents are working in the fields. Programs are center-based and full day to meet the needs of the parents who work long days.

The American Indian/Alaska Native Head Start program provides children and their families with health, nutritional, social, educational, and developmental services aimed at promoting school readiness. The program encourages parental involvement and embraces the rich cultural heritage of these groups through activities such as dance, language, and artwork.

Early Head Start was initiated in the mid-1990's to meet the needs of low-income pregnant women, infants, and families. Much of the research which emphasized the critical nature of the early years of development and the need to optimize those early years including prenatal development provided the framework for Early

Head Start. The purpose of the program is to support the emotional, social, physical, and cognitive development of children; provide parenting education; and help families move toward self-sufficiency (Morrison, 2012). Early Head Start has taken the lead in the field of infant and toddler education, emphasizing the necessity for responsive educare, a holistic approach to supporting all domains of children's development, and building strong, respectful relationships with parents.

Standards

THE HEAD START CHILD DEVELOPMENT
AND EARLY LEARNING FRAMEWORK
Promoting Positive Outcomes in Early Childhood Programs
Serving Children 3-5 Years Old

The Head Start Performance Standards provide the compulsory guidelines that Head Start and Early Head Start programs are required to implement. These standards define the objectives and services of a quality Head Start program, they stipulate the services that should be provided to both young children and their families, and they necessitate a group to monitor and enforce quality standards (Morrison, 2012). The structure of the Performance Standards includes seven principles: 1) Child development, 2) Family development, 3) Community building, 4) Staff development, 5) Administration and management, 6) Continuous improvement of the programs, and 7) Children with disabilities. The responsibility for the professional development of the teaching and support staff falls on the shoulders of the local agencies. The local agency, utilizing the Head Start Standards, is responsible for creating programs which meet the unique needs of the children and families in the agency's community.

The new 2015 Head Start Early Learning Outcomes Framework replaces the 2010 version that was heavily literacy-based. The new Framework respects the holistic nature of young children's development and learning. The framework is grounded in a comprehensive corpus of research of what children should know across the domains of Approaches to Learning, Social and Emotional development, Language and Literacy, Cognition, and Perceptual, Motor and Physical development. The Framework helps adults better understand how they should be providing learning opportunities that support learning outcomes.

The Early Learning Outcomes Framework is supported by 7 Guiding Principles (NHSA, 2016):

1. Each child is unique and can succeed
2. Learning occurs within the context of relationships
3. Families are children's first and most important caregivers, teachers, and advocates
4. Children learn best when they are emotionally and physically safe and secure

5. Areas of development are integrated, and children learn many concepts and skills at the same time
6. Teaching must be intentional and focused on how children learn and grow
7. Every child has diverse strengths rooted in their family's culture, background, language, and beliefs.

The Framework is organized into Domains, Sub-Domains, Goals, Developmental Progressions, and Indicators. These elements are research-based, comprehensive, inclusive, manageable and measureable. The Framework combined with teacher knowledge of the content material and understanding of each child's cultural background, ensures that children's unique ways of learning are recognized.

Family Involvement

Parents are respected as the child's first teachers and the family unit is always valued as a supportive network for the child. Parents are included in planning, community outreach, and programming decisions. Parents are encouraged to volunteer in classrooms and are given preference for hiring when paid positions are made available. Training and informational sessions are held to enhance the parents' abilities to care and advocate  for themselves and their children. Through empowerment of both families and children, Head Start programs endeavor to empower the family unit as a member of the larger social community (Peth-Pierce, 2000). As services are provided, it is important to respect the culture of the families and the larger community context in which children live their lives.

Concerns about Head Start

One of the largest challenges facing federally funded programs is answering the pervasive questions: Does the Head Start program provide a good return on its large investment? How can the tax-paying public be assured that this program servicing young children coming from low-income homes achieves its intended goals?

Cognitive and language development are two areas that are evaluated on an ongoing basis. The 2006 FACES study (USDHHS, 2006) includes data gathered from 1997 to 2003. The research shows that the large gap in the literacy and numeracy skills of children entering Head Start programs is narrowed as a result of attendance in the program. Those children with the most substantial delays made the greatest gains, particularly in the areas of vocabulary and early writing. English language learners made noteworthy gains in vocabulary growth. Despite these positive data points, children in Head Start programs still score below the national average in many areas including reading readiness for kindergarten (USDHHS, 2006).

Social skills and competence is a major goal of Head Start. The research shows that significant advances were found in children's social development, reduced hyperactive behavior, and increased cooperation in the classroom (USDHHS, 2006). Early Head Start data reports gains in parent-child relationships and attachment, child responsiveness to parents and caregivers, and improvements in parenting skills (USDHHS, 2006). The importance of positive social skills as a factor in later school success is a cornerstone of early childhood educare. Head Start and Early Head Start strives to build those social skills that lay the foundation for pre-schools and elementary school readiness.

Wash-out of the skills learned in Head Start is a real concern about the program. The wash-out effect refers to the reality that many of the positive gains in early childhood programs often decrease or "wash-out" by third grade, with much of the effect occurring by the end of first grade. This fading effect may be due to the fact that kindergartens have many more children with less adult support, health and welfare  services may not be continued into kindergarten, intervention services may be discontinued, and many of these low-income children and children in poverty enter some of the poorest schools (Follari, 2011). However, the FACES report does offer a glimmer of hope in the long term positive effects of Head Start in the areas of vocabulary, early writing, early math, and social skills that continue to develop in kindergarten (USDHHS, 2006).

Teacher credentialing for program improvement is an issue addressed periodically by the federal government. The 2004 reauthorization requires all Early Head Start to have a child development associate (CDA) credential by 2010, at least half of all Head Start teachers to have a bachelor's degree by 2013, and all Head Start teacher assistants to have at least a CDA by 2013. By 2011 all Head Start teachers were required to have at least an associate's degree in early childhood education with teaching experience (USDHHS, 2006). By 2015, 73% of all Head Start center-based preschool teachers had a baccalaureate degree or higher in early childhood education, or in a related field with experience. Ninety-six per cent had an Associate's Degree or higher. The more rigorous professional requirements reflect Head Start's and the Department of Health and Human Services' commitment to improved program quality and best classroom practice.

The goals of Head Start and Early Head Start programs, created in 1965 and 1994 respectively, were to close the achievement gap, prepare children to be successful in school settings, and to support families with education and services. The success of Head Start and Early Head Start in its efforts to fight poverty and to give every child a leveled playing field for school success endures today.

High/Scope

The High/Scope curriculum model was originated by the late David P. Weikart, the former president of the High/Scope Educational Research Foundation. In 1962, Weikart and his colleagues started the Perry Preschool Project in Ypsilanti, Michigan to address the persistent failure of high school students in Ypsilanti's poorest neighborhoods. The premise of the Perry Project was that purposeful, constructivist early childhood education could have a lasting positive effect on  children's long-term success in school (Schweinhart, Barnes & Weikart, 1993). During the project, teachers worked with 3- and 4-year old children in a classroom setting, made weekly home visits, and met in daily staff meetings.

A significant accomplishment of Weikart's project was a longitudinal study of the participants as well as a group who did not have the benefit of the Perry Preschool Project through the age of 40. This landmark study found that in various indicators of the quality of life (e.g. high school graduation, adult earnings, home ownership, educational attainment, occupation, lifetime arrests), those who participated in the project's preschool had much more positive outcomes.

The High/Scope educational model is based on Piaget's cognitive development theory and Vygotsky's theory of sociocultural development. The curriculum emphasizes that children need to be engaged in active learning, partnering with teachers in building a community of learners. Children actively participate in choosing and organizing their learning while teachers carefully guide, observe, and document children's learning. The curriculum encourages student choice as well as providing teachers with a framework of sequential learning goals that children need to accomplish.

High/Scope teachers provide an environment enriched with a variety of materials and tools for learning as well as large blocks of time to experiment, explore and problem-solve. Teachers are guided by a curriculum of sequenced outcomes that frame the daily learning activities. Five basic principles – active learning, a consistent daily routine, a richly supplied and carefully arranged classroom environment, a precisely designed, developmentally appropriate curriculum, and ongoing assessment – shape the High/Scope program.

Active learning is modeled in the High/Scope program through supportive adult-child interactions. Adults scaffold children's learning utilizing a variety of effective strategies – establishing authentic relationships with children, sharing control of the learning with children, reviewing materials and activities with children, taking a strengths-based approach to children's abilities, leading large- and small-group activities, observing and evaluating children's learning, and adopting a problem-solving approach.

"Introduction to Large-Group Time"

"Introduction to Small-Group Time"

Daily routines follow a predictable series of events and activities, providing the security and consistency young children need. The routine provides children with large blocks of time over which they have control of their choices for learning. The daily routine is comprised of:

- Small-group time where children meet together and with the teacher to experiment with new materials and problems using emerging skills
- Large-group time where children and teachers learn through limited direct-instruction, music and movement, read alouds, and sharing experiences
- Plan-do-review is a process unique to the High/Scope program. Children take 10-15 minutes to *plan*, organize, and announce what they want to work on that day. Next, children have approximately

an hour to *do* the activities – usually in learning centers – the activities they have planned. During this time teachers circulate, using intentional questioning and comments to promote deeper thinking and to encourage positive conflict resolution. After the work period, children *review* what they have accomplished during a 10-15 minute debriefing time. This time offers a learning closure time and the opportunity for developing analysis, language, and social skills

- Outdoor time is approximately 30 minutes every day
- Daily adult planning time occurs before or after children are at school and during rest times

The **classroom environment** and organization of routines and materials supports children's learning in the High/Scope program. Materials are varied, plentiful, and organized and stored in places that children can easily access. The classroom has a meeting space as well as at least five activity centers which foster independence and choice and reflect children's interests.

The High/Scope **Curriculum** is based on 58 **key developmental indicators** organized in five content areas: approaches to learning; language, literacy, and communication; social and emotional development; physical development, health and well-being; and arts and sciences (High/Scope Education Research Foundation, 2009). Within each content area specific skills, concepts, and behaviors are identified as appropriate outcomes for young children. Teachers use the 58 indicators for planning, designing the learning environment, and assessment of learning.

Assessment data is gathered through daily observations and interactions, and recorded in anecdotal notes. Teacher observations are structured around the High/Scope Child Observation Record (COR) which identifies and evaluates children's progress in key developmental indicators. The COR is a checklist of 30 developmental outcomes across all the domains of development and learning (social-emotional, cognitive, physical, and language) that are aligned to the 58 key developmental indicators (Schweinhart, 2003). Assessment data is collected over time and in natural, authentic situations where children are participating in learning activities and interacting with peers and adults.

There is also an assessment of the program utilizing a program assessment tool called the High/Scope Preschool Program Quality Assessment (PQA). The purpose of the PQA is to "evaluate the quality of early childhood programs and identify staff training needs" (High/Scope Education Research Foundation, 2003). The assessment, using a

5-point scale, rates the program in the areas of learning environment, schedules, interactions, curriculum, family involvement, staff development, and program management. Data collection includes observations, interviews of teachers, administration, and children.

High/Scope also offers programming for infants and toddlers. The infant and toddler curriculum includes 41 vital experiences covering the following developmental and content areas (High/Scope Educational Research Foundation, 2009):

- Sense of self
- Social relations
- Movement
- Music
- Creativity
- Communication and language
- Exploring objects
- Space
- Time
- Early quantity and number

Teacher interactions with infants and toddlers are especially crucial, establishing the secure relationships that encourage infants' and toddlers' active exploration of their environments. The willingness of infants and toddlers to explore their world is enhanced by being surrounded by approving and attentive adults who are attuned to the individual children's needs and cues.

The use of centers, the belief in active learning, and the plan-do-review cycle allows children to progress at their individual pace. This benefits all children including children who are diverse learners. Through continuous and perceptive observation, High/Scope teachers ascertain where children are developmentally and then provide a broad range of appropriate learning opportunities.

Creative Curriculum

Over 30 years ago, Diane Trister Dodge developed Teaching Strategies – the curriculum framework of Creative Curriculum – to support early childhood educators as they planned and implemented developmentally appropriate, content-rich programs that facilitate active learning and promote pre-school and kindergarten children's progress in all developmental areas. Over a decade ago, the Creative Curriculum for Infants, Toddlers, and Twos was added to assist teachers as they develop daily routines and meaningful activities that meet the needs, strengths and interests of our youngest children.

The Creative Curriculum is based on the work of six main theorists. Using their views of children as the organizational framework, the curriculum serves as a guideline for how to provide the best care and education for young children. T. Berry Brazelton and Abraham Maslow believed that children's basic needs such as safety, security, and esteem need to be met. Erik Erikson and Stanley Greenspan focused on children's need for trusting, secure relationships with adults that foster emotional and social growth. Jean Piaget and Lev Vygotsky theorized how interactions with others and the environment are crucial for cognitive development (teachingstrategies.com).

The Creative Curriculum for Infants, Toddlers and Twos has five components that guide teacher decision-making about routines and activities they provide for children birth to 36 months of age. The components are:

1. **Knowing infants, toddlers, twos** – the teacher is responsible for utilizing the provided Developmental Continuum to evaluate each child's development; then plan individually appropriate experiences and routines; consider the child's temperament, culture, life circumstances and any disabilities; and assess each child's progress.

2. **Creating a responsive environment** – the physical environment is designed to be welcoming, home-like, pleasant and efficient for learning and teaching. Daily and weekly, individualized lessons and routines are planned and implemented.

3. **What children are learning** – teacher observation of each child's progress across all developmental domains allows the teacher to plan meaningful lessons. Traits for pre-school and kindergarten readiness include confidence, curiosity, intentionality, self-control, relatedness, cooperativeness and capacity to communicate.

4. **Caring and teaching** – teachers use their knowledge of child development and individual children's strengths and needs to build trusting, responsive relationships with children. An ongoing assessment plan is in place in every classroom.

5. **Building partnerships with families** – welcoming programs help to build positive relationships with families; teachers encourage families to actively participate in their child's experiences, thus alleviating some of the stress of placing a child in an educare setting.

The Creative Curriculum for Pre-School is based on five principles:

1. **Positive interactions and relationships with adults provide a critical foundation for successful learning.**

2. **Social-emotional competence is a significant factor in school success.**

3. **Constructive, purposeful play supports essential learning.**

4. **The physical environment affects the type and quality of learning interactions.**

5. **Teacher-parent relationships promote development and learning (teachingstrategies.com).**

The Creative Curriculum offers for purchase a planned curriculum and assessment system (GOLD) for four age groups/educare environment: Infants, Toddlers, and Twos; Pre-School; Kindergarten; and Family Childcare. The teachingstrategies.com website also provides research and theory papers on a variety of topics such as executive function, letter recognition, phonological awareness, and curriculum for English and Dual-Language Learners.

"The Creative Curriculum for Preschool"

"Intentional Teaching in the Creative Curriculum Classroom"

Project Approach

The use of project-based learning was influenced by the work of educators in the British Infant Schools in the early 1900's and later by John Dewey in his lab school at the University of Chicago (Follari, 2011). This curriculum framework emerges out of children's interests and is taught through hands-on investigations and active inquiry. The Reggio Emilia approach is a prime example of an effective project approach.

Topics can be suggested by children or can be introduced by the teacher based on teacher observations of children in their play and interactions. The project can be a whole group, small group, or individual study. "A key feature of project work is that it is an investigation – a piece of research that involves children seeking answers to questions they have formulated" (Katz & Chard, 2000, p.2). Interest in a topic is a strong motivator for learning; children are allowed to investigate projects in which they are interested. Being excited, engaged and motivated about the topic fulfills one of the four key learning goals addressed in the project approach (Katz & Chard, 2000):

- Knowledge
- Skills
- Dispositions
- Feelings

As soon as the topic is selected, teachers and children first, plan the investigation, then carry out the investigation, and finally, share the project in a culminating activity. In the planning phase, children and teachers brainstorm what they already know about the topic, using graphic organizers such as KWL's, Venn Diagrams, and concept maps. In the investigation phase children collect, record, analyze, and share data. The culminating activity includes charts, displays, Power Point presentations, reports, plays, open houses, etc.

During the investigation, teachers keep a detailed, daily account of the path of the project, the children's learning, and the standards covered. Authentic documentation is an important aspect of the project approach. Direct-teaching of embedded skills and knowledge is balanced with child-directed hands-on inquiry and exploration. One of the benefits of the project approach is the ability to support diverse learning styles and multiple ways that children can represent their learning.

In Conclusion

It is important that early childhood educators know about a variety of programs for children, their historical roots, and practical application in the lives of children. In addition, it is important that early childhood educators are knowledgeable in their field and are able to compare and contrast the wide range of approaches. The knowledge gained provides a frame of reference as the early childhood educator crafts her philosophy of early learning which then shapes her classroom and teaching.

Summary

- Quality in early childhood care and education refers to the excellence of the program. High-quality programs benefit children and their families, while poor-quality programs are disadvantageous to children's development and learning.

- According to the Montessori Method, the four most important aspects in understanding how children learn are: the absorbent mind, prepared environment, sensitive periods, and autoeducation.

- The core values of Reggio Emilia – an early childhood approach that emerged in northern Italy after World War II – affirm an abiding respect for children's capabilities, the importance of families, and attention to aesthetics and detail.

- Waldorf education strives to instill a love of learning in children, to ensure that children develop as a whole person with all three developmental elements addressed – mind, body, and spirit – and to support a child's evolution into a free and creative thinker.

- Head Start's purpose is to serve children from low-income households by providing extensive early childhood education, nutrition and health services, and parent programs. The main purpose of an entitlement program such as Head Start is to offer an enriched program from lower incomes – the "head start" that could reverse the cycle of poverty, and ensure children's readiness for kindergarten.

- The High/Scope educational model is based on Piaget's cognitive development theory and Vygotsky's theory of sociocultural development. The curriculum emphasizes that children need to be engaged in active learning, partnering with teachers in building a community of learners.

- The Creative Curriculum is based on the work of six main theorists: Brazelton, Maslow, Erikson, Greenspan, Piaget and Vygotsky.

- The Project Approach curriculum framework emerges out of children's interests and is taught through hands-on investigations and active inquiry around a problem or question.

Key Terms

absorbent mind
active learning
atelierista
autoeducation
CDA
curriculum model
early intervention
educare
emergent curriculum
eurythmy
key developmental indicators
migrant families
pedagogista

poverty level
prepared environment
seasonal families
sensitive periods

Suggested Readings

Children's Defense Fund. (2003). *Head Start reauthorization: Questions and answers.* Washington, DC: Children's Defense Fund.

Edwards, C.P., Gandini, L., & Forman, G. (Eds.). (2012). *The hundred languages of children: The Reggio Emilia approach to early childhood education.* (3rd Ed.). Santa Barbara, CA: ABC-CLIO, LLC.

Katz, L. & Chard, S. (2000). *Engaging children's minds: The project approach.* Stanford, CT: Ablex Publishing.

Montessori, M. (1967). *The discovery of the child.* New York: Ballantine.

Schweinhart, L.J. (2003). *Validity of the High/Scope preschool education model.* Ypsilanti, MI: High/Scope Educational Research Foundation.

Waldorf Kindergarten Association. (1994). *Understanding young children: Excerpts from lecture by Rudolf Steiner.* Silver Spring, MD: Waldorf Kindergarten Association.

Suggested Websites

American Montessori Society
www.amshq.org

Creative Curriculum
www.teachingstrategies.com

Head Start
www.eclkc.ohs.acf.hhs.gov

HighScope Educational Research Foundation
www.highscope.org

Reggio Emilia Approach
www.reggioemiliaapproach.net

The Project Approach
www.projectapproach.org

Reflections

1. Why do the benefits of Head Start seem to fade out in grade one? Be sure to consider such things as the way children are taught in kindergarten through first grade. What are some of the ways you can help assure that the fade out effect does not happen?

2. Observe at an infant/toddler child care facility. Ask the teachers how they decide what they will do with the children. Reflect on whether there is a "curriculum" in the program and the developmental appropriateness.

3. How can you advocate for children with disabilities to receive the services they will need in classrooms using the early childhood models presented in this chapter?

References

Begeny, J. C. & Martens, B. K.(2007). Inclusionary education in Italy: A literature review and call for more empirical research. *Remedial and Special Education, 28,* 80-94.

Biddle, B. J. & Berliner, D. C. (2002, February). Small class size and its effects. *Educational Leadership, 59*(5), 12-23.

Bowman, B. T., Donovan, M. S., & Burns, M. S. (2001). *Eager to learn: Educating our preschoolers.* Washington, DC: National Academy Press.

Bredekamp, S. (2008). Malaguzzi's metaphors: The power of imagery to transform educational practice and policy. In L. Gandini, S. Etheredge, & I. Hill (Eds.). *Insights and inspirations from Reggio Emilia: Stories of teachers and children from North America* (pp. 48-49). Worchester, MA: Davis Publications.

Caldwell, L. B. (1997). *Bringing Reggio Emilia home.* New York: Teachers College Press.

Copple, C. & Bredekamp, S. (2009). *Developmentally appropriate practice in early childhood programs* (3rd Ed.). Washington, DC: National Association for the Education of Young Children.

Creative Curriculum. www.teachingstrategies.com

Edwards, C. Gandini, L. & Forman, G. (1998). *The hundred languages of children: The Reggio Emilia approach – Advanced reflections* (2nd ed.). Greenwich, CT: Ablex.

Edwards, C. P. (2003). "Fine designs" from Italy: Montessori education and the Reggio Emilia approach, believing in the power of the child. *Scholastic Early Childhood Today, 15*(8), 46.

Fenner, P. J. & Rivers, K. (1995). *Waldorf education – A family guide.* Amesbury, MA: Michaelmas Press.

Follari, L. M. (2011). *Foundations and best practices in early childhood education.* (2nd Ed.). Upper Saddle River, NJ: Pearson Education.

Gandini, L. (1997). The Reggio Emilia story: History and organization. In J. Hendrick (Ed.), *First steps toward teaching the Reggio way.* Upper Saddle River, NJ: Merrill/ Prentice Hall.

Gandini, L. (2002). The story and foundations of the Reggio Emilia Approach. In V. Fu, A. Stremmel, & L. Hill (Eds.), *Teaching and learning: Collaborative exploration of the Reggio Emilia approach.* Upper Saddle River, NJ: Merrill/Prentice Hall.

High/Scope Educational Research Foundation. (2003). *Preschool program quality assessment* (2nd ed.). Ypsilanti, MI: High/Scope Press.

High/Scope Educational Research Foundation. (2009). *Key developmental indicators.* Ypsilanti, MI: High/Scope Press.

Hume, K. Bellini, S. & Pratt, C. (2005). The usage and perceived outcomes of early intervention and early childhood programs for young children with Autism Spectrum Disorder. *Topics in Early Childhood Special Education, 24*(4), 195-207.

Instituzione of the Municipality of Reggio Emilia. (2012). *One city, many children: Reggio Emilia, a history of the present.* Reggio Emilia, Italy: Reggio Children.

Kagan, J. (2002). Empowerment and education: Civil rights, expert-advocates, and parent politics in Head Start, 1964-1980. *Teachers College Record, 104*(3), 516-562. *In Developmentally appropriate curriculum: Best practices in early childhood education.* (5th ed.). Upper Saddle River, NJ: Pearson.

Katz, L. & Chard, S. (2000). *Engaging children's minds: The project approach.* Stamford, CT: Ablex.

Ludwig, J. and Phillips, D.A. (2007). The benefits and costs of Head Start. *Society for Research on Child Development, Social Policy Report.* Volume XXI, Number 3.

Malaguzzi, L. (1998). History, ideas, and basic philosophy: An interview with Lella Gandini. In C. Edwards, L. Gandini, & G. Forman (Eds.). *The hundred languages of children: The Reggio Emilia approach – Advanced reflections* (2nd ed. 49-97). Greenwich,CT: Ablex.

Montessori, M. (1966). *The secret of childhood.* New York: Ballantine Books.

Montessori, M. (1967). *The discovery of the child.* New York: Ballantine Books.

Mooney, C. G. (2000). *Theories of childhood: An introduction to Dewey, Montessori, Erikson, Piaget, and Vygotsky.* St. Paul, MN: Redleaf Press.

Morrison, G. S., (2012). *Early childhood education today.* Upper Saddle River, NJ: Pearson Education.

National Association for the Education of Young Children. (2012). http://naeyc.org/accreditation

National Center for Children in Poverty, (2016). *United States early childhood profile.* Retrieved January 6, 2017, from http://www.nccp.org/profiles

National Head Start Association (2016). www.nhsa.org

Nicholson, D. (2000). Layers of experience: Forms of representation in a Waldorf school classroom. *Journal of Curriculum Studies, 32*(4), 575-587.

Palsha, S. (2002). An outstanding education for ALL children: Learning from Reggio Emilia's approach to inclusion. In V. R. Fu, A. J. Stremmel, & L. T. Hill (Eds.). *Teaching and learning: Collaborative exploration of the Reggio Emilia approach* (pp. 109-130). Upper Saddle River, NJ: Merrill Prentice Hall.

Peth-Pierce, R. (2000). *A good beginning: Sending America's children to school with the social and emotional competence they need to succeed.* Bethesda, MD: Child Mental Health Foundations and Agencies Network (FAN), National Institute of Mental Health.

Schweinhart, L. J. (2003). *Validity of the High/Scope preschool education model.* Ypsilanti, MI: High/Scope Educational Research Foundation.

Schweinhart, L. J., Barnes, H. V., & Weikart, D. P., (1993). *Significant benefits: The High/Scope Perry Preschool study through age 27.* Ypsilanti, MI; High/Scope Press.

Seefeldt, C. (1995). Art – serious work. *Young Children, 50*(3), 39-45.

USDHHS (U.S. Department of Health and Human Services). (2006). Head Start fact sheet. Retrieved on June 15, 2012, from www.acf.hhs.gov/opa/fact_sheets/headstart

USDHHS (U.S. Department of Health and Human Services). (2009). The 2015 poverty guidelines. *Federal Register*.

USDHHS (U.S. Department of Health and Human Services). (2012).

Wolfe, J. (2000). *Learning from the past: Historical voices in early childhood education*. Mayerthorpe, Alberta: Piney Branch Press.

Chapter 6
Infants and Toddlers – A Time for Responsive Educare

The Importance of the First Three Years of Life

Thinking Ahead

1. What are the influences on infant and toddler development?
2. How does a responsive, relationship-based educare program provide the most effective environment and curriculum for infants and toddlers?
3. How does poverty influence development?
4. What are some of the cognitive and language milestones across the first 36 months of development?
5. What are some of the social and emotional milestones across the first 36 months of development?
6. What are some of the large and small muscle development milestones across the first 36 months?

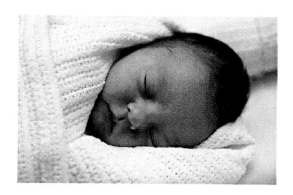

The first three years are a period of incredible growth across all domains of development: cognitive, social, emotional, physical, and language. This is an exciting and challenging moment in history for babies, families, and their teachers. The excitement is generated because scientific research has confirmed the critical importance and has advanced our appreciation of the first three years of life. The challenge becomes real because of the overwhelming responsibility we have in caring for our young children.

"Making the Most of the First 3 Years"

What we do with infants and toddlers – our interactions, the opportunities and experiences we provide children, and our nurturing skills – exert a powerful influence on how children build relationships, learn about the world, and succeed in their lives. As teachers of infants and toddlers, we have a unique opportunity to build strong relationships with children and their families, making a difference in all their lives. The  opportunity to make this difference and to provide a positive influence on children and families depends on the quality of the program. Organizations like ZERO TO THREE and the National Association for the Education of Young Children (NAEYC) have defined the standards of quality programming for children birth to 3 years. Additionally, NAEYC has developed standards for the educational preparation of early care and education teachers. Well-prepared teachers learn that they must utilize every moment with children intentionally through maximized experiences, routines, and nurturance. Responsive, reflective, and relationship-based practice are the hallmarks of quality infant and toddler educare.

Current brain research has provided evidence of the connection between quality educare and a baby's ability to develop all the human skills needed for school success and a healthy, satisfying life. "Warm, responsive care is not only comforting for an infant; it is critical to healthy development" (Shore, 2003, p. 12). Brain research also stresses the importance of building strong, respectful, reciprocal relationships with infants, toddlers, and their families. The needs of young children are met through these partnerships which view children, families, and educators as capable, competent, and caring.

A knowledgeable, passionate early childhood educator's job is to promote competence, well-being, healthy development, and quality of life for infants, toddlers, and their families. Competence refers to a child's adaptability and flexibility in daily changes. Well-being is "how a child feels and thinks about him- or herself and the joy and satisfaction that the child experiences in regard to his or her relationships and accomplishments" (Erickson & Kurz-Reimer, 1999, p. 26). Quality of life "refers to the child's feelings about the value, worth, living conditions, and relationships that he or she experiences" (Wittmer & Petersen, 2010, p. 2). It is imperative that educare providers develop a community of caring that honors and respects the importance of the infant and toddler years.

Relationship-Based Educare

Infants' and toddlers' emotional and social needs include feeling safe, loved, valued, and connected to their culture, family, important adults and peers. Building relationships meets these needs of young children and creates the environment in which children's development flourishes. A relationship-based model of education and care respects how the individual child's characteristics and the environment affect the quality of the child's relationships. These relationships then serve as the channel for children's development and feeling of well-being.

A relationship-based model acknowledges that caring, productive relationships are essential to human growth and development. Infants and toddlers benefit from relationship-building skills such as problem solving and initiating interactions; these skills are vital for later success in schools, families, and society. Infants and toddlers need loving adults who will nurture, protect and support their learning, as well as provide respectful, loving responsiveness to children's needs. Responsiveness refers to how well an adult can understand what the young child is trying to communicate through his or her cues such as facial expressions, gestures, words, and postures, and how the adult reacts to the child. A responsive adult is "in sync" with the child and responds with care and sensitivity. In educare settings, young children feel more secure to learn and care for others when the teachers are involved with the children, engaging them in conversations and activities, comforting them, and showing affection (Wittmer & Petersen, 2010). The more sensitive, attentive and engaged the teacher is with children as compared to being harsh, critical, punitive or detached, the more secure the child feels with the teacher (Howes & Hamilton, 1992).

Development

Development is often divided into four broad domains: *physical, cognitive, language,* and *emotional-social.* We think of these domains as being distinct, yet we know they combine in an integrated, holistic way to mold an individual, unique child. Each domain is influenced by the others. For instance, new motor capabilities such as crawling (physical) which allows greater exploration of the environment, contribute to the infant's cognitive development.

"Developmental Milestones from Infancy to Toddlers"

Development in the first three years of life is a fascinating complex process because all the domains are interdependent. Emerging capabilities in one area enables change in another. For instance, as an infant's neck muscles develop, allowing her to lift her head, the infant's vision sharpens, thus allowing her to focus on smaller objects in her purview. Development does not always follow a continuous path; a child may move forward, attain a new skill and then reach a plateau during which development seems to stand still. Often what is occurring is a consolidation and establishment of the new accomplishment.

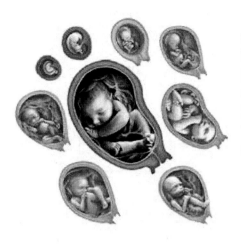

Development is not only divided into integrated domains, but also into time periods. What follows are the commonly accepted age division of the prenatal period and first thirty-six months of life: **Prenatal development (conception-birth),** normally a 9-month period, marks the most rapid time of change from a one-celled organism into a human baby with great facility for acclimating to life in the world. After infants are born, early childhood teachers plan for and provide care in four age groups: **young infants (birth-9 months), mobile infants (8-18 months), toddlers (16-25 months), and twos (24-36 months).**

The overlap of ages occurs because individual development follows its own path and proceeds at its own rate. Development is often benchmarked based on what constitutes "normal" growth and developmental milestones. Developmental milestones are based on averages of children's growth within a chronological age span. Knowing the milestones of different stages of development allows early childhood educators to assess children's growth or lack of.

"Ages of Infancy- Caring for Young, Mobile, Older Infants"

It is important that educators also consider the unique development of each individual child. One child may be efficiently using the toilet at age 2 while another child may still be "having accidents" at age 3. One infant may walk at 9 months of age while another does not walk until 14 months. Because of the wide range of individual differences, it is sometimes difficult to differentiate between an individual difference in development and what might be a developmental delay that requires intervention. Being cognizant of cultural contexts and reviewing developmental sequences aids in one's assessment of the individual child.

Cultural contexts – the basic values, language, religion, beliefs, food and cultural practices – influence the development of children through the child-rearing practices, experiences, habits, and routines in the raising of children. Everyone views the world through the lens of their own culture (Small, 1998) and these culturally-based outlooks define the child and family's interactions, traditions, and way of life. The influence of culture will be discussed later in this chapter.

In Developmentally Appropriate Practice (DAP), educators use these three core understandings to meet the needs of each child: 1) what is known about child development and learning; 2) what is known about each child as an individual; and 3) what is known about the social and cultural contexts in which children live. Understanding the complex process of development requires the early childhood educator to be knowledgeable about child development to make relatively accurate predictions about children's expertise based on their chronological age ranges. Understanding the complex process that is development allows the early childhood educator to get to know and appreciate children as the unique individuals they are; each child brings her or his own interests, strengths, needs, and culture. Armed with this knowledge, it makes it possible for the early childhood educator to become more culturally competent as one begins to understand the similarities and differences among families. As a result, one becomes a more responsive and effective teacher.

Influences on Development

Nature-Nurture

When discussing development, the age-old **nature-nurture controversy** pits genetic factors against environmental factors as the most important influence on development. **Nature** refers to the biological make-up inherent in the hereditary code we receive from our parents at the second of conception. **Nurture** refers to the complex amalgamation of social experiences and physical factors that influence our biological and psychological makeup before and after birth. If one believes that development is predominantly due to nature, then providing rich, early experiences as intervention has little value. If however, one believes that nurture is most important then early intervention in the form of high-quality, intentional experiences is believed to make the difference in children's development. Most modern educators now acknowledge that heredity and environment are inextricably interwoven, each influencing the other (Berk, 2008).

"Nature vs. Nurture: Psych 101"

Brain Development

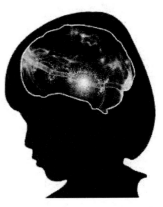

The brain begins developing in the days following conception and continues throughout a human's life. Over several weeks of prenatal growth, fetal brain cells – **neurons** – are created at about the rate of 250,000 a minute and become differentiated into the forebrain, the midbrain, and the hindbrain. The forebrain becomes the **cerebrum** which controls thinking and language; the midbrain becomes the **thalamus** and **hypothalamus** which controls the generation of sensory information; and the hindbrain becomes the **cerebellum** and the brain stem which control heartbeat, respiration, and motor development (Wittmer & Petersen, 2010). In the last three months of gestation, the previously smooth surface of the brain becomes folded and grooved due to the rapid growth that makes the brain fold in on itself. Additionally, the brain is divided into two hemispheres with a crease down the middle.

At birth, babies have about 100 billion brain cells which will be "pruned" down to half that number by adulthood. The job of the neurons is to make connections with other neurons, exchanging information. Each neuron has an **axon** (transmitter), a thin filament that conducts electrical pulses containing information from the neuron to the **dendrites** (receptors) in other cells. Each neuron has many dendrites that receive electrical pulses from other neurons, receiving the information through a connection called a synapse (Shore, 1997). The experiences and stimuli in the fetus', and later, the baby's life are responsible for the formation of the connections, or synapses. The synapses that are used repeatedly in the infant's life are strengthened and fortified, while those synapses that are not revitalized through use are eradicated via a process called **pruning** (Chugani, 1998). Those synapses which are activated frequently are protected from pruning. All of an infant's learning will follow this process of being built and strengthened by repetition; conversely, the learning will fail to emerge due to lack of experience and pruning will result. It is apparent that frequent, positive and nurturing experiences have an enormous and lasting effect on the brain and the proliferation of neural pathways.

"The Secret Life of the Baby's Brain"

Importance of Early Experiences

During an infant's first year of life, the brain grows to nearly 70% of its adult size and by age three to 90% of an adult, establishing most of the composition that will direct future social, behavioral, and emotional performance throughout the child's life. These domains of development are positively built through responsive, nurturing relationships

with adults. The adults in the infant's life provide the experiences through their relationship with the infant that build her brain synapses. The quality, frequency, and pattern of these repeated synapse-building experiences and interactions "trains" the brain for either positive or negative social, behavioral, and emotional performance throughout the child's life.

Infants and toddlers are born with a curiosity for exploring their environment. They have goals for their own construction of knowledge and develop strategies – language, motor, social and cognitive tools – to reach these learning goals. In addition to being curious, infants and toddlers are motivated to solve problems and possess great stores of energy to sustain their exploration. This exploration materializes optimally with adults to whom the child has a strong attachment, who makes her feel safe, nurturing the child and supporting her learning.

"Discussing the Curious Learner Style / Early Child Development 18-24 months / Baby Genius"

Attachment theory focuses on the basic feelings of trust, safety, and security (Bowlby, 1980). John Bowlby posited that children have an exploratory system that motivates them to venture out and learn about their world. In addition, children have an attachment system which motivates them to stay close to trusted, nurturing adults who will protect and make them feel secure. The two systems work in tandem to provide a sheltered base from which the child can safely and securely venture out to play, explore, and discover the world, checking back with the **attachment relationship** – the person they can count on to keep them safe and meet their needs. The secure attachment between the young child and the adult is built over time through consistent, responsive, sensitive and nurturing interactions.

**"John Bowlby: Attachment Theory
Across Generations"**

Over time as the secure attachment is nurtured, the young child also learns **self-regulation.** Self-regulation is the ability of a human to adapt one's reactions to feelings, sensory experiences, people, and the environment. Self-regulation allows a child to concentrate and focus on a task, act in a socially acceptable way, and control emotions positively (Kopp, 2000). The development of self-regulation blazes the trail for the development of **executive functioning** – the ability to plan, sequence, organize behavior, and show flexibility and control of one's behavior (Wittmer & Petersen, 2010). The importance of building secure attachments cannot be over-emphasized – it is the support, security, and nurturance offered by adults in the very early years of a child's life that establishes the foundation of later cognitive, social, and emotional development.

Temperament

Temperament is defined as the stable individual differences in quality and intensity of emotional reaction, activity level, attention, and emotional self-regulation (Rothbart & Bates, 1998). Research shows that temperament increases the chances that a child will either be protected from the stresses of daily life or succumb and experience psychological problems. Parenting practices, to a large degree, can modify a child's temperament (Thomas & Chess, 1977).

"Understanding a Child's Temperament"

Thomas and Chess (1977) created a model of temperament that includes nine dimensions: activity level, rhythmicity (regularity of body functions), distractibility, approach/withdrawal, adaptability (to new environments), attention span and persistence, intensity of reaction, threshold of responsiveness (intensity of stimulation required to evoke a response), and quality of mood. Data collection on individual characteristics was then clustered into three descriptors of children:

- The **easy child** quickly establishes regular routines, is generally cheerful, and adapts easily to new situations
- The **difficult child** is irregular in daily routines, is slow to adapt to new experiences, and tends to react negatively and strongly
- The **slow-to-warm-up child** is inactive, shows mild, low-key reactions to stimuli, possesses a negative mood, and adjusts slowly to new experiences

"Goodness to Fit – One Size Does Not Fit / Carly Jeffrey"

Temperament is not firmly set in infancy; it develops with age. For example, a "fussy" infant can become calmer as his nervous system develops and better regulates his reaction to environmental stimuli. Genetic makeup has been shown to contribute to approximately half of individual temperamental makeup (Saudino & Cherny, 2001). Environment also exerts a powerful influence on temperament. For example, severe malnutrition generally causes a child to be more distractible and fearful (Wachs & Bates, 2001). Parenting styles also exert an influence on temperament. Jansen and his fellow researchers found that infants in lower income families were more likely to have a difficult temperament that may be partly explained by family stress, maternal depression, and food and housing insecurity (Jansen, Raat, Mackenbach, Jaddoe, Hofman, Verhulst, et al., 2009).

Early research proposed that temperament styles were fixed and stable throughout life (Caspi & Silva, 1995). However, more recent research suggests that child-rearing styles and environmental influences such as poverty and poor childcare settings can significantly alter temperament during the first three years of life (Worobey &Islas-Lopez, 2009). Thomas and Chess (1977) offered a **goodness-of-fit model** to explain how temperament coupled with environmental factors can produce favorable results. Goodness of fit requires child-rearing environments that recognize children's individual temperaments while consistently helping children to adapt to their behavior to be socially acceptable. The type of temperament a child has is less important to their development than the temperamental match between the infant and the care provider.

The Effects of Poverty

The 2015 statistics on poverty show an alarming number of American children under the age of 5 – 4,704,000 children – living in poverty. The term poverty is defined by income thresholds. One of those designations is *low income* which is used to denote families whose income is at or below twice the federal poverty level (NCCP, 2016). For instance, the 2015 National Poverty Guidelines indicate that a family of three with an income of $20,160 is at the *poverty level* and that a family of three making twice that

amount or less would be considered at the *low income* level. Children from homes that experience low income or poverty are more likely to suffer from inadequate nutrition, insecure housing, abuse and/or neglect, and lack of adequate health care.

Although poverty cuts across ethnicity, gender, and age, the National Center for Children in Poverty (2012) offers some alarming statistics:

- Every 35 seconds a baby is born into poverty in the U.S
- There are more than 11 million infants and toddlers under age 3 in the United States. 48 percent – 5.7 million – live in low-income families. 25 percent – 3.0 million – live in poor families

- 35 percent of white infants and toddlers – 2.1 million – live in low-income families
- 70 percent of black infants and toddlers – 1.1 million – live in low-income families
- 30 percent of Asian infants and toddlers – 0.2 million – live in low-income families
- 70 percent of American Indian infants and toddlers – over 65,000 – live in low-income families
- 47 percent of infants and toddlers of some other race – 0.3 million – live in low-income families
- 66 percent of Hispanic infants and toddlers – 1.9 million – live in low-income families
- 35 percent of infants and toddlers with married parents – 2.6 million – live in low-income families
- 75 percent of infants and toddlers with a single parent – 3.0 million – live in low-income families

The effects of poverty are injurious and pervade all aspects of young children's lives as children, and later on as adults. Families in poverty have difficulty providing adequate nutrition, health care, and decent housing for their children. Families struggle to find adequate paying jobs; quality, affordable childcare; and basic services. When people are in poverty, children's development is seriously threatened. The stress level that accompanies poverty weakens the family unit. Families in poverty struggle to pay bills and find safe childcare; live from paycheck to paycheck, often running out of money before the week is up; and often have to move because they cannot afford the rent. Parents become irritable, depressed, and aggressive behavior can increase, resulting in children's arrested development. A palpable effect of poverty is on brain growth. Neuroscientists at the University of California Berkley have shown differences in the brain function of low-income children comparable to those in stroke patients (Sanders, 2008). It makes sense that high quality childcare, universal health care, and increased services in nutrition and housing can positively affect the lives of children living in poverty.

Development and Culture

Infant and toddler development can only be fully understood when it is viewed in its larger cultural context. Cultural values and practices affect the environmental contexts in which children develop. A range of beliefs and practices define who children and families are, their traditions and way of life, as well as their interactions. Cultural values shape the home and community environments, childcare settings, schools, and all aspects of daily life.

"Cultural Dimension: Me or We"

These community and home subcultures may reflect the values of the larger culture in which they reside, but often may not share the same beliefs. A good example of this is the clash of an **individualistic society** as exists in the United States – one in which independence and self-reliance are the hallmarks, and in which families are believed to be responsible for the care and educational decision-making and payment – versus a more collectivist society which views the individual as part of a larger group and deems the good of the larger group takes precedence. A **collectivist society** recognizes the rights of its citizens, including children, and invests in long-term policies that benefit the individual – health care, quality childcare and education – which ultimately contribute to the betterment of the entire community. Many ethnic minority groups provide their own collectivist structures such as the community church and the extended family.

Many African-American, Hispanic, and Asian-American families enjoy the tradition of **extended-family households** in which the nuclear family of parents and children live with other relatives. Within this extended family, grandparents provide childcare and guidance for the youngest in the family, share financial support and household chores with the adults in the household, and provide their wisdom regarding child-rearing (Berk, 2008). The extended-family plays an important role in transmitting the home culture to the other members of the family. This may include the moral and religious values, traditions and celebrations, and possibly, the language of the cultural group.

Just as children bring their cultural contexts to the childcare settings and schools which they attend, each educare provider brings his or her unique cultural experiences and belief system to the educare setting. It is imperative that the early childhood professional is sensitive to the cultural diversity of the children and families in their care. Every culture has different customs, beliefs and attitudes about childcare and education. Prejudging these culturally embedded principles is an example of **bias.** Educare providers must examine and be aware of their biases for certain cultural styles and practices. Each child is a unique individual whose development is determined by universal child development factors as well as his cultural contexts.

Emotional and Social Development

Healthy emotional and social development begins with the establishment of a healthy attachment to another human, typically the parent. Grounded in this trusting relationship, infants and toddlers can gradually venture out to explore and expand relationships and learn about their world that they view as a good place. Emotional development refers to children's ability to manage, recognize, and express their feelings as well as to understand and appropriately respond to the  feelings of those around them. Social development refers to children's ability to create and sustain relationships with those around them. Healthy development in the social and emotional domains ensures healthy development in all domains of learning.

"Early Years In Action – Personal, Social and Emotional Development"

Birth to Four Months

This is the period of a child's development when the foundation of security and attachment are being built. Parents and care providers offer the kind of relationships, consistency, and experiences that facilitate the development of this security. Relationships and how the child is treated provide the contexts in which trust and security are formed. Immediate and consistent responsiveness to the child's cues is most important in helping the infant feel secure (Swim & Watson, 2011).

 **Temperament** – the infant's principal style of behavior and reaction to stimuli – emerges during this period of development. The activity level of the infant becomes predictable. Highly active infants get plenty of activity kicking, squirming, and wiggling. Quiet infants may seem easier to care for, yet they need to be moved around to stimulate their activity level. Infants have differing levels of **sensory threshold** – how a child responds to environmental stimuli such as light. Emotional development requires consistent and focused responsiveness to the child's needs, verbal and non-verbal interaction, and comforting nurturance.

During this early phase of development, when a unique attachment is being formed with the mother, the infant also develops an attachment to their primary caregiver, whether a father, grandparent, or a provider in a childcare setting. The infant's emotional and social development flourishes in the context of attachment. Infants use their senses to develop a sense of the world and to test the strength of the attachment by sending out signals that require a response. Mary Ainsworth (1982) identified infants' social behavior during the first few months of age; she called Phase 1 the Undiscriminating Social Responsiveness phase. In this phase infants demonstrate orienting behaviors such as visual fixation and tracking, rooting, and listening; sucking and grasping; and signaling behaviors such as smiling and crying.

Four to Eight Months

Infants learn best when they are alert and calm. Infants' expressions of emotion are widened and becoming more refined. The infant uses a variety of sounds such as cooing, wailing, and chuckling and physical movement such as smiling and waving arms to express happiness, fear and frustration.  During the latter half of this phase of development many infants develop **stranger anxiety** of people they do not know or do not see frequently (McDevitt & Ormrod, 2010). This is also a period of development in which an infant may exhibit anxiety when separated from their mother or primary care provider. The infant is beginning to form the concept that they are separate from others, thus the anxiety that occurs when separated from the primary attachment figure.

"Is Your Baby Afraid of Strangers or Being Too Clingy?"

As an infant's temperament style emerges, it is important to assess the child's view of the world based on the behavioral categories: activity level, rhythmicity (regularity of body functions), distractibility, approach/withdrawal, adaptability (to new environments), attention span and persistence, intensity of reaction, threshold of responsiveness (intensity of stimulation required to evoke a response), and quality of mood. The primary caregiver then can help the infant to cope with the daily experiences and stresses of life. Goodness-of-fit through responsive care aids the caregiver in creating appropriate learning experiences for each infant.

Attachment to the primary caregiver is deepening and becoming stronger. The caregiver needs to provide the infant consistent, responsive, and nurturing care. Infants are moving around more, socializing with other children and adults and learning how to interact with other humans. Ainsworth (1982) classified the budding social skills during this period of growth Phase 2 – Discriminating Social Responsiveness and Phase 3 – Actively Seeking Proximity and Contact. Phase 2 emerges at around age six months and is typified by a child's discrimination of and response to familiar and unfamiliar people. As stated before, this period of development is characterized by the onset of stranger anxiety. Phase 3 emerges at about seven months and is demonstrated in an infant's increased mobility to be in proximity to her caregiver using crying, smiling, and babbling to gain the attention of the attachment figure; to gain control over the movement of the extremities; and to stay in close contact with the caregiver.

"The Strange Situation – Mary Ainsworth"

Eight to Twelve Months

As the attachment to the primary caregiver deepens, infants at this stage are increasingly able to express and communicate their emotions which can range from delight to anger. When a parent leaves, the infant may crawl to the door, cry, and/or try to follow the parent. The caregiver is instrumental in helping to establish routines at the beginning and end of the day that support the infant and family. "Hello and goodbye" rituals allow the child to comfortably separate from and then reunite with parents at the end of the day. The infant will seek out the primary caregiver to keep her in his sight; as well, stranger anxiety is prevalent and making the infant less fearful and more secure is one of the jobs of the caregiver.

Infants at this age exhibit increasing independence and need to control their environment. They are helping more with self-feeding and dressing; this is a time for patience on the part of the caregiver to allow the child to experiment and try out these new skills. Persistence in learning how to walk varies in infants at this stage; persistent infants will try relentlessly to pull themselves up and walk, while less persistent children will become discouraged quickly after a few falls.

Infants at this age are beginning to respond to a verbal "no" or "stop". Praise and firm, positive re-direction are more effective strategies with infants this age; using "no" sparingly helps infants determine the importance of responding to potentially dangerous and hurtful situations. Increased mobility allows the infant to interact more with those in their vicinity. However, infants become more possessive of toys and important people and may become occasionally "clingy".

"Still Face Experiment: Dr. Edward Tronick"

Twelve to Eighteen Months

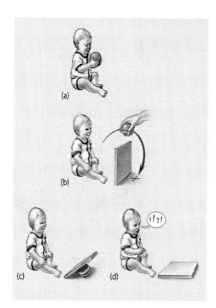

This stage of development can be considered a transitional period where mobile infants become toddlers, and due to their increased mobility, a larger world opens up to them. The mobile infant/toddler hovers between a need for independence and lingering dependence. Erikson's (1963) second stage of development is autonomy versus shame and doubt; the child is gaining new mental and motor skills and wants to choose and decide on his own. It is important that the primary caregiver allows increased reasonable free choice and does not shame the child or make the child doubt their capabilities. This increased sense of accomplishment enhances the child's feelings of self-worth – a quality that will carry into adulthood.

Mobile infants/toddlers at this stage of development actively explore their independence as they learn how to respond appropriately to the feelings of others. They also are learning to gain better control over their own emotions, however their emotions may overwhelm them, and their frustration may culminate in temper tantrums. Mobile infants/toddlers at this age vacillate between wanting to be "big" and wanting to stay "little" at the same time. In communicating their need for increased independence, toddlers may convey negativism by using the word "no" a great deal. Responsive, caring educare providers understand that children want to practice new skills, do things themselves, and make their own decisions. At the same time, educators need to help children distinguish between right and wrong while accepting each child as a valuable person. Giving mobile infants/ toddlers authentic choices, determining and removing the cause of the tantrum, and providing play props for the child to act out their fears and frustration are all strategies that responsive educators use to guide children to increased self-regulation.

Children at this stage are egocentric, seeing the world from their own perspective. As the concept of **object permanence** develops, children are able to distinguish between themselves and their play objects as well as other people. Mobile infants/toddlers begin to develop self-image at this stage; acceptance of the child is subsumed and becomes part of the child's sense of himself.

The mobile infants/toddler may accept people to varying degrees; the child may be shy with some people, particularly those with whom she has infrequent contact. It is important that the child is not forced to interact with everyone. Again, the responsive educare provider will provide a secure base of attachment and will allow the child to regulate their own distance from, and degree of interaction with strangers.

Eighteen to Twenty-Four Months

Toddlers are primarily concerned with understanding who they are; identity becomes a major principle of development. Much of toddlers' drive is tied to their desire for independence and control. Educare providers can support toddlers to find appropriate ways to assert themselves, by introducing social guidelines, and providing them with choices (Copple & Bredekamp, 2009).

Toddlers at this stage of development continue to display intense emotions through their behavior. Their emotions swing back and forth from moments of absolutely delighted laughter to moments of shrieking displeasure or withdrawal. The responsive educare provider needs to provide nonverbal and verbal approval of the child as an individual, and of the child's socially acceptable behavior. In addition, the educator needs to provide consistent routines that will support toddlers' growth in independence and competency, and consistency of rules and expectations that will serve as a reminder to the toddler.

Children at this stage continue to build their sense of self and self-worth. Consistency of feedback and behavior guidelines enable the child to feel positive self-worth and avoid "mixed messages" of what is acceptable behavior. At this point, the child is beginning to separate the idea of his/her self as a person from his actions. This concept is reinforced by emphasizing that the child is still a worthy person, even when they display negative or angry feelings. If, during the first 24 months of life, the child has enjoyed the establishment of a strong attachment to parents and the primary caregiver, the toddler can begin to successfully separate and begin to act more like a separate social being (Caplan & Caplan, 1980). Children begin to establish relationships with others, and consequently, they are honing their skills recognizing others' feelings and understanding others' perspectives (Swim & Watson, 2011).

Although toddlers at this stage of development are beginning to consider others' points of views, the child continues to be egocentric and can easily misinterpret the intent of other children. The toddler still clings selfishly to her belongings and toys, being hesitant to share. The responsive educare provider helps a child to identify and verbalize her own feelings as well as the feelings of other children. Providing enough materials and equipment may encourage sharing but will not require it until the child is ready.

Children's fantasies and fears may increase in number and deepen in intensity during this period of development. As a child's imagination and experience expands, so does the child's level of stress due to negative fantasies and fears. Listening to the child, validating his fears, and reassuring the child are strategies the care provider can utilize. Comforting and reassuring the child of his safety provide a sense of security for the toddler.

Twenty-Four Months to Thirty Months

Children at this age experience an increasing confidence in their competence and sense of self. This stage of development represents another transitional period; at the beginning of the stage, the 24 month old child has acquired enough language to better communicate, is able to attend to activities for longer periods of time, and enjoys increased independence. However, the 30 month old child becomes more demanding and less patient – the "terrible twos" that typically is the descriptor of children's behavior at this juncture of development. Toddlers at the age may become frustrated, fluctuating between being affectionate and being defiant, and using the word "no" a great deal.

The quest for identity development continues through this stage of development Erikson described as autonomy versus shame and doubt. Responsive educare providers need to offer toddlers consistent routines with flexibility, as well as varied opportunities to explore. Activities that utilize the child's senses and maturing physical capabilities provide the opportunity for increased independence and self-reliance. Play offers children this age a vehicle to discover themselves and what they may become (Elkind, 2007). Through role-playing and social play with peers, children develop emotionally, socially, and cognitively. Play also provides experiences which enable the child to appreciate others' feelings and emotions, and to develop the emotion of empathy.

Thirty to Thirty-Six Months

At this stage of development toddlers are becoming more adept at expressing their emotions in socially acceptable ways, yet they continue to express negativity as a way to declare their independence This intense display of emotions shows itself in classroom work as well as social play. Children are keen learners, enjoying hours of exploration and discovery which reinforce their desire for independence. This is a stage of development where children build persistence in their play and work; using children's interests to develop curriculum that engages and motivates them is part of the early childhood educator's job.

"0 to 5 in 30 Minutes! Toddler Independence"

As toddlers approach age 3, generally, their emotions become more controlled and less resistant. They become more responsible and caring; often, this increased pro-social behavior can be used by the educare provider in curriculum planning. Completing classroom chores, helping peers, and sharing materials all provide opportunities for building social competence. Children this age enjoy control over their personal possessions, yet they are more amenable to sharing, taking turns, and engaging in cooperative play. Caring and responsive educare providers teach children positive pro-social behaviors through daily modeling of empathy, respect, concern, and nurturance toward others.

Cognitive and Language Development

Cognitive development encompasses the way children think, develop understanding of the world around them, and use their knowledge to solve problems. Current theories of learning claim that children construct knowledge through their experiences in the world (Piaget, 1954). In addition, they learn through the scaffolding of information and experience provided by adults (Vygotsky, 1978). Theory also asserts that infants are born with basic cognitive systems that predispose them to be keen on learning about things that ensure their survival – numbers, literacy, adaptability to the environment (Spelke & Kinzler, 2007).

Two aspects of emotional development are vital in a child's ability to pay attention to the world to foster his cognitive growth: self-regulation and an attachment relationship to a primary caregiver. Self-regulation helps a child control her actions, and maintain alertness to people and activity. An attachment relationship provides a sense of security that guarantees the child safety as she ventures out to explore the world.

Newborns use all their senses to learn about their world. Their ability to focus on and explore objects and people increases as their grasp and visual acuity develops. Mobile infants show an increased ability to use tools, act with intention, and understand the concept of cause and effect (Dodge, Rudick, Berke & Dumbro, 2006). They begin to categorize information and objects on their world. Toddlers' ability to remember in addition to increased language skills allows them to separate and explore their world. As their attention span improves, toddlers persist in investigation and problem-solving.

Language acquisition is one of children's greatest accomplishments during the first 36 months of life. Throughout the first three years, infants and toddlers learn to make the sounds of their language, how to combine the sounds into words, and the words into sentences. The child will acquire a working vocabulary of hundreds of words by communicating with the adults in their world. The child will also learn the rules of the language through frequent and nurturing conversations with adults. The quantity and significance of this vocabulary acquisition is wholly mediated by the adults and opportunities the adults provide in the child's life.

Infants are born with a predisposition to pay attention to language and the people around them. Newborns begin by communicating their needs through gestures, facial and body expressions, and crying, to communication through verbal means or sign language. Mobile infants understand more than they can verbalize. They point to objects that have been named, use gestures, make sounds, and begin to utter single words such as *mama* or *ball*. Toddlers enjoy the picture book reading that was begun when they were infants; they enjoy more complex stories. They are beginning to put two words together such as "me do"; this skill will increase during ages 2 to 3 as the toddler's vocabulary increases dramatically. Receptive vocabulary remains larger than the expressive vocabulary.

Birth to Four Months

Much has been written about the cognitive growth and brain development of infants and toddlers; the importance of the educare young children receive cannot be overstated. Healy (2004) expresses it best:

> Amazingly, although the number of cells actually decreases, brain weight can double during the first year of life. As neurons respond to stimuli seen, heard, felt, or tasted, they fire off messages that build new

physical connections to neighboring cells....During the first six months after birth, they become extremely active as sensory messages bombard the infant brain, which must learn to receive them and then pass them from one area to another....Synaptic connections are strengthened by repeated use; if they fail to connect, they die off....Every response to sights, sounds, feelings, smells, and tastes makes more connections. (pp. 17-20)

The frequency and quality of interactions stimulates all the senses of the infant, building important synaptic connections.

Piaget's Sensorimotor stage frames the cognitive growth in the first four months of life. Sub-stage 1 of this stage is reflexive behavior; the newborn uses his senses to first react to, and then search his environment. In sub-stage 2 the previously independently working senses begin to coordinate and work together (e.g., eye-hand coordination). Newborns enjoy looking at faces, particularly female faces (Ramsey, Langlois, & Marti, 2005). During this period of development infants should be in environments that stimulate their senses – mobiles, music, pictures of faces, rattles. Objects should be placed in the range of the infant's vision and objects such as rattles should be placed in her hands.

Crying is the major means of communication during early infancy. As they develop, their crying takes on differing vocalizations depending on the need being communicated – hunger, discomfort, sensory overload, etc. Immediate and consistent response to the infant, and attending to the infant's needs are of prime importance. Around 10 weeks of age socializing language – cooing and laughter – begin. These vocalizations begin to build the physical structures that produce speech. This is a time when the primary caregiver should use every opportunity to talk and sing to the infant, and carry on running conversations. A verbal "dance" is established between the infant and adult as the infant mirrors the adult mouth movements and facial expressions.

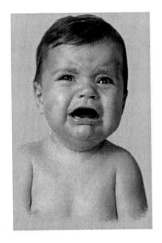

"Nourishing Language Development in Early Childhood"

Four to Eight Months

The infant at this stage – the Reproduction and Coordination sub-stages of Piaget's Sensorimotor Stage – is building brain synapses through repetition of activities that attract him. The infant is learning cause and effect as he or she hits the crib activity center and hears the music play. The infant visually follows objects that appear and begin to disappear. Infants are beginning to realize that objects are entities separate from their bodies.

The neural pathways that are being created play a significant role in infants' development of speech sounds. The cooing that began in the first four months continues to be refined. Cooing is soon accompanied by babbling. Cooing sounds are extended vowel sounds like *ahhh, ooo,* and *eee.* During cooing infants begin to manipulate their mouths and tongues, building coordination for later speech production. Babbling is rudimentary playing with sounds – primarily some of the "hard" consonant sounds (b, t, m). Babbling then progresses to consonant-vowel strings such as *ba-ba-ba.* Babbling is a social event in which infants listen to sounds around them and imitate those sounds and the conversations adults have with them. Intensity, volume, rhythm, and pitch begin to emerge at this stage (Otto, 2010).

Eight to Twelve Months

Mobile infants are in the Coordination sub-stage of the Sensorimotor stage. The infant can better manipulate objects to more thoroughly explore using their senses. **Object permanence** is a major developmental milestone during this stage. The mobile infant remembers people, objects, and events for longer periods of time, and will search for objects that disappear. Infants are developing symbolic representation by making a mental picture of the object, person, or past event. Cause and effect is a deepening concept and at the same time imitation becomes keener.

"Piaget – Stage 1 – Sensorimotor, Object Permanence"

The babbling the infant has been engaging in up to this point begins to take the form of distinguishable words such as "no" and "mama". The infant makes conversational sounds that mirror the structure of adult conversation. In the area of receptive language, the infant is learning frequently heard nouns and names of objects and people around her, and labeling objects with these words. Shared book readings afford the opportunity for basic concepts to be reinforced and new vocabulary to be built through questioning and labeling of objects in the pictures.

Twelve to Eighteen Months

Children at this developmental stage are in Piaget's sub-stage 5 – the Experimentation stage – of the sensorimotor stage of cognitive development. In this experimentation stage the child is consolidating much of the accumulated knowledge and with challenging but achievable opportunities, is developing the skill of problem-solving (Healy, 2004). Exploration is pursued through trial and error, using a rudimentary scientific method of hypothesizing, testing and concluding. Mobile infants are also learning more about cause and effect as they explore and experiment with the materials in their environment.

Children this age are relying more and more on their burgeoning vocabulary as opposed to their grunts and babbling. Due to their still limited vocabulary, children this age tend to overgeneralize so that *dada* may mean all men and *dog* stands for all four-legged animals. Specific vocabulary is built through constant conversation and oral labeling of objects and through storybook reading. Emergent literacy building is fostered by providing books; writing and art materials; space; modeling of reading, writing and creating; and opportunity to "dabble" in emergent literacy practice (Otto, 2010).

Eighteen to Twenty-Four Months

This developmental stage is a transitional stage where toddlers are moving from the sensorimotor stage to the preoperational stage – a stage during which the child begins

to form ideas based on his perceptions and shows an increased ability to think symbolically and conceptually as evidenced in his increased use of imaginative play and language. The toddler is able to use her mental capacities to think through and solve problems instead of having to manipulate objects, using trial and error. A toddler's memory skills are being refined, allowing one to follow one- and two-step directions. The child's mental representation skills are expanding so that she can begin to play symbolically, using props to re-play experiences embedded in her memory. Role-playing becomes important as both a way to experiment with adult roles and to work out emotions.

"Piaget's Preoperational Stage"

Vocabulary acquisition continues to be fast-paced, particularly for children who are fortunate to have consistent, prolific, and grammatically correct adult modeling of language (Hart & Risley, 1995). Toddlers use language for two purposes: 1) to name, describe and make remarks and, 2) to express desires and to reject (Otto 2010). Children at this developmental stage produce **telegraphic speech** – a sequence of words that conveys a thought using only the most important key words. Shared readings continue to provide opportunities for cognitive growth and emergent literacy. Writing is represented by scribbles that children may be able to "read back" to adults.

Twenty-Four Months to Thirty Months

Toddlers at this age are firmly in the pre-operational stage where children use mental operations to construct and organize knowledge into categorized schema files. Mental operations are consolidating so that children are able to mentally manipulate events and objects (Piaget, 1952). Symbolic play is becoming more abstract at this stage; for example, the child may substitute a block for a play phone. Children at this stage are more capable when using open-ended materials to develop their imagination and creativity. Mental images are embedded through the child's use of private speech (Vygotsky, 1987) allowing the child to self-regulate and guide his own activity.

Toddlers at this stage of development begin to construct sentences that include function words such as *the*, *in,* and *to*. They are moving into producing 3- and 4-word sentences that are predominantly structured in a subject-verb-direct object sentence pattern. Toddlers make some linguistic mistakes, but these are developmentally appropriate mistakes that show us that toddlers are beginning to apply some grammatical rules they have synthesized as a result of their exposure to language. Often they overgeneralize by applying the same rule to all words of the same parts of speech (e.g., mouse-mouses) or they undergeneralize a word and do not use it for all the cases to which it applies (e.g., a dog is only a dog if it is black – if it is white, children think it is named something else). Toddlers are beginning to understand and utilize prosody – intonation and stress that express their ideas – "*that* boy" means something different than "that *boy*" (Swim & Watson, 2011).

Shared readings should include stories with more sophisticated and repetitive language that supports more highly-developed vocabulary and oral language. Children are more aware of environmental print and need increased access to writing materials, easels, chalkboards and whiteboards. Toddlers' scribbling is more developed and may contain early picture-writing.

Thirty to Thirty-Six Months

As children reach their third birthdays, the cognitive and language growth in the first thirty-six months is nothing short of amazing! Children have evolved into curious problem-solvers who persistently manipulate, question, hypothesize, and test. Piaget (1952) stated that children are learning three different categories of knowledge: physical knowledge, social-arbitrary knowledge, and logico-mathematical knowledge. Physical knowledge includes understanding the properties of objects (e.g., attributes such as size and shape) as well as understanding the effects of human interaction with objects (e.g., dropping, pushing, squeezing, etc. the object). Social-arbitrary knowledge includes forms of communication (DeVries, 2000) such as learning vocabulary, grammatical rules and information that allows children to function in their social world. Logico-mathematical knowledge includes attributes of objects such as number, time, quantity, and size. Toddlers approaching their third birthdays will engage in more content- bound activities – mathematical, science-based, and literacy – that are integrated across the content areas (e.g., reading a book about shapes, making patterns of shapes, and making creative artwork out of shapes).

"Counting the Benefits of Teaching Math to 3-year olds"

Children continue to accumulate vocabulary, to refine their grammatical correctness and prosody skills, and to increase the length and accuracy of their sentences. The thirty-six month accumulation of story sharing experience, writing endeavors and artwork, as well as the introduction to social, dramatic play all provide opportunities for children to build sound language and emergent literacy skills. Much of children's knowledge at this stage is built through direct, adult modeling. Adults

model how book reading requires a prosodic voice; how more complex sentences are structured; the shades of meaning in vocabulary; and the use of print in writing names, lists, and sentences (Otto, 2010).

Physical Development

Motor development occupies much of a young child's effort and time; the infant and toddler strive to move their bodies, stabilize their body positioning, and reach and hold objects to look at and mouth. Motor development is not a simple, linear progression of maturation, but is instead, a complex, ongoing process of learning (Adolph, 2008). While the initial movements after birth are reflexive, the process of learning quickly becomes the motivating force in motor development. Each new skill – whether it is walking, grasping, or sitting – is refined by repetition, adjustment, and merging previous achievements with new goals.

"Physical Development Milestones"

The reflexive movements of newborns protect them from harm, help them find food, and keep their head, arms, trunk, and legs controlled. As the infant grows, the motor skills combine to create a dynamic and efficient system. For example, as a 4-month old is gaining head and neck control, he will enjoy "tummy time" where he may look around to explore the environment and move to reaching for objects within reach. Esther Thelen (2000) describes motor development as systematic problem solving of the conflict between a child's goals and the constraints of her body structure. The young child is constantly attempting to move, having to adjust for her changing body weight, postures, and proportions.

"Motor Development – Baby Body Sense (Esther Thelen)"

Am I Big Like You Yet?

Physical development is **cephalocaudal**, meaning that voluntary muscle control begins at the head and neck, progressing to the chest, trunk and extremities. Development is also **proximaldistal**, commencing at the midline and progressing outward and downward. Muscle control begins with large muscle sets, proceeding to small muscle sets (Wittmer & Petersen, 2010). The areas of motor development that are acquired during the first three years are locomotion, stability, and manipulation. Locomotion is crawling, walking, and running; stability is sitting and standing upright; and manipulation includes reaching, grasping, and releasing (Swim & Watson, 2011).

Birth to 4 Months

During the four months of this stage of development, infants rapidly progress from reflexive movements such as **rooting** – searching for the nipple – and **sucking,** to increased muscular control of most of their body. The **Moro reflex** – startle reflex – is a response to a loud sound or the sense of falling. The newborn throws back her head, flails her arms and legs and then pulls them back in toward her body. The **tonic neck reflex** causes the infant's arms to move in concert with his head movement when lying on his back (**supine** position). When the baby's head turns to the right, their right arm thrusts out and their left raises up; the opposite happens when the infant turns her head to the left. This reflex disappears when the infant begins to clasp his hands together, at the midline. The **palmar grasp reflex** allows the infant to close his fingers around an object that is in the palm such as an adult's finger or a toy.

During this stage of development, the infant moves from these reflexive movements to increased muscular control. By the time the infant reaches four months of age, he or she is holding their head, shoulders and chest up when placed on their tummy; may enjoy sitting up with arm or pillow support; and is rolling from stomach to back. The infant is grasping toward toys placed within reach, opening and closing her hands as well as playing with her hands, grasping objects, and refining her eye-hand coordination when reaching for an object.

"Primitive Reflexes"

Four to Eight Months

The infant's movements are becoming more coordinated; infants can grasp and move objects intentionally and roll over, are developing muscular strength that allows

them to sit up for longer periods of time, and may be creeping. By the end of this stage, infants are able to stand and take steps with support. The infant's manipulation skills involve the coordination of the entire arm from shoulder to fingers as well as acuity of eye-hand coordination to grasp objects. The child is now able to shift objects from hand to hand and is beginning to experiment and refine the **pincer grasp** which utilizes the thumb and forefinger. Infants this age begin to manipulate finger food, as solid foods are introduced.

During this four month stage of development, the infant's locomotion skills advance from rolling from stomach to back, to pulling to a standing position and taking steps. In between, they will roll from back to stomach, pull their body up and balance on their arms and legs, learn to creep, and then to crawl. The infant's head, neck, and trunk muscular control is developing so that the infant holds their head independently and can sit for longer periods of time, eventually pushing up to a sitting position.

Infants usually begin teething during this stage of development and may need special comforting through their pain and discomfort. As their tongue and swallowing muscles mature, infants are able to move to solid food (pureed food) fed with a spoon. Mealtime is becoming more of a social occasion that is important for future social development.

Eight to Twelve Months

During this stage of development, standing with support soon becomes traveling, as the mobile infant takes a few cautious steps along the edge of a table. All this practice is leading up to the mobile infant taking the first steps without support. The first attempts at walking are wobbly and weaving, with several falls, but with persistence, continued attempts, and strengthened muscles and coordination, the mobile infant becomes much more adept at walking.

The mobile infant is refining his pincer grasp and eye-hand coordination by using the thumb and forefinger as well as the thumb and two fingers. He or she also is able to bring their hands together in front when clapping and playing patty cake. The mobile infant is able to use both of their hands in a coordinated way when manipulating objects. These enhanced fine motor skills aid the mobile infant in feeding finger foods and by using utensils. As infants approach their first birthday, infants hold their own bottles and move from solely bottle-feeding to using a cup with a cover. Mobile infants are beginning to hold and use writing utensils such as fat crayons and markers.

"Baby Playing Patty Cake"

Twelve to Eighteen Months

This stage of development is a transitional period where mobile infants enjoy an expanding world and with increased stability, enter toddlerhood. These young children are becoming steadier in their gait as they make the necessary adjustments based on their changing center of gravity. Even falling is a valuable experience (Joh & Adolph, 2006) as the child learns persistence. Often, the child who had just begun to walk prefers going back to crawling because they can get from one place to another faster. The budding toddler is showing increased curiosity about ascending and descending stairs, first by crawling and later by climbing and holding onto a handrail.

The young child in this developmental stage is honing more exacting fine motor skills and is beginning to prefer one hand over the other, although handedness is not finalized at this point. Children are using their "pointer finger" effectively as they look at storybooks and point to pictures and they are deftly using writing materials to scribble. They are beginning to show interest in dressing and undressing by buttoning, unbuttoning, zipping, and unzipping. Throwing and rolling balls are favorite activities for toddlers this age, although much of this action is not at intended targets.

Eighteen to Twenty-Four Months

Once toddlers have mastered those first months of unsteady walking, they become much more serious about moving – hopping, jumping, skipping, and leaping. The ability to toddle from place to place frees up the child's hands to carry things and to push and pull toys. Toddlers are able to climb up and down stairs holding the handrail, yet they are not alternating their feet. Kicking balls, pedaling tricycles, and throwing at intended targets are all skills that the toddler becomes more proficient at by the end of this developmental stage.

"Baby on the Move: Walking"

"Babies and Toddlers Cruising & Walking"

Young children's strengthening fine motor skills are demonstrated in increased control of their fingers and wrist movements. Toddlers are more able to grasp and release objects and to turn their wrist to turn objects. Due to the fact they are showing more interest and independence in dressing and undressing, it is important to provide opportunities to zip, unzip, button, and unbutton. Hand dominance is beginning to be established as a toddler may prefer one hand over the other; occasionally, the toddler may use the non-dominant hand for specific tasks, such as throwing a ball. It is important that the educare provider allows the child to use the hand they prefer and does not try to change the handedness of the child.

Twenty-Four Months to Thirty Months

Two--year olds are active, energetic participants in all their large muscle pursuits – bending, walking, running, jumping, climbing, hopping, kicking, and throwing. Toddlers' increased stability and flexibility (Adolph, 2008) allow them to engage in all these activities with greater intensity and curiosity. This developmental stage offers the opportunity for consolidation of both large muscle coordination and fine motor accuracy.

"Simply Parenting – Playing with your Two Year Old"

Toddlers begin to become more skilled with art activities such as bead threading, large pegboards, scissor-cutting, drawing, and painting. In dramatic play, toddlers are using their new accomplishments to dress in play clothes, pour from pitchers during tea parties, and build blocks. With maturing eye-hand coordination, children are able to grasp, twist, and manipulate objects. They enjoy fitting pieces of objects together and take them apart; shape-sorters and puzzles with knobs are popular items for children this age. Toddlers are using

spoons to feed themselves with increasing expertise and are experimenting with manipulating forks.

The increased competence in self-help skills often leads to an interest in toilet learning. Educare providers can introduce the potty chair and encourage the child to use the chair. Positive feedback and gentleness are necessary at this stage of development. Much of the readiness for toilet learning involves the child's awareness of the sensations of the sphincter muscles, the ability to control the muscles and then to relax the muscles for elimination. This large muscle control often begins at around 24 months, but it may take many children until ages three or four to have full control of bowel movements and urination (American Psychiatric Association, 1994).

Thirty to Thirty-Six Months

The first thirty-six months of physical growth is a time of amazing development in the young child! As the child approaches their third birthday, the toddler is stable when running and walking forward and backward. The child is jumping, hopping, dancing, and balancing, as well as alternating their feet when going up stairs. In the area of fine motor skills, he or she is able to put their clothes on with zippering, snapping, and buttoning them. Children enjoy art projects not only to demonstrate their fine motor accomplishments but also to express their emerging creativity. Handedness is established, and most activities are accomplished with the dominant hand.

Using their healthy muscles and brains, babies make extraordinary progress in their capability to use initially their bodies' reflexes to process information and then mature in their ability to process, move toward, and manipulate objects. Infants make amazing passage from using reflexive movements to becoming toddlers demonstrating intentional and purposeful hopping, jumping, buttoning, and scribbling.

Responsive, Relationship-based Planning

Curriculum planning requires the teacher to perceptively observe children, sensitively document their learning, and utilize the data for planning supportive interactions and environments for children. The needs and interests of the children and their families must underpin the planning process. An effective program does not begin with an activity plan, but instead with the observation of the individual child's development across all learning domains. For instance, when a child is beginning to walk around furniture in anticipation of walking independently, the teacher will document the gains the child can make socially, emotionally, cognitively as well as physically, by learning to ambulate. Once the child is walking, the teacher will scaffold the child's ability to carry objects, greet other children, join into play and will verbally label objects the child encounters. Wittmer and Petersen (2010) emphasize a 3 R approach to responsive, relationship-based curriculum planning for infants and toddlers. **Respect** – value what the child is trying to do and how the child feels. Admire the child's feelings, goals, and how the child is learning. **Reflect** – observe, think, and feel. How is the child showing you how he or she feels? What are the child's goals? What is the child learning? How is the child trying to learn it? What does the child need? **Relate** – be responsive by observing with interest, interacting, communicating, sharing feelings, or changing the physical environment (p. 288).

Ensuring that infants and toddlers feel safe, secure, and nurtured is one of the most important roles of the teacher. Responsive teachers intentionally plan for and scaffold children's emotional, social, cognitive, language, and physical development. Additionally, teachers develop strong, positive relationships with families to build a support system that meets all the needs of infants and toddlers. These powerful relationships are built through mutual respect and positive dialogue.

Early Intervention Services

Since 1986, federal law providing special education services for 3-21 year olds in the United States also provides early invention for infants and toddlers. Part C of the Individuals with Disabilities Education Act (IDEA) provides services designed to:

- Strengthen the capacity of families to meet their child's needs
- Enhance the development of infants and toddlers with disabilities
- Reduce educational costs by decreasing the need for special education through early intervention
- Minimize the possibility of institutionalization and maximize independent living (NECTAC, 2005)

Part C requires each state to determine its own criteria for eligibility and to define "developmental delay". However, states are required to provide services to children who have conditions deemed a risk. This includes:

Chromosomal abnormalities; genetic or congenital disorders; severe sensory impairments, including hearing and vision; inborn errors of metabolism; disorders reflecting disturbance of the nervous system; congenital infections; disorders secondary to exposure of toxic substances, including fetal alcohol syndrome; and severe attachment disorders. Many states add to this list biological conditions that increase the likelihood of, but do not necessarily result in, developmental delay. These would include low birth weight, intraventricular hemorrhage at birth, chronic lung disease, and failure to thrive. (Wittmer & Petersen, 2010, p.363)

If a child is eligible for services, the child goes through a developmental evaluation administered by an early intervention team. The family and the team then develop an Individualized Family Service Plan (IFSP) that states the goals for development and the services and supports needed to be successful. The IFSP takes into serious consideration the strengths, needs, and priorities of the family as well as the child.

It is incumbent upon professionals to always use person-first language – the child is a person first and the disability is only a part of who that child is. Teachers need to be informed about the nature of disabilities the infants and toddlers in their classrooms may need to have accommodated, and have the opportunity to have their questions answered and their concerns taken seriously. Teachers will incorporate many strategies to adapt materials and activities for their successful use by infants and toddlers with disabilities. The greatest indicator for success is that a teacher is willing to accept, and is welcoming to, children with disabilities and their families.

Summary

- Infants and toddlers are incredibly delightful and engaging beings who need responsive, consistent, and sensitive educare so that they can become responsive, competent, and caring adults.

- Secure attachments, enriched environments and relationships, and intentionally planned opportunities support the infants and toddlers as they gain knowledge about themselves, their relationships, and their world.

- A knowledgeable, passionate early childhood educator's job is to promote competence, well-being, healthy development, and quality of life for infants, toddlers, and their families.

- Development is often divided into four broad domains: *physical, cognitive, language,* and *emotional-social.* We think of these domains as being distinct, yet we know they combine in an integrated, holistic way to mold the individual, unique child.

- In a responsive, relationship-based curriculum the needs and interests of the children and their families guide the planning process. A responsive planning process must include the 3 R's – respect, reflect and relate – to support relationship building with infants, toddlers, and their families.

Key Terms

attachment relationship
axons
bias
cephalocaudal
cerebellum
cerebrum
dendrites
domains of learning
educare
executive functioning
goodness-of-fit
mobile infants
Moro reflex
nature
neurons
nurture
object permanence
palmar grasp
pincer grasp
proximal-distal
pruning
quality of life
responsiveness
rooting
self-regulation
sensory threshold
stranger anxiety
supine
telegraphic speech
toddlers
tonic neck reflex
well-being
young infants

Suggested Readings

Geist, K. & Geist, E.A. (2008). Do re mi, 1-2-3: That's how easy math can be – Using music to support emergent mathematics. *Young Children, 63* (2), 20-25.

Nelson, C.A., de Haan, M. & Thomas, K.M. (2006). *Neuroscience of cognitive development: The role of experience and the developing brain.* Hoboken, NJ: John Wiley & Sons, Inc.

Weitzman, E. (2000). *Learning language and loving it: A guide to promoting children's social and language development in early childhood settings.* Toronto, Ontario: The Hanen Center.

Suggested Websites

Circle of Inclusion. This is a website full of information for the service provider and for families.
www.circleofinclusion.org

Council for Exceptional Children Here you will find the Individuals with Disabilities Education Act (IDEA)
www.cec.sped.org

National Council for Children in Poverty (NCCP)
www.nccp.org

Reflections

1. Observe an inclusive infant-toddler program. What works well? What would you change?

2. Observe infants or toddlers in an educare setting. Identify the skills that two children of different ages have in receptive and expressive language.

3. Visit an infant-toddler program. How does the teacher set up an engaging, responsive learning environment that facilitates cognitive development? What would you change?

4. Visit an infant-toddler program. What strategies does the teacher use to encourage peer interactions? What else could be done to promote positive peer interactions?

References

Adolph, K. E. (2008). Learning to move. *Current Directions in Psychological Science, 17,* 213-218.

Ainsworth, M. D. (1982). The development of infant-mother attachment. In J. Belsky (Ed.), *In the beginning: Readings on infancy.* New York: Columbia University Press.

American Psychiatric Association. (1994). *Diagnostic and statistical manual of mental disorders* (4th ed.). Washington, DC: APA.

Berk, L. E. (2008). *Child development* (5th ed.). Boston: Allyn & Bacon.

Bowlby, J. (1980). *Attachment and loss. Volume 3. Loss.* New York: Basic Books.

Caplan, F. & Caplan, T. (1980). *The second twelve months of life.* New York: Bantam/Grosset and Dunlap.

Caspi, A. & Silva,P. A. (1995). Temperamental qualities at age three predict personality traits in young adulthood: Longitudinal evidence from a birth cohort. *Child Development, 66,* 486-498.

Chugani, H. T. (1998). A critical period of brain development: Studies of cerebral glucose utilization with PET. *Preventive Medicine, 27,* 487-497.

Copple, C. & Bredekamp, S. (2009). *Developmentally appropriate practice in early childhood programs* (3rd Ed.). Washington, DC: National Association for the Education of Young Children.

DeVries, R. (2000). Vygotsky, Piaget and education: A reciprocal assimilation of theories and educational practices. *New Ideas in Psychology, 18*(2-3), 187-213.

Dodge, D. T., Rudick, S. & Berke, K. & Dumbro, A. (2006). *The creative curriculum for infants, toddlers, & twos* (2nd ed.). Washington, DC: Teaching Strategies.

Elkind, D. (2007). *The power of play: How spontaneous, imaginative activities lead to happier, healthier children.* Cambridge, MA: Da Capo Press.

Erickson, M. E. & Kurz-Reimer, K. (1999). *Infants, toddlers, and families: A framework for support and intervention.* New York: Guilford Press.

Erikson, E. (1950/1963). *Childhood and society* (2nd Ed.). New York: Norton.

Hart, B. & Risley, T. R. (1995). *Meaningful differences in the everyday experience of young American children.* Baltimore: Brookes.

Healy, J. (2004). *Your child's growing mind: A guide to learning and brain development from birth to adolescence.* (3rd ed.). New York: Broadway Books.

Howes, C. & Hamilton, C. E. (1992). Children's relationships with caregivers: Mothers and childcare teachers. *Child Development, 63,* 859-866.

Janson, P., Raat, H., Mackenbach, J., Jaddoe, V., Hofman, A., Verhulst, F., Tiemeier, A. (2009). Socioeconomic inequalities in infant temperament. *Social Psychiatry & Psychiatric Epidemiology, 44*(2), 87-95.

Joh, A. S. & Adolph, K. E. (2006). Learning from falling. *Child Development, 77*(1), 89-102.

Kopp, C. B. (2000). Self-regulation in children. In J. J. Smelser & P. B. Baltes (Eds.). *International encyclopedia of the social and behavioral sciences.* Oxford, England: Elsevier.

McDevitt, T. M. & Ormrod, J. E. (2010). *Child development: Educating and working with children and adolescents* (4th ed.). Upper Saddle River, NJ: Pearson Prentice Hall.

National Center for Children in Poverty, (2016). *United States early childhood profile.* Retrieved January 6, 2017 from http://www.nccp.org/profiles

NECTAC (National Early Childhood Technical Assistance Center).(2005). *Minimum components under IDEA for statewide, comprehensive system of early intervention services to infants and toddlers with special needs (Including American Indian and homeless infants and toddlers).* Retrieved 11/23/2012, from http://nectac.otg/partc

Otto, B., (2010). *Language development in early childhood* (2nd ed.). Upper Saddle River, NJ: Pearson.

Piaget, J. (1954). *The construction of reality in the child.* New York: Basic Books.

Ramsey, J. L. Langlois, J. H.& Marti, N. C. (2005). Infant categorization of faces: Ladies first. *Developmental Review, 25*(2), 212-246.

Rothbart, M. K. & Bates, J. E. (1998). Temperament. In W. Damon (Ed.), *Handbook of child psychology: Volume 3. Social, emotional, and personality of development* (5th ed.). New York: Wiley.

Saudino, K. L. & Cherny,S. S. (2001). Sources of continuity and change in observed temperament. In R.N. Emde & J. K. Hewitt (Eds.), *Infancy to early childhood: Genetic and environmental influences on developmental change* (pp.89-110). New York: Oxford University Press.

Shore, R. (1997). *Rethinking the brain: New insights into early development.* New York: Families and Work Institute.

Shore, R. (2003). *Rethinking the brain: New insights into early development (2nd Edition).* New York: Families and Work Institute.

Small, M. F. (1998). *Our babies, ourselves: How biology and culture shape the way we parent.* New York: Anchor.

Spelke, E. S. & Kinzler, K. D. (2007). Core knowledge. *Developmental Science, 10*(1), 89-96.

Swim, T. J. & Watson, L. (2011). *Infants and toddlers: Curriculum and teaching.* Belmont, CA: Wadsworth Cengage Learning.

Thelen, E. (2000). Grounded in the world: Developmental origins of the embodied mind. *Infancy, 1,* 3-30.

Thomas, A. & Chess, S. (1977). *Temperament and development.* New York: Bruner/Mazel.

Vygotsky, L. S. (1978). *Mind in society.* Cambridge, MA: Harvard University Press.

Vygotsky, I. S. (1987). Thinking and speech. In N. Minick (Trans.). *The collected works L. S. Vygotsky: Volume 1. Problems in general psychology.* New York: Plenum.

Wachs, T. D. & Bates, J. E. (2001). Temperament. In G. Brenner & A. Fogel (Eds.), *Blackwell handbook of infant development* (pp. 465-501). Oxford, U.K.: Blackwell.

Wittmer, D. S. & Petersen, S. H. (2010). *Infant and toddler development and responsive program planning: A relationship-based approach.* Upper Saddle River, NJ: Pearson.

Worobey, J. &Islas-Lopez, M. (2009). Temperament measures of African-American infants: Change and convergence with age. *Early Child Development and Care, 179*(1), 107-112.

Chapter 7
Planning the Curriculum Using Intentional Teaching

An Introduction to Curriculum Planning

Thinking Ahead

1. What is the role of curriculum?
2. How are learning standards used in curriculum planning?
3. What is integrated curriculum and how can it be used in early childhood settings?
4. What are the aspects that should be considered when planning the environment, materials and schedule in an early childhood classroom?
5. What is the role of intentional teaching in the early childhood classroom?
6. How can child-guided learning and adult-guided instruction complement each other?
7. How is intentional teaching used in planning each of the content areas?

The early childhood curriculum should be planned around the developmental strengths and needs of young children. The National Association for the Education of Young Children (NAEYC) and the National Association of Early Childhood Specialists in State Departments of Education (NAECS/SDE) advise early childhood educators to "implement curriculum that is thoughtfully planned, challenging, engaging, developmentally appropriate, culturally and linguistically responsive, comprehensive, and likely to promote positive outcomes for all children" (NAEYC & NAECS/SDE, 2003, p.1). Intentional teaching guarantees thoughtful and purposeful planning which is both developmentally appropriate and challenging. Developmentally appropriate practice incorporates the cultural and linguistic contexts of children to help children make sense of their world and to build a bridge from home to school. Curriculum activities should support children's thinking, reasoning, inventing, and problem solving.

**"Make the Most of Every Minute With
The Creative Curriculum System for Preschool"**

The joint statement on curriculum from NAEYC and NAECS/SDE (2003, p.2) states the following principles of effective curriculum:

- Children are active and engaged
- Goals are clear and shared by all
- Curriculum is evidence-based
- Valued content is learned through investigation, play, and focused, intentional teaching
- Curriculum builds on prior learning and experiences
- Curriculum is comprehensive
- Professional standards validate the curriculum's subject-matter content
- Curriculum is likely to benefit children

Curriculum should include active learning through hands-on problem-solving and real-world experiences. Curriculum should be based on children's interests and should take children's input seriously. Curriculum should provide opportunities for development across all the domains of learning – social-emotional, cognitive, language, physical, and motor.

Role of Curriculum

Curriculum is the foundation of what to teach, why we teach what we teach, and how to teach it, based on a philosophy of how children learn. The NAEYC and the NAECS/SDE (2003) have issued a joint position statement defining curriculum as "an organized framework that delineates the content children are to learn, the processes through which children achieve the identified curricular goals, what teachers do to help children achieve these goals, and the context in which teaching and learning occur" (p. 21). Regardless of the age of the child, there is no universal curriculum that meets the needs of every child. The outcomes, or goals and objectives of the planned curriculum need to be tailored to connect with the developmental levels and individual needs of the children. In addition, the curriculum helps in the decision-making of classroom design and expectations for behavior.

Curriculum should focus on promoting the cognitive, physical, social-emotional, and language growth of each child. Units of study should meld the unique interests of the children with established, expected outcomes for learning. Although the design of curriculum varies from teacher to teacher and program to program, the reasons for planning are universal. Planning helps teachers to (Kostelnik, Soderman, & Whiren, 2011, p.71):

- Organize their thoughts and actions
- Think creatively about they want to do
- Gather needed equipment and materials in advance
- Connect their teaching to state standards and program goals
- Address the needs of the "whole child"
- Tailor activities to accommodate the needs of specific children, including children with special needs and children who are English language learners
- Address differences among learners
- Communicate to others what they are doing
- Identify the standards by which learning and teaching can be accurately and appropriately evaluated

Effective and intentional teaching considers the needs of children individually and groups of children. Curriculum planning focuses on short-term objectives as well as long-term goals, is tied to state standards, and reflects the teacher's knowledge of how young children learn and develop. Planning also needs to be flexible enough to embrace the "teachable moment" that arises almost daily, and individualized enough to accommodate children's unique needs and interests. Curriculum can be developed at the classroom level by teachers; at the local level by agencies, school districts, or childcare programs; and at the national and international level, by publishing companies.

The *why* of curriculum planning are the goals and objectives that constitute the purposes of the teaching. *Goals* are the long-term desired outcomes of the curriculum while *objectives* are the short-term, measurable ways in which goals are achieved. Objectives are specific, clearly stating the purpose of the lesson or activity, and articulating the desired outcome. Objectives are planned from the perspective of "What do I want my students to *know*, *do*, or *feel* as a result of this lesson or activity?" Goals and objectives must be purposeful, valuable, and benefit student learning.

Bloom's Taxonomy is a framework of learning objectives that classifies the goals of learning and provides a basis for building curricula. A revised version of the taxonomy was designed in 2000. In the cognitive domain, the base of the taxonomy is *knowledge*, while moving up the taxonomy the levels in increasingly higher order are: *comprehension, application, analysis, synthesis*, and *evaluation*. Learning at the higher levels is dependent on attaining prerequisite knowledge and skills at lower levels.

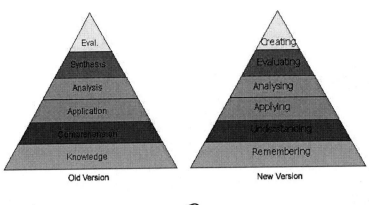

Old Version — New Version

"Bloom's Taxonomy According to Seinfeld"

"Bloom's Taxonomy"

The *why* is also contained in the state and locally mandated learning standards; as part of the curriculum planning, teachers need to review those standards. Curriculum alignment is very important and occurs when the goals, objectives, learning activity/lesson procedure, and assessment of the learning match each other.

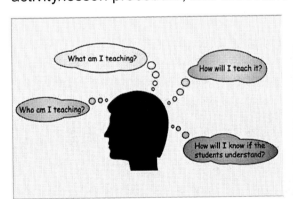

The *what* of curriculum planning is the activities and materials needed to achieve the desired goals and objectives. The curriculum is planned around developmentally appropriate themes, projects, and units of study. Once the goals and objectives of learning are established, the activity or lesson must be designed to align with those goals and objectives, to enable children to meet them. The curriculum must incorporate the prior knowledge of children as well as their interests, while adhering to the framework of professional learning standards.

The *how* of curriculum planning is the ways that the activities and materials (the *what)* are presented so that the *why* (the goals and objectives) can be achieved. This component of curriculum planning includes the preparation and planning of the teaching method as well as gathering and organizing the materials needed to implement the lesson plan. The teacher is thoughtful and purposeful in thinking through the sequence of the activity, as well as the assessment of learning.

Curriculum planning compels the teacher to assess the abilities and needs of children. The position statement by NAEYC and NAECS/SDE (2003, p. 3) proposes that the purposes of assessment are to:

- Make sound decisions about teaching and learning
- Identify significant concerns that may require focused intervention for individual children
- Help programs improve their educational and developmental interventions

The purpose of assessment is to provide teachers with valid data that best informs the teaching of each child. Ethical, appropriate, and reliable assessment allows the teacher to support the learning with teacher-initiated learning, while promoting self-directed learning that results in intrinsic rewards. The assessment of learning must align with the goals and objectives of the learning activity.

Role of Learning Standards in Curriculum Planning

In determining the curriculum, a teacher carefully and intentionally attends to established learning standards, as well as the individual strengths and needs of children. In most classrooms today, the goals and objectives of curriculum are planned with specific standards. Nearly all of the states in the US have embraced the new, largely uniform Common Core State Standards (CCSS) for the teaching of ELA and math. The creation of CCSS was led by the Council of Chief State School Officers (CCSSO) and the National Governors Association (NGA), building on the previous work of states in their crafting of high-quality learning standards. The standards are research and evidence-based, aligned with college and work expectations, rigorous, and internationally bench-marked (NYSED, 2012). These standards require that, at each grade level, students and teachers focus their time and energy on fewer topics, in order to form deeper understandings, gain greater skill and fluency, and more powerfully apply what is learned.

**"Common Core State Standards:
A New Foundation for Student Success"**

Focus in the curriculum is meant to give students an opportunity to understand concepts and daily practice with them in order to reach a deep and fluent understanding. Coherence in the curriculum requires sequences that span grade levels to build students' understanding of ever more sophisticated and abstract concepts and applications. The CCSS contain explicit guidance about the reading, writing, speaking, listening, language, and math skills. One of the first grade reading standards demonstrates this specificity in the CCSS (RF. 2):

Demonstrate understanding of spoken words, syllables, and sounds (phonemes):

   a. Distinguish long from short vowel sounds in spoken single-syllable words
   b. Orally produce single-syllable words by blending sounds (phonemes), including consonant blends
   c. Isolate and pronounce initial, medial vowel, and final sounds (phonemes) in spoken single-syllable words
   d. Segment spoken single-syllable words into their complete sequence of individual sounds (phonemes)

The CCSS explain that the new standards are to be taught within the context of a "content-rich curriculum". The CCSS do not stipulate what content students need to master; the responsibility for developing the curriculum falls to the individual state, districts, and schools:

While the Standards make references to some particular forms of content including mythology, foundational U.S. documents, and Shakespeare, they do not – indeed, cannot – enumerate all or even most of the content that students should learn. The Standards must therefore be complemented by a well-developed, content-rich curriculum consistent with the expectations laid out in this document. (Common Core Standards Initiative, 2011)

As much as the CCSS provide guidelines for goals and objectives of learning, there are limitations to what the standards offer (NYSED, 2012, p. 4):

1) The Standards define what all students are expected to know and be able to do, not how teachers should teach.

2) While the Standards focus on what is most essential, they do not describe all that can or should be taught.

3) The Standards do not define the nature of advanced work for students who meet the Standards prior to the end of high school.

4) The Standards set grade-specific standards but do not define the intervention methods or materials necessary to support students who are well below or well above grade-level expectations.

5) It is also beyond the scope of the Standards to define the full range of supports appropriate for English language learners and for students with special needs. The Standards should also be read as

allowing for the widest possible range of students to participate fully from the outset and as permitting appropriate accommodations to ensure maximum participation of students with special education needs.

6) While the ELA content area literacy components described are critical to college and career readiness, they do not define the whole of such readiness. Students require a wide-ranging, rigorous academic preparation and, particularly in the early grades, attention to such matters as social, emotional, and physical development and approaches to learning.

In addition, the CCSS are not to be used as a curriculum, assessment checklist, as a mandate for specific teaching practices, or as a firm benchmarking system that bars children from kindergarten. The CCSS is a resource to guide the design and implementation of a high-quality curriculum, for planning activities that enable children to meet the standards, and as a guide for selecting assessment tools that are appropriate for young children with differing abilities and challenges (NYSED, 2011). Standards provide clear expectations for the learning and development of young children across all the domains of learning, and provide a guide for teachers as they create intentional, integrated curriculum.

Defining Integrated Curriculum

A curriculum can focus on one subject area such as science or reading, or it can be wide-ranging, addressing all the learning domains and goals for a defined grade level or age. In developmentally appropriate classrooms, teachers endeavor to integrate topics

such as math, science, social studies, with developmental domains such as social-emotional and language. In integrated curriculum, teachers use both informational text and fiction; set up centers with activities that support the goals and objectives of learning as well as the topic; and develop thematic units on specific topics such as families, healthy living, and seasons, that incorporate all the developmental domains. NAEYC's position regarding curriculum development (Bredekamp & Copple, 1997) states: "Effective curriculum plans frequently integrate across traditional subject-matter divisions to help children make meaningful connections and provide opportunities for rich conceptual development; focusing on one subject is also a valid strategy at times" (p. 20). Integrated curriculum helps to address the challenge of covering many learning goals in a limited amount of instructional time. For instance, instead of having separate literacy and science time, one extended period of time can be spent reading informational text, exploring in the science center, and then writing the results of a science experiment in a science journal.

"Integrated Learning"

Planning developmentally appropriate, integrated curriculum is more important today than ever before. During the past few years, early childhood education has become increasingly scripted and restrictive, with assessment becoming the focus. As a result, the "whole child" often gets forgotten, and teaching an integrated curriculum has become more challenging. Presently, early childhood educators and research hold the view that young children learn best using a combination of adult-guided and child-guided learning spiraling from a curriculum that integrates subject areas by connecting and weaving the subject areas with the multiple domains of learning. John Dewey's progressive education included an integrated curriculum that was related to real life problems and situations. The Reggio Emilia approach believes that learning occurs through inquiry projects of children's creation using integrated content, making learning meaningful for children. Piaget and Vygotsky both believed that children construct knowledge through interaction with their environment and the people in it.

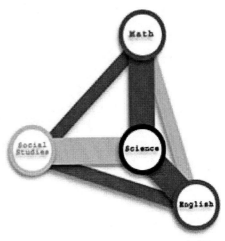

"MCPS Elementary Integrated Curriculum"

Despite the evidence that substantiates the value of hands-on, integrated curriculum, there are influences that work against this approach. Presently, the pervasive atmosphere in education is one of accountability, both of teachers and students. This has led to widespread testing of even young children, and scripted, uniform approaches to teaching that are developmentally inappropriate. For many early childhood educators, it is a challenge to preserve the kind of teaching they know is most effective and appropriate for young children. Yet, with the advent of uniform and broad Common Core State Standards and granting freedom of standards-based curriculum design to the local and state levels, integration may become more possible.

Often early childhood educators struggle with making an integrated curriculum that is meaningful, and effective – a curriculum that maintains the integrity of each subject area, provides in-depth learning, and does not overwhelm either the teacher or the children. Krogh and Morehouse (2008, pp. 22-23) provide clear parameters for creating effective, appropriate, integrated curriculum:

- Each subject should be addressed individually before being integrated in the various topics
- Ways to meet the standards should be explicit in the planning of activities and lessons
- Ways of achieving depth, as well as breadth of learning need to be provided throughout the curriculum
- While there are ideas for giving children some control over their own learning, there also must be ideas for the teacher, who plays an important role in children's learning. There must be a good balance of adult-guided and child-guided learning
- Introduction of integration and inquiry-based learning must be introduced gradually into the classroom, and daily modeled to prepare children to take partial control of their learning

"Joyful Learning: The Reggio Inspired Approach to Education"

Thematic curriculum planning is one strategy for creating integrated curriculum; it is a process by which the curriculum is organized around topics (**units of study**) that children find interesting and engaging, and which have the underpinning of a "big idea". Big ideas are concepts that are rich enough to be studied in depth, lead to new learning, and provide the focus for building connections across the learning domains. Animals' and humans' preparation for winter, for example, can be the organizing structure for cross content study over several weeks. Thematic teaching is not simply a collection of related activities, but an integrated approach where the teacher supports learning across all domains of learning. This type of integrated approach is powerful in that it is meaningful, engaging, and allows children to see the connection between experiences (Chaille, 2008).

Webbing is a visual curriculum-planning tool that offers a great deal of flexibility in creating the scope and content of the theme that aids in planning the learning activities. The web is an illustration of what could be included in a thematic unit or project. To produce a thematic web, the teacher can either brainstorm a topic on her own, or with students. As the web is being refined and activities are being planned, the teacher needs to identify a preliminary list of learning standards that are being addressed in each of the activities. **It is vital that the teacher does NOT design the activity first, but instead simultaneously consults the learning standards as the lesson or**

activity is being created. In addition, the web needs to contain adaptations and accommodations for children with individual learning strengths or needs.

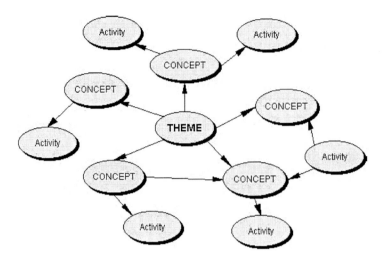

One of the most effective ways the teacher can collaboratively create a web of a topic to be studied is first observe children's conversations to identify their interests. Then, gather children to brainstorm topics to be studied, and generate questions about the agreed upon topic students want answered. Completing a graphic organizer such as a KWL chart can visually organize children's thoughts. In the KWL, children answer the questions "What do you know?" "What do you want to know?" and at the end of the study, "What did you learn?" Webbing is a valuable way to graphically represent the answers to the K and W portions of the KWL, as it organizes the integration of the curriculum. Webbing is particularly effective when used in the Project Approach, a topic to which we discuss next.

Thematic units often extend into long-term projects. The **Project Approach** is not a curriculum, but rather, a way of guiding children through in-depth studies of real topics of interest, or problems that children want to solve. Well-planned and effectively implemented projects engage children's interest, curiosity, persistence, and initiative for learning. Bredekamp (2011, pp.306-308) offers an excellent project that integrates social studies and other content areas:

> One morning at the Active Learning Center, the organic milk delivery service mistakenly left chocolate milk. Before she notices, the teacher, Diane, asks Lamont and Sara to bring it to the kitchen because they have the "milk deliverer" job today. Lamont and Sara shriek as they lift a glass bottle filled with chocolate milk out of the box. They head for the classroom to find Diane, but along the way they tell each child in the class about the yummy mistake, "We got chocolate. It's brown!"
>
> By the time they reach Diane, there is a long line of children asking if they can have the chocolate milk for their snack. After Diane agrees, a more dedicated line of inquiry ensues. "Who left this for us?" "How do they make it brown?" "Does it cost more money?" 'Can we have it

again?" Diane sees that the milk mistake has the potential for an interesting project.

At group time, Diane asks the children to list what they know about chocolate milk and what else they want to find out. She records their ideas on chart paper. During the next two weeks, the children learn a lot about chocolate milk. They write stories about the "milk mistake" in the writing center. They write letters to the milkman, thanking him for the mistake. They examine the price list to compare the cost of chocolate and plain milk. They make chocolate milk and graph how many children like chocolate versus plain milk (a skewed distribution for sure!).

The milk investigation goes into greater depth when the children take a field trip to the dairy and learn about "organic" milk, and why people might prefer it to non-organic. They observe dairy cows and see milking machines. The children also learn how the milk is transported to the customers, and why they use glass bottles. On the trip they discover that the empty bottles are recycled, which prompts one of the children to propose a "recycler" job in the classroom. The children learn that not all people drink milk and the reasons why. They learn why regular milk is healthier than chocolate.

During the last week, the children decide to have a "chocolate milk celebration" with their families. They make invitations, propose and vote on the menu, and help develop displays documenting their field trip and what they've learned. They also offer a book signing for the class book they title *The Chocolate Mistake*.

At the end of the project, Diane revisits the chart created a few weeks ago and asks the children what they have learned. It is clear that they thoroughly enjoyed the project and learned a lot about chocolate milk. But they learned much more about social studies, including concepts about culture, health, community, the environment, diverse beliefs, production of goods and services, and economics, and they also engaged in reading, writing, mathematics, and science.

"REC and the Project Approach to Learning"

When planning a project, the teacher must first assess and identify children's interests and prior knowledge, then prepare the scope and sequence of inquiry into the topic, and finally plan a culminating event (Chard, 2001). In the above vignette, Diane successfully completes each part of the project approach design.

Organizing the Physical Environment, Materials, and Time for Integrated Thematic Units

The design of the physical environment in early childhood programs should take into consideration how young children learn, influencing what they do, how successfully they achieve their goals, and how they behave (Chard, 2001). The environment should be inviting to children; the areas and materials should foster the behavior and activities that are inherent in the philosophy of the program. Arranging the environment is significant to the curriculum development,

classroom management, and accomplishment of goals and objectives. Organizing the learning space, providing developmentally appropriate materials and activities, and putting in place a schedule that promotes optimum learning are the tasks of early childhood educators.

"Inspiring Spaces for Young Children"

Safety must be the highest priority when planning the environment. Teaching children how to use equipment and materials safely, making sure the space is daily assessed for safety hazards, and using materials that are appropriate for the age and ability of the children are all ways to ensure a safe environment. Additionally, young children must be supervised continuously to ensure their safety.

Comfort is important to guarantee that children can use all areas of the classroom easily and comfortably while engaging in meaningful activities. A consistent temperature of the classroom should be kept from 68-72 degrees, but should be adjusted for comfort based on the outside temperature. Indoor lighting should be adequate for doing close work and should include some natural light in addition to artificial lighting. Children need time in natural light to activate the Vitamin D their bodies need to absorb minerals that help them grow strong. Noise can compromise students' ability to remain focused on learning. Children who have difficulty remaining attentive and children who are still learning the English language have difficulty processing verbal messages in noisy environments. Hard surfaces are easier to clean but increase the reverberation of noise, while soft surfaces absorb noise but are more difficult to clean. Yet there needs to be an area of hard flooring with a sink nearby where children can "dabble" in messy projects and carpeted areas where children will be playing actively and sitting on the floor.

"A Tour of The Learning Experience Child Care Centers"

Space design needs to support the early childhood program; the organization of the space is a sound predictor of program quality as it influences what children can do and how they use materials, and the ease with which children can carry out their goals. An integrated and inquiry-based curriculum is based on the belief that children take an active role in constructing their own knowledge, and that interaction with their environment and the people in it are vital in making the learning relevant. For this type of learning, children need an environment with clutter-free spaces, few obstacles, and non-slip floors. The child-sized furniture in the environment needs to be moveable to make the learning space flexible. There needs to be a balance of large and small spaces; the large spaces are used for whole-group instruction, classroom meetings, story reading, and music and movement, while the small spaces are used for two to six children for centers and small group meetings. There should be a variety of well-defined **learning centers** where materials are used in special activities that support and extend the learning. The following learning centers are appropriate for early childhood programs:

- Books, language, literacy, listening
- Writing
- Dramatic play, home area
- Puppet theater
- Sensory activities – cooking, water, sand, crafts
- Blocks
- Music and movement
- Science discovery
- Math and manipulatives
- Computers/technology

Children need **private space** where they can work individually or may be given the opportunity to gain control of their emotions. **Pathways** between activity areas allow free and safe movement from one activity to another however these pathways should not be long lanes that may invite children's running. The pathways may need to be widened to accommodate wheelchairs. Noisy activities should be located away from quieter activities.

In addition, the space needs plenty of **storage** for both teachers' supplies and students' belongings, windows, and empty wall space where student work can be displayed. Materials that are used daily by the children must be accessible; in contrast, materials that only the teacher should access need to be stored away from the mainstream

of activity. Transparent boxes are good storage choices for materials that are small and have pieces. For all early childhood classrooms, but especially those smaller classrooms, portable and stackable storage units are extremely efficient.

Equipment and materials should be appropriate for the age and size of the children. Children need to comfortably fit in the chairs so that their feet touch the floor, and their legs should fit comfortably under tables without bumping knees. Bins and shelves of materials need to be labeled with both words and pictures. There needs to be sturdy, high-quality equipment and materials in the classroom, and the teacher needs to demonstrate the proper use, care, and storage of the equipment and materials.

"Managing Flow in the Early Childhood Classroom"

Aesthetics in an early childhood classroom is a foundational principle in environment design. The Reggio Emilia approach recognizes that the layout of the physical space should be welcoming and aesthetically pleasing, with plenty of space for objects and activities which inspire discovery in the pursuit of learning. In addition, when adults demonstrate their appreciation for attractiveness and neatness, children often emulate this behavior. The environment should be neat and organized yet homelike, with artwork, lighting, furniture, and live plants and flowers. The room should not be over-decorated so as to avoid over-stimulation of children's senses; simplicity is the key to the physical setting. There should be plenty of clear wall space to showcase children's creations.

Materials are another important consideration in developmentally appropriate integrated curriculum. A variety of materials is needed to support the content areas – literacy, math, science, art, music, and social studies, as well as dramatic play, block building, sensory experiences, and theme-based activities. As materials are used, they need to be replaced and a variety needs to be added so that centers do not become "stale" to students. Children need concrete materials to manipulate, construct, and create. The materials should be developmentally appropriate, with duplicates to eliminate disputes among children, in excellent condition, and flexible enough to be used for learning more than one concept. There should be literacy-based materials in each center. For example, there should be seashell books in the center that has been transformed into a "beach" and shopping lists in the home area. The materials should be reflective of cultural diversity, showing children with special needs, and people of both genders.

Sample Classroom Schedule

Childcare	7:00am – 8:30am
7:00 – 7:45	Welcome & activities with combined ages
7:45 – 8:00	Clean up
8:00 – 8:25	Outdoor play time
8:25 – 8:30	Bathroom, wash up, proceed to classroom

Classroom	8:30am – 11:45am
8:30 – 8:35	Welcome
8:35 – 8:50	Group time
8:50 – 9:30	Learning Centers/Games/Art
9:30 – 9:40	Inside Clean up time
9:40 – 10:00	Nutrition
10:00 – 10:45	Outdoor play time
10:45 – 11:00	Physical Development
11:00 – 11:15	Clean up, bathroom, and wash up
11:15 – 11:30	Bible group time
11:30 – 11:45	Music and Movement
11:45 – 12:15	Lunch in classroom or at tables under patio
12:15 – 12:30	Bathroom, wash up prepare for rest time

Child Care	12:30am – 6:00pm
12:30 – 2:30	Rest
2:30 – 3:00	Wake up, stack cots/mats, bathroom and wash up
3:00 – 3:15	Story/Activity Time
3:15 – 3:30	Nutrition
3:30 – 4:20	Outdoor play time
4:20 – 4:30	Clean up, bathroom, wash up
4:30 – 4:45	Group time
4:45 – 5:00	Music and motor development
5:00 – 6:00	Quiet activities as children depart

The **daily routine** set in a predictable schedule provides a context where children feel secure and relaxed, able to concentrate on learning. The predictability allows the child to enjoy a sense of continuity throughout the day and from day to day. The pace at which children work, the lengths of time blocks needed to accomplish child-guided work, the lengths of time blocks that are appropriate for young children to sit through adult-guided instruction, and the balance of instructional strategies make up the structure of the daily routine. Allowing large blocks of uninterrupted time to explore, experiment, move from center to center, build, and create allows for flexibility in pacing. A common strategy that early childhood educators use in center-based learning is to make some of the weekly centers required and some of the centers optional. This way a child who works more slowly has plenty of time to complete the assigned tasks without feeling pressured, while the faster working child can either visit more of the optional centers or spend more time in one or more of those centers. The teacher must offer a variety of activities and monitor the activity in each of the centers; often this is a time that teachers gather informal assessment data. There is a need for the daily routine to have a balance of: child-guided learning and adult-guided learning, of small group activities and whole group activities, of physically active tasks and quiet tasks. What follows are typical daily schedules for programs serving 3- and 4-year olds and kindergarten (left).

Role of Intentional Teaching

The historical role of early childhood education has been to socialize children and to provide them with opportunities to grow emotionally, physically, and to some degree cognitively. This was accomplished through environments set up with materials and experiences that encouraged child-initiated learning. This philosophy was supported by the 1987 and 1997 editions of Developmentally Appropriate Practice (Bredekamp & Copple 1987, Copple & Bredekamp 1997). However, with the advent of the No Child Left Behind Act in 2001, the early childhood education pendulum swung toward increased adult-directed instruction. This controversy pitted the extreme interpretations of "child-initiated" (teacher as passive "guide on the side") and "adult-initiated" (direct instruction, scripted lessons) against each other. The 2009 edition of Developmentally Appropriate Practice (Copple & Bredekamp, p. 49) calls for a balanced approach that respects both child-initiated learning and adult-initiated instruction:

- Children *both* construct their own understanding of concepts *and* benefit from instruction by more competent peers and adults
- Children benefit *both* from engaging in self-initiated, spontaneous play *and* from teacher-planned and –structured activities, projects, and experiences
- Children benefit *both* from predictable structure and orderly routine in the learning environment *and* from the teacher's flexibility and responsiveness to children's emerging ideas, needs, and interests

"Intentional Teaching: Extending Children's Ideas 1/4"

The concept of balance is supported by research such as the report, *Eager to Learn,* commissioned by the Committee on Early Childhood Pedagogy of the National Research Council:

> Children need opportunities to initiate activities and follow their interests, but teachers are not passive during these child-initiated and directed activities. Similarly, children should be actively engaged and responsive during teacher-initiated and –directed activities. Good teachers help support the child's learning in both types of activities. (National Research Council, 2000, p. 8-9)

Developmentally appropriate practice calls for both children and adults actively planning, implementing, and assessing children's learning.

The *what* of teaching – the content – has been debated by early childhood educators as well as the *how* – the pedagogy. The preponderance of early childhood educators agree that the curriculum should include the academic content areas as well as the traditional domains of social-emotional, physical, and creative development. The Prekindergarten and Common Core Standards for Grades K-3 – adopted by 45 states – provide the guidelines for early childhood curriculum development. The New York State Prekindergarten Foundation for the Common Core (2011), for example, looks holistically at young children's learning. Content areas as well as the traditional domains of learning are addressed; approaches to learning which includes engagement, creativity, imagination, persistence, curiosity, and initiative are also given lengthy and thoughtful consideration. The New York State Prekindergarten Foundation for the Common Core (NYSED, 2011) states: "Children are active learners. A primary approach to learning is through purposeful play. *Intentional planning* (italics are mine) promotes rich learning experiences that invite participation, involve multiple contexts, and engage the senses that help children explore their environment" (p. 8).

"EYLF PLP Talking About Practice – Intentional Teaching"

So what is *intentional teaching and planning*? It is purposeful teacher planning of knowledge (content) and skills that children will need for school and life success.

> Intentional teaching does not happen by chance: it is planful, thoughtful, and purposeful. Intentional teachers use their knowledge, judgment, and expertise to organize learning experiences for children; when an unexpected situation arises (as it always does), they can recognize a teaching opportunity and are able to take advantage of it, too. (Epstein, 2007, p.1)

Intentional teaching requires the teacher to use the three foundational tenets of developmentally appropriate practice: 1) What is known about child development and learning; 2) What is known about each child as an individual; and 3) What is known about the social and cultural contexts in which children live (Copple & Bredekamp, 2009). In the area of child development, the teacher must have knowledge of the wide range of typical development and then offer strategies that accommodate the individual needs and interests of children. Often, children will learn through child-guided experiences – using their own explorations, experiences, and interactions to gain knowledge. At other times – particularly for the introduction of new content – children learn best from adult-guided experience; these experiences include teacher direct instruction, modeling, and demonstration (Epstein, 2007). The early childhood teacher also must know the child's social and cultural contexts to ascertain the child's experiential knowledge as well as the family's expectations for success.

"Intentional Teaching: Responding to Children's Ideas & Interests 2/4"

The intentional teacher, when planning curriculum, discerns between the skills and content children learn through their own exploration and interactions, and those that require teacher-guided instruction and scaffolding. It is then the teacher's job to plan the appropriate learning experience to maximize student learning. Intentional teaching utilizes local, state, and national standards: 1) to clearly define the goals and objectives for learning, 2) to design instructional strategies that teach so children can meet the goals and objectives, 3) to assess the learning, and 4) to use the assessment data to plan future instruction. Intentionality of teaching paves the way for effective teaching that supports deep, purposeful learning.

Berliner's (1992) characteristics of effective teaching provide guidelines for successful intentional teaching:

- Teacher's **high expectations** for student engagement and learning
- The classroom as a **valued learning environment**
- **Thought-provoking questioning** to stimulate thinking
- Careful **planning** and **effectual management** of the classroom
- **Engaging activities** within the child's zone of proximal development
- **Supportive and specific feedback** that focuses on the child's learning

At any time of the day, the teacher should be able to clearly explain the *why* of what they are teaching. In-depth and systematic planning to meet both learning objectives and the needs of individual students is one of the hallmarks of intentional teaching.

Intentional teaching includes factors other than the actual daily instruction. It includes the design of the room and the materials and activities that are offered. The physical room arrangement should include a meeting area, interest/content centers, plentiful and diverse equipment and materials, and small group work areas. Student work samples and artwork should be displayed around the room and the school. The Reggio Emilia program uses documentation panels to visually chart the progress of student learning (Edwards, Gandini, & Forman, 1998). Many American schools have adopted this strategy to "make the learning visible".

"Intentional Teaching: Learning Through Routines 3/4"

Another factor in intentional teaching that the early childhood educator must bear in mind is the schedule of the school day. Establishing a consistent, flexible routine provides security and predictability but allows for the "teachable moments" that need to be captured. A predictable routine aids the teacher in planning an integrated curriculum that meets the needs of all students and incorporates all domains of learning. It also should allow time for children to spend long blocks of uninterrupted time to explore materials and activities and to re-visit the same centers for further investigation.

Within the consistent daily routine, the teacher needs to vary the type of activities; there should be opportunities for student choice, whole group activities for teacher-directed "stage-setting", small group activities, and debriefing and reflection times. Teachers need to be sensitive to combinations of children when planning group work; there should be a balance between teacher choice of groups and student choice. There should also be options for individual and pair work.

The teaching/learning system, **SPEDRA** (Dyer, 2004) purposefully structures the teaching and learning cycle to allow children plenty of focused inquiry. SPEDRA – **S**et the stage, **P**lay, **E**xplore, **D**ebrief, **R**evisit, and **A**ssess-**A**pply – is a recursive planning-learning-assessing system that employs intentional teaching through both teacher-directed instruction and investigative play. The teacher designs scenarios, problems, or dilemmas that **set the stage** for student investigation involving essential concepts; setting the stage may also include a purposeful read aloud accompanied by intentional questioning and the creation of supportive graphic organizers. The **play and explore** stages begin as students experiment with materials and ideas, constructing and testing hypotheses intended to resolve the dilemma. In the **debriefing** session the teacher provides a forum for discussion of student ideas. During the discussion, students are encouraged to respect the ideas of others; the teacher checks for student understanding, and clarifies misconceptions. The teacher poses questions that challenge children's thinking and stimulates an excitement for further investigation. During the revisit stage, children use the same materials or additional materials and hypotheses to carry out more complex investigations leading to more extensive understanding. During the final **assess-apply** stage, the teacher poses scenarios, questions, and dilemmas related to the concept or skill previously explored but often transported to new contexts. By completing this recursive cycle the teacher is able to assess student learning and to plan for new learning.

In the area of independent problem-solving, teachers must strike a delicate balance between allowing children enough time and effort to try solutions to problems, while not allowing the child to become discouraged and frustrated. This balance is achieved by effective teachers being vigilant, allowing the child time to articulate what he or she is attempting and then time to try out the solutions, and often by intervening and doing limited direct instruction or by providing suggestions.

Teacher-student interactions as well as peer interactions provide the relationships that are foundational in the teaching/learning cycle. These critical connections are created when children feel respected and secure in taking risks in their quest for knowledge. This positive classroom climate is constructed through warm, nurturing interactions – both verbal and nonverbal, focused listening and inquisitive questioning on the part of the teacher, and strong, individual relationships.

Teacher-student interaction also occurs in the "stage setting" phase of learning, when the teacher provides content knowledge by explicitly introducing information or modeling specific skills. "Children construct their own understanding of concepts, and they benefit from instruction by more competent peers and adults" (Bredekamp & Copple, 1997, p. 23).

It is important for the teacher to encourage initiative in each child by allowing opportunities to plan, carry out, and reflect upon his or her learning. Encouragement and specific feedback goes much further in guaranteeing student success than general praise:

Effective teachers know many ways to recognize and encourage children's intentions and accomplishments: to comment specifically on what the child has done; ask questions to learn more about the child's plan and thoughts (not stock questions to which the adult knows the answer, but authentic queries to elicit information); repeat the child's ideas and imitate his actions; write down or tape the child's ideas; draw connections between the child's current words and actions and events or information that came up at other times or places; refer children to one another for information or assistance; display children's work; and share the child's ideas, contributions, and products with peers, other staff, and family members. (Epstein, 2007, p.18)

"Intentional Teaching: Group Learning 4/4"

Positive peer relationships are facilitated by modeling kind, respectful and reciprocal relationships; creating a classroom environment that encourages positive peer relationships; structuring plenty of possibilities for collaborative play and inquiry; and encouraging students to ask for peer assistance in solving problems.

Assessment is an important part of intentional teaching; authentic, consistent, and objective assessment provides valuable data to all stakeholders – teachers, children, families, and policymakers. "Ongoing…assessments enable teachers to appreciate children's unique qualities, to develop appropriate goals, and to plan, implement, and evaluate effective curriculum" (NAEYC, 2005, p.33). Ongoing, daily assessment provides a comprehensive, holistic view – much like a video – of  a child's ability, as opposed to a one time test which is more like a snapshot of the child's ability at one moment in time. Assessment data should be used to "make sound decisions about individual and group curriculum content, teaching approaches, and personal interactions" (NAEYC, 2005, Criterion 4.14). Assessment data may also be used to identify areas of need in professional development. "…By enhancing their own understanding and expertise – of specific content areas, in using instructional strategies, or both – teachers will be able to more effectively plan and execute activities that advance children's knowledge and understanding" (Epstein, 2007, p. 21).

The task of the intentional teacher is to ensure that young children attain the knowledge and skills that ensure school- and life-success. This undertaking is fulfilled by addressing every domain of learning – cognitive, social-emotional, physical and motor, and creative – through a thoughtfully planned balance of child-guided and adult-guided experiences. Reflection and self-evaluation by both children and teachers is an integral part of lifelong learning – a basic tenet of intentional teaching. We now turn our attention to the application of intentional teaching across the subject areas of early childhood education.

Intentional teachers play a crucial role in establishing a community of learners through a combination of adult- and child- initiated activities. Additionally, the positive classroom environment is built through teacher-student interactions and collaborations among peers; supplying materials and activities, modeling and providing information in a timely manner, guiding discussions, asking purposeful questions, and posing new challenges.

Intentional Teaching in Math and Science

Young children are beginning to understand and be able to: 1) think symbolically in terms of numbers representing quantities, 2) understand conservation of numbers in that materials and objects remain the same regardless of change of form or arrangement, and 3) think semi-logically, being able to keep only one relationship in their mind at one time (Seefeldt & Wasik, 2006). These cognitive limitations restrict the amount of mathematical reasoning young children are capable of. However, children need experiences and daily opportunities to build the foundation of complex mathematical reasoning.

"Building Mathematical Competencies in Early Childhood"

Although much of the early childhood mathematics curriculum is dedicated to numbers, counting, and number operations, the Common Core Mathematics Standards also include the concepts of operations and algebraic thinking; measurement and data; and geometry. Young children, of their own volition, explore topics such as patterns, shapes, adding, and subtracting. In 2002, NAEYC published a joint position paper with the National Council of Teachers of Mathematics (NCTM) supporting the NCTM's Principles and Standards in School Mathematics, offering suggestions for early mathematics education. The Common Core Mathematics Standards attempt to build a strong foundation of mathematical knowledge by focusing each grade level's standards on a

deeper study of fewer topics – an effort to turn around the "inch deep and mile wide curriculum" that traditionally has been "covered" in American schooling. For example, the New York State Prekindergarten Common Core Standards Overview includes the following concepts (NYSED, 2011, p.8):

1) Counting and Cardinality –
   - Know number names and the count sequence
   - Count to tell the number of objects
   - Compare numbers

2) Operations and Algebraic Thinking
   - Understand addition as adding to, and understand subtraction as taking from
   - Understand simple patterns

3) Measurement and Data
   - Describe and compare measurable attributes
   - Sort objects and count the number of objects in each category

4) Geometry
   - Identify and describe shapes (squares, circles, triangles, rectangles)

"Why Students in the US Need Common Core Math"

In addition to learning the mathematical conceptual knowledge, children are expected daily to use mathematical practices such as making sense of problems and persevere in solving them, reasoning abstractly and quantitatively, constructing viable arguments and critiquing the reasoning of others, and modeling with mathematics.

In addition to rethinking the *what* children should learn in mathematics, the *how* of mathematics education is being revolutionized:

> Because young children's experiences fundamentally shape their attitude toward mathematics, an engaging and encouraging climate for children's early encounters with mathematics is important. It is vital for young children to develop confidence in their ability to understand and use mathematics – in other words, to see mathematics as within their reach. (NAEYC & NCTM, 2002).

The processes of problem-solving and reasoning constitute the core of the mathematics content delivery.

"Common Core and Science A-Z"

Scientific inquiry is closely related to mathematics; when young children are engaging in scientific inquiry they are (Epstein, 2007, p.43):

- Raising questions about objects and events around them
- Exploring objects, materials, and events by acting upon them and noticing what happens
- Making careful observations of objects, organisms, and events using senses
- Describing, comparing, sorting, classifying, and ordering in terms of observable characteristics and properties
- Using a variety of simple tools
- Engaging in simple investigations in which they make predictions, gather and interpret data, recognize simple patterns, and draw conclusions
- Recording observations, explanations, and ideas through multiple forms or representation including drawings, simple graphs, writing, and movement
- Working collaboratively with others
- Sharing and discussing ideas

Children gain inquiry skills as they investigate interesting subject matter and build theories through child- and adult-initiated experiences.

The intentional teacher "sets the stage" for mathematics and science education by taking care to design the setting, purposefully planning engaging lessons which meet the goals and objectives for learning. By utilizing the gradual release of responsibility model, the teacher first builds the concepts, principles, and vocabulary children will need to support their mathematical and scientific explorations. The teacher then needs to plan blocks of time and substantive investigations that are thought-provoking and planned in a logical sequence, while providing well-stocked learning centers. Children then need many opportunities to manipulate materials, solve problems, share hypotheses and interpretations, question each other, observe and listen, play games, and interact with peers.

The following is an example of intentional teaching in the area of data analysis in mathematics. There is an initial adult-initiated lesson to introduce the concept of data analysis and display and then there are purposefully planned choices for child-initiated learning:

Data analysis has three elements: classifying and organizing data, representing data, and interpreting data.

- **Adult-initiated** – The first grade teacher would introduce a simple bar graph as a "picture that tells information", showing an example of a bar graph of "Pets We Have at Home" that has already been completed with data previously gathered from children. The lesson would include the parts of the graph, how to sort, count, and plot the graph as well as an analysis of the data, using the terms "total amount", "more", "less", "equal", "___more than", and "___less than". This direct-instruction can be delivered in two lessons.
- **Child-initiated** – In groups of four, have children choose a set of data to sort, count, and plot on a graph that has been supplied. Some of the data to be used could be items in trail mix, students' favorite ice cream flavor, eye color of students, a collection of fall artifacts such as acorns, leaves, and gourds, etc. During a de-briefing session, students can present the analysis of their graph.

The adult initiates the learning through modeling and direct instruction; often the teacher will use fiction and non-fiction literature to introduce the topic and pertinent vocabulary along with graphic organizers such as KWL charts to record the plans for learning. Subsequently, the teacher's role during the child-initiated experiences is to encourage and support children's exploration, model and coach, observe and listen to children's questions and justifications, encourage children to reflect and self-correct, and encourage peer interaction (Epstein, 2007).

Intentional Teaching in Language and Literacy

In early childhood education, there are some important principles of literacy acquisition that provide the basis for best practice for young children. First, literacy is the holistic development of reading, writing, speaking, listening, and creative and analytic strategies used to comprehend text (Snow, Burns, & Griffin, 1998). Second, literacy development begins long before formal instruction; emergent literacy begins in infancy and when children enter preschool they bring varying levels of competency in

oral language, writing, and reading. Third, learning to read and write is critical to children's success in school (Bowman, Donovan, & Burns, 2001). The reading and writing experiences in preschool and kindergarten build a critical foundation for future literacy development. Preschool should be a time, not for formal literacy instruction, but for a combination of child-initiated and adult-initiated experiences that support and extend language and emergent literacy competency with intentionality.

"A Window to the World: Promoting Early Language and Literacy Development"

Reading research has generated the following information, which supports intentional teaching (Ranweiler, 2004):

- Language and literacy are connected from infancy onward
- Children differ in their learning; some grasp skills easily and quickly while others need explicit and repeated instruction
- Some language and literacy learning is "ancillary", arising naturally from play and everyday interactions. Other learning requires explicit instruction and modeling through formal instruction. Children actively construct their own knowledge, but also need adult support.
- Children learn to talk, read, and write because they are social beings and need to communicate with others
- Language and literacy acquisition occurs in activities children initiate such as exploring print, role-playing, and invented writing. It also happens in adult-initiated instruction such as shared reading, letter identification activities, and creating rhymes
- Children learn best when instruction is meaningful and relevant to their lives
- Differences in home language and culture can affect language and literacy development. Intentional teaching must take these variances into account when planning.

The intentional teacher uses assessment data to identify the individual literacy strengths and needs of her students. The National Reading Panel's (2000) report identified four abilities preschoolers must develop to become proficient readers, writers, and speakers:

- Phonological awareness which includes awareness of speech sounds and rhythms, recognition of similar and differing sounds, and phonemic awareness
- Comprehension which is built through intentional thinking and questioning to build meaning
- Print awareness that print carries a message
- Alphabet knowledge which builds the idea of a relationship between symbols and sounds

The intentional teacher of kindergarten, first- and second-graders uses purposeful teaching which builds on the literacy and language foundation laid by the preschool teacher, to make reading and writing not only useful, but pleasurable.

With all this research in mind, the intentional teacher purposefully plans a balance of adult-initiated and child-initiated experiences that allow children freedom to explore, yet provide adult support to sustain motivation and supply vital information. Knowledge and skills acquired through explicit adult-initiated instruction require child-initiated investigation and practice to gain depth of understanding (Epstein, 2007). What follows is a good example of the synergy of child-initiated and adult-initiated learning:

Print Awareness, also called concepts about print, includes familiarity of how print and books work – front and back of the book, title page, left-to-write and return sweep, etc. Through repeated exposure, children gain print awareness.

- **Adult-initiated** learning would include daily whole group read alouds using big books, predictable charts, morning messages, dictated stories, etc. During the read alouds, the teacher would point out book and print features such as the front cover, author, illustrator, title page, page numbers, reading left-to-right, and return sweep.
- **Child-initiated** learning would deepen the understanding of concepts about print. One example of this independent exploration would be the opportunity for children to create their own books which would contain all the parts of a book they learned about during the adult-initiated read aloud. The intentional teacher would provide books in the writing center for children to refer to while creating their own books. When children complete their books, they would place them in the library corner for other children to "read".

Intentional Teaching in the Visual Arts

The learning values in the arts are both intellectual and emotional. The arts provide children with a feeling of competence and empowerment, and offer communication and self-expression. In some cases, such as the Reggio Emilia approach, the arts are used to support and document children's learning. The arts are valuable in that they promote development in other domains of learning:

> For all children, at all ability levels, the arts play a central role in cognitive, motor, language, and social-emotional development. The arts motivate and engage children in learning, stimulate memory and facilitate understanding, enhance symbolic communication, promote relationships, and provide an avenue for building competence. (Arts Education Partnership, 1998, p. *v*)

Research supports the role that visual arts plays in lifelong human development. The arts were included in the reforms proposed by the Goals 2000: Educate America Act passed by Congress (National Education Goals Panel, 1994). The Task Force on Children's Learning and the Arts: Birth to Age Eight (Arts Education Partnership, 1998) recognizes the role of arts in fostering language and literacy skills.

"Early Childhood at Potomac Arts Academy"

Intentional teaching in the visual arts should focus on both developmental abilities of creating visual arts and appreciating visual arts. **Creating** visual arts includes four developmental stages (Epstein & Trimis, 2002):

1) Moving from accidental or spontaneous representation to intentional representation – moving from taking an accidentally created form and deciding what it looks like, to purposefully translating a mental image into an artistic creation
2) Moving from simple to elaborated representations
3) Moving from making marks and lines to shapes and figures
4) Moving from making random marks to making colors and objects form relationships in artistic expression. Colors and objects are combined in art because they "go together"

Appreciating visual arts is also a skill that that develops in stages from the concrete to the abstract (Parsons, 1987):

1) Sensorial – Young children respond to works that please their senses, and their concern is only with how something looks, not with how it was made
2) Concrete – Children like artwork that expresses ideas they can relate to and is done in a realistic way. The purpose of art at this stage is to tell a "story" about a person, event, or object (Epstein, 2007)
3) Expressive – Children at this stage can begin to view works of art from the artist's perspective, venture a theory on the artist's intentions, and judge the success of the artwork based on their reaction as the viewer (Seefeldt, 1999)

It is important that creating and appreciating the visual arts become components of the early childhood curriculum. The most effective way to foster a child's development in expressive and perceptual development is through a balance of adult-guided and child-guided activities.

Children's use of two- and three-dimensional art materials and tools becomes refined with time and practice. Adults need to model techniques and make suggestions, and then provide the time and opportunity for children to experiment and refine their technique in the use of materials and tools.

- **Adult-guided** – During the study of an author/illustrator such as Eric Carle or Jan Brett, analyze the artistic style of the author/illustrator and the materials he or she uses. For instance, Eric Carle uses hand-painted papers, which are layered and then cut into the shape of the object in the picture. Model some of the illustrators' techniques for children – using cut paper with paint, tissue paper and water color, etc.

- **Child-guided** – Set up a spacious, well stocked, permanent art area with labeled bins of materials. Provide large spaces so children can work independently or in groups. Make sure the floor is easy to clean and the area is near a water source. There should be a drying area for finished work and ample wall space on which to work, store works-in-progress, and to display finished products. After demonstrating the illustrator's technique, make sure there is a wide and abundant variety of tools and materials, as well as books and illustrations from several authors and illustrators. Combine this activity with the book students are creating in the literacy assignment. Have students choose a style of illustration for the book they are writing.

Intentional teachers (Epstein, 2007):

- Create rich learning environments
- Encourage student exploration
- Know the content (facts, vocabulary, conceptual knowledge, skills) of each topic
- Know and use effective, general teaching strategies
- Know and use specific teaching strategies that are effective in different content areas
- Are planful, purposeful, and thoughtful

For children to acquire information and skills, adult- and child-guided learning experiences are essential. Intentional teachers know they have a role to play in both, and they do so using their professional knowledge and skills. We need to reject the idea that teachers need scripted lessons in order to teach children effectively. However, as professionals, teachers need to know the core body of knowledge of content, child development, and learning theory in order to teach children so their learning is meaningful.

Essential Life Skills that All Children Need

Life today can be stressful, fast moving, and complicated. It can also be fulfilling, joyous, with multiple, exciting options. Educators in their quest for providing children with a quality education – facts, concepts, understandings – need to understand that there are also life skills that are essential for children.

Ellen Galinsky (2010) in her seminal work *Mind in the Making: The Seven Essential Life Skills Every Child Needs* examines the skills that all children need in order to thrive in our world. Galinsky also investigates at length the ways that educators and parents can support children's maturing in each of the skills.

Skill 1 – Focus and self-control – Focus and self-control involve many executive functions of the brain such as paying attention, remembering the rules, and inhibiting one's initial response to achieve a larger goal, and they can be taught (p.5). To promote focus, one of Galinsky's suggestions is to play games that require children to focus; to promote self-control, Galinsky's suggestions include making sure that both children and adults are rested and take breaks.

Skill 2 – Perspective taking – "Perspective taking involves the intellectual skill of discerning how someone thinks and feels...putting aside our own thoughts and feelings, and trying to feel and think as another person must feel and think" (p. 71). Galinsky recommends that parents and educators model this skill by helping children feel known and making sure their perspectives are understood.

Skill 3 – Communicating – communicating well encompasses the language and literacy skills such as vocabulary and fluency, as well as executive functioning such as reflecting upon the goal of the communication and inhibiting our point of view, to understand the viewpoint of others (p. 7). Galinsky advocates for the creation of environments both at home and school where words, reading, and listening are important.

Skill 4 – Making connections – "Making multiple connections is a skill that becomes possible during the later preschool and early school age years and beyond as the prefrontal cortex of children's brains matures...making connections is the basis of creativity" (p.9). These are the moments when children can see connections among facts, statistics, or concepts, and involves the use of executive functions. Teachers and parents are encouraged to impress upon children that making mistakes is not only okay, but is a part of learning.

Skill 5 – Critical thinking – "Critical thinking draws on executive functions of the brain. It parallels the reasoning used in the scientific method because it involves developing, testing, and refining theories about 'what causes what' to happen" (p.9). Galinsky suggests a balance of encouraging children's curiosity and having an adult as expert, providing accurate and valid information to children.

Skill 6 – Taking on challenges – "Children who avoid challenges have a *fixed mindset*; they see their intelligence as a fixed trait and therefore are reluctant to undertake challenges that 'stretch' them" (p. 10). In order to foster a *growth mindset* where children take on challenges and view their abilities as entities they can develop, Galinsky suggests that parents don't shield children from everyday stresses, but instead, teach a child how to "get back on the horse after falling off".

Skill 7 – Self-directed, engaged learning – Social-emotional and intellectual learning are linked. It is paramount that parents and teachers support children in finding something they care about investigating and then pursue that ambition. Galinsky believes establishing a "community of learners" whether at home or in a classroom is vital in modeling lifelong, engaged learning.

Summary

- The National Association for the Education of Young Children (NAEYC) and the National Association of Early Childhood Specialists in State Departments of Education (NAECS/SDE) advise early childhood educators to "implement curriculum that is thoughtfully planned, challenging, engaging, developmentally appropriate, culturally and linguistically responsive, comprehensive, and likely to promote positive outcomes for all children" (NAEYC & NAECS/SDE, 2003, p.1).

- The NAEYC and the NAECS/SDE (2003) have issued a joint position statement defining curriculum as "an organized framework that delineates the content children are to learn, the processes through which children achieve the identified curricular goals, what teachers do to help children achieve these goals, and the context in which teaching and learning occur" (p. 21).

- In integrated curriculum, teachers use both informational text and fiction; set up centers with activities that support the goals and objectives of learning as well as the topic; and develop thematic units on specific topics such as families, healthy living, and seasons, that incorporate all the developmental domains.

- When planning a project, the teacher must first assess and identify children's interests and prior knowledge, then prepare the scope and sequence of inquiry into the topic, and finally plan a culminating event (Chard, 2001).

- Intentional teaching is purposeful teacher planning of knowledge (content) and skills that children will need for school and life success. "Intentional teaching does not happen by chance: it is planful, thoughtful, and purposeful. Intentional teachers use their knowledge, judgment, and expertise to organize learning experiences for children; when an unexpected situation arises (as it always does), they can recognize a teaching opportunity and are able to take advantage of it, too" (Epstein, 2007, p.1).

- Assessment is a vital part of intentional teaching; authentic, consistent, and objective assessment provides valuable data to all stakeholders – teachers, children, families, and policymakers. "Ongoing…assessments enable teachers to appreciate children's unique qualities, to develop appropriate goals, and to plan, implement, and evaluate effective curriculum" (NAEYC, 2003, p.33).

- Ellen Galinsky (2010) in her seminal work *Mind in the Making: The Seven Essential Life Skills Every Child Needs* examines the skills that all children need in order to thrive in our world. Galinsky also investigates at length the ways that educators and parents can support children's maturing in each of the skills.

Key Terms

adult-initiated learning
Bloom's Taxonomy
child-initiated learning
Common Core State Standards (CCSS)
curriculum
intentional teaching
learning centers
Project Approach
SPEDRA
thematic curriculum
units of study
webbing

Suggested Readings

Gardner, H. (1991). *The unschooled mind: How children think and how schools should teach.* New York: Basic Books.

Gronlund, G. (2006). *Make early learning standards come alive: Connecting your practice and curriculum to state guidelines.* St. Paul, MN: Redleaf Press.

Katz, L.G. & Chard, S.C. (2000). *Engaging children's minds: The Project Approach.* 2nd ed. Greenwich, CT: Ablex.

Suggested Websites

Association for Supervision and Curriculum Development (ASCD)
www.ascd.org

Bank Street College of Education
www.bankstreet.edu

Project Approach
www.projectapproach.org

Reflections

1. Interview an experienced kindergarten, first-, or second-grade teacher. Ask how he or she thinks the standards movement has affected the curriculum. Write a short essay that discusses the positive and negative impacts of standards on curriculum.

2. Observe a class that incorporates thematic learning or curriculum units of study. Take notes on the following:

- Adult-initiated learning activities
- Child-initiated learning activities
- Spontaneous learning
- Social interaction
- Noise levels
- Traffic patterns and freedom of movement
- Congruency of the room arrangement and the philosophy of teaching/learning

3. What are the advantages and disadvantages of learning centers as an important part of the early childhood classroom?

4. In what contexts do child-guided experiences seem to predominate? In what contexts do adult-guided experiences seem to dominate? How can understanding adult modes of learning inform how we intentionally teach young children?

References

Arts Education Partnership. (1998). *Young children and the arts: Making creative connections – A report of the Task Force on Children's Learning and the Arts: Birth to Age Eight.* Washington, DC: Arts Education Partnership.

Berliner, D. C. (1992). The nature of expertise in teaching. In *Effective and responsible teaching: the new synthesis,* , F. K. Oser, A. Dick, & J. L. Patry, 227-248. San Francisco: Jossey-Bass.

Bowman, B. T., Donovan, M. S., & Burns, M. S. (2001). *Eager to learn: Educating our preschoolers.* Washington, DC: National Academy Press.

Bredekamp, S. (Ed). (1987). *Developmentally appropriate practice in early childhood programs serving children from birth through age 8.* Washington, DC: NAEYC.

Bredekamp, S. (2011). *Effective practices in early childhood education: Building a foundation.* Upper Saddle River, NJ: Pearson Education.

Bredekamp, S. & Copple, C. (Eds.). (1997). *Developmentally appropriate practice in early childhood programs serving children from birth through age 8* (2nd ed.). Washington, DC: NAEYC.

Chaille, C. (2008). *Constructivism across the curriculum in early childhood classrooms: Big ideas of inspiration.* Boston: Pearson Education.

Chard, S. (2001). *The project approach: Book 1.* New York: Scholastic.

Common Core Standards Initiative. (2011). Retrieved December 8, 2012 from http://www.corestandards.org

Copple, C. & Bredekamp, S. (Eds.). (2009). *Developmentally appropriate practice in early childhood programs serving children from birth through age 8* (3rd ed.). Washington, DC: NAEYC.

Dyer, D.L. 2004. *SPEDRA: A learning/teaching framework that supports success for all children.* In editing.

Edwards, C. Gandini, L. & Forman, G. (1998). *The hundred languages of children: The Reggio Emilia approach – Advanced reflections* (2nd ed.). Greenwich, CT: Ablex.

Epstein, A. S. (2007). *The intentional teacher: Choosing the best strategies for young children.* Washington, DC: NAEYC.

Epstein, A.S. & Trimis, E. (2002). *Supporting young artists: The development of the visual arts in young children.* Ypsilanti, MI: High/Scope Press.

Galinsky, E. (2010). *Mind in the making: The seven essential life skills every child needs.* NYC, NY: HarperCollins.

Kostelnik, M. J., Soderman, A. K. & Whiren, A. P. (2011). *Developmentally appropriate curriculum.* Upper Saddle River, NJ: Pearson.

Krogh, S. & Morehouse, P. (2008). *The early childhood curriculum: Inquiry learning through integration.* New York: McGraw-Hill.

National Association for the Education of Young Children. (2009). *NAEYC Standards for Early Childhood Professional Preparation Programs.* Washington DC: NAEYC.

National Association for the Education of Young Children (NAEYC) & National Association of Early Childhood Specialists in State Departments of Education (NAECS/SDE). (2003). *Early childhood curriculum, assessment, and program evaluation: Building an effective, accountable system in programs for children birth through age 8.* Retrieved December 8, 2012, from http://www.naeyc.org

National Association for the Education of Young Children (NAEYC) & National Council of Teachers of Mathematics (NCTM). (2002). *Early childhood mathematics: Promoting good beginnings.* Joint position statement. Washington, DC: NAEYC.

National Research Council. (2000). *How people learn: Brain, mind, experience, and School.* Washington, DC: National Academy Press.

New York State Education Department (NYSED). (2011). http://www.nysed.org

Parsons, M. J. (1987). *How we understand art.* Cambridge, UK: Cambridge University.

Ranweiler, L. (2004). *Preschool readers and writers: Early literacy strategies for teachers.* Ypsilanti, MI: High/Scope Press.

Seefeldt, C. (1999). *The early childhood curriculum: Current findings in theory and practice* (3rd ed.). New York: Teachers College Press.

Seefeldt, C. & Wasik, B. A. (2006). *Early education: Three, four, and five-year-olds go to school* (2nd ed.). Upper Saddle River, NJ: Pearson.

Snow, C. E., Burns, M. S., Griffin, P., (1998). *Preventing reading difficulties in young children.* Washington, DC: National Academy Press.

Chapter 8
Preschool Today

Today in Preschool

Thinking Ahead

1. How do young children develop socially and emotionally?
2. How do young children develop language from birth to age 4?
3. What are the influences on emergent literacy development?
4. How can teachers foster children's development of motor skills?
5. What is the importance of executive functioning in cognition?
6. What role do standards and assessment play in pre-k education?

Success in the primary grades and in the later grades has its roots in quality pre-kindergarten. Early childhood educators, parents, and society at large view exceptional preschool education as the foundation of success; these years are recognized as an important period of learning and development, not just a time to "get ready" for learning. Preschool programs meet the needs of three- and four-year old children before they enter kindergarten. In 2014, approximately 80 percent of 3- and 4-year olds were  enrolled in either a public or private preschool full day or half-day program (NIEER, 2015). A large body of research validates that high-quality early childhood programs can have a lifelong positive effect for children, especially for those who come from economically disadvantaged backgrounds (Galinsky, 2006). Two longitudinal studies – the Perry Preschool Project and the Chicago Child-Parent Center Study– followed children for decades, confirming the importance of early childhood education, greatly influencing policy makers.

"Why Preschool is So Important"

 **The Perry Preschool Project** – one of the first studies to justify the enduring effects of high-quality preschool education on future economic and educational outcomes – began in the early 1960's in Ypsilanti, Michigan. The results of the research found that the graduates of the Perry Preschool had better achievement test scores than children who did not attend preschool and were less likely to need special education services or to be retained in a grade. Almost a decade later, the

data showed that preschool participation was correlated to a higher rate of high school graduation, and lowered involvement in crime and delinquency (Schweinhart, Barnes, & Weikart, 1993). When the study was forty years old, the participant data showed higher levels of educational achievement, higher wages, and less likelihood to be on welfare (Schweinhart, et al., 2005). The Perry Preschool Project later became the High/Scope Educational Research Foundation that has developed one of the most widely-used early childhood constructivist curricula.

The Chicago Parent-Child Center Study was a study of the large-scale, Title I federally funded Chicago Child-Parent Centers, involving more than 1,500 children (Temple & Reynolds, 2007). Since 1985, the Chicago Child-Parent Centers (CPC) has provided preschool and kindergarten to children from low-income families. Family support services and continued intervention services in the primary grades are also supplied through this Title I grant. Children participating in CPC showed higher school achievement, less frequent grade retention, lower dropout rates, better social adjustment, and lower rates of juvenile arrests (Temple & Reynolds, 2007). The most positive data emanates from children who participated in preschool and had continued intervention in elementary school up to and including third grade.

The issue of **social justice** threads throughout early educational research. One of the greatest challenges the US faces is the continuing achievement gap that exists between school achievement of children in poverty and low-income homes, and that of middle- and upper-income homes. Family income is more closely related to cognitive ability than race or ethnicity (Lee & Burkam, 2002). Many Americans believe that early education aids in  closing the achievement gap by promoting equal opportunity for all children, and "leveling the playing field" for children entering public education. The argument is that low-income children begin school behind their same-age middle- and upper-income peers, so commencing education earlier for low-income children is the socially just thing to do.

"Early Learning: America's Middle Class Promise Begins Early"

Another factor that influences the achievement gap is the quality of public schooling once children enter kindergarten. Children from low-income families are more likely to encounter poorer quality schools than their middle- and upper-income peers (Neuman, 2008, Edleman, 2012). Higher student achievement, more qualified teachers, better neighborhoods and school conditions, and more resources are factors that determine school quality. Poor quality schools exacerbate the existing achievement gap kindergartners from low-income families already possess (Lee & Burkam, 2002). Some policymakers are concerned with the cost of providing high-quality preschool and primary education. However, sweeping research shows that investing in children can actually be a bargain (Heckman).

High-quality pre-school education benefits not only the participants, but society as a whole. Economists have estimated that for each dollar spent, the return on the investment is as much as $17. The savings was in decreased costs in special education, grade retention, welfare, and crime (Heckman). In addition, quality early education programs help reduce social problems such as drug abuse and high school dropout rates (Schweinhart et al., 2015). The number of young children in poverty in the US is increasing, with the largest number being children under the age of 5 and children of color (NCCP, 2010). The achievement gap produces profound consequences for the American society in the larger global competitive arena and in individuals' futures.

Trends in Early Childhood Education

UPK

Universal prekindergarten means different things to different people. By its definition "universal" means" including or covering all or available equitably to all members of a society" (Merriam Webster, 2012). Head Start and Universal Pre-K target children from low-income families or those deemed at-risk for school failure, but those four-year olds who do not fall within the income guidelines for Head Start may not receive the high-quality prekindergarten education that research has shown ensures school success. Universal prekindergarten (UPK) is quickly becoming a permanent part of American public schooling, however, it is far from universal – not all American four-year olds have access to free prekindergarten. Although we have seen tremendous growth in public support and funding for universal, voluntary preschool for all 4-year olds, few states offer it at this time. Despite the economic downturn in 2008, a limited number of states, including Florida, Georgia, Vermont, and Oklahoma make true, voluntary universal prekindergarten available to all 4-year olds regardless of family income (NIEER, 2015). Families do not have to participate, but have the unfettered opportunity to do so; the result is that in some states the number of children in UPK's exceeds the number of children in Head Start (Bredekamp, 2011).

"Seeing Success, Conservative Oklahoma Banks on Universal Preschool"

Universal preschool is the beginning of public school therefore there is greater involvement of the public schools and increased alignment of curriculum and learning standards. This presents a challenge in that curriculum alignment and standards can be positive forces in providing purposeful, well-coordinated learning; yet on the negative side, alignment and standards can force curriculum to be inappropriately "pushed down" into early grades.

"What Children Learn in Pre-K"

Standards and Accountability

In the early 1990's, learning standards – benchmarks of what children should know and learn at certain ages – have come to the forefront of curriculum planning and assessment. In 2002, Good Start, Grow Smart – a government initiative – called for early learning standards in literacy, mathematics, and language that were adopted in Head Start and other federally funded programs. The new 2015 Head Start Early Learning Outcomes Framework replaces the 2010 version that was heavily literacy-based. The new Framework respects the holistic nature of young children's development and learning. The framework is grounded in a comprehensive corpus of research of what children should know across the domains of Approaches to Learning, Social and Emotional development, Language and Literacy, Cognition, and Perceptual, Motor and Physical development. The Framework helps adults better understand how they should be providing learning opportunities that support learning outcomes.

The Early Learning Outcomes Framework is supported by 7 Guiding Principles (NHSA, 2016):

1. Each child is unique and can succeed
2. Learning occurs within the context of relationships
3. Families are children's first and most important caregivers, teachers, and advocates
4. Children learn best when they are emotionally and physically safe and secure
5. Areas of development are integrated, and children learn many concepts and skills at the same time
6. Teaching must be intentional and focused on how children learn and grow

7. Every child has diverse strengths rooted in their family's culture, background, language, and beliefs.

As of 2015, all 50 states have published comprehensive early learning standards for preschool children in areas such as literacy, math, and language (NIEER, 2015). In addition to state standards, professional organizations have also identified outcomes in content areas that children should achieve at particular grade levels. Most of the states (45) initially adopted the Common Core State Standards that articulate a clear, consistent understanding of what students are to learn in grades Pre-K to 12th (CCSSO, 2012). However, eight of those states have withdrawn their adoption of the CCSS's. These learning standards will be discussed later in this book.

Teacher accountability for student learning is emphasized along with student accountability for reaching benchmarks of learning. The belief is that schools and teachers who receive public money need to be held accountable for children's achievement of the learning standards. The teacher is responsible for knowing and using the local, state, and national standards in daily lesson planning. The planning also includes assessment of each child's progress meeting the standards. In most preschool programs, the teacher will be asked to teach content areas and topics and will be given standards with benchmarks, goals, objective, and, possibly, a prepared curriculum guide to follow. In addition, the teacher will be given the formative and summative assessment format to be used to evaluate children's progress.

Assessment

The development of academic learning standards by organizations and states was accompanied by assessment of children's progress toward these standards. Early childhood teachers feel the increased pressure of wide-scale, high-stakes accountability testing. However, experts in the early childhood field are aware of the shortcomings of standardized assessment with young children – poor test construction, low validity and reliability, unsuitability for culturally and linguistically diverse children, and the undue influence of tests and testing on children's learning (Snow & Van Hemel, 2008).

Teachers assess children to determine individual developmental status at a given time, and their progress over time. Assessment of young children is more appropriately done using informal, formative evaluation over a long period of time. The data collected over time are used to: 1) monitor children's development and learning, 2) guide classroom planning and decision-making in order to help children learn, 3) identify children who might benefit from special help, and 4) report to and communicate with parents and school officials. In pre-kindergarten teachers assess by documenting observations of children in the form of observational/anecdotal notes, work products from classroom activities, checklists, rating scales, audio and video recordings, participation charts, rubrics, and photographs.

Portfolios are a good place to collect and organize the data. After compiling, reflectively analyzing and summarizing the assessment findings, teachers then use the information to plan ways to meet each child's assessed strengths and needs. Curriculum planning then incorporates the information, resources, and strategies to support children's learning.

Higher Teacher Qualifications

Early childhood educators are responsible for ensuring that the preschool program enhances the development and learning of each individual child it serves. To secure this, teachers must have a great deal of skill, knowledge, and training. As the field of early education changes dramatically, so do the skills and knowledge associated with it. To meet the challenge of the changing field, there has been an increased emphasis on making sure teachers receive college degrees in early childhood education and/or child development (NAEYC, 2005).

"Teacher Qualifications in Early Childhood Education: What is Quality?"

Research shows that teachers having a bachelor's degree with specialization in early childhood education provide educational opportunities with better outcomes for young children (Barnett, 2003; Whitebook, 2003). Raising teacher qualifications may go far in improving quality for children and raising the professional status for teachers. Head Start provides a good example of a commitment to raising teacher qualifications. In the past, Head Start teachers could hold a CDA (Child Development Associate) credential which requires 120 hours of training, 480 hours of experience with children, and a written exam. The Head Start Act of 2009 requires that by 2013, 50% of the teachers must possess a bachelor's degree. This will go far in providing high-quality education for many of our 3- and 4-year olds. Yet, a teacher's education does not stop with attaining a degree; constant and continuous education will become paramount in a teacher's professional development. One way professional development is facilitated is through membership in professional organizations such as NAEYC.

Alignment of Pre-school and K-3

A trend that early education has been experiencing in the past decade is the increased responsibility for curriculum and learning guidelines for preschools being housed in state departments of education (Morrison, 2012). Traditionally, because preschool attendance is not mandated by most states, preschool and K-3 have resided in two separate worlds with very little communication between them. But as preschools have grown in popularity and number, the purpose of their programs have changed.

Once a bastion of socialization and play with its purpose being to prepare students emotionally and socially for kindergarten, preschool has become a center of academic preparation. Literacy, math, and science skills are now taught in preschools in addition to providing the traditional play and socialization opportunities.

This increased emphasis on academic preparation of 4 year-olds has necessitated an increased attention on curriculum **alignment**. Alignment is the coordination of the curriculum from one level of education to the next. Alignment means the preschool education lays a foundation for the kindergarten curriculum, ensuring that children can easily build their knowledge. The premise is that easier transitions are built for students between schools and from one school level to the next, enhancing continuity of learning (Foundation for Child Development, 2008).

"Exceptional, Personalized Learning: Eastern Carver County Schools"

One of the concerns with curriculum alignment is that it will encourage the policymakers to allow "curriculum pushdown", expecting young children to accomplish skills that are developmentally inappropriate for their age and then testing young children inappropriately. In addition, there is concern that alignment will narrow the curriculum to academic domains such as mathematics and literacy, neglecting physical, social, and emotional development (NAEYC, 2009). Early childhood educators are especially troubled by the potential elimination of valuable experiences that include the arts and play, and by the possibility of a "fractured curriculum" that lacks integration of content areas. The NAEYC stresses curriculum alignment that reflects what children can and should learn at each developmental stage and age, and the need for well-prepared teachers who know how to help children learn and progress (NAEYC, 2009).

Preschool Development Across the Domains

Effective curriculum planning for 3- and 4-year olds addresses the development and learning of the whole child: physical and motor development; social and emotional development; cognitive and language development; and approaches to learning such as persistence and curiosity (Copple & Bredekamp, 2009). The curriculum should build knowledge and skills in mathematics, literacy, science, social studies, and the arts. The most effective way to build preschool and kindergarten curriculum is through **curriculum integration.**

Curriculum integration addresses learning goals across multiple content areas at the same time. For example, a single read aloud about butterflies can address literacy

standards as well as science knowledge. Integrated curriculum addresses the time issue – there is never enough time to teach everything – by covering several goals in one lesson. Integrated curriculum enhances student learning by connecting knowledge and skills across the content areas and building deeper conceptual understanding (Bredekamp, 2011). Returning to our example of the butterfly read aloud, children can learn to utilize the structure of informational text to investigate the scientific information about butterflies. Students will then recall the literacy skill they have learned in this lesson during future read alouds of informational text on other science topics.

"Science and Math Integrating Literacy in Early Childhood"

Thematic curriculum is curriculum that is organized around interesting and engaging topics. A broad topic creates "big ideas" or essential questions; an example might be the topic of the lifecycle of butterflies, answering the essential question, "How does the lifecycle of a living thing guarantee its survival?" This essential question can be answered within many thematic units and could provide the organizing structure for a large part of the preschool and kindergarten curriculum. The important thing to remember is that the teacher needs to build thematic units around essential questions and big ideas that provide in-depth study, not on frivolous, shallow topics.

Approaches to learning are the dispositions and learning styles of children which engage them in the activities that promote learning. Children who possess some or all of the approaches to learning find great lifelong learning success. Approaches to learning include: engagement, problem-solving, creativity and imagination, curiosity and initiative, and persistence. **Engagement** is demonstrated when a child actively engages in play as a

means of exploration and learning; interacts with a variety of materials in her play; uses "trial and error" methods to figure out a task or problem; and demonstrates an awareness of connections between prior and new knowledge. **Problem-solving** is identifying a problem and trying to solve it independently; attempting multiple ways to solve a problem; communicating more than one solution to a problem; and engaging with peers to solve problems. A child who is using their **creativity and imagination** uses materials and props in novel ways to represent ideas, characters, and objects. The child attains clarity in knowledge acquisition; communicates more than one solution to a problem; and seeks out assistance from peers and adults to complete a task. **Curiosity**

and initiative is demonstrated by asking questions, using the "6 w's and 1 h" – who, what, why, when, where, what if, and how; actively exploring how things "work"; investigating areas of interest; seeking out activities and materials that support curiosity; willingly engaging in new experiences and activities; and taking objects and materials apart and attempting to reassemble them. **Persistence** is maintaining focus on a task; seeking assistance when the next step appears unclear; and modifying strategies used to complete a task (NYSED, 2012).

Social-Emotional Development

From ages 3 to 5, children make great strides in their relationships with others and with themselves, as well as in their ability to understand and regulate their own emotions. Positive emotional and social development provide the framework for not only prosocial skill building, but for academic and cognitive growth (Raver, 2002). To support their development, children need caring and supportive adult relationships; these strong attachments assist the child in establishing positive attitudes and behaviors towards learning. Positive and encouraging experiences with adults in early learning settings and at home support a child's enthusiasm for learning and approaches to learning.

"Pre-School-U – Introduction to Social and Emotional Development"

Development of Self-Regulation

During the preschool years children are honing their self-regulation skills – the ability to plan, initiate, and complete an activity; delay gratification; maintain attention; control emotions and behaviors; and build positive social relations with others (NIEER, 2006). Three-year olds are gaining better control of their tantrums and uncontrolled outbursts. They still have conflicts over ownership of possessions, yet they are less likely to hit or bite. Four–year olds, though they are gaining control of their emotions and behavior, may use their developing language skills to intentionally offend their peers and hurt their feelings. This relational bullying can evolve into physical bullying by the end of preschool (Hanish et al., 2004). Aggression is often a common reaction in children with difficult temperaments or children who themselves have been victims of bullying and/or abuse (Copple & Bredekamp, 2009).

"Full House Clip – Michelle and Aaron pinch each other"

Building strong self-regulation skills is facilitated by the teacher through the classroom relationships that are formed, the set-up of the classroom environment, the learning opportunities, and the established guidelines for behavior. Positive relationships that children establish with their peers and teachers are an important influence on the development of self-regulation. Positive peer relationships can be fostered within a caring community of learners where cooperation is stressed. Child-adult relationships are built when the teacher treats students with dignity, communicates warmth and respect, and coaches students in expressing their frustration and anger appropriately. A well-organized classroom allows a student more independence, eliminates periods of wait time where children can lapse into challenging behavior, and allows the teacher to remain totally focused on the students. Rich, interesting learning opportunities engage students and pique their curiosity. By establishing clear guidelines and consequences for behavior, the teacher is communicating respect and caring for individual students, the community of learners, and their learning environment.

Development of Relationships and Friendships

The social world of the preschooler is widening from the world he or she lived in when he or she was an infant and toddler. Preschoolers form strong, enduring attachments to their teachers; these valuable relationships help to sustain the child's engagement and interest in learning and ensure the likelihood that the child will be socially competent in later years (Morrison, 2007). Preschoolers are also building friendships with their peers, although these budding relationships may have their share of conflict, particularly over ownership of objects. Children who have built their self-regulation skills are more likely to have an easier time building their friendships; they are more skilled at controlling their emotions, more skilled at resolving conflicts in nonaggressive ways, and they have a better understanding of others' feelings (Bredekamp, 2009).

"Teaching Moment: Social and Emotional Skills"

By building a "caring community of learners" the first day of preschool, early childhood educators create the connections with students by making them feel part of a supportive "classroom family". Teachers can model kind, caring, and respectful behavior and language. In classroom meetings, rituals and discussions provide openings for children to share their ideas and have them validated by their teacher and peers. Center-based and project learning in small groups contribute to the sense of communal problem-solving. Large blocks of time for play support interaction that builds strong, enduring friendships.

Development of Prosocial Behavior

Prosocial behavior is a concern for the well-being of others and the ability to share and maintain friendships with others by knowing how to communicate, share, and cooperate with others (Seefeldt, Castle, & Falconer, 2010). Because three-year olds can be very egocentric, they have difficulty taking another's perspective, thus they have difficulty sharing and cooperating with others. Yet as the child gets closer to their fourth birthday, they become more aware of their impact on others' feelings and emotions, and begin to develop the prosocial behavior of empathy (Beaty, 2008).

"Providing Opportunities to Practice Pro-Social Skills"

Often, school is the first occasion that three- and four-year olds will have to negotiate and use their emerging prosocial skills to get along with peers their own age. Young children have varying levels of prosocial skill; some preschool children are more prosocial than others. Preschoolers are learning appropriate responses in social  situations; they will frequently observe other children and adults to learn how to enter social groups and interact. Children with secure attachments with adults who make them aware of others' perspectives are more likely to be prosocial and considerate of their peers. Early childhood educators can create prosocial skill-building activities as part of the curriculum. Developing the skill of taking another's perspective can be structured into activities and the thoughtful choice of children's literature that can be shared and discussed.

The greatest gift a teacher can give students is a nurturing, responsive relationship with each child. Secure attachments provide the secure base from which children can develop positive peer relationships, engendering prosocial growth. Children who have warm, secure relationships with adults use the adults' interactions as models for prosocial skill-building. The secure relationship helps children become aware of others' distress and supports the children's empathy building (e.g., "Bobby, I think Sarah is missing her mom. Will you please take her over to the block corner and build the castle for our fairytale read aloud?"). Early childhood educators need to use modeled demonstrations to help children recognize their own emotions and what they signal, and then improve their ability to take the perspectives of others.

Development of Emotional Competence

Emotional regulation involves internal feelings, states, and emotion-related physical responses (Jalongo & Isenburg, 2012). Research shows that preschoolers' emotions – both positive and negative – serve important purposes, motivating each facet of development and learning (Saarni, 1999). Interest, curiosity, motivation, and pleasure are positive emotions which propel children in their exploration of the world. Conversely, sadness, anxiety, fear, and uncontrolled anger will hinder children from establishing relationships, cooperatively exploring problems, and building knowledge. Preschoolers are gaining better understanding and regulation of their emotions, the ability to more articulately voice their feelings, and a clearer sense of right and wrong (Copple & Bredekamp, 2009).

Most preschoolers are able to describe their and others' emotions through words, gestures, facial expressions, and artwork. They are also learning to express their emotions in increasingly acceptable ways. These emotional regulation skills build the foundation for school and lifetime success; children who cannot manage their negative emotions or who have difficulty understanding and responding positively to others' feelings are not as successful in school as those who are more emotionally competent (Raver, 2002). Parenting styles influence children's level of emotional regulation; warm, nurturing parents who support children in dealing with their emotions produce more emotionally competent children, while callous, rejecting parents and volatile home environments sabotage children's emotional growth (Saarni et al., 2006).

Establishing emotional security for a child is one of the most important jobs of an early childhood educator. A nurturing, consistent, and responsive relationship and a daily predictable routine can go far in promoting emotional competence. The classroom environment needs to be predictable, responsive, and flexible, while the curriculum needs to engage children, be based on student interest, and require cooperative learning. Educators assist

children in building emotional competence by helping them "use their words" to appropriately express themselves; curricula should also include read alouds and activities that help with children's emotional regulation skill-building.

Development of Resilience and Coping Skills

Stress is a body's way of rising to a challenge, preparing to meet a difficult situation with strength, focus, stamina, and keen alertness. Stress arises in children when they feel that a situation is more than they are capable of managing. The events that provoke stress are called **stressors**; humans respond to stressors with our behavior (the "fight or flight" response), our bodies (the release of adrenaline and cortisol which speed up the heart and breathing rates, blood pressure, and metabolism), and our feelings (anxiety or anger) (Gunnar, 2000).

"The Effects of Stress on a Child's Brain Development"

Preschoolers experience stress from several sources – insecure housing and food, parents' divorce, chronic illness, changing schools, etc. Children's stressful feelings that result can become overwhelming and if unsupported by responsive adults can result in long-lasting emotional problems (National Scientific Council on the Developing Child, 2010). Young children learn many coping skills to handle the stress in healthy ways; the adults in the child's life can aid in the development of effective coping skills by remaining sensitive and responsive and by providing secure, nurturing attachments. Sound relationships aid children in developing resilience to overcome the effects of many of the daunting stressors young children face.

Resilience helps humans to "overcome adversity with courage, skills, and faith" (Grotberg, 1993). Resilience is the ability to adapt to trauma, tragedy, threats, and significant stress. Resilience is important because it provides lifelong skills that allow a human to overcome the adversities of life. Resilient preschoolers have the ability to be autonomous, yet are able to ask for help when necessary (NAEYC, 2012).

Resilience is built by the presence of a nurturing, supportive adult (Copple & Bredekamp, 2009). Other factors are a positive sense of self-worth, the ability to think positively, the ability to think of alternative solutions to problems, and good communication skills (Haggerty et al.,1996). These skills can all be taught in a supportive preschool setting.

A close, nurturing relationship with the teacher can help shield the child from the negative effects of stress, particularly if the child is returning to a stressful home situation after her school day. Dramatic play, creative art, and **bibliotherapy** – the use of literature to help solve personal, emotional, or psychiatric problems – can all provide activities that teach coping skills. Adults can offer a listening ear, comfort, calming strategies, and positive responses to help children build their own coping strategies.

Utilizing Play as a Social Activity

Developing social relations is an important milestone for young children. Between the ages of 3 and 5, children begin to understand that the people around them – peers and adults – have feelings, yet in their egocentrism young children assume that these feelings are similar to their own. Dramatic play often reflects this level of development, yet it provides a valuable opportunity to build social skills. Social play provides a vehicle for children to interact with others and learn social skills; to learn how to compromise and resolve conflicts; and how adult roles are played.

"The Bakery – Supporting Children to Succeed in the Dramatic Play Center"

Three-year olds become "social animals" by showing increased interest in other children and adults, yet they often prefer to play alone or parallel to other children. As they approach their fourth birthday, children become increasingly capable of entering play groups and remaining involved in mature sociodramatic play. Four-year olds are gradually becoming adept at taking on more complex roles, and sustaining play with other children for longer periods of time (Bodrova & Leong, 2007). Along with the opportunity for experimenting with objects and roles that play provides, play provides scenarios that teach young children how to play cooperatively and fairly. Helping children understand sharing, taking turns, and being respectful to their peers is part of the early educator's job. Activities can be constructed to facilitate cooperative social skills, often with the thematic topic as the organizing focal point (e.g., learning how to work together in a pizza parlor can be part of a "Healthy Foods" unit).

Five-year-olds have developed more effective cooperative skills and are adept at getting along and playing with peers. Play activities usually occur in one-to-one situations or small groups; at this point children begin to show preferences for the children they want to play with. This is the beginning of the warmth of friendship-building and the hurt of social rejection. The teacher needs to continue to help children become sensitive to other children's feelings and develop respect for others.

Cognitive Development

Children's thinking during ages 3-5 is a combination of reality and fantasy; three-year olds have difficulty with thinking in terms of the past and future, but four-year olds begin to think beyond the "here and now". Three-year olds have good memories for events in the immediate past, but have difficulty recalling information over longer periods of time. With accrued experiences and increased memory, four-year olds are able to think about events that happened weeks ago and foresee what has not yet happened. The four-year old can usually recall and retell  main events in a story sequence. As well, young children can remember things if they have direct experience with what is being taught; this is the reason hands-on experiences with authentic materials are essential.

One of the most significant shifts in thought that occurs from age three to age four is the development of symbolic thought – the ability to symbolically represent concrete objects, actions, and events (Piaget, 1952). Four-year olds are able to take a concept or idea and create elaborate play scenarios using objects to represent the imaginary people and items in their play.

"Early Childhood Cognitive Development"

Preschoolers are in the preoperational stage of cognitive development. In this stage, children are using more symbolic thought, are centering on one thought or idea at a time, and relying solely on the concrete appearance of objects, thus, often thinking illogically (Piaget, 1969). A good example of children's thinking in this stage is demonstrated in Piaget's example of conservation of number. A child looks at two rows of cups – the top row has the cups placed further apart than the bottom row. When asked which row has more cups, the child says the top row has more, because the row is longer. The child makes his decision based on the appearance of the rows of cups and doesn't pay attention to the logic of counting the number of cups.

"Piaget's Preoperational Stage: Conservation"

Preschoolers' thinking and reasoning are concrete; young children at this age reason from the particular to the particular (Siegler, 1997). For instance, four-year old Emma loves spaghetti, so everyone she knows must love spaghetti. Organization of information into concepts is based on attributes that classify the object or an idea. The categories that define concepts or ideas arise from the appearance or action of the object. Emma calls a lamb a "dog" because the lamb fits all the criteria of a dog: furry, small, and having four legs. At this age, children can sort objects based on only one attribute – size, shape, or color, for example. The ability to sort by more than one attribute develops between ages 4 and 6. Three- and four-year old children ask many "why" questions stemming from their compelling need to find out about their world.

Executive Function

Executive function is a broad term for cognitive processes that regulate, control, and manage other cognitive processes such as attention, memory, planning, problem-solving, and reasoning. The prefrontal cortex is responsible for control over emotions and for focused attention, planning and monitoring cognitive processes (Bodrova & Leong, 2006). Preschool children's executive function is a strong predictor of their later academic success (Blair & Razza, 2007). As pre-school children are given the opportunity and practice in activities where the cognitive processes of executive function are utilized, young children's skills will improve.

"Executive Function: Skills for Life and Learning"

Attention is vital to the learning process as this skill directs the learner's concentration on the information needed to successfully complete a task. The ability to filter out extraneous information, and concentrate for periods of time enhances a child's academic and problem-solving skills (Murphy et al. 2007). Three-year olds have incredibly short attention spans, however as children mature and gain experience through activities that require longer periods of attentiveness, their attention becomes more sustained. To build longer attention spans, the knowledgeable early childhood educator ensures large blocks of time for children to play and explore. The educator is

also responsible for providing props, space, and engaging ideas for the play and content area exploration; this guarantees that the learning is purposeful and directed toward building attentiveness.

Memory is the process by which information is stored and then retrieved. Memory requires that we maintain information over short (short-term memory) and long periods of time (long-term memory). Retrieval of stored information requires the mind to locate it and bring it forward to our consciousness. Four-year old pre-schoolers can learn simple memory strategies such as **mnemonics** – a learning technique that translates information into a form that the brain can retain and remember better – with repeated opportunity and scaffolding to practice them (Berk, 2016). However, young children are not developmentally ready to use the strategies effectively. Four-year olds can group the objects and the ideas they have had experience with into categories (e.g., grouping the play food in the housekeeping corner into breakfast food and lunch food). The important thing for educators to remember is that young children gain memory strategies from hands-on experiences. It is important that pre-schoolers are given opportunities for active involvement in their learning. This demands a well-planned environment, intentionally planned and diverse activities that facilitate learning across all the domains and all content areas, and engaging materials that motivate children to explore.

Planning is one of the **metacognitive activities** – activities that require children to think and reflect about their own learning – necessary for building higher-level thinking. Planning entails children making intentional choices and identifying goals, weighing all the options for achieving goals, making predictions, and anticipating consequences (Epstein, 2003). If planning is the prologue of metacognition, then **reflection** is the epilogue. Reflection is the analysis and recall of the planned events (Epstein, 2003).

Reflection – also known as **debriefing** – is a teaching strategy in which the teacher supports children in remembering what they accomplished and learned, what was interesting and successful, how they felt about their learning, and what they can do to extend and elaborate on the experience (Bredekamp, 2011). The High/Scope strategy, **Plan-Do-Review**, is an approximately 90-minute metacognitive sequence in which children plan what they want to do during work time, carry out the activity, and then review and reflect upon the activity.

When children engage in planning, they actively use their minds to plan, initiate, and problem-solve. Educators can make planning a routine classroom activity at morning meetings. Planning can be done with the whole group, small groups, pairs, or individually; whatever the format, each child needs to be able to express their ideas fully. For more shy children or children with little experience planning, the teacher will need to use effective questioning and scaffolding to elicit their ideas. Writing down children's plans and ideas validate their thinking and demonstrate respect for young children as learners. Older four-year old children may be able to write some of their own ideas with phonetic spelling and/or pictures (Epstein, 2003).

Problem-solving is another metacognitive strategy that can be taught in a structured format – the **scientific method** – which involves beginning with a hypothesis, testing it, observing and gathering data, and then confirming or rejecting the initial hypothesis. Utilizing this strategy, pre-schoolers can activate their schema, while deepening their understanding of concepts. When children explain their thinking, their understanding is deepened (Marzano et al., 2001). The scientific method is not designed just for the science content area, but can be applied to all content areas such as social studies, art, and block-building. For example, the teacher can pose a problem such as "How will we be able to take care of our polar bears in our block corner zoo? What will the polar bears need? Use the materials in your block corner and your art center to find a solution to the problem."

"Preschool Problem Solving"

Reasoning is having the capacity to make sense of things by establishing and verifying facts, to come to a conclusion or find a result. Reasoning precedes and develops from problem-solving; it necessitates taking another's perspective, which is very difficult for egocentric pre-schoolers. Three-year olds do not have this capability, but a four-year old child is able to take a different perspective, to a limited degree. Pre-schoolers think in concrete terms and focus on the observable traits of an object; logical reasoning entails using abstract concepts such as time and space – concepts young children do not yet possess. However, young children do have some ability to reason when the tasks are simple and relevant to their daily lives (Berk, 2008).

Reasoning is often associated with mathematical thinking; mathematical understanding includes numbers and operations, geometry, spatial relations, measurement and data. The processes of problem-solving and reasoning encompass all of these mathematical operations. The skill of reasoning comes with a great deal of practice and support. That adult support comes from well thought out cues, focused questioning, direct instruction and scaffolding. The **gradual release of responsibility** model is very effective in teaching/learning across the content areas, but it is especially useful in teaching mathematical reasoning. In this model, the teacher initially takes on the responsibility for the instruction/learning through direct instruction and modeling. Then gradually through guided practice, independent practice, and meaningful application, the teacher releases the responsibility for learning to the child, until eventually the child can succeed on their own.

Utilizing Play as a Cognitive Activity

One of the most important things that expert early childhood educators do to promote children's learning and development is to plan large blocks of time for play and exploration. The interconnectedness of learning is embodied in sociodramatic play – social and language development is used in play to stimulate cognitive growth, while cognitive development fosters social and language skills. Play also provides a venue for building attentiveness, memory, planning, problem-solving, reasoning, and self-regulation.

Froebel believed in the power of play for cognitive growth, using his gifts and occupations. Montessori designed concrete materials for children to engage with to build cognitive development. Piaget's theory purports that play is a cognitive process and is the way children develop the ability to use symbols to understand their world (Piaget, 1952). Piaget believed that children can only learn the physical properties of objects by playing and manipulating them; through play, children begin to build schema  about the characteristics of objects and ideas. Vygotsky (1978) believed that play leads development; that the rules and roles of dramatic play build self-regulation, attentiveness to the play format, and negotiation with peers. Vygostsky theorized that children at play are functioning at the highest level of their zone of proximal development as they are functioning independently and challenging themselves in their learning.

Some of the ways that early childhood educators can promote preschool children's cognitive development through play (Seefeldt & Wasik, 2006):

- Offer open-ended materials that children can control and experiment with in multiple ways. Make sure that children have large blocks of time to use their senses to experiment with, label, classify, and describe objects and ideas.

- Use hands-on activities so that children can be actively involved in their learning. Through these activities children build schema – mental concept files – about the materials they are manipulating.
- Use children's familiar experiences on which to build novel and challenging activities. For example, allow children to use familiar 2-dimensional shapes with newly introduced 2- and 3-dimensional shapes to create interesting designs.
- Scaffold tasks by modeling and direct instruction, and then allow children the opportunity for guided and independent practice.
- Provide a literacy-rich environment to engage and motivate children. Begin units of study with enchanting read alouds of fiction and informational texts. Supply children with literature and writing materials as well as a well-stocked art center.
- Provide for the involvement of children with special needs. Make sure materials and space are flexible to accommodate the needs of all your students. Offer sufficient materials for all children and structure activities that require groups of children to collaborate.

Teacher Role in Play

The teacher has to assume a balanced role in children's play; if the teacher is too involved or not involved enough in the play, there can be a negative effect. If the teacher is too involved, the children will be intimidated and withdraw from the play; if the teacher is not vigilant enough, the play may become mindless, raucous, and with little purpose. The delicate balance requires a teacher who can serve as either the person who leads the play, plays with the children, or sets the stage for learning by playing.

"The Teacher's Role in Play"

The play leader helps children who are having difficulty initiating the play. He or she will give children ideas for play scenarios, roles, and rules for carrying out the play. The play leader is also responsible for posing thought-provoking questions that elicit further reflection and exploration. The co-player acts as an equal partner in the play and usually takes the minor player's role so that the children can take the lead in the play. As a co-player, the teacher can model how to enter a play group, how to maintain a play role, the language that should be used, and taking turns. As the person who sets the stage for the learning, the teacher is responsible for providing time, space, and props;

for suggesting ideas and concepts for the play; for integrating the curriculum into the play to achieve learning outcomes; and then to step away and allow the play to flourish (Bredekamp, 2011).

Many educators plan curriculum based on the assumption that all children come to pre-school knowing how to engage in pretend play. This is a misunderstanding of many parents and educators. Many children from low income as well as some middle-income homes are inexperienced in rich, productive pretend play; the role of the teacher is to coach children, and model and scaffold appropriate pretend play. No matter what role the teacher is taking she is responsible for providing a healthy and safe environment with plenty of high quality materials that are appropriate for the development of the children and tailored to the specific play setting. Additionally, the play should be free of cultural and gender stereotypes.

Language and Literacy Development

For three- and four-year olds, this is a time of great growth in language and emergent literacy skill. Vocabulary acquisition is exploding, and semantics and syntax are becoming more complex, conveying more precise communication than that of toddlers. These advances have a substantial impact on development across the domains of learning – social, emotional, and cognitive. For instance, language development is necessary for emergent literacy development while a  literacy-rich environment fosters higher levels of language. Language can be defined very broadly as any system of symbols that is used to transmit meaning. For our purposes, we will use the school-based definition of language and literacy – oral language is communicating via speaking and listening, and literacy is reading and writing (communicating through print).

Important language skills include **receptive language** – the language a person is able to comprehend in reading and listening, **expressive language** – the language that a person is able to produce. Language includes **phonology** – the sound system of language (the smallest unit of sound is a **phoneme**), **morphology** – the smallest unit of meaning in language, **syntax** – the grammar of a language, **semantics** – word meanings and vocabulary, and **pragmatics** – the conventions, such as intonation, that enable one to become a competent language user.

Language

Three-year olds have acquired approximately 900 to 1,000 words; they can clearly produce three- and four-word sentences. Three-year olds can express their needs and feelings verbally, while responding to a variety of questions. They also ask a great deal

of questions often responding to the answers they are given, with multiple "whys". Three-year olds are beginning to use correct grammar if the structure follows regular syntactical rules.

Four-year olds experience a steep trajectory of language development. Their vocabulary contains 4,000 to 6,000 words and they can easily put five to six words into sentences that are for the most part grammatically correct. In part, because four-year olds have such an extensive vocabulary, they are extremely talkative as they experiment with language.

"Small Group Oral Language Sample for Early Childhood Education"

Language is directly connected to levels of cognition; Vygotsky (1978) believed that language is a "tool" for "verbal mediation" – labeling objects and concepts –which leads to thought. Another way that children use language as a mediator is in their private speech – the use of language to think out loud or to regulate one's behavior. As a child matures, their private speech helps plan and implement their work; at its highest level, private speech is internalized and used silently to plan ahead and manage actions and behaviors(Vygotsky, 1978).

**"How to Talk to Your Child:
The Best Strategies for Effective Communication"**

Influences on Language Development

Preschool children's language acquisition is rooted in the environments in which children live and interact – home, and preschool or childcare settings. Language competence is shaped considerably by children's environment and experiences. Research supports the importance of supportive, language-prolific contexts – homes and schools/childcare. Educare providers can carry out much of the same strategies with young children in their settings.

The importance of parent and care provider interactions and the quality and quantity of language in home contexts has been widely documented (Beals,

2001; Hart & Risley, 1995; Heath, 1983). Parents/care providers foster the child's language development through effective scaffolding within the child's zone of proximal development. Scaffolding is accomplished when the parents/care providers engage the child in verbal tasks which he cannot perform independently. Parents/care providers modify the amount of help they provide and gradually decrease the assistance until the child is engaging successfully and independently. Scaffolding can occur in tasks such as problem-solving, shared reading and writing, conversations, and daily routines. Verbal exchange can be scaffolded through questioning, expansion, and extension of the language.

Conversation offers an opportunity to build give-and-take skills that are important for effective conversation, to enrich vocabulary that fosters cognitive development, and to build schema about experiences and concepts. Vocabulary building can emanate from in-depth study of interesting topics, and from project work and play. Early childhood educators need to intentionally build vocabulary by introducing new words every day and encouraging children to use the new vocabulary in conversations. Conversation also provides the opportunity to model correct grammar to assist children in self-correcting the speech errors they often make.

For children whose first language is not English, the goal of English proficiency acquisition is critical. However, it is equally important to provide support for maintaining and advancing the home language at the same time the child is acquiring English (Espinosa, 2008). Quality bilingual programs are most effective in closing the achievement gap between English speakers and ELL's (Espinosa, 2008). The pre-school program needs to be respectful of culturally and linguistically diverse children, their families, and their communities. Educators need to forge strong partnerships with all families, yet it becomes paramount that these partnerships are strengthened with the parents of English Language Learners. Educators need to encourage families to speak to, read to, and teach children in their home language. Honoring and using the home language in the classroom enriches the lives of all children (Barnett et al., 2007).

Literacy

Literacy instruction has been a debated topic in the past few decades; two basic approaches – emergent literacy and scientifically-based reading approach – have had their passionate proponents, arguing for their respective philosophies of effective literacy instruction

Emergent literacy is the view that children begin learning about reading and writing at a young age by observing and interacting with adults and other children as they use literacy in everyday life activities (Vukelich, Christie, & Enz, 2010,). It is a meaning-centered perspective based on children's observations and activities; children can construct their own conceptual knowledge about the functions and structure of print.

Eventually with repeated opportunities engaging in meaningful literacy activities, interactions with adults and peers, and some appropriate instruction, children become proficient readers and writers. A program based on emergent literacy includes:

- Frequent read alouds of fiction and informational texts
- Shared reading of big books to build concepts about print
- Shared writing
- Thematic units that integrate literacy with content knowledge
- A print-rich classroom
- Hands-on small group center time

"Teaching Emerging Literacy"

Scientifically-based reading approach is a skills-based approach that has identified a core of knowledge and skills that children need to become successful readers (Snow, Burns, & Griffin, 1998). These skills include: oral language including vocabulary development, phonological awareness, alphabet knowledge, print awareness, book concepts, and sight word recognition. Research has shown that strength in these areas is positively correlated with reading ability in later years, and that explicit, systematic instruction increases these core early literacy skills (National Early Literacy Panel, 2008). Instruction can occur in whole- or small-groups; instruction can be through games and activities using the gradual release of responsibility model of direct instruction/modeling, guided practice, and independent practice.

Balanced approach incorporates the belief in offering boundless literacy opportunities with the guidance and instruction from teachers. This approach includes a print-rich classroom, daily read alouds of fiction and informational text, projects, shared writing, center-based instruction combined with direct instruction and practice on basic language and literacy skills. The balanced approach offers the best aspects of emergent literacy and the scientifically-based reading approach. Most pre-school early literacy curricula are blended programs utilizing large-group (circle) time, small group center time, and small group instructional time (Vukelich, Christie, & Enz, 2010). Early childhood educators carefully plan and implement the meaningful activities and lessons that combine emergent literacy and the scientifically-based reading approach.

The goal for three- and four-year old is to have opportunities to "explore their environment and build the foundations for learning to read and write" (Neuman, Copple, & Bredekamp, 2000). Children do this by:

- Listening to and discussing storybooks
- Engaging in reading and writing attempts
- Participating in rhyming games, finger-plays, and chants
- Playing in literacy-based centers such as a fishing pond where children "fish" for alphabet letters or sight words
- Understanding that print carries a message and daily participating in activities such as morning message
- Identifying labels and signs in their print-rich environment
- Identifying some letter and letter-sound matches
- Using known letters or approximations of letters to represent written language (Seefeldt & Wasik, 2006, p. 216)

Influences on Literacy Development

Language development is foundational to literacy development. The babbling and cooing of the infant lead to oral language which uses words and then sentences. Children learn language from interactions with the peers and adults around them; it is important that the adults in their world answer children's questions, rephrasing and elaborating on children's utterances, modeling complex sentences, and asking questions that need children to respond (Seefeldt & Wasik, 2006).

One of the most important predictors of literacy acquisition is language development (Otto, 2010). The words and sentences children hear and use set the stage for phonemic awareness, phonics usage, vocabulary, fluency and comprehension. Four-year olds, with rich language experiences and access to literacy experiences develop skills such as phonemic awareness.

Phonemic awareness development is the understanding that words are made up of sounds that can be manipulated. The phoneme is the smallest unit of speech; for example, "cat" has 3 phonemes – /k/ /a/ /t/. Children who are proficient in phonemic awareness can segment words into their phonemes, can blend and substitute phonemes, are able to rhyme words, and understand words that sound the same. This is not the same as phonics awareness; children can be aware of the sounds in words without knowing the letter-name.

Important findings about phonemic awareness:

- Children as young as three-years old can possess phonemic awareness skills (Maclean, Bryant, & Bradley, 1987), but typically phonemic awareness is a four- and five-year old skill.
- Phonemic awareness is highly predictive of success in learning to read, particularly in decoding words (Snow, Burns, & Griffin, 1998).
- Opportunities to play with language in the context of natural play support phonemic awareness development (Yopp & Yopp, 2000).

Nursery rhymes, poems, tongue twisters, and choral reading of predictable text all promote phonemic awareness development.

Family literacy creates a firm foundation of language and literacy development. Research confirms that a family's role in the child's language and literacy development is correlated with the child's communication competence, positive attitudes toward reading and writing, and literacy achievement (Hart & Risley, 1995). Home literacy studies have identified several factors that contribute to a child's early literacy acquisition:

- Adult modeling of literacy behaviors. Children need to observe family members using literacy in everyday activities such as writing shopping lists, reading the newspaper, and completing crossword puzzles. Children begin to see the practical applications of reading and writing in daily living (Otto, 2010).
- Access to print and books. Plentiful supplies of children's books have been linked to early reading and positive attitudes toward schooling (Nord et al.,1999).
- Storybook reading is positively correlated with language growth, reading achievement, and early literacy (Otto, 2010).
- Children need supportive adults who answer their questions; read storybooks daily; point out print in the environment; take children to the library; provide children with a wide variety of experiences such as trips to parks, the post office, and museums; and share literacy activities (Hart & Risley, 1995).

"Family Literacy"

Learning how to proficiently read and write necessitates a solid base of language and literacy skills as well as conceptual development; early childhood educators need to provide both skill-building opportunities in the areas of: phonemic awareness, phonics understanding, vocabulary, fluency, and comprehension, and content building through read alouds, artifacts which can be manipulated, field trips, and hands-on activities. Purposeful, engaging projects and investigations provide opportunities for children to expand and apply their knowledge.

Physical and Motor Development

Pre-schoolers are extremely active little human beings – they are in perpetual motion. As they grow, pre-schoolers are developing and refining their gross and fine motor skills. Physical development follows a relatively predictable sequence, yet some variation exists, particularly in the pace of development. Physical growth can be sporadic and uneven; sometimes development is in spurts, while at other times development is steady and incremental. Gender differences are often apparent, with girls being more advanced in fine motor skills and gross motor skills which require precision such as skipping and hopping; boys' strengths are in gross motor skills that require force and power, such as jumping and running (Berk, 2016).

Children this age need physical activity throughout the day to burn off excess energy in order to remain focused on more structured tasks. Additionally, physical activity and healthy lifestyles are connected; regular physical activity helps children:

- Build and maintain healthy bones, muscles, and joints
- Control weight
- Build lean muscle and reduce fat
- Prevent or delay the development of high blood pressure (AHA, 2008)

Fine motor skills refers to accuracy and control of small muscle movement such as those needed to pick up things, to write, to cut with scissors, and to use a keyboard. Fine motor skills allow children to dress themselves, manipulate small objects, and explore how things work. Strength is needed for many of these tasks, as well as control and coordination of hands, fingers and wrists. Most paper-pencil activities are inappropriate for three- and four-year old children. Fine motor skills are most effectively built through activities such as working with clay, building block structures, manipulating small objects, using scissors, stringing beads, etc.

Gross Motor Development

Three-year olds are gaining control of their large muscle coordination through daily activities; the skills of running, climbing, and jumping are becoming more automatic and

coordinated. Three-year olds have an increased awareness of their own abilities so they are more understanding of potentially unsafe behaviors, although they can still lose self-control (Bredekamp, 2011). When they do fall down, three-year olds quickly jump back up and try again. Children this age, ride tricycles but have difficulty coordinating their feet to pedal; they are progressing in their ability to walk up stairs using alternating feet, yet walking downstairs using alternating feet is a challenge.

Four-year olds are becoming even more coordinated; they can run, stop, and change direction with greater control. With growth, four-year olds' center of gravity is lower to the ground, providing stability, balance and a sense of equilibrium. They enjoy hopping and skipping, and are more accurately throwing and catching a ball. Children this age enjoy pedaling tricycles and some are even starting to ride two-wheelers with training wheels.

"Early Childhood Gross Motor Development"

Fine Motor Development

Three-year olds can sit attentively for a period of time, particularly if they are interested in the activity. They are happiest when they are actively engaged in interesting activities. Three-year olds' hands and fingers are gaining more strength and control; children this age still have some difficulty manipulating small objects so large block play is more satisfying than working with small objects like Legos. Children this age can successfully dress themselves yet they have some trouble with buttoning, zipping, and tying. Three-year olds usually exhibit a preference for one hand, although they sometimes switch hands for certain tasks, like coloring. Children are more comfortable coloring and writing with oversized crayons and pencils, and cutting with scissors can be a challenge (Seefeldt & Wasik, 2006).

Four-year olds are high-energy and are beginning to demonstrate increased impulse control. Four-year olds are advancing in their fine motor strength, control, and coordination. They are able to complete board and floor puzzles, cut simple shapes and lines with scissors, dress themselves completely (although tying is still a challenge for most four-year olds), are beginning to copy letters and numbers correctly, and enjoy coloring and painting. Four-year olds' ability to write their name can vary from writing only one letter to writing their name completely; grasping and holding the pencil is challenging for many children this age.

Three- and four-year olds love the challenge of fine motor skills, but their manual dexterity is limited. Many of the skills mentioned above are difficult for children this age and they may experience frustration if they are pushed to perform tasks that are not developmentally appropriate (e.g., precise letter and number writing). Instead, pre-schoolers need opportunities to participate in open-ended activities that develop fine motor skills and small muscles in their hands, fingers, and wrists. These activities can include working with clay; easel and finger painting; stringing beads; drawing; and cutting and constructing. Early childhood educators need to provide children with materials, large blocks of time, and encouragement in practicing and refining their fine motor skills.

"Early Childhood Fine Motor"

Children develop many motor skills through play and exploration, but direct instruction is also needed and can be implemented through planned activities that embody verbal instructions and modeling. Educators need to be sensitive to individual developmental levels and the interests of the children. In addition, early childhood educators need to alternate activities that require sitting and listening with those that allow unstructured physical activity and hands-on moving and exploring. Pre-school children need daily opportunities to manipulate materials and objects, exploring and learning through their senses. They also need at least 120 minutes of structured and unstructured large motor activity every day (National Association for Sport and Physical Education, 2002).

Gross motor skills can include taking observation walks inside and outside, moving to music, walking a balance beam, jumping on a trampoline, and building with large blocks. Outdoor activities are important for both the development of gross motor skills and to ensure that children acquire a lifelong commitment to healthy living. Outdoor equipment should be matched to the development of young children, needs to be varied in skill level, with strict adherence to safety regulations.

Fine motor skills can be fostered through abundant opportunities to use appropriate tools with adult support and supervision. Scaffolding children's skill-building is most efficient when the teacher knows the capabilities (ZPD) of each child. Pre-schoolers need small objects to sort and count; clothing to zip, tie, and button; scissors, paint, and clay; dolls and dollhouses; drawing and writing materials; and a well-stocked housekeeping corner where children can pour, open and close jars, and set the table (Copple & Bredekamp, 2009).

Summary

- Early childhood educators, parents, and society at large view exceptional preschool education as the foundation of success; these years are recognized as a vitally important period of learning and development, not just a time to "get ready" for learning.

- Universal preschool is the beginning of public school therefore there is greater involvement of the public schools and increased alignment of curriculum and learning standards.

- As the field of early education changes dramatically, so do the skills and knowledge associated with it. To meet the challenge of the changing field, there has been an increased emphasis on making sure teachers receive college degrees in early childhood education and/or child development (NAEYC, 2005).

- Positive emotional and social development provide the framework for not only prosocial skill building, but for academic and cognitive growth (Raver, 2002). To support their development, children need caring and supportive adult relationships; these strong attachments assist the child in establishing positive attitudes and behaviors towards learning.

- The interconnectedness of learning is embodied in sociodramatic play – social and language development is used in play to stimulate cognitive growth, while cognitive development fosters social and language skills. Play also provides a venue for building attentiveness, memory, planning, problem-solving, reasoning, and self-regulation.

- Preschool children's language and emergent literacy acquisition are rooted in the environments in which children live and interact – home, and preschool or childcare settings.

- Children develop many of their motor skills through play and exploration, but direct instruction is also needed and can be implemented through planned activities that embody verbal instructions and modeling.

Key Terms

alignment
bibliotherapy
curriculum integration
emergent literacy
executive function
fine motor development
Gradual Release of Responsibility
gross motor development
metacognition
mnemonic
phonemic awareness
prosocial behavior
resilience
scientific method
social justice
stressor

Suggested Readings

Berk, L.E. (2016). *Infants and toddlers: Prenatal through middle childhood* (8th Ed.) Boston, MA: Pearson/Allyn & Bacon.

Epstein, A.S. (2009). *Me, you, us: Social-emotional learning in preschool.* Ypsilanti, MI: HighScope Educational Research Foundation.

Roskos, K.A., Tabors, P.O., & Lenhart, L.A. (2009). *Oral language and early literacy in preschool: Talking, reading, and writing* (2nd Ed.). Newark, DE: International Reading Association.

Suggested Websites

International Association for the Child's Right to Play
www.ipausa.org

National Center for Family Literacy
www.famlit.org

Pre-K Now – A website dedicated to the advancement of high-quality pre-kindergarten for all preschool-age children.
www.preknow.org

Reflections

1. Listen to parent-child interactions – in the grocery store, on the bus, at the playground, at the doctor's office. How do parents talk to their children? Do they respond with extended answers? Do they initiate the conversation? Do they "hush"

children when the child initiates the conversation? How does the child react? In your opinion, what is the effect of the quantity and quality of parents' interactions on their child's language development?

2. Observe a preschool classroom for a half-day. How much time do children spend in whole group, small group, learning centers, routines and transitions? Describe how children's time is used. Reflect on "teachable moments" that were maximized, and/or missed opportunities for teaching and learning.

3. Observe a preschool classroom. What evidence of social-emotional learning do you observe? What happens when children have difficulty sharing or playing cooperatively? How does the teacher teach prosocial skills? Reflect on "teachable moments" that were maximized, and/or missed opportunities for teaching and learning social-emotional skills.

4. Review the NAEYC program accreditation standards on health (www.naeyc.org/accreditation). What are your responsibilities as a teacher in meeting these standards and how important are they in keeping children safe and healthy in early childhood settings?

References

AHA (American Heart Association). (2008). *Exercise (physical activity) and children* *http://www.americanheart.org*

Barnett, W. S. (2003). Better teachers, better preschools: Student achievement linked to teacher qualifications. *Preschool Policy Matters, 2.* New Brunswick, NJ: National Institute for Early Education Research.

Barnett, W. S., Yarosz, D., Thomas, J., Jung, K. & Blanco, D. (2007). *Two-way and monolingual English immersion in preschool education: An experiment comparison.* New Brunswick, NJ: National Institute for Early Education Research.

Beals, D. (2001). Eating and reading: Links between family conversations with preschoolers and later language and literacy. In D. Dickenson & P. Tabors (Eds.). *Beginning literacy with language: Young children learning at home and school* (pp. 75-92). Baltimore: Paul H. Brookes.

Beaty, J. (2008). *Observing development of the young child* (7th ed.). Upper Saddle River, NJ: Pearson/Merrill/Prentice Hall.

Berk, L. E. (2016). *Infants and children* (8th ed.). Boston, MA: Allyn & Bacon.

Berreuta-Clement, J. R., Schweinhart, L. J., Barnett, W. S., Epstein, A. S. & Weikart, D. P. (1984). *Changed lives: The effects of the Perry preschool program on youths through age 19.* Ypsilanti, MI: High/Scope Press.

Blair, C. & Razza, R. C. (2007). Relating effortful control, executive functional and false belief understanding to emerging math and literacy ability in kindergarten. *Child Development, 78*(2), 647-663.

Bodrova, E. & Leong, D. J. (2007). *Tools of the mind: The Vygotskian approach to early childhood education* (2nd ed.). Upper Saddle River, NJ: Pearson/Merrill Prentice Hall.

Bredekamp, S. (2011). *Effective practices in early childhood education: Building a foundation.* Upper Saddle River, NJ: Pearson Education.

CCSSO. (2012). http://www.corestandards.org

Copple, C. & Bredekamp, S. (2009). *Developmentally appropriate practice in early childhood programs* (3rd Ed.). Washington, DC: National Association for the Education of Young Children.

Edelman, P. (2012). *So rich, so poor: Why it's so hard to end poverty in America. NY: The New Press.*

Epstein, A. S. (2003). How planning and reflections develop young children's thinking skills. *Young Children, 58*(5), 28-36.

Espinosa, L. M. (2008). English language learners as they enter school. In *School readiness and the transition to kindergarten in the era of accountability.* R. C. Pianta, M. J. Cox, & K. L. Snow (Eds.). Baltimore: Paul H. Brookes.

Foundation for Child Development. (2008). *America's vanishing potential: The case for pre-k-3rd education.* New York: Foundation for Child Development.

Galinsky, E. (2006). *The economic benefits of high-quality early childhood programs: What makes the difference?* Washington, DC: Committee for Economic Development.

Grotberg, E., (1993) Promoting resilience in children: A new approach. *The Ahfad Journal 10*(2), 5-14.

Gunnar, M. R. (2000). Early adversity and the development of stress reactivity and regulation. In *Minnesota symposium on child psychology. Vol. 31. The effects of adversity on neurobehavioral development.* C. A. Nelson (Ed.). 163-200. Mahwah, NJ: Lawrence Erlbaum.

Haggerty, J. Sherrod, L. R., Garmezy, N. & Rutter, M. (1996). *Stress, risk and resilience in children and adolescents – processes, mechanisms, and interventions.* Cambridge, UK: Cambridge University Press.

Hanish, L. D., Kochenderfer-Ladd, B., Fabes, R. A., Martin, C.L. & Denning, D. (2004). Bullying among young children: The influence of peers and teachers. In *Bullying in American schools: A social ecological perspective on prevention and intervention.* In D. L. Espelage & S. M. Swearer, (Eds.). 141-160. Mahwah: NJ: Lawrence Erlbaum.

Hart, B. & Risley, T. R. (1995). *Meaningful differences in the everyday experience of young American children.* Baltimore: Brookes.

Heath, S. B. (1983). *Ways with words: Language, life, and work in communities and classrooms.* Boston: Cambridge University Press.

Heckman, J. http://www.heckmanequation.org.

Jalongo, M. R. & Isenberg, J. P. (2012). *Exploring your role in early childhood education.* Upper Saddle River, NJ: Pearson Education.

Lee, V. E., & Burkam, D. T. (2002). *Inequality at the starting gate: Social background differences in achievement as children begin school.* New York: Economic Policy Institute.

Maclean, M., Bryant, P. & Bradley, L. (1987). Rhymes, nursery rhymes, and reading in early childhood. *Merrill-Palmer Quarterly, 33*(3), 255-281.

Marzano, R. J., Pickering, D. J., & Pollock, J. E. (2001). *Classroom instruction that works: Research-based strategies for increasing student achievement.* Alexandria, VA: Association for Supervision and Curriculum Development.

Merriam Webster (2012). http://www.merriam-webster.com

Morrison, F. J. (2007). *Contemporary perspectives on children's engagement in learning.* Symposium presented at the biennial meeting of the Society for Research in Child Development, March 29-April 1, Boston, MA.

Morrison, G. S., (2012). *Early childhood education today.* Upper Saddle River, NJ: Pearson Education.

Murphy, L. M. B., Laurie-Rose, C., Brinkman, T. M., & McNamara, K. A.(2007). S Sustained attention and social competence in typically developing preschool-aged children. *Early Child Development and Care, 177*(2), 133-149.

National Association for Sport and Physical Education. (2002). *Active start: A statement of physical activity guidelines for children birth to five years* (2nd ed.). Reston, VA: National Association for Sport and Physical Education.

National Association for the Education of Young Children. (2005). *NAEYC Early Childhood Program Standards and Accreditation Criteria: The mark of quality In early childhood education.* Washington, DC: NAEYC.

National Association for the Education of Young Children. (2009). *NAEYC Standards for Early Childhood Professional Preparation Programs.* Washington DC: NAEYC.

National Center for Children in Poverty, (2015). *United States early childhood profile.* Retrieved January 10, 2017, from http://www.nccp.org/profiles

National Early Literacy Panel. (2008). *Developing early literacy: Report of the National Early literacy panel. A scientific synthesis of early literacy development and implications for intervention.* Washington, DC: National Early Literacy Panel.

National Institute for Early Education Research. (2006). Executive function: A critical skill for preschoolers. *Preschool Matters, 4*(5). Retrieved December 26, 2012, at http://www.nieer.org/psm

National Institute for Early Education Research. (2014). Cost of providing quality preschool education to America's 3- and 4-year olds. Retrieved January 10, 2017, at http://www.nieer.org/psm

National Scientific Council on the Developing Child. (2010). *Persistent fear and anxiety can affect young children's learning and development: Working paper no. 9.* Retrieved January 25, 2013, from http://www.developingchild.harvard.edu

Neuman, S. B. (Ed.). (2008). *Educating the other America: Top experts tackle poverty, literacy, and achievement in our schools.* Baltimore: Paul H. Brookes.

Neuman, S. B., Copple, C., & Bredekamp, S.(Eds.). (2006). *Learning to read and write: Developmentally appropriate practices for young children.* Washington, DC: NAEYC.

New York State Education Department (NYSED). (2012). http://www.nysed.gov/commoncore/

Nord, C., Lennon, J., Liu, D., & Chandler, K. (1999). *Home literacy activities and signs of children's emergent literacy, 1993-1999.* U.S. Department of Education, Office of Educational Research and Improvement.

Piaget, J. (1952). *The origins of intelligence in children.* New York: International Universities Press.

Piaget, J. (1969). *The mechanisms of perception.* London: Rutledge & Kegan Paul.

Raver, C. C. (2002). *Emotions matter: Making the case for the role of young children's emotional development for early school readiness.* Ann Arbor, MI: Society for Research in Child Development.

Saarni, C. (1999). *The development of emotional competence.* New York: Guilford.

Saarni, C, Campos, J.J., Camras, L. & Witherington, D. (2006). Emotional Development: Action, communication, and understanding. In *Handbook of child psychology, Vol. 3: Social, emotional, and personality development,* (6th ed.). N. Eisenberg (Ed.), 226-249. New York: John Wiley & Sons.

Schweinhart, L. J., Barnes, H. V., & Weikart, D. P., (1993). *Significant benefits: The High/Scope Perry Preschool study through age 27.* Ypsilanti, MI; High/Scope Press.

Schweinhart, L. J., Montie, J., Xiang, Z., Barnett, W. S., Belfield, C. R. & Nores, M. (2005). *Lifetime effects: The High/Scope Perry Preschool study through age 40.* Ypsilanti, MI: High/Scope Press.

Scott-Little, C., Lesko, J., Martella, J.,& Milburn, P. (2007). Early learning standards: Results from a national survey to document trends in state-level policies and practices. *Early Childhood Research and Practice, 9*(10), 1-22.

Seefeldt, C., Castle, S., & Falconer, R. C. (2010). *Social studies for the preschool/primary child* (8th ed.). Upper Saddle River, NJ: Pearson.

Seefeldt, C. & Wasik, B. A. (2006). *Early education: Three, four, and five-year-olds go to school* (2nd ed.). Upper Saddle River, NJ: Pearson.

Siegler, R. (1997). *Emerging minds: The process of change in children's thinking.* New York: Oxford University Press.

Snow, C. E., Burns, M. S., Griffin, P., (1998). *Preventing reading difficulties in young children.* Washington, DC: National Academy Press.

Snow, C. E., Van Hemel, S.B. (Eds). (2008). *Early childhood assessment: Who, what and how.* Washington, DC: National Academies Press.

Temple, J. & Reynolds, A., (2007). Benefits and costs of investments in preschool Education: Evidence from the Child-Parent Centers and related programs. *Economics of Education Review, 26,* 126-144.

Vukelich, C., Christie, J., & Enz, B.J., (2010). *Helping young children learn language and literacy: Birth to Kindergarten* (3rd ed.). Boston, MA: Allyn & Bacon.

Vygotsky, L. S. (1978). *Mind in society.* Cambridge, MA: Harvard University Press.

Whitebook, M. (2003). *Early education quality: Higher teacher qualifications for better learning environments – A review of the literature.* Berkeley, CA: University of California, Institute of Industrial Relations, Center for the Study of Child Care Employment.

Yopp, H. & Yopp, R. (2000). Supporting phonemic awareness development in the classroom. *The Reading Teacher, 54*(2), 130-145.

Chapter 9
Kindergarten Today

Today in Kindergarten

Thinking Ahead

1. What are the characteristics of a typical kindergarten today?
2. What are some of the controversial issues in kindergarten education?
3. What are the social-emotional, physical, and cognitive characteristics of kindergarten children?
4. What compromises a typical kindergarten curriculum?

Based on Froebel's work, "the children's garden" revolutionized the approach to educating very young children. Kindergartens came to the US from Europe in the mid-1800's, yet for many years only a very few children attended them. In the 1900's, kindergarten became more mainstream, and eventually became part of public schooling. In chapter 2, we discussed the evolution of kindergarten from its early beginnings to the mid-1950's. We now turn our attention to the kindergarten of the past 60 years.

Two events had great significance in the development of kindergarten as we now know it. The first one was the launch by the Soviet Union of Sputnik I in 1957. Though it did not affect kindergarten immediately, the US's humiliation by this event brought wide-spread pressure to focus more on academics in the kindergarten. Thus began the "push-down" of the primary curriculum into the kindergarten. The second event was a renewed interest in the academic content of kindergarten. Robinson and Spodek (1965), in their book *New Directions in the Kindergarten,* argued against the emphasis in kindergarten being solely on the physical, emotional, and social development of the child. Their book laid out a curriculum of appropriate activities in Social Studies, Science, and Math. Robinson and Spodek's book was met with sharp criticism by the kindergarten professional community, and was not accepted, however, the absence of content in kindergarten has fueled a debate for the past almost fifty years. During this period of time, attendance in kindergarten has grown from 80% of eligible kindergartners being enrolled in 1977 to over 96% of age-eligible children enrolled in 2014 (NCES, 2015). Kindergarten is generally regarded as the first year of school, rather than a preparatory year for "first" grade.

The period of the mid-1960's to the present has been extremely prolific in terms of knowledge about the social, physical, emotional, language, literacy, and cognitive growth of young children. The works of Jean Piaget, Lev Vygotsky, and Jerome Bruner have given us new insight into the cognitive processes in young children. Children's emerging methodology for decoding, understanding, and gaining meaning from written representation became better understood in the past fifty years (Clay, 1972; Holdaway, 1979). **Emergent literacy** – a term coined by Marie Clay – defines the development of literacy long before children enter formal schooling, and negates much of the previous "reading readiness" curriculum that states children have to accrue a store of reading skills *before* literacy acquisition is possible. Holdaway (1979) determined that literacy development (reading, writing, listening, and speaking) begins to be acquired long before formal instruction, occurs in real-life settings, and is learned through children's active engagement with their environment and the people in it.

"Building Blocks: The Sequence of Emergent Literacy Skills"

Probably the most significant development in kindergarten education has been NAEYC's interpretation and articulation of what constitutes "developmentally appropriate practice" for the education of children from birth to age eight (Bredekamp, 1987; Bredekamp & Copple, 1997; Copple & Bredekamp, 2009). The influence of research in emergent literacy paved the way for the NAEYC to address the need for standards of practice for young children by writing the Developmentally Appropriate Practice (DAP) and Code of Ethical Conduct statements. The NAEYC marshaled its forces "...in an effort to stave off the increasing demands for academic instruction in early childhood programs" (Marsh, 2003, p. 26). In addition to pushdown curriculum, DAP evolved to address two other significant early childhood issues: lack of universal high-quality early education programs and growing concerns over lags in achievement among certain groups of children, particularly children living in poverty.

"High-Quality Kindergarten Today"

Yet the forces behind increased academics have had a full effect on the modern kindergarten. In 1989, President George H. W. Bush met with the governors of the states at their annual Governor's Conference. At this meeting, a list of learning goals –

Goals 2000 – for all American children was established: by the year 2000, "all children in America will start school ready to learn." States responded by putting in place learning standards articulating measurable outcomes for all grades including kindergarten. Another profound influence was the No Child Left Behind Act of 2001 which stipulated that states must administer assessments to all students at select grade levels in order to receive federal school funding. NCLB expanded the federal role in public education through annual testing, annual academic progress, report cards, teacher qualifications, and funding changes. These political initiatives have had a critical effect on kindergarten.

ESSA (Every Student Succeeds Act), the latest reauthorization of the fifty-year old Elementary and Secondary Education Act, was signed into law on December 10, 2015 by President Obama. In many ways ESSA is a reverse from the No Child Left Behind Act in that states have significant leeway in a wide range of areas, and the role and power of the U.S. Department of Education is diminished. The major tenets of the law are:

- States are required to adopt academic content standards in reading, mathematics, and science. Standards in other content areas are optional. These standards do not have to be the Common Core State Standards.

- Annual testing in reading and mathematics is still required for all students in grades 3 through 8, and once in high school. However, states can opt to administer shorter, frequent assessments throughout the school year that result in a single score rather than administering one comprehensive test.

- Schools must continue to report student achievement by subgroup and to issue an annual state report. States may substitute the SAT or ACT for the high school state achievement test. States must continue to administer a science test once in grades 3 through 5, once in grades 6 through 8, and once in high school.

- Schools must use at least three academic indicators such as student proficiency on state tests, student growth on state tests, and English Language Proficiency. At the high school level, schools must also include graduation rates. There is no longer the requirement for 100 percent proficiency and adequate yearly progress has been eliminated.

- Once every three years, states are to identify schools for comprehensive district support. These schools include those at the lowest 5 percent of Title 1 schools, high schools with graduation rates of less than 67 percent, and schools with one or more low-performing subgroups among the lowest 5 percent of all title 1 schools. If the district is unable to help underperforming schools meet the state's improvement criteria within four years, states are required to implement "more rigorous actions". States can include factors such as student engagement, faculty engagement school climate/safety, or whatever else the state feels is significant. Schools will no longer be labeled as failing if they miss a single target for a single group of students.

The term "highly qualified teachers" has been replaced with a provision that all teachers working in programs supported by Title 1 funds must meet their state's certification and licensure requirements. This provision stipulates that teacher evaluation based on student growth measured on a standardized test will cease to exist, but states may elect to make it part of their individual teacher evaluation process (www.ed.gov/essa).

"New Education Law Shifts Federal Influence over Public School"

Kindergarten used to be the year of transition created to smooth the adjustment from being at home to being in school. Formal academics were begun in the first grade, with kindergarten serving as a bridge between home or childcare, and mainstream schooling. Kindergarten teachers were responsible for "getting children ready" for the behavioral, social, and learning expectations of school, emphasizing development over learning. Curriculum emphasized "reading readiness" and "math readiness" focused on getting children "ready to learn" as opposed to actual learning. But all this has changed.

Expectations for increased kindergarten performance on specific academic skills have changed the kindergarten classroom. Part of the reason kindergarten is becoming increasingly academic is a growing understanding of brain development and the capabilities of young children. Brain-based learning has compelled schools to commence earlier formal reading instruction. Another pressure on schools is to prepare children for testing in 3rd grade; this has eradicated the dramatic play and block areas in many kindergarten classrooms. In many kindergarten classrooms formal reading instruction has replaced the blocks of creative play in these centers.

The movement toward more academics in the kindergarten has required more highly educated kindergarten teachers who understand child development; the influences of culture, language, and pre-kindergarten experiences on children's individual development; and the individual child's strengths and needs. Additionally, the well-informed teacher must understand how to intentionally teach the skills and knowledge inherent in the state and local learning standards through meaningful and engaging, developmentally appropriate thematic units. Complicating the kindergarten teacher's focus on balancing appropriateness with accountability is the inclusion of diverse learners in the general education classroom. Diversity includes children with special needs, children living in poverty, and those for whom English is a second language. Highly educated kindergarten teachers use all the tools and knowledge they possess to create learning opportunities that enhance children's learning to improve their life chances. We now turn our attention to current issues in kindergarten education.

Issues in Kindergarten Education

Entry age – In many of the 50 states, kindergarten may be offered but is not mandated. The age at which children are eligible to begin kindergarten varies from state to state; most children enter at age 5 but the age range can be 4 ¾ to 7 ¼ (Berk, 2016). Schools almost always set an entry cut-off date – a child needs to have turned five before that date to qualify for kindergarten entry. The majority of states require that the kindergarten entrance age of 5 is reached before September 1. Eleven states, including New York and Kentucky, have a later kindergarten age requirement, which for some states could be January 1 (NCES, 2015). However, some of these states are in the process of changing the cut-off date to earlier in the year, eliminating more of the older four-year olds in kindergarten.

The entry age is not all that important; what matters is how close the child's birthday is to the entry age. A child with a birthday of August 30, entering a kindergarten that has a cut-off date of September 1, will be just five years old while a child who turned five the previous October will be 5 years, 11 months upon entry to kindergarten. Some kindergartners will be almost a year older than others; just by accident of birth date, the older kindergarten child will have nearly 20% more time for exposure to experiences and language. Thus, there may be a wide distribution of abilities, even if parents send their children on schedule; but many parents do not send their children when they are age-eligible for kindergarten.

"Kindergarten Entrance Age / Transitional Kindergarten"

Redshirting in sports is the policy of holding an athlete out a year so that he/she can be more mature and physically stronger to play during his/her years of eligibility. Many school districts endorsing maturationist theories believe that they can ensure student success by assessing children's performance in terms of norms that compare children to the performance of other same-age children with the purpose of "holding children out" of school. The Gesell Developmental Scales (1954) provided the developmental benchmarks by which children were evaluated. Those who did not perform according to the norms for their age were often denied entrance into kindergarten or recommended for a year in "developmental kindergarten" before entering "regular kindergarten".

"Is Delaying Kindergarten good for your Child?"

Some parents, feeling pressure from their community or from the school, hold their age-eligible child out of kindergarten because they believe that by holding them back their child will excel when they do begin kindergarten. About 6% of parents whose children were eligible for kindergarten held them back for a year. More boys than girls and more white children than minorities are usually held back (NCES, 2015). Much of parental decision is determined by their perceptions of what constitutes kindergarten readiness. Kindergarten readiness will be discussed later in this chapter.

There are blatantly negative effects of denying children access to kindergarten on the basis of a test or because of age. First, it is unconstitutional and constitutes educational neglect to deny eligible children access to public education. By excluding children from early educative experiences, those children who are deemed "unready" become progressively more behind their peers. Children labeled as "unready" are deprived of instruction that could promote learning. It is important that schools are ready for children by responding to their individual needs and strengths, instead of children having to be ready for an intractable school environment and curriculum.

Instead of holding children out of kindergarten due to their age or perceived lack of school readiness, school systems could do the following (Seefeldt & Wasik, 2006):

- Create kindergartens that are responsive to the needs of individual children by understanding child development and learning
- Set a reasonable entry age for kindergarten where most of the children in the kindergarten are five years old
- Offer continuous progress from kindergarten to the primary grades
- Include parents in the decision-making about best placement for their children
- Implement developmentally appropriate curriculum that meets the needs and interests of individual children as well as groups of children

Readiness for kindergarten is a controversial topic that has been bantered about for the past few decades. Readiness is defined as being prepared for performance, however, what does it mean that a child is "ready" for kindergarten? Three major theories attempt to define kindergarten readiness: maturationist, behaviorist, and constructivist. Maturationists hypothesize that development and learning are the result of inner maturation (Gesell, 1940) therefore all children will learn if they are given enough time to develop. Directly opposite in thought are the behaviorists who believe that growth and learning are external to the child and controlled by the environment. To the behaviorists, all children can learn if their learning environment is prepared and properly structured. Constructivists suggest that both environmental and biological factors shape human development in a synergistic manner. Maturation is part of constructivist thought, but children grow and learn optimally through interaction with their social and physical environments. The maturationist theory that development is a process of biological "unfolding" is still a prevalent force in public schooling. However, development does not occur in exactly the same way for each child; it is greatly influenced by socioeconomic status, language, culture, and maternal education (Duncan, et al., 2007). Creating supportive and enriched learning environments help secure children's development and readiness for learning.

"Kindergarten Readiness"

As the US moves toward universal preschool for four-year olds, preparedness issues have again pushed to the forefront of the kindergarten readiness discussion. Preschool experience sets the stage for how well children achieve in kindergarten and beyond. Unfortunately, not all preschool programs are created equally; gaps in preparedness for learning still exist, particularly among children coming from low socioeconomic status. It is important that preschool programs address the issue of leveling the playing field for children who have vastly different abilities and experiences entering their programs. Early Learning Guidelines provide guidance in preparing meaningful standards-based instruction. The NAEYC (2001) has responded to the call for kindergarten readiness standards with a position paper that reminds educators and policymakers that preparedness for school entry has to be considered in relation to three factors:

- the diversity and inequity of children's early life experiences
- the wide range of variation in young children's development and learning

- the degree to which school expectations of children entering kindergarten are reasonable, appropriate and supportive of individual differences

All fifty states and the District of Columbia have published Early Learning Guidelines to guide preschool teachers and programs. The newly published New York State Early Learning Guidelines (2012) have identified five broad domains that encompass the development of the whole child:

- Domain I – Physical Well-Being, Health, and Motor Development
- Domain II – Social and Emotional Development
- Domain III – Approaches to Learning
- Domain IV – Cognition and General Knowledge
- Domain V – Language, Communication, and Literacy

Preschool educators need to be familiar with their state's Early Learning Guidelines and use them daily in their planning and teaching. Rich learning environments with intentional teaching can go far in preparing children for the rigors of kindergarten.

Kindergarten retention is another policy often practiced by school districts. States and local districts may decide to grant access to kindergarten, but if the child's progress does not meet the benchmarks set by the district, it would be recommended that he or she repeat kindergarten, or be placed in a transitional or "developmental" program prior to entering first grade. Retention comes in the form of "developmental" or "junior" kindergarten the year before kindergarten, transitional first grade between kindergarten and first  grade, or simply repeating kindergarten (Marshall, 2003). The belief is that this "gift of time" will ensure a child doesn't "fail", but in reality children who are retained or spend time in a transitional program either before or after kindergarten, generally have poorer attitudes toward school and lower self-esteem when compared to children who followed the normal pathway from kindergarten at age 5 to first grade at age 6 (Shepard & Smith, 1989).

That extra year in kindergarten is not only detrimental to the child's self-esteem and attitude toward school, but it is costly to school districts. The cost of an extra school year for as much as 30% of the kindergarten class (NCES, 2015) can cost public education billions of dollars over time. Children who experience some form of kindergarten retention do seem to achieve better during the second year of schooling, however there is a "wash-out" effect mostly by third grade when any gains made dissipate and the child who was retained performs at the same level or below her peers (Shepard & Smith, 1989).

Half-day programs were for decades the norm in kindergarten education but **full day programs** have become more common during the last twenty years. Today, 77 percent of kindergarten children are enrolled in full day programs (NCES, 2015). Full day programs are far superior to half day programs if the program is well-planned, intentional, and developmentally appropriate. Yet, if kindergarten children are expected to fill out worksheets, sit long periods for direct instruction, and be exposed to a great deal of drill day after day in a full day program, children would be better served in a developmentally appropriate half-day program that allows children to explore, learn, grow, and socialize in a supportive environment (Morrison, 2012).

"Full Day vs. Half Day Kindergarten"

With the evolution of a more rigorous curriculum beginning in kindergarten and continuing throughout a child's school experience, well-run, full day programs give children many advantages:

- Children adapt to longer school days earlier in their school career.
- There is more flexibility of time and activities in which children can participate. Often, academics are emphasized in the morning, leaving time for centers, indoor and outdoor play, literacy extension projects, and special classes such as music and art in the afternoons.
- Children who are at risk or have developmental delays have more time for socialization, opportunities for rich language exposure, and time for support services such as speech and language therapy.
- Gives teachers more time for in-depth study of thematic units, greater opportunity to address state learning standards, and more possibility for authentically assessing each child's progress.

"Lisa Guernsey: The Benefits of Full-Day Kindergarten"

As of 2015, thirteen states and the District of Columbia (NCES, 2015) have made full day kindergarten mandatory for all five-year olds in schools. Full day kindergarten meets the societal needs for quality full day educare as well as for economic and academic reasons. More and more districts, recognizing the benefits, are adopting full day kindergarten programs.

Kindergarten Development Across the Domains

Students enter kindergarten with a range of experiences. Approximately five out of six children will have had some preschool experience (NCES, 2015): full day programs, half-day programs, programs meeting fewer than five days a week, home-based child care, and center-based child care. Some children have spent most of their time in English language-rich environments while other children are learning English for the first time.

It is the kindergarten teacher's job to find a way to make each child welcome and be able to flourish in the classroom; the teacher accomplishes this by knowing the needs of individual children, knowing about the social and cultural contexts in which children live, and knowing about child development and learning.

Social-Emotional Development

Acquiring social and emotional competence has long-lasting effects on a human's life including school and career success, and lifelong social and psychological regulation (Raver, 2002). As children develop and have increased experiences and interactions, they grow in their ability to socialize, act in a socially acceptable way, and to interpret the cues of other people. With modeling and guidance children learn to interact in empathetic, skilled, and positive ways.

Establishing and maintaining relationships are very important skills for kindergarten age children to achieve; social acumen relates not only to peer acceptance and healthy emotional adjustment but to school success (McClelland, Acock, & Morrison, 2006). Some kindergarten children struggle with sustaining healthy, well-adjusted relationships while other children are adept at these skills. Children who display positive behaviors and show better overall social skills have more friends, leading to increased peer acceptance.

Kindergarten children, ages 5 and 6, enter Erikson's industry vs. inferiority stage of social-emotional development. **Self-regulation** is a skill that began in the previous stage – initiative vs. guilt – and involves children either making themselves not do something (such as hitting another child out of frustration), or making themselves do something when they don't really want to do it (such as stopping play and cleaning up). Children are more aware of themselves as individuals and work hard to be responsible, share, and cooperate. Kindergarten children are more able than younger children to regulate their emotions as they interact with other people. Children who have been exposed to good models of self-regulation – teachers and parents who demonstrated warmth, patience, and positive guidance – can learn self-regulation. However, five year-olds still enter kindergarten with varying self-regulation skills. Being able to modulate one's emotional state is an important skill for succeeding in school, being productive, and working cooperatively (Copple & Bredekamp, 2009).

Teachers can support children's development in self-regulation by modeling positive responses in relation to social and emotional situations. Teachers can interpret social situations for children by modeling caring behaviors ("We must help Kevin clean up the blocks because that's what good friends do"). Using bibliotherapy by reading and discussing books about feelings is another positive strategy. Whole group read alouds and thematic units focused on emotions are explicit ways to reach a large group of children, while identifying an individual child's needs and then reading to just that child is a way to tailor the bibliotherapy. Teacher attention to children's emotional needs is incredibly important; children who develop self-regulation skills early on, tend to have better peer acceptance and the ability to regulate their emotions as adults (Sroufe, Carlson, & Shulman, 1993).

Another way a kindergarten teacher can support five- and six-year olds in their development of self-regulation skills is through careful organization of the environment and establishment of clear rules. Kindergarten children are much more likely to strengthen their self-regulation skills, as well as develop independence and problem solving skills if they are given some control over and choice in their activities (Ryan & Deci, 2000). This requires a classroom that is intentionally prepared and organized to offer activity and material choices.

The environment needs to have a good balance of materials and activity choices that neither under-stimulate nor overstimulate children, that are thoughtfully planned and  organized, with enough time for intentional inquiry. Teachers need to model constructive strategies for settling disputes – a "peace table" for negotiation, "drawing straws" to share roles and materials, and "giving children the words" to express themselves. Dramatic play is essential for children to practice their self-regulation and pro-social skills. Additionally, the classroom rules and guidelines for expected behavior need to be concise, positive, and simple, with the rationale and the consequences made explicit to children. Kindergarten children can reason and brainstorm solutions to problems in the classroom; they can also understand why certain rules are necessary, giving them control over and responsibility for their actions (Bodrova & Leong, 2008). It is important to provide children with opportunities to use all their domains of learning to problem-solve; playing games that require strategic thinking, putting together intricate puzzles, and playing roles in the dramatic play center all offer possibilities for learning.

Emotional understanding and empathy for others are lifelong skills developing in kindergarten children at a stage in their maturation when they are more aware of others' thoughts, emotions, and intent. Children at this age can correctly identify both the causes and consequences of others' emotions and their emergent prosocial skills allow them to comfort peers who are in emotional distress. Empathy helps children get along with others, paving the way for peer acceptance and other emotions such as kindness and consideration (Copple & Bredekamp, 2009). A small percentage of kindergarten children are limited in their ability to "feel another's pain" and to take the perspective of other children. Teachers need to model true empathy, help  children correctly interpret social situations, and learn ways to cope with their negative emotions (Pettit, 2004). Dramatic play helps foster self-regulation in more impulsive children by allowing the child to practice made-up rules in make-believe roles (Bodrova & Leong, 2008).

Sociability and positive self-concept both develop in warm, secure attachments with adults; the kindergarten teacher is especially important in the life of the child who at this stage of development is seeking approval. Sociability is cultivated in early childhood settings where teachers provide consistent emotional and academic support; a predictable, organized environment; and warm, positive feedback (Wilson, Pianta, & Stuhlman, 2007). Positive self-concept is fostered in much the same type of environments with teachers who convey affirmative messages to kindergarten children about their academic gains as well as their social and prosocial behaviors. Conversely, children who receive frequent negative messages may develop poor self-concept, increased self-criticism, and compromised academic progress (Burhans & Dweck, 1995).

The teacher serves as a positive model of sociability and positive self-concept that the kindergarten child can emulate. Teachers must share a warm, positive, and predictable relationship with *all* the children in their classes and need to demonstrate kindness, caring, and respect so children can pattern these behaviors. Teachers also must provide time, opportunities, and activities that require social interaction. Part of the teacher's role is to observe children's social interactions and scaffold their social problem-solving, aid in settling disputes, and keeping interactions fair (Katz & McClellan, 1997).

Physical and Motor Development

Five- and six-year old children in kindergarten are full of energy; both their fine and gross motor skills are beginning to be more directed and focused in their actions (Berk, 1997). Kindergarten children are becoming more advanced and coordinated in their physical endeavors, balance, and eye-hand coordination. This development is a result of a synergistic developmental system: kindergarten children's leaner bodies; their motivation to set and attain new goals; their evolving cognition; and their expanding prosocial skills in social settings (Thelen & Smith, 1998). As with all domains of development and learning, no two children are alike; much of their development is determined by cultural, social, and familial contexts. Some children will need more scaffolding and practice in various skills; as with other domains, teachers need to modify or individualize the task based on each child's needs, strengths, and interests. Generally, girls are more advanced than boys in fine motor skills, and in gross motor skills requiring accuracy such as skipping and dancing. Boys tend to be more skilled in gross motor activities that require force and power such as running and jumping (Berk, 2016).

**"Kindergarten Readiness –
Physical and Motor Skills"**

Fine motor skills are becoming increasingly honed as the muscles that control the extremities develop; children have greater control over writing implements and the use of scissors is less frustrating. Children struggle at first with laborious tasks that require precision, accuracy, and patience such as cutting and writing. Kindergarten is a time where children should have daily opportunities to work with clay, construct with Legos, sort objects, pour liquids, put puzzles together, easel and finger paint, and use tools such as eggbeaters and hole punches. Dressing becomes easier through practice with zippers, buttoning, and tying.

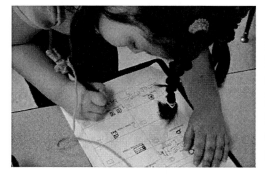

Writing is a critical skill in the area of fine motor development, particularly because there are increased demands in the modern kindergarten for children to communicate via written expression. Proper pencil grip allows the child to control and manipulate the writing utensil efficiently. By the end of kindergarten, most children have mastered adult style pencil grip that can be used in writing and drawing. Also, handedness is established in many five-year olds and most six-year olds. Both right- and left-handedness that is firmly established facilitates the use of fine motor activities, leading to refined coordination and dexterity (Puckett & Black, 2005).

Gross motor skills in kindergarten children show more agility and coordination. Children can run quickly, smoothly, and can change directions effortlessly. They throw and catch with force and increasing accuracy. By the end of kindergarten, children may have begun to ride a two-wheeler with training wheels and may have enough eye-hand coordination to swing a bat to accurately connect with a pitched ball. **Motor planning** – the ability of the brain to invent, organize, and carry out a series of actions – becomes an important skill during the kindergarten year as children gain control over their bodies (Berk, 2016).

Gross motor activities are very important for the kindergarten child so as to maintain his focus and on-task behavior during the structured learning periods in the school day. Children develop their bodies through play and being outdoors, yet children also need instruction besides play to develop their bodies (Manross, 1994, 2000). A combination of intentionally taught activities and play-based opportunities for experimentation and creativity with the skills taught by the teacher offer the balanced learning children require. The intentional teacher coaches, encourages, and provides modification of equipment and materials to ensure success for all children. The teacher needs to design activities in which all children will enjoy success by providing (Copple & Bredekamp, 2009, pp.190-191):

- Inside and outside physical activity areas with adequate space for children to move freely and safely without bumping into each other
- Opportunities for daily, high-quality movement instruction with plenty of time for practice – exclusive of the outdoor play time that should also occur
- Appropriate equipment so that each child benefits from maximum participation

One of the most effective uses of space is to create a separate gross motor room with space and equipment for children to create obstacle course, ride trikes and scooters, throw and catch a ball, jump rope, etc. There, teachers can design challenging but attainable activity choices that are open-ended and in which individuals, pairs, and groups can participate. As with any other domain of learning, teachers need to make accommodations and modifications based on the strengths, needs, and interests of each child, and to ensure that children with disabilities participate as fully as possible. **Universal Design for Learning (UDL)** is the belief that materials and environments need to be functional for everyone, including those with disabilities, to the greatest degree possible (Chapter 2).

Cognitive Development

The kindergarten year is a time for rapid language and cognitive growth; five- and six-year old children display maturity in flexibility in their thinking, reasoning, problem-solving, attentiveness, and greater awareness of their world. Kindergarten children use their curiosity and imagination to learn more about their world, largely through pretend play. However, they are able to distinguish between when they are pretending and when they are not.

Much of what we now know about young children's cognitive growth is based on brain research. The first seven years of life present great opportunity for cognitive growth if the child is appropriately stimulated in her environment and in her daily activities. The brain grows rapidly during the pre-school and kindergarten years, increasing from 70 percent to 90% percent of the eventual adult size (Thatcher et al., 1996). The brain is more adaptable at this age and more responsive to stimulation; pruning of the unused neural networks allows for robust growth in the areas that are being used. This is a sensitive period, giving kindergarten children a high capacity for learning; this is an optimum time for accelerated learning and intervention.

Children in this age range are refining their thinking to be more accurate and complex – they have a greater capacity for organizing categories of information. Five- and six-year olds are becoming more sophisticated in their organization of conceptual knowledge. With increased interaction with objects and greater opportunity for experiences, the kindergarten child begins to see how different objects fit into different categories. The classroom has a hamster and a turtle as classroom pets; the hamster is furry and eats hamster food while the turtle has a hard shell and drinks water and eats lettuce. Yet, the child understands they both fit into the category of "animal" – a concept that is becoming more refined with each interaction the child has with animals and objects that do not fit into the "animal" category. Kindergarten children are also more flexible in their thinking and are able to take more than one perspective, whether it is in the cognitive domain when visualizing objects from different perspectives or in the social domain when considering others' feelings (Berk, 2008).

Kindergarten children build on their prior knowledge and experiences and they use the materials in their environment to practice their cognitive skills, for instance by measuring the length of the table in the classroom. Children this age, like children of all ages, learn from social interaction with adult and peers. Intentional teachers plan activities in which children can collaborate and interact to build cognitive skills. Five- and six-year old children learn best when they are allowed choices in their learning; choice-making empowers children and leads to greater engagement and motivation. Choice can be offered in means of assessment performance, play opportunities, and activities.

Math, Science, and Social Studies

In recent years math and science education in early childhood have come to the forefront of educational research and policymaking. Much of this attention is due to the global competitiveness for high-quality jobs and a concern for the achievement gap in American schooling. Research shows that early mathematics and science instruction can go far in addressing these two issues, yet young children often have not been given the opportunity (National Research Council, (NRC), 2016). Children in other nations consistently outperform American children in STEM – science, technology, engineering, and mathematics (Mullis, Martin, & Foy, 2008). As a result, The National Association for the Education of Young Children (NAEYC) and the National Council of Teachers of Mathematics (NCTM), in 2002, issued a joint statement on early math education with recommendations for strengthening instruction and exposure to major concepts.

Math. Some of the major points in recent research that supports increased focus on mathematics education:

1) Although we have been focused on literacy instruction in American schools, math skills at kindergarten entry are a much stronger predictor of school success (Duncan et al., 2007).
2) Using a math-focused early childhood curriculum can significantly improve mathematics achievement of children in poverty (Preschool Curriculum Evaluation Research Consortium [PCERC], 2008).
3) Teaching mathematics in preschool and at home has a greater priority in Asian countries like China and Japan – even with children living in poverty – than in the US (Starkey & Klein, 2008).
4) In the US we make the assumption that achievement in mathematics is because of natural, innate ability afforded only particular people, while Eastern countries believe that with hard work, all children can achieve high levels of mathematical understanding (NRC, 2016).

Today's kindergarten is a place where mathematical and scientific inquiry is built along with literacy. Teaching mathematics requires teachers to have a working knowledge of the math standards set forth by the National Council of Teachers of Mathematics (NCTM); for states using the Common Core State Standards, which are grounded in the NCTM standards, teachers need to consult the CCSS for all curriculum and lesson planning.

**"Teaching Kindergarten Math:
How to Tell Kids Addition Stories"**

What does this mean for the kindergarten mathematics curriculum and instruction? First, we need to review the developmental skills and knowledge five- and six-year old children normally demonstrate.

Numbers and Operations. Children use numbers to count (**enumeration**), represent quantities, to solve quantitative problems such as counting the objects in a set, to join and break up groups of objects, to create sets of objects given a number, and to order sets and numerals using cardinal and ordinal numbers. Most kindergarten children are competent in counting with the understanding that numbers always are said in the same order. The concept of **one-to-one correspondence** – only one number word is attached to each object being counted – needs to be practiced almost daily in the 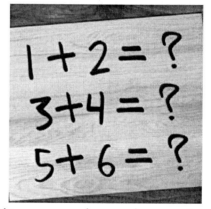 kindergarten class – counting blocks, toys, puzzle pieces, snack crackers, etc. Kindergarten children also will either come to kindergarten knowing about **cardinality** – the concept that when counting a set the last number stated stands for the total number in the set – or they will become competent in this skill with repeated practice. Five- and six-year old children should be able to count objects in a set up to 20 and be able to write the numeral representing the set. The term **operations** represents solving problems in addition and subtraction, as well as being able to use the terminology, *more than*, *less than*, and *equal* when discussing relationships of numbers and quantities. The kindergarten year is replete with opportunities to develop and practice skill in operations.

"Numeracy Learning in Kindergarten: Counting"

The topic of Numbers and Operations is taught in kindergarten through activities that use counting, one-to-one correspondence, ordinal and cardinal numbers, adding and subtracting numbers, and using a variety of methods and tools for computation including manipulatives, mental computation, paper and pencil, pictures, and calculators. Kindergarten children can create sets of manipulatives that match a numeral in a card, use a number line and manipulatives to compute problems such as "find 4 more than 1", use dice to add or subtract the numbers shown on the dice, or use a 1-100 number chart to count by 10's.

Geometry, spatial relations, and measurement. Kindergarten children's thinking is becoming increasingly flexible. Five- and six-year old children are more metacognitive in

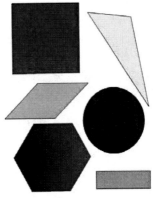

Shapes

that they can think about their own thinking. This is shown in their ability to predict and plan (*"Let's make a list of all the things we will need for our field trip"*) and to make connections with prior learning (*"This reminds me of a book we read last week"*). This flexibility can be seen in the area of mathematical thinking, particularly in geometric and spatial concepts. Geometry involves position, size, direction, and movement. Kindergarten children will learn about angles, and 2- and 3-dimensional objects by manipulating them. Geometry can be taught by recognizing, building, drawing, and sorting shapes; creating pictures that have symmetry, or analyzing spatial relationship names such as "above", "near", "below', using a map. Kindergarten children are far more competent in geometry than we often give them credit for – they can create designs with shapes and identify shapes in a design, as well as name the shapes (Bredekamp, 2011). Five- and six-year old children can take apart shapes with smaller parts and re-assemble them, as well as divide objects such as a pizza to share equally with friends. Spatial competency is shown in block building and puzzle construction. Kindergarten children use measurement to determine weight, length, quantity, and time.

"The Shapes Song"

Kindergarten children observe and analyze relationships in the world around them by using measurement. Children use attributes such as length and weight which can be used to compare and order objects. Five- and six-year old children will compare two objects by comparing them with each other to see which one is longer, larger, or heavier, and by comparing two objects with a third object. Young children use nonstandard units such as blocks, yarn, or a part of their body with which to measure. Kindergarten children also enjoy experimenting with rulers as they gain competence in rudimentary standard measurement.

The concept of time is still difficult for kindergarten children to understand (Flavell, Green, & Flavell, 1995). Time is relative to events and objects in the child's immediate world; for example, the child can conceptualize the length of time to travel to the movie theater on a Saturday afternoon if he or she is told it is the same amount of time they ride on the bus from home to school. **Measurement of time** can be taught daily using the calendar and posted schedules; **measurement of money** can be taught playing "coin Bingo", by using newspaper advertisements with price tags, and turning the dramatic play corner into a grocery store where children can "shop". **Measurement of length** can be taught by letting children use non-standard units of measurement such as crayons and paper clips to measure desks, chairs, tables, etc. ('The desk is 9 crayons wide."), using yarn or string to measure the height of each child, and can be explored at the water table when children measure the number of smaller containers (cups) are contained in the larger containers (gallons). **Size** can be taught by having kindergarten children seriate objects such as Styrofoam balls from smallest to largest, by supplying different sizes of boxes and tops mixed together for children to match, and using yarn to measure the circumference of various fruits and vegetables.

"Telling Time for Kindergarteners"

Algebra and patterns. The ability to identify patterns is an important skill for all areas of mathematics – algebra, geometry, spatial relations, and numbers. Classification of objects by an attribute involves patterns. Teachers can provide strategies throughout the day such as identifying, matching, extending, and creating patterns with blocks, beads, shapes, etc. Children can also clap patterns, move to rhythms, and look for patterns in their environment, such as stripes on clothing. Algebra can be taught by giving kindergarten children the opportunity to sort objects by attributes such as shape, color, and size to use in data representation such as a bar graph; by creating and extending patterns of objects; and by using the block building corner to build repeating patterns of blocks.

Problem solving and reasoning. Mathematics is about thinking and reasoning; it is not simply about computation. To think mathematically, children need opportunities to solve problems and reason about geometry, spatial relations, measurement, and numbers and operations. They need to know how to solve problems in multiple ways and to be able to explain their thinking.

As children mature, they develop a greater capacity for memory and more complex thinking; kindergarten children are on the cusp of this development. Kindergarten children often lack in memory for information that is meaningless to them however, their memories become refined when it comes to experiences in their own lives. Sometimes five- and six-year old children revert back to concrete, simplistic thinking but often demonstrate more advanced, abstract thinking. An example of this can be seen in sorting objects; the young kindergarten child will only be able to sort colored shapes by one attribute such as color, yet the older kindergarten child may be able to classify by two attributes – the color and the shape.

Science education in the kindergarten needs to follow the natural curiosity children have about the world. Five- and six-year old children are eager to explore and learn about their world; they do that by asking the "What if…?" questions, formulating hypotheses, testing them, and finding out answers. As the teacher you will also observe, question, make predictions, carry out experiments, and confirm your conclusions with your students. "A good science program is skillfully integrated into the total life of the classroom" (Copple & Bredekamp, 2009, p.141). The kindergarten teacher should take this into consideration when planning the room arrangement to emphasize small group investigations, setting the schedule so as to include plenty of indoor and outdoor exploration time, and to collect a variety of materials that can be manipulated and reconstructed.

"Kindergarten Science Lab - Matter"

Science is important in the kindergarten for the following reasons (Morrison, 2012, pp.321-322):

- Science is an ideal vehicle for developing children's questioning minds about the natural world
- Implementing the National Science Education Standards helps students take their place in a scientifically literate society
- When children explore science they acquire oral and written language for scientific expression – and learn to read in new contexts
- Science teaches children to appreciate the diversity of life and its interconnectedness

- When children learn about nature they respect and care for our planet and its natural resources
- Learning scientific methods teaches children to view themselves as scientists
- Exciting lessons in science can foster a lifelong love for the subject

Science is a combination of **process skills** (*how* children learn) and **content** (*what* children learn). These process skills include **inquiry** – a questioning mode which encourages natural curiosity and exploration. Science inquiry requires frequent opportunities for children to question, investigate, predict, and communicate their findings. Wortham (2010, p.201)) states, "Children learn science concepts in a social milieu. While observing and working with other children in learning centers, cooperative groups, and paired activities, children exchange ideas, engage in science projects, and discuss their findings". It is important that the kindergarten teacher provides the time, opportunity, and materials that foster scientific inquiry.

The National Research Council (1997) has identified the following categories as the fundamental concepts and knowledge that children, including kindergarten age, should be investigating:

- Life science – the study of living people, plants, and animals
- Physical science – the study of nonliving materials – matter, energy, and chemistry
- Earth and space – the study of objects in the sky, materials on earth (such as rocks), and changes in the sky and earth
- Ecology – the study of living things and their relationship with their environment and each other
- Science and technology – studying and using the tools needed for inquiry

One of the fundamental goals of early childhood curriculum is to develop young children's inquiry skills. These skills include exploring, questioning, observing, describing, comparing, classifying, using tools, making predictions, gathering and interpreting data, perceiving patterns, coming to conclusions, recording, working with others, sharing, discussing, and listening (Worth & Grollman, 2003). The role of the teacher is to facilitate children's scientific exploration. This happens when the teacher models curiosity about a topic by asking probing and motivating questions. Then, the teacher can set up the environment so that children can discover the answers to their questions through exploring, reading, questioning, experimenting, and observing.

Science should be taught through activities that encourage kindergarten children to engage, explore, explain, elaborate, and evaluate. For example, children can explore the topic of "gardening" by engaging in collaborative brain-storming about everything they know about gardens and how they will use their knowledge to design their garden. Children explore gardening and science books to determine how the garden should be set up, what seeds to grow, what materials will be needed, etc. The kindergarten children will then explain and record the jobs each child will be responsible for in the garden; using shared writing, students and teacher will plan the schedule and finalize the garden design. As the children carry out the construction and maintenance of the garden, they will modify and record the progress. Elaboration can be done through daily reflections in science journals; evaluating the completion of the gardening unit can be contained in the final reflections in the journals and incorporated in pictures, graphs and charts, and oral presentations.

Problem–solving is a necessary component when working with all mathematical and scientific processes and content. Problem-solving and mathematical-scientific thinking are fostered through challenging and open-ended questions that lead to thinking, experimenting, and discussion. The process of problem-solving is as valuable as arriving at the solution. As the teacher is evaluating children's learning, it is important to assess the thinking that they demonstrate, not just the specific skills they are learning. This is done through focused observation and daily recording of children's thinking, as well as the solutions to problems children produce. Problem-solving paves the way for the higher-level thinking children will need throughout their lives.

Social Studies, like math and science, should be presented in an authentic and hands-on way. Through interactions with their families and community, children can learn about the core subjects of social studies:

- Sociology – the study of the way groups live, cooperate, and take on responsibilities
- History – the study of what has happened in the life of a country or people
- Geography – the study of the earth's surface, and resources, as well as the concepts of direction, distance, and location
- Economics – the study of production, distribution, and consumption of goods and services
- Anthropology – the way people live, their beliefs and customs

The 2010 revised social studies curriculum standards, written by the National Council for the Social Studies (NCSS) are organized into ten thematic strands:

- Culture
- Time, continuity, change
- People, places, environments
- Individual development and identity
- Individuals, groups, and institutions
- Power, authority, governance

- Production, distribution, consumption
- Science, technology, society
- Global connections
- Civic ideals and practices

The kindergarten social studies curriculum emphasizes self-reliance; contributing to society in their families, communities, and school; awareness of the world; making wise decisions, developing a sense of responsibility and respect for themselves and others. The kindergarten curriculum goals are focused on developing a child's positive self-concept, furthering an understanding of a child's role in the family, providing an inclusive, multicultural classroom environment, teaching the need for rules and laws, and developing an awareness of a child's own cultural heritage and that of others.

Language and Literacy Development

From the first moment of birth, most children learn how to communicate by watching and listening to the people around them. Children "learn what language is through what language *does*" (Novick, 2000, p. 70). Kindergarten is a time for children to refine their communication skills by increasing their competency in speaking, listening, reading, writing, and representing. We know that oral language provides the bedrock of literacy acquisition and that this foundation needs to be built in infancy, yet many of the five- and six-year old children entering kindergarten will not have had the experiences necessary to build language and literacy skills. It is the kindergarten teacher's job to provide a language–rich classroom and curriculum with intentional teaching which builds children's language and literacy skills.

"Language and Literacy Development: Diary Web"

Language. By kindergarten entry, children have learned amazing amounts in the areas of language and emergent literacy. Because language builds the foundation for literacy acquisition, kindergarten teachers must "set the stage" in their classrooms for language and literacy development. By the time children enter kindergarten they have a large vocabulary, and speak in sentences. Five- and six-year old children have an incredible capacity for learning and playing with words. In the early grades, children learn approximately 20 new words every day (Anglin, 1993). Six-year old children typically have a vocabulary of 10,000 words, if they have been immersed in a language-rich environment (Bloom, 1998). However, many children, largely due to socioeconomic reasons, begin kindergarten with a vastly limited knowledge of words and the way language works (Hart & Risley, 1995). Between the ages of 5 and 7 children attain most of their grammatical understanding, although it will take longer for children to master the complex structure of grammar in their expressive language. Kindergarten children love to talk and should be encouraged to expand their language facility through singing, storytelling, reading books and being read to, dramatic play, and alliteration games.

"Kindergarten Language Arts"

Semantics – the meanings of words – develops as children accumulate life experiences and engage in interactions with those in their environment. Background knowledge (schema) and a comprehensive bank of vocabulary are vital for comprehension. The more experiences – authentic experiences or those children learn through books and media – children have, the more their vocabulary will expand and deepen. The kindergarten teacher needs to consistently interact, share and extend language, read and discuss vocabulary-rich books, and label words that children encounter in their experiences. The teacher also needs to use specific words that expand children's vocabularies and teach word meanings.

The basic fundamentals of **syntax** – the order and structure of words in a sentence (grammar) that make sentences understandable – are set by age four in most children. Children's ability to construct grammatically correct sentences is not only a language skill but also an indication of their development in cognitive skills. Kindergarten children gain increased competence with syntactic structures by being exposed to grammatically correct language. Teachers need to be high-quality models speaking articulately, with exacting vocabulary, and using correct grammar.

Pragmatic language is based on the principles of competent language use. These principles include imitating and maintaining a conversation, taking turns in conversation, using cues to indicate subject interest, and learning how to tactfully interrupt and/or change subjects (Otto, 2006). Pragmatics also includes the use of language to communicate one's intention; this is done with oral language, body language, facial expression, and vocal inflection. Conversation with rich oral language and emotive expression provides a model for children. Dramatic and pretend play provides a vehicle for children to try out roles, vocabulary, mannerisms, inflection, and attitudes that convey a message.

Literacy. When kindergarten children enter school, they become increasingly knowledgeable in reading, writing, listening, speaking, and representing. They know the phonemes of their home language and can identify environmental sounds. Knowledge of books and knowledge of the world are both factors that support literacy proficiency (RAND, 2002). Knowledge of books and the world are built through adult-child experiences first in "lap time" story reading and conversations with parents and childcare providers. Later, pre-school and kindergarten teachers continue building literacy skills through read alouds, conversations, and story-telling. Story reading and discussion about the book build a base of conceptual knowledge and vocabulary. This

emergent literacy approach states that reading is meaning-centered and children accomplish this by observing and modeling after adults interacting with print. On the basis of their observations, children construct their own perceptions about the functions and systems of print and then experiment with print in reading and writing.

Yet, **scientifically-based reading research (SBRR)** has identified a core of knowledge and skills that young children must have to become successful readers (Snow, Burns & Griffin, 1998). Research has shown that children's oral language, vocabulary development, phonological awareness, and alphabet knowledge are valuable predictors of reading achievement in elementary school. Print awareness, book concepts, and sight word recognition have also been positively correlated with reading ability (National Early Literacy Panel, 2008). Not only is there a skill set that children need to ensure proficient literacy, but that skill set is most effectively learned through explicit, systematic instruction which incorporates games, direct instruction, teacher modeling, guided practice, and independent practice.

Most kindergarten teachers and school district policy-makers advocate literacy instruction that blends an emergent literacy approach with a scientifically-based reading research approach. This **blended approach** highlights print-rich classrooms, read alouds of high-quality children's literature, shared reading and writing, engaging center-based literacy activities with intentionality, as well as direct instruction, modeling, and guided practice on core language and literacy skills.

Print awareness. According to the National Research Council (1997, p. 27), "a child's sensitivity to print is a major first step toward reading." Print awareness is a broad term that encompasses children's skills at recognizing print in their environment as well as in books. Print awareness also refers to concepts about print including book concepts (author, illustrator, title, front, back, etc.) and conventions of print (capitalization, punctuation, directionality). There is a moderate correlation between knowledge of concepts of print and reading ability (National Early Literacy Panel, 2008), thus, the importance of daily exposure to books that is seen in the kindergarten.

Kindergarten teachers can teach print awareness by providing a print-rich environment, and teaching concepts about print during read alouds of literature. Word walls containing students' names, **sight words**, words from units of studies, and number and color words can be utilized in shared and independent writing. Furniture and materials in the classroom (table, chair, door, etc.) can be labeled as a way to teach sight vocabulary.

Phonological awareness is the awareness of the sound structure of oral language. A "massive body of work has established that phonological awareness is a critical precursor, correlate, and predictor of reading achievement" (Dickinson, McCabe, & Sprague, 2003, p. 476). **Phonemic awareness** is the awareness that spoken words are composed of individual sounds or phonemes; the ability to differentiate the units of language (words, segments, syllables, phonemes) is linked to successful reading (National Early Literacy Panel, 2008). Phonological and phonemic awareness are two, closely connected skills that are important to early literacy development and constitute a large part of the kindergarten curriculum. Later phonics instruction is built on a firm foundation of phonological and phonemic awareness.

"Phonological Awareness"

Research suggests a developmental continuum in phonological processing skills that moves from larger units – word awareness – to syllable awareness, then onset-rime awareness to finally, phonemic awareness (Adams, 1990). However, phonological awareness "is not a stage model in which a child has to master one level before moving to the next. Rather, children show beginning levels of skills on more complex levels while still working toward mastery of less complex levels" (Phillips, Clancy-Menchetti, & Lonigan, 2008, p. 5). **Onset-rime** is the skill of blending, segmenting, and substituting the beginning part of a word (onset) with the ending part of the word (rime).

Children's ability to detect words that rhyme (e.g. hat rhymes with cat but not with ham) is an example of children's onset-rime awareness. "Playing with words", and repeated exposure to phonological awareness through reading and story-telling are all worthwhile but they are not enough. Explicit instruction is required to build the foundation that young children need.

"Onset & Rime"

Kindergarten children learn phoneme isolation by playing games in which they match phonemes to pictures of words beginning with the phoneme, and isolating the sound that is heard at the beginning, medial, or ending position in a word. Games can be played where children blend three phonemes to make a word – "/k/-/a/-/t/" – cat, and then take the word "cat" and segment it into /k/-/a/-/t/. Phoneme manipulation games can be played with "word families" such as the "_at" family (e.g. take the /b/ off bat and add /c/ - cat).

Alphabet recognition. Alphabet recognition is a strong predictor of later success in reading skill (National Early Literacy Panel, 2008). Additionally, research shows that phonemic awareness instruction is more effective when accompanied by alphabet knowledge instruction (Ehri et al., 2001). The **alphabetic principle** is grasping the concept that sounds of the language (phonemes) are represented by letters. Most kindergarten children, dependent on their early exposure, come to school knowing at least the letters in their names. Many of them recognize all the uppercase letters and many of the lowercase. The Common Core State Standards set a benchmark for kindergarten children to recognize all upper- and lower-case letters by the end of the kindergarten year.

Adams (1990) suggests that letter recognition is extremely important in the development of word recognition:

> For children with little letter knowledge on entry to school, current learning theory suggests it is unwise to try to teach both uppercase and lowercase forms of all twenty-six letters at once. For children who do not know letter names on school entry, special care should be taken to avoid confusion of names and sounds. (p.26)

Kindergarten instruction in letter recognition usually begins with the letters in the child's name and then may move to the eleven letters that have basically the same shape in both upper- and lower-case (Cc, Kk, Oo, Pp, Ss, Uu, Vv, Ww, Xx, Yy, Zz). The next seven letters that may be taught are similar in upper- and lower-case (Bb, Hh, Ii, Jj, Mm, Nn, Tt). The remainder of the letters in upper- and lower-case have the greatest difference and may require more exposure and direct instruction. As children begin to recognize words, they make the connection between the letter and the sound that it represents. Children learn the alphabetic principle in context, as they interact with written language, and through direct instruction.

Alphabet recognition can be taught by using environmental print such as newspapers, cereal boxes, etc. to find certain letters (e.g. "Find all the C's on the cereal box."). Using children's names in daily activities is a good way to call attention to the letters in the names. The kindergarten classroom is usually stocked with materials that children can use to solidify their recognition of the alphabet – magnetic letters, letter stencils, alphabet puzzles, and white boards. Alphabet books – commercially produced

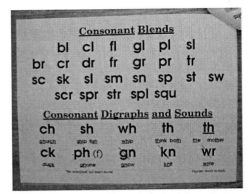

and student created – offer a pleasurable way to introduce children to letters and the sounds they represent.

Phonics Instruction. Phonics involves utilizing the alphabetic principle (letters represent the sounds of language) to decode and recognize printed words. Phonics instruction in the kindergarten is taught implicitly and explicitly as well as incidentally and systematically. **Systematic phonics instruction** refers to the scope (the content) and sequence (the order) for teaching the letter-sound relationships. **Explicit phonics instruction refers** to lesson delivery that is teacher-directed. Mesmer and Griffith (2006, p. 376) state that when children pay "attention to letter and sound correspondence through the application of phonics to decode unknown words…(this) helps the beginner master a multitude of spelling patterns, and become a fluent reader."

"ABC Phonics Songs for Children"

Phonics instruction includes working with letter-sound relationships, spelling patterns that combine consonants and vowels, and rhyming words. Adams (1990) reminds us that the patterns of written and oral language and words enable humans to learn to decode and read. As children work with and manipulate words through implicit and explicit exposure, incidental and systematic instruction, they accrue a bank of word and spelling patterns. **Sight words (high-frequency words)** are words that are not sounded out, but instead must be memorized (e.g. *the, and, give*). During the kindergarten year, children need to learn many of these words that do not have regular spelling patterns. Children become more fluent readers when they build a repertoire of sight words; if sight words are not learned, children will attempt to decode these words, affecting reading fluency and comprehension.

Writing is a strategy that children can use to learn phonics (Stahl, 1992). **Invented spelling (phonetic spelling)** encourages children to use their knowledge of letter names and letter-sound relationships to spell words. The invented spelling stage of writing is a temporary stage that actually promotes children's decoding skills (Clarke, 1988). Kindergarten children's invented spellings for words aids the teacher in assessing their level of understanding of letter-sound relationships and sight word memorization.

ce minte — cement
oShin — ocean
PuniSh mit — punishment
moShih — motion
tomato — tomato
Kratie — karate
vakaShih — vacation

Kindergarten children will vary greatly in their need for instruction in decoding skills. "Some will learn to decode on their own, without any instruction. Others will need some degree of instruction, ranging from pointing out of common spelling patterns to intense and systematic instruction" (Stahl, 1992, p. 620). Many kindergarten children who seemingly need direct instruction of phonics, in actuality, are lacking the foundational skills of phonemic awareness and letter recognition. The teacher needs to build up the foundation of these skills while providing informal phonics instruction.

Vocabulary instruction in the kindergarten involves the teaching of high-frequency words as well as new and less frequently used words, and content-specific words. Cunningham (2008) states that about 100 words account for 50% of all the words young children read. Thus, direct instruction and wide reading build knowledge of both sight words and concept-specific vocabulary. Repeated exposure to new vocabulary is necessary in order to embed words in the child's working oral and sight vocabulary. Implicit vocabulary instruction can occur during read aloud discussion and questioning, in conversations, and in group activities and play that necessitate verbal interaction.

"Boone County Schools Kindergarten Readiness – Vocabulary/Language Skills"

Direct instruction of vocabulary in the kindergarten includes:

- Teaching targeted words that are connected to the thematic unit, math lessons, field trips, or literature that is being read. Intentionally teaching these word meanings is important for daily interactions and comprehension.
- Teaching word learning strategies to comprehend word meanings using the context of the word. Strategies can be taught through direct modeling in a read aloud-think aloud.
- Acquiring social and emotional competence that has long-lasting effects on a human's life including school and career success, and lifelong social and psychological regulation (Raver, 2002).

Comprehension is the ultimate goal of reading and writing; comprehending and creating meaning are the skills that we want kindergarten children to attain. In order for comprehension to occur, children must have a solid foundation of phonemic awareness, phonics knowledge, print awareness, and a bank of sight words. However, a balanced literacy approach does not wait until kindergarten children are "skill ready" to read. Reading comprehension, as well as the foundational skills for reading, is built through repeated experiences with books and stories. The more we experience and learn language to label our experiences and create new schema, the more fluently we will read about topics we have been exposed to. For example, reading stories about the postal system and how our mail travels is most appropriate when planning for a field trip to the post office. The intentional kindergarten teacher uses both **informational** and **narrative** texts to increase children's background knowledge, conceptual knowledge, and vocabulary.

Coupled with the use of graphic organizers such as KWL charts, T-charts, webs, and predictable charts, kindergarten children's schema and reading skills can be developed through read aloud-think alouds and beginning reading instruction. Young children can learn specific subject information (e.g. Science, Social Studies) in informational text as well as making inferences, analyzing, comparing and contrasting, making connections, drawing conclusions, and asking questions in both informational and narrative texts (Harvey & Goudvis, 2000).

Writing. Reading and writing are interconnected; as children learn to read, they learn to write and conversely, as they write, their reading skills are consolidated. When kindergarten children are regularly involved in writing, their reading ability grows significantly (Reutzel & Cooter, 1992). In kindergarten, the purpose of writing is to communicate meaning through the use of sight words and invented spelling. The mechanics – conventional spelling, punctuation, and neatness – come later. The principal focus of writing in the kindergarten should be on creating ideas and meaning.

There are multiple opportunities for children to write and interact with print in different contexts – the writing center, circle time, dramatic play, math and science journals, etc. Kindergarten children can write grocery lists, invitations, menus, telephone messages, and customer orders in the dramatic play corner. Letters to friends, creative stories to accompany artwork, and holiday cards can all be written in the writing center. Circle time invites five- and six-year old children to participate in shared writing and LEA (Language Experience Approach) experiences (Veatch et al., 1979). In the language experience approach children first dictate a story about a personal event such as building a snowman, the teacher writes the story down, reads the story back to the children, and then the children read it together.

"Writers Workshop"

Summary

- The period of the mid-1960's to the present has been extremely prolific in terms of knowledge about the social, physical, emotional, language, literacy, and cognitive growth of young children.

- Probably the most significant development in kindergarten education has been NAEYC's interpretation and articulation of what constitutes "developmentally appropriate practice" for the education of children from birth to age eight (Bredekamp 1987; Bredekamp & Copple, 1997; Copple & Bredekamp, 2009).

- As with any other domain of learning, teachers need to make accommodations and modifications based on the strengths, needs, and interests of each child, and to ensure that children with disabilities participate as fully as possible. **Universal Design for Learning (UDL)** is the belief that materials and environments need to be functional for everyone, including those with disabilities, to the greatest degree possible.

- The first seven years of life present great opportunity for cognitive growth if the child is appropriately stimulated in her environment and in her daily activities.

- Children in this age range are refining their thinking to be more accurate and complex – they have a greater capacity for organizing categories of information. Five- and six-year olds are becoming more sophisticated in their organization of conceptual knowledge.

- We know that oral language provides the bedrock of literacy acquisition and that this foundation needs to be built in infancy, yet many of the five- and six-year old children entering kindergarten will not have had the experiences necessary to build language and literacy skills. It is the kindergarten teacher's job to provide a language –rich classroom and curriculum with intentional teaching, building children's language and literacy skills.

Key Terms

alphabetic principle
behaviorist theory
blended approach
cardinality
constructivist theory

emergent literacy
emergent literacy approach
enumeration
explicit phonics instruction
high-frequency words
informational text
inquiry
invented spelling
maturationist theory
motor planning
narrative text
one-to-one correspondence
onset-rime
operations
phonemic awareness
phonological awareness
pragmatic language
redshirting
scientifically-based reading research (SBRR)
self-regulation
semantics
sight words
syntax
systematic phonics instruction
Universal Design for Learning (UDL)

Suggested Readings

Charlesworth, R. & Lind, K.K. (2016). *Math and science for young children* (8th ed.). Clifton Park, NY: Wadsworth Cengage Learning.

Children's Book Committee of Bank Street College of Education. (2009). *Celebrating 100 years: The best children's books of the year.* New York: Bank Street Children's Committee & Teachers' College Press.

Hyland, N. E. (2010, January). Social justice in early childhood classrooms. Young Children, 65 (1), 82-87.

Kennedy, L.M., Tipps, S., & Johnson, A. (2011). *Guiding children's learning of mathematics.* Clifton Park, NY: Wadsworth Cengage Learning.

Suggested Websites

Kindergarten Connection
 www.kconnect.com

National Kindergarten Alliance
 www.nkateach.org

American Library Association
  www.ala.org

National Council of Teachers of Mathematics
  www.nctm.org

Reflections

1. Go to your state's department of education website to bookmark your state's preschool and kindergarten learning standards. Compare what your state expects preschool children to know with what the state expects of kindergarten children. Then compare what children have to know in first grade. Why is it important to know this information? How can you use this knowledge?

2. Interview parents of preschool age children. Ask them what they think their children need to know and be able to do before they enter kindergarten. How do parents' views match with those of the theorists and philosophers? Of school district policy?

3. Interview two kindergarten teachers and ask them to describe their philosophy of kindergarten readiness and how they apply this philosophy.

4. Design plans for a literacy-enriched play center. Describe how this center might be created in a classroom. What literacy props should be placed in the play center? How might you scaffold children's play and literacy knowledge in the center?

References

Adams, M. (1990). *Beginning to read: Thinking and learning about print.* Cambridge, MA: MIT Press.

Anglin, J. M. (1993). *Vocabulary development: A morphological analysis.* Monographs of the Society for Research in Child Development, vol. 58, no. 10, serial no. 238. Chicago: University of Chicago Press.

Berk, L. E. (1997). *Infants and children: Prenatal through middle childhood.* (2nd ed.). Boston: Allyn & Bacon.

Berk, L. E. (2006). Looking at the kindergarten child. In D. F. Gullo (Ed.), *K today: Teaching and learning in the kindergarten year* (pp.11-25). Washington, DC: National Association for the Education of Young Children.

Berk, L. E. (2016). *Infants and children* (8th ed.). Boston, MA: Allyn & Bacon.

Bloom, L. (1998). Language acquisition in its developmental context. In *Handbook of child psychology, Vol. 2: Cognition, perception, and language,* 5th ed., D. Kuhn & R. S. Siegler, 309-370. New York: John Wiley & Sons.

Bodrova., E & Leong, D. J. (2008). Developing self-regulation in kindergarten: Can we keep all the crickets in the basket? *Young Children, 63*(2), 56-58.

Bredekamp, S. (Ed.). (1987). *Developmentally appropriate practice in early childhood programs serving children from birth through age 8.* Washington, DC: NAEYC.

Bredekamp, S. (2011). *Effective practices in early childhood education: Building a foundation.* Upper Saddle River, NJ: Pearson Education.

Bredekamp, S. & Copple, C. (Eds.). (1997). *Developmentally appropriate practice in early childhood programs serving children from birth through age 8.*(2nd ed.) Washington, DC: NAEYC.

Burhans, K. K. & Dweck, C. S. (1995). Helplessness in early childhood: The role of contingent worth. *Child Development, 66*(6), 1719-1738.

Clarke, L. K. (1988). Invented versus traditional spelling in first graders' writings: Effects on learning to spell and read. *Research in the Teaching of English, 22,* 281-309.

Clay, M. (1972). *Reading: The patterning of complex behavior.* Portsmouth, NH: Heinemann.

Copple, C. & Bredekamp, S. (2009). *Developmentally appropriate practice in early childhood programs.* (3rd ed.). Washington, DC: NAEYC.

Cunningham, P. (2008). *Phonics they use: Words for reading and writing* (5th ed.). New York: Longman.

Dickinson, D. K., McCabe, A., & Sprague, K. (2003). Teacher rating of oral language and literacy (TROLL): Individualizing early literacy instruction with a standards-based rating tool. *The Reading Teacher, 56*(6), 554-564.

Duncan, G. J., Dowsett, C. J., Claessens, A., Magnuson, K., Huston, A. C., Klebanov, P. (2007). School readiness and later achievement. *Developmental Psychology, 43,* 1428-1446.

Ehri, L., Nunes, S., Willows, D., Schuster, B., Yaghoub-Zadeh, Z., & Shanahan, T. (2001). Phonemic awareness instruction helps children learn to read: Evidence from the National Reading Panel's meta-analysis. *Reading Research Quarterly, 36,* 250-287.

Flavell, J.H., Green, F.L., & Flavell, E.R (1995). The development of children's knowledge about attentional focus. *Developmental Psychology, 31,* 706-712.

Gesell, A. (1940). *The first five years of life.* New York: Harper & Row.

Hart, B. & Risley, T. R. (1995). *Meaningful differences in the everyday experience of young American children.* Baltimore: Brookes.

Harvey, S. & Goudvis, A. (2000). *Strategies that work: Teaching comprehension to enhance understanding.* Portland, ME: Stenhouse.

Holdaway, D. (1979). *The foundations of literacy.* Toronto: Ashton Scholastic.

Katz, L. G. & McClellan, D. E. (1997). *Fostering children's social competence: The teacher's role.* Washington, DC: National Association for the Education of Young Children.

Manross, M. A. (1994). *What children think, feel, and know about the overhand throw.* Master's thesis. Virginia Tech University, Blacksburg, VA.

Manross, M. A. (2000). *Learning to throw in physical education class: Part 3, Teaching Elementary Physical Education.* New York: Oxford University Press.

Marshall, H. (2003). Research in review. Opportunity deferred or opportunity taken? An updated look at delaying kindergarten entry. *Young Children, 58*(5), 84-93.

Marsh, M. (2003). *Social fashioning of teacher identities.* New York: Peter Lang.

McClelland, M. M., Acock, A. C., & Morrison, E.J. (2006). The impact of kindergarten learning-related skills on academic trajectories at the end of elementary school. *Early Learning Research Quarterly, 21*(4), 471-490.

Mesmer, H. A. E. & Griffith, P. L. (2006). Everybody's selling it –But just what is explicit, systematic phonics instruction? *The Reading Teacher, 59*(3), 366-376.

Morrison, G. S., (2012). *Early childhood education today.* Upper Saddle River, NJ: Pearson Education.

Mullis, I. V. S., Martin, M. O., & Foy, P. (2008). *TIMSS 2007 international report and technical report.* Chestnut Hill, MA: TIMSS & PIRLS International Study Center, Lynch School of Education, Boston College.

National Association for the Education of Young Children (NAEYC). (2001). *NAEYC at 75: Reflections on the past, challenges for the future.* Washington, DC: NAEYC.

National Center for Education Statistics (NCES). (2015). Available online at http://nces.ed.gov/programs.

National Early Literacy Panel. (2008). *Developing early literacy: Report of the National Early Literacy Panel. A scientific synthesis of early literacy development and implications for intervention.* Washington, DC: National Early Literacy Panel.

National Research Council. (1997). *National Science Education Standards (NSES).* Washington, DC: National Academy Press.

National Research Council (NRC). (2016). *Mathematics learning in early childhood: Paths toward excellence and equity.* Washington, DC: National Academies Press.

New York State Early Learning Guidelines. (2012). http://www.ccf.ny.gov/ECAC/ECACResources/ELG.pdf

Novick, R. (1999/2000). Supporting early literacy development: Doing things with words in the real world. *Childhood Education, 76*(2). 70-75.

Otto, B. (2006). *Language development in early childhood* (2nd ed.). Upper Saddle River, NJ: Merrill.

Pettit, S. G. (2004). Violent children in developmental perspective. *Current Directions in Psychological Science, 13,* 194-197.

Phillips, B.M., Clancy-Menchetti, J., Lonigan, C.J. (2008). Successful phonological awareness instruction with preschool children: Lessons from the classroom. *Topics in Early Childhood Special Education, 28,* 3-17.

Preschool Curriculum Evaluation Research Consortium [PCERC]. (2008, July). *Effects of preschool curriculum programs on school readiness.* Washington, DC: U. S. Department of Education, Institute of Education Sciences, National Center for Education Research.

Puckett, M. B. & Black, J. K. (2005). *The young child: Development from prebirth through age eight* (4th ed.). Upper Saddle River, NJ: Pearson.

RAND Reading Study Group. (2002). *Reading for understanding: Toward an R&D program in reading comprehension.* Santa Monica, CA: RAND Education, Science & Technology Policy Institute.

Raver, C. C. (2002). *Emotions matter: Making the case for the role of young children's emotional development for early school readiness.* Ann Arbor, MI: Society for Research in Child Development.

Robinson, H. F. & Spodek, B. (1965). *New directions in the kindergarten.* New York: Teachers College Press.

Ryan, R. M. & Deci, E. L. (2000). Self-determination theory and the facilitation of intrinsic motivation, social development, and well-being. *American Psychologist, 55,* 68-78.

Seefeldt, C. & Wasik, B. A. (2006). *Early education: Three, four, and five-year-olds go to school* (2nd ed.). Upper Saddle River, NJ: Pearson.

Shepard, L. A., & Smith, M. L. (Eds.). (1989). *Flunking grades: Research and policies on retention.* Philadelphia: The Falmer Press.

Snow, C. E., Burns, M. S., Griffin, P., (1998). *Preventing reading difficulties in young children.* Washington, DC: National Academy Press.

Sroufe, L. A., Carlson, E., & Shulman, S. (1993). Individuals in relationships: Development from infancy to adolescence. In *Studying lives through time: Personality and development.* D. C. Funder, R. D. Parke, C. Tomlinson, & K. Widaman, pp. 315-342. Washington, DC: American Psychological Association.

Stahl, S. A. (1992). Saying the "p" word: Nine guidelines for exemplary phonics instruction. *The Reading Teacher, 45,* 618-625.

Starkey, P. & Klein, A. (2008). Sociocultural influences on young children's mathematical knowledge. In O. N. Saracho & B. Spodek (Eds.), *Contemporary perspectives on mathematics in early childhood education* (pp. 253-276). Charlotte, NC: Information Age Publishing.

Thatcher, R. W., Lyon, G. R., Rumsey, J., Krasnegor, J. (1996). *Developmental neuroimaging.* San Diego, CA: Academic Press.

Thelen, E. & Smith, L. B., (1998). Dynamic systems theories. In *Handbook of child psychology, Vol. 1: Theoretical models of human development* (5th ed.). R. M. Lerner (Ed.), 563-634. New York: John Wiley & Sons.

Veatch, J., Sawlicki, F., Elliott, G., Flake, E., & Blakey, J. (1979). Key words in reading. Columbus OH: Merrill.

Wilson, H. K., Pianta,R. C., & Stuhlman, M. W. (2007). Typical classroom experiences in first grade: The role of classroom climate and functional risk in the development of social competencies. *Elementary School Journal, 108*(2), 81-96.

Worth, K. & Grollman, S, (2003). *Worms, shadows and whirlpools: Science in the early childhood classroom.* Portsmouth, NH: Heinemann.

Wortham, S. C. (2010). *Early childhood curriculum* (5th ed.). Upper Saddle River, NJ: Merrill.

Chapter 10
Primary Grades Today

Today in the Primary Grades

Thinking Ahead

1. What is education in the primary grades like today?
2. What are the social-emotional characteristics of six- to eight-year olds?
3. What are the physical development characteristics of six- to eight-year olds?
4. What are the cognitive characteristics of six- to eight-year olds?
5. How can teachers of primary age children support their development across all the domains of learning?

"The primary grades are a time for children to shine. They gain increasing mastery in every area of their development and learning. They explore, read, and reason, problem solve, communicate through conversations and writing, and develop lasting friendships" (Tomlinson, cited in Copple & Bredekamp, 2009, p. 257). Despite the increased emphasis on assessment, and "push-down curriculum" that requires first and second graders to cover more  content, six to eight year olds still benefit from teachers who focus on the needs of the whole child, integrate the learning, offer warm and sensitive teaching and provide a carefully planned balance of child-guided and teacher-guided activities.

"Whole Brain Teaching: Grade 1 Classroom"

Children in this age range experience a slower but continuous body growth; motor coordination is improving (Manross, 2000), and six to eight year olds' play is in more organized play, such as soccer, that requires increased eye-hand coordination as well as stopping and starting, and running and changing direction. Six- to eight-year olds are interested in making friends and they are increasingly savvy in their ability to take the perspective of their peers. Seefeldt and Barbour

(1998) state: "They're developing the ability to see things from another perspective and are able to be more empathetic. At the same time, they're very sensitive and their feelings get hurt easily" (p. 212). Children at this age need strong support from the adults around them, both parents and teachers.

Intellectually, children at this age learn best when the curriculum is challenging, engaging, meaningful, and built on their interests (Hyson, 2008). Primary grade children's communication skills have increased dramatically as they move from oral communication alone to oral and written self-expression. These children are developing their ability to concentrate their attention for longer periods of time. Engagement and motivation for learning are important entities as children in this age range are learning to read and doing higher level mathematics. It is important that the intentional teacher instills the desire for learning – a lifelong, necessary skill (Epstein, 2007).

"Teaching Children Good Communication Skills"

Teaching today in the primary grades presents a set of challenges that teachers must face. Mandatory assessment in language arts and mathematics begins in third grade, yet preparation in terms of academics and skill work begins in the earlier grades. This compulsory assessment has taken the control of curriculum planning and pacing out of the hands of most classroom teachers; the administration as well as school boards and state officials set much of the curriculum which is narrowed to focus in on the specific topics which are tested. Implementing what teachers know is best practice that is developmentally appropriate while preparing children for the inevitable testing, is often problematic (Bredekamp, 2011). Yet, often teachers are not given the support or the time to use a more balanced approach to instruction. This chapter will discuss the development of primary grade students across domains of learning and what constitutes best practice for six to eight year olds in each learning domain.

**"First Year Teaching (Elementary Grades) –
Success from the Start"**

Primary Development Across the Domains

Children in this age range, because of their accumulated life experiences, display a great deal of individuality and uniqueness, yet they share common traits across all the domains of learning. Knowledge of these commonalities helps guide our teaching practice to meet the needs of all primary age children.

Social-Emotional Development

Six to eight-year old children work hard at making friends; peer relationships become increasingly important to them. As children mature through the age range, they become more adept at sustaining friendships by helping, cooperating, sharing, and finding ways to maintain and extend their play (Hyson, 2008). When conflict does arise, problem-solving to negotiate a solution becomes more sophisticated; children attempt to balance their needs with the needs of their peers. The adults in children's live can serve as knowledgeable supports and models in learning social skills.

"Personal, Social, and Emotional Development"

The strong friendships children are establishing make them feel accepted and part of a group; identity with a group gives the child a sense of belonging and fosters imitation of his or her group members. Seven and eight-year olds crave peer acceptance more than six-year olds, leading them to form "clubs" which include and exclude peers (Bandura, 1997). Even though children at this age enjoy feeling part of a group, they occasionally take pleasure in working by themselves in a quiet space.

During these years, gender identification becomes more clear-cut, as children accept the permanence of gender. During the primary grades, children's own gender identification becomes intertwined with culturally imposed gender roles and rules, and it strongly influences children's choice of friends (Berk, 2008). Children generally show a preference for same-gender friends and can become vocal in excluding the opposite sex from their play and school activities.

Children this age are in Erikson's industry vs. inferiority stage where they are accomplishing more complex tasks and gaining confidence and self-satisfaction from completing the tasks. The industry that is demonstrated by pride and persistence in completing a task is the positive side of the conflict in this stage of Erikson's theory. Children in this stage compare themselves to their peers and may be self-critical if they think they do not measure up to their peers. Unlike four- and five-year olds who overvalue their competence, six- to eight-year old children may judge themselves too punitively. They may lose self-confidence, which can set them up for a lifetime of not feeling capable (Bredekamp, 2011). This represents the inferiority side of Erikson's stage of development.

During the primary years of schooling, children's sense of self-worth - reflected in their opinion of their own self-efficacy – becomes increasingly realistic. They can more accurately assess their competence in some areas and limited abilities in other areas. The result is self-evaluation through comparison to others: this self-critique, if positive, can propel the child forward in his development, or if negative, can stifle his motivation (Bandura, 1997). If the child has a negative self-image, he is more likely to be aggressive, resulting in social isolation; this cycle of aggression and shunning serves to deepen the feelings of low-esteem in the child. This may then cycle into bullying – the child with low self-esteem may be bullied, become a bully, or both.

"Tips for Building Self Esteem in Your Child"

Physical bullying, which is practiced mostly by boys - often rooted in low self-esteem – perpetuates a negative spiral leading to further social isolation and rejection (Kenny et al., 2007). The child often is bullied and then becomes the bully, which leads to peers and adults disliking and avoiding him. This isolation debilitates the bully because he is marginalized and not given the opportunity for positive interaction which would allow him to develop the skill of "reading" people's intentions and behaviors accurately (Bandura, 1997). Bullying is a serious issue since boys who practice bullying in the primary grades are more likely in adolescence and adulthood to experience depression, suicidal thoughts, violent behavior, and other problems (Klomek et al., 2008).

"Kids Talk About Bullying"

Relational bullying – deceiving, being mean to, or excluding another child – often begins as early as age four and intensifies in the primary grades. Girls are usually thought to be relational bullies, although boys too participate in it. Family expectations, media exposure, and cultural principles influence the depth and frequency of physical and relational aggression (Brown et al., 2007).

The victim of bullying can be a bully themselves, or can be a seemingly physically or emotionally frail child who is an easy target. The victims, too, can become socially isolated, lonely, and depressed. It is part of the teacher's role to recognize that bullying is not a normal part of growing up, to intervene in the bullying, and to teach both the bully and the bullied alternative social skills. One of those skills is enabling the victim to stand up for his rights, to seek intervention, and to build a cadre of friends who will also learn how to intervene (Copple & Bredekamp, 2009).

Persistence at a task is the ability to maintain focus on the task, to seek assistance when the next step seems unclear or too difficult, and the ability to modify strategies needed to complete the task. Primary children learn the disposition of persistence when they build competency in the knowledge and skills that are deemed important. Primary children persist in activities in which they are confident and knowledgeable however, if they feel incompetent, they are likely to develop feelings of inferiority and ineptitude.

Over time, children can develop **learned helplessness** – "a condition in which children attribute their failures to a lack of ability…these children are passive and have learned to feel they are helpless" (Morrison, 2012, p.336). Teachers need to provide children with challenging but achievable tasks, and scaffold the children until they can complete the tasks independently.

Emotional understanding of themselves and of others is a skill that is built across the primary years. Children become less egocentric and begin to consider others' perspectives and feelings. By age 8, the disposition of empathy is developed to the degree that this awareness of others' needs extends to children with special physical, cognitive, and emotional needs (Berk, 2016).

Self-regulation is the internally developed ability to practice self-control of one's behavior and emotions. Children learn self-regulation through direct instruction, scaffolding, and adult support; self-regulation is a necessary skill that can ensure school and life success. Bandura (1997) hypothesized that children learn by modeling the self-regulated behavior of others, reflecting on their performance, and then by rewarding or punishing themselves. Teachers can support children's development in self-regulation by helping them set goals, allowing them to self-evaluate, and to meaningfully praise every success. Role-playing and dramatization are strategies that allow children to problem-solve, come up with alternatives that demonstrate self-regulation, and learn the skill of negotiation.

The teacher role in social-emotional development of young children is very important; the teacher has the job of creating environments and opportunities in which all children can develop positive self-esteem, self-regulation, social competence, and persistence in learning. The classroom environment should emphasize cooperation instead of competition, offer engaging and intrinsically motivating learning, and heighten children's joy of learning (Copple & Bredekamp, 2009). The activities in the classroom should be tailored to individual needs so that all children are challenged yet feel successful. Role-playing helps children see situations from perspectives other than their own. Making children feel invested in the classroom by having them build the classroom rules is another strategy that supports social-emotional development in young children. Cooperative learning where children work together fosters the sense of collaboration and community while strengthening peer relationships.

Physical and Motor Development

Primary age children are more confident due to their increasing independence, refined motor skills, and physical strength. Children in this stage of development, on average, grow two to three inches and gain three to five pounds annually (Copple & Bredekamp, 2009). Muscle mass increases in boys and girls while the body elongates and broadens. By age 8, the brain has achieved about 90% of its full adult growth, and by age 6 the eyes are coordinated in binocular vision (Berk, 2016).

"Promoting Physical Development in Children"

Access to quality healthcare and nutritious foods are factors which can result in variation of sizes of children. Yet poverty is a factor which increases children's potential risk for health problems – poor quality or non-existent health care, inadequate nutrition, and sub-par housing. Additionally, the growing childhood obesity problem in the United States puts a large number of American children at risk. Childhood obesity has more than doubled in children 6-11 in the past 30 years. The percentage of children aged 6-11 years in the United States who were obese increased from 7% in 1980 to nearly 18% in 2012. In 2012, more than one-third of children and adolescents were overweight or obese (CDC 2013). Obesity in childhood is a precursor for adult obesity, and contributes to heart disease, diabetes, high blood pressure, and many other physical conditions. Children who have balanced nutritious meals and plenty of exercise have a reduced risk for obesity.

"Gross Motor Skills"

Gross motor development. As children in this age range get stronger, more coordinated, and possessing high energy levels, they attempt new challenges in structured and unstructured sports. Six- to eight-year old children emboldened by their improving physical skills become more "dare-devilish" and take greater risks. Due to their greater balance, coordination, increased endurance, and ability to plan out the sequence of games and play, primary age children are interested in team sports.

Fine motor development. Children come into the first grade with varying fine motor abilities, yet with practice they become more adept and controlled at fine motor skills. The primary grades are a time for refinement of fine motor skills. Writing skills become more uniform and precise. During this time girls tend to be developmentally ahead of boys (Haywood & Getchell, 2005). However, gender differences are in part the result of opportunity – girls usually gravitate to fine motor activities such as writing, drawing, and crafts.

The teacher role in children's physical and motor development is to support children's individual interests as well as create environments and opportunities for children to engage in fine and gross motor activities. Fine motor skills can be strengthened by offering possibilities for art and construction activities. Six- to eight-year olds need to develop their growing facility in drawing, writing, and building. These activities can be integrated across content areas as options or as means of assessing mastery of the learning objectives. Children this age need to be active to both expend excess energy and to keep up energy levels (Berk, 2016). The classroom teacher needs to provide daily movement activities in addition to the structured activities in physical education.

This is a time when children become self-critical; teachers and coaches should encourage children to participate in organized sports to gain cooperation skills, team-building, and self-esteem. Adults should avoid putting children in overly competitive situations where children can be overly critical of themselves. Competition should be individual and framed as goal-setting and goal-meeting.

Teachers need to make accommodations for children with disabilities so that they can participate in an activity as much as possible. Modified equipment inside and outside on the playground can enable children with physical disabilities to participate fully. Physical education is important for children with special needs to participate in because it builds coordination, social skills, listening skills, and rule following (Pica, 2004). It is important that children with special needs are successful in physical activities to build their self-confidence.

Cognitive Development

Children in the primary grades are curious learners who value both the product and process of their learning. Six- to eight-year old children are entering Piaget's Concrete Operational Stage when children can begin to structure time and space as well as think logically. They still learn best through active participation and concrete experiences however, as children in this age range approach eight years old they have the ability to think abstractly as long as what they are thinking about has its roots in something that is familiar or relevant. For instance, children can learn about maps of countries and the world by having experience in making maps of their school or community. Across this age range, children develop their ability to think logically; they enjoy hands-on experimentation and are able to plan,  execute and organize their experiences mentally. They are able to reverse mathematical operations in addition and subtraction; for example, children can understand that six plus three equals nine, and nine minus six equals three. Imaginative play remains an important outlet for children in the primary grades, but it progresses into more complex role-playing such as puppet shows and skits (Seefeldt & Barbour, 1998).

The development that occurs in children's cognitive abilities during the primary grades prepares children for the rigors of mental operations that are part of schools' literacy, mathematics, and content curricula. This growth affects all the domains of learning – cognitive, physical, language, and social-emotional.

Executive function is the ability to focus attention, plan and think ahead, and monitor cognitive processes against the teacher's expectations (Bodrova & Leong, 2007)). Additionally, children must be able to hold information actively in their minds while performing tasks – "working memory". Executive function is dependent on a child's level of self-regulation, is emerging in the primary grades, and should be taught and practiced (Mahone & Silverman, 2008).

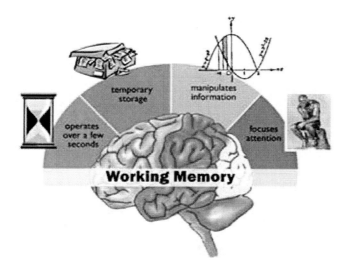

Remaining focused on a task and ignoring extraneous, distracting stimuli is a skill that is refined as children grow and with experience. This skill allows children to concentrate to complete their work; difficulty paying attention and staying on task can impede a child's learning and school success. The ability for primary children to self-regulate and remain focused on a task is a definitive indicator of success both in school and in adulthood. We can understand the correlation of self-regulation to success in school and its importance when we consider the example of primary school children being expected to delay the gratification of play with friends in order to concentrate and complete a reading lesson.

Planning is another aspect of executive function; planning requires the ability to look ahead in a task to think out and break down the steps of the sequence, apportioning the appropriate level of attention to each of the steps in the sequence. Even though primary students have varying capacity to plan and then carrying out a task sequentially, they use their increased sorting skills to organize a task. By age 8, primary children have enough of a concept of time to be able to successfully sequence tasks and events. Teachers can scaffold children in strengthening their planning and organizational skills through think alouds that model how to break apart a task, decide the sequence of steps, and then "talk" children through the task.

Memory is a facet of executive function that is essential for success in school and adulthood. Primary children's increased working memory provides an important support for learning. As children this age improve their ability to store information, retrieve the stored information, use their mental processes and become more metacognitive, they become better problem-solvers (Copple & Bredekamp, 2016). While adults can hold seven pieces of information in short-term memory, most seven year olds can hold only five. In order for information to be retained, the bits of information that are in short-term memory have to be transferred to long-term memory (Berk, 2008). Children need plenty of time, opportunities, and review of conceptual knowledge to consolidate knowledge so that it can be retained. All this capacity for memory does not come naturally; it is the job of the teacher to model memory skills. They can do this by cueing children that material has to be remembered, through games where children use mnemonics and other devices to memorize, and by modeling using mental imagery in think alouds to create mental pictures.

"Cognitive Development of Middle Childhood: Memory Skills"

Concept acquisition and reasoning. Six- to eight-year olds' cognition is moving toward having the capability for more abstract reasoning; children in the concrete operations stage of cognitive development are increasingly able to use mental images and symbols while they are thinking. They are now able to perform operations such as  more complex classification and are able to reverse operations by thinking backwards through a problem. However, children this age still need a great deal of concrete, hands-on experience. New concepts need to be introduced in authentic, experiential ways so that children can manipulate ideas and objects to grasp the concept in a developmentally appropriate way. Primary age children can mentally manipulate symbols such as numbers, yet they still need concrete objects while computing abstract problems.

Intentional teaching and effective learning for primary children should include concrete, learning experiences that are built on children's prior knowledge and have relevancy to them. Conceptual knowledge is most effectively learned when it is related to children's daily lives It is also built through in-depth, integrated studies and long-term projects that deepen the learning. Cooperative learning activities allow children to progress in planning, focusing attention, and development of memory.

Math, Science, and Social Studies

Math in today's primary grades, in most states in the US, is aligned to the Common Core State Standards for Mathematics. The National Council of Teachers of Mathematics (NCTM) has identified five areas of content understanding: numbers and operations, algebra, geometry, measurement, and data and probability, and five areas of process competencies: problem-solving, reasoning and proof, communications, connection, and representation. The Common Core State Standards for grades 1-3 are framed around the following content areas: operations and algebraic thinking, number and operations in base ten, measurement

and data, and geometry; and the process skills identified by the NCTM. Additionally, the CCSS have adopted the strands of mathematical proficiency identified by the National Research Council (2009): adaptive reasoning, strategic competence, conceptual understanding, procedural fluency, and productive disposition (seeing mathematics as sensible and worthwhile).

"Using Guided Math to Strengthen Students' Math Learning, Grades K-2"

In order for primary age children to move the mathematical knowledge in their short-term memory into long-term memory, children must use many of their modalities – particularly visual, auditory, and tactile. Using manipulatives such as coins, parquetry  blocks, counters, and dice makes learning mathematics more meaningful to young children, giving them more confidence in their ability. Making mathematics relevant to their daily lives is another way to embed mathematics understanding. A logical way to teach mathematics thinking is to build on the skills children bring to school, encourage them to use these skills in a purposeful way, and plan experiences that promote learning new skills while solving problems they come across every day. One of the ways this happens is when children **mathematize** – understanding and thinking about everyday problems and experiences in mathematical terms (NRC, 2009). Mathematics is abstract and to have a better understanding of it, children have to create concrete models. When they mathematize, children think about the mathematical aspects of a problem and then they create a model or representation to solve the problem. The model can be drawn, represented by objects, or acted out. A good example is when children decide to survey all their peers in the class about their pets. After tallying the number of pets of each type, the children can draw a bar graph, and analyze and interpret the data.

Numbers and operations has traditionally been the central focus of the primary grade math curriculum and the basis upon which children's mathematical ability and achievement are evaluated. Understanding number concepts includes three levels of understanding:

- *Number*, e.g., the meaning of 5
- *The relationship between numbers*, e.g., five is less than eight, thirty is 3 times 10
- *The result of operations on numbers*, e.g., if you subtract one number from another you get a smaller number

Throughout the primary grades, children have real-life experiences counting, estimating, connecting, grouping, and interpreting numbers to develop a substantive understanding of number and operations concepts. Children need many opportunities to group and manipulate numbers to learn how the placement of the number determines its value. For example, children need to know what the "5" means in 15, and 50. Exploring numbers with authentic materials such as manipulatives and bundling sticks deepens children's understanding. Games are a great activity for children to practice and bolster number concepts. Playing cards, dominoes, board games, and dice games require children to count, calculate sums and differences, recognize equivalency, and comprehend number relationships.

Geometry, spatial relations, and measurement in the primary grades offer six- to eight-year old children another way to organize data in their world. In geometry, children in the primary grades learn about the attributes of geometric shapes, compare and transform shapes, and explore spatial relationships. Children learn about the attributes of shapes by constructing shapes; matching, describing, naming, and reproducing shapes; investigating solid geometry such as cylinders and spheres; and classifying shapes by specific attributes (e.g., all the shapes that have right angles). Comparing and transforming shapes are more complex skills that  primary grade children are beginning to develop: recognizing congruent shapes; comparing difference in geometric solids; comparing the number of sides, lines of symmetry and angles of shapes; and sorting and classifying shapes according to more complex attributes such as straight sides or two long sides. Children explore spatial relationships by filling an area with geometrical shapes (e.g., using parquetry blocks to fill in a design such as a house), solving area problems such as filling a space using rectangular or square tiles, and studying symmetry.

Through their study of measurement, primary children learn how to use the tools and strategies of measurement. They can use meter sticks, unifix cubes, or popsicle sticks to measure the width of the classroom. Children in this age range understand that the unit-length of measurement needs to be uniform and that the smaller the unit of measurement, the more units they need to cover a given length. Using their knowledge of linear measurement, children are able to calculate the perimeter of an object. Primary age children also use estimation with measurement; they use their knowledge of conservation and their developing logic to estimate how many cups of M&M's a container holds and how many total M&M's will be in the container if they know how many are in one cup. Children can also compare and determine the difference in weight between two objects, even if they are the same size.

Patterns and algebra. Patterns are all around us in the organization of nature's cycles, numbers, and events. An understanding of patterns is necessary for higher level work in geometry, numbers, and data analysis. As primary children develop higher levels of abstract thinking, they move from the concrete patterning of preschool and kindergarten into more complex uses of patterns. Consistent and recurring patterns support children's understanding of operations. For example, if children learn that an object is ten inches long, then 2 of the objects laid end to end make twenty inches long and 3 of them make a length of thirty inches. By providing opportunities for children to notice patterns, we help them to understand functions and algebraic relationships, so that children can make connections to solve problems. Primary children need repeated activities to identify, extend, and create patterns both visually and in auditory experiences such as music and literature.

"Learning Math: Patterns, Functions, and Algebra"

Teachers need to plan lessons in which children identify patterns: examining numbers on a hundreds chart and extending number patterns such as -3, 0, 3, 6, 9, ?, 15. Children can create patterns, for example, making patterns with a string of beads and eventually being able to make a number pattern using two rules such as add 2, subtract 1. Extending patterns by using algebraic reasoning is demonstrated when a pattern continues that repeats itself and also grows (2, 4, 2, 6, 2, 8…). Children can describe relationships by grouping objects in more than one way and sorting by more than one attribute.

Visual Math

Directions: Draw the object that should come next for each sequence below.

○◇○○○◇○○○   _____

□□○○□◇○□○○□◇   _____

○○◻☆△○○◻   _____

▱○▱◇☆□▱▱○▱   _____

☆☆○☆□☆   _____

☆□▱☆□▱☆   _____

Data analysis, statistics, probability are a part of primary age children's authentic experience when they roll dice, predict what numbers are going to come up, analyze and graph the results. Probability problems challenge children, are interesting and engaging to children, and make numbers a meaningful part of their daily lives. Primary grade children make predictions and develop arguments by predicting outcomes and testing them (e.g., roll a die 15 times and predict which number occurs most often). Children in this age range learn to collect, organize, and record data by first creating graphs with real objects such as different color M&M's and later being able to create picture, bar, pie, and line graphs. Reading graphs and drawing conclusions are skills that six- to eight-year old children develop and become adept at. Children can answer questions using information on a graph, eventually being able to locate and read graphs in newspapers and magazines.

"Problem Solving Strategies"

Not only do teachers of primary age children plan lessons teaching the above topics of mathematical content, but they also focus on the process skills of problem-solving, reasoning and proof, making connections, communicating and representing mathematical information. To solve problems, children need problem-solving strategies that enable them to comprehend, interpret the meaning of the problem, and then make a plan to solve the problem. Children learn to reason and prove by noticing patterns, making logical conclusions from the data they notice, and arguing their conclusions as proof of their original hypothesis. Children make connections when they can relate math to their daily lives such as finding numbers and patterns in books they are reading. Communicating is apparent when children can talk about math using mathematical signs symbols, and language. Children can represent their mathematical thinking in drawings, models, drama, games, and journals.

Science in the primary grades continues the **inquiry-based** learning that began in preschool and kindergarten. Inquiry-based learning involves children directly in asking questions, observing carefully while gathering and analyzing information, and ultimately proposing explanations that can be tested. Six- to eight-year old children possess the insatiable curiosity and the developing skills to carry out scientific investigations that are inquiry-based. Children – like adult scientists - are consistently asking questions about the world around them and science curriculum for primary age children is most effective when it is intentionally built on children's penchant to find answers for their questions and their inclination for hands-on investigations.

"Elementary Science, Grades K-3, Cells, Genetics"

The steps in the inquiry process of scientific thinking include: 1) posing a question, 2) observation, 3) researching to build background knowledge about the subject being investigated, 4) suggesting solutions and predicting what will happen for each solution, 5) testing a solution, 6) gathering data and interpreting it. For primary age children, any topic that addresses scientific knowledge – living environment, earth and space, energy, matter – can be a vehicle for teaching scientific thinking. An example is a second grade class that displays interest in shadows after listening to a read aloud about shadows in morning meeting. Children discuss their experiences with shadows, while the teacher poses some thought-provoking questions such as "What do you think makes our shadows show up and then disappear?" The teacher then designs a series of activities including tracing children's shadows at different times of the day while the children investigate, measure, record, chart, and graph the data they collect. Children use their mathematical skills to graph and analyze comparative charts; as well, they study sources of light, angles of light that change the shadows, and absence of light. All children are involved in this engaging and purposeful scientific investigation and are thinking, questioning, explaining, and assessing.

The Science curriculum is divided into three categories: physical science, life science, and earth and space science. **Physical science** includes the knowledge of properties of matter and the relationship of the matter's properties to its purpose. Physical science also includes the topics of sound, heat, light, electricity, and motion. **Life science** includes the knowledge of the needs of animals and plants, as well as of their behavior, characteristics, life cycles, and habitats. **Earth and space science** is knowledge that is related to day and night, climate and weather, the earth's surface, and the moon and stars. As with all curriculum content, superficial coverage of several topics should not be the goal; teachers need to focus science instruction on in-depth study of a few topics. Primary children need long-term units of study that are organized around developmentally appropriate scientific investigations.

The topics that six- to eight-year old children learn about should be connected to their experience and the world around them; children need direct observation of materials and objects around them. All three categories in science should be taught in depth in each academic year. For instance, children could engage in an extended study of the life cycle of plants and animals, their basic needs, and their adaptation; weather and seasons and the sun's effect on both; and the properties of materials and their different states.

Often, teachers do not feel comfortable teaching science; this is due in part because teachers do not feel comfortable with the content as well as the time and messiness of true scientific investigations. One way to make science part of children's everyday life and to inspire children to become scientists is to provide experiences, a classroom space, and materials for investigation. The classroom needs to be stocked with the tools of inquiry, collections of objects such as seashells and seeds, and living things such as plants and small pets. Primary grade children need a teacher who can model how a scientist thinks; teachers need to demonstrate enthusiastic curiosity as well as pose probing questions (e.g., What would happen if…?, How can we find out…?).

pppst.com

Children need a time for debriefing where they can share what they have found in their investigations, and entertain suggestions from their peers and teacher. Six- to eight-year old children also need to talk about discoveries they have made outside of school. Birds' nests, seashells, and plants are all scientific "treasures" that can elicit scientific conversations, questions, and encouragement for further study. The traditional "show and tell" time provides an opportunity that may be better used for scientific conversations.

Long-term studies such as graphing the daily temperature over several months or observing a tree and journaling its changes over the school year provide plenty of scientific observations that lead to rich, inquiry-based discussions. Long-term studies support primary children as they assume the role of investigative scientist – a lifelong disposition that educators can instill in young children. By studying a variety of topics in depth, children can see threads of common concepts (e.g., cycles and patterns can be seen in weather, seasons, life cycles, etc.). There should be a balance in long-term studies so that life science, physical science, and earth and space science are all studied in depth. Long-term studies, as well as shorter studies, need to be based on children's interests; a flexible curriculum affords the time for studies that are child-generated.

Social Studies in the primary grades is built upon children's knowledge of themselves, their families, their communities, and their school. The curriculum should be derived from the fields of study in geography, history, economics, civics and political science, anthropology, and sociology. One of the most important functions of social studies is to teach responsible citizenship in a community, using the classroom as their first real experience in a community. Children learn how to make and follow rules, the rights and responsibilities of living in a democracy, how to make thoughtful choices, how to treat others with tolerance and respect, and how to consider others' perspectives and viewpoints.

The National Council for Social Studies (2010) has published curriculum standards which encompass ten themes: culture; time, continuity, and change; people, places, environments; individual development and identity; individuals, groups, institutions; power, authority, governance; production, distribution, consumption; science, technology and society; global connections; and civic ideals and practices. In 2008, the NCSS emphasized the importance of making the social studies curriculum meaningful, integrated, value-based, challenging, and active. "The primary purpose of social studies is to help young people develop the ability to make informed and reasoned decisions for the public good as citizens of a culturally diverse, democratic society in an interdependent world" (NCSS, 2008). State and local districts use these standards as a guideline for their own social studies standards.

"Social Studies Lesson Plan- Alyssa Rehder"

Social Studies is a combination of content and process. The content encompasses the ten themes on which the learning standards are based, focusing on what children know – first, their families and communities and then expanding to wider contexts such as regional, state, country, and then global communities. The process of social studies

includes skill and knowledge building such as critical thinking, becoming a researcher, and being a contributing member of a democratic community. Primary age children best learn the content and process of social studies by studying what is familiar to them – their school, family, and community – and through their own curiosity about the world around them. They can learn about how people in groups function at a local level before they investigate the national and world community.

Although we think of social studies as being a series of facts and dates, social studies needs to concentrate on broad concepts in which the facts and dates are learned only in relationship to the broader concept. Bickart, Jablon, and Dodge (1999, p. 347) have categorized social studies concepts into six components:

- Human similarities and differences
- Basic human needs
- Human interdependence
- Rights and responsibilities
- People and the places where they live
- People and the past

In the primary grades, social studies instruction in each of the six components usually includes (NCSS, 2008) :

- **Human similarities and differences** – similarities in lifestyles, family configuration, customs, language, habits, and heritage. Young children learn about the similarities and differences of people through the stories that the teacher reads as well as by sharing information about themselves and their families while listening to the perspectives of others.

- **Basic human needs** – money can be exchanged to obtain food, shelter, clothing, and belongings. Young children learn about needs and wants which is a universal concept among all people; the ways in which different people meet their needs and wants differ.

- **Human interdependence** – people have different roles in their families, work, and the broader society. People depend on each other for goods and services; children learn about the world of work and how these goods are produced and the services are performed.

- **Rights and responsibilities** – rules are necessary in families and societies to protect rights and property; group decision-making and problem-solving is for the common good. As children make and follow the classroom rules, they learn respect for each other, responsibility to their classroom community, and the skill of cooperation and negotiation.

- **People and the places where they live** – the environment, climate, and resources shape the way people live; maps are symbols for real places. Hopefully, the topics in social studies will teach children an appreciation for the world's precious natural resources, their importance in our lives, and how to preserve them. Map study is a major part of this component of social studies; children learn to both read and construct maps.

- **People and the past** – human life is continuous from the past to the present; time is chronological in a sequential order. History is best taught to young children through an analysis of their own life stories. As children develop an awareness of time, they can examine how people change over time through storytelling and read alouds.

Much like the scientific method of investigation, social studies inquiry teaches six- to eight-year old children how to be researchers. Young "researchers" can **investigate a problem** such as "There is no park in our community". They can **gather information** through surveys, on-site field trips, searching the internet, reading books, and studying maps. Children can then analyze their research through discussions, classifying information into topics, and debating each other's opinion. Finally, children can **draw their conclusions** and construct a plan of action – possibly, writing a letter, proposing a volunteer project, or starting a fund raiser.

Long-term studies give children the opportunity to become experts on a chosen topic by applying the social studies inquiry method to topics of interest in an in-depth study. By carefully planning out a long-term study based on student interest, the teacher can ensure that all the ten themes in the curriculum standards are studied in purposeful and relevant ways. Topics need to be cooperatively based on student interest and community resources. Six- to eight-year olds' thinking changes with time; how six-year olds view the world is very different from eight-year olds. First graders tend to view the world through the lens of their own personal experience, while second and third graders are able to expand their thinking beyond their own personal experience. For instance, first graders can most effectively study their own families, neighborhoods, and immediate community, while third graders are able to use their growing abstract abilities to study other cultures and/or period of time. Second graders are able to think more vicariously than first graders (e.g. studying their country), but with not as much abstractness as a third grader. An intentionally planned long-term study requires teacher planning by considering:

- What should children **investigate**? What are they interested in? What are the resources we can use? What topics do they have some knowledge of?
- How can children **demonstrate** their learning? What are the different modalities of learning – art, writing, acting, construction, etc. – that children may use to represent their learning?
- What will be the opportunities in which children can **reflect** on their learning? Will children utilize learning logs? Where in the daily schedule will children be given time to reflect?

Teaching social studies in the primary grades is most effectively accomplished through thematic integration in all the content areas – literacy, math, science, and the arts. State learning standards can provide the guidance teachers need in planning integrated units of study, whether these studies are short-term or long-term.

Language and Literacy Development

Literacy and language receive the greatest amount of instructional time and curricular emphasis in early childhood education and the primary grades reflect this. Dependent on prior experiences and familiarity with printed materials and vocabulary, children move into the primary grades with a range of literacy and language capabilities.

Children's receptive language skills develop by listening and reading, and their expressive language expands from spoken to written communication (Copple & Bredekamp, 2009). An important goal of the primary grades is to assist six- to eight-year olds in acquiring language and literacy skills that are used in meaningful and purposeful ways, connected to their everyday lives. Reading, writing, listening, speaking, and representing can be integrated into all the daily activities of the primary classroom.

The Common Core State Standards provide guidance to teachers in their planning of literacy and language; specifically, the standards are grouped in the following topics: Reading for Literature (RL), Reading for Informational Text (RI), Foundational Skills (RF), Writing (W), Speaking and Listening (SL), and Language (L). Using these standards, the teacher can identify themes and topics that interest children and can offer them a better understanding of the world. Through the study of these themes and topics, teachers can plan lessons and integrate units of study that systematically develop the knowledge base of six- to eight-year olds while promoting language and literacy development.

The purposes for making children "good listeners" is so that they can synthesize the meanings of conversations and discussions, understand stories, follow directions, and listen attentively to others. Listening is developed when primary children have the opportunity to participate appropriately in a discussion, follow oral directions, listen carefully for interesting language in books, and understand the message that is conveyed in oral language.

With heightened listening ability, children's speaking skills become more refined; children often need scaffolding in organizing and expressing their thoughts. As children mature, they require less teacher scaffolding. Speaking skills are developed through discussions, response to open-ended questions, presenting stories and reports, and asking questions. Listening and speaking skills are fostered throughout the school day in whole and small group activities, and in reading, writing, and representing endeavors.

Reading, as well as conversation, is supported by vocabulary knowledge; comprehension of text is increased with fluent reading and understanding of both decodable words and sight words. Vocabulary development from age six to eight experiences a tremendous spurt – by age eight many children have doubled their six year old vocabulary to 20,000 words (Berk, 2016). Much of this growth is due to children's expanding reading and writing abilities and abstract thinking which allow them to deconstruct words into prefixes, root words and suffixes (Snow, Burns, & Griffin, 1998). Through daily reading and listening to, and discussions of, read alouds, children amass an impressive bank of vocabulary words. As children grow and develop through this age range, their expanding vocabulary, increased fluency, and their awareness of the multiple meanings of words allow children to engage socially and to understand others' perspective. Six- to eight-year olds' social skills become more sophisticated and collaboration becomes refined.

Reading narrative and informational texts allows children to study a topic over a sustained period of time. The knowledge children learn about certain topics in earlier grades can be expanded and developed in later grade levels, thus ensuring a deeper

understanding of these topics. Appropriate informational text should be used in whole group read alouds, small group guided reading, and individual reading. Informational text lays a conceptual foundation as well as an understanding of increasingly complex text in the upper grades. By the time children have turned eight years old they can read and discuss both narrative and informational texts, identify themes and conceptual information, read chapter books independently, synthesize main idea and supporting facts, and distinguish between fact and opinion (Snow, Burns, & Griffin, 1998). Six- to eight-year olds' reading transitions from "learning to read" to "reading to learn".

For children to become proficient readers by the end of third grade they must be encouraged in their growing capabilities for spoken and written language, and they must be taught the skills and strategies needed to decode written language and to comprehend it. Children need to be read to everyday, read and discuss text at their instructional and independent levels, produce and use environmental print, develop a sight vocabulary, attend to letter-sound correspondence, learn new vocabulary, analyze text, and write every day.

Utilizing a **balanced approach** to literacy instruction, teachers provide both explicit skill instruction and consistent use of authentic texts. In first and second grade, children continue to have practice in phonemic awareness and letter/print awareness. By the end of first grade children should be able to read aloud with reasonable fluency and comprehension and accurately decode phonetically regular words (Fountas & Pinnell, 1996). Children at this age should also have a bank of irregularly spelled sight words that they recognize. At the end of second grade, children are more facile at reading and comprehending narrative and informational texts at their reading level. They use their phonics knowledge to decode multi-syllable words; fluency and expression is better developed due in part to the repeated practice of reading more complex sentences.

Reading aloud quality narrative and informational texts that are above the students' reading abilities every day significantly increases children's conceptual knowledge, reading skill level, and love for reading. Listening to engaging read alouds introduces children to a myriad of literature genres, builds vocabulary and knowledge relating to many topics, provides children with models of writing, and sets the stage for science and social studies inquiry. Children learn the difference in purpose and text structure between narrative and informational texts. Many teachers strive for "five-a-day" – five read alouds spread out across the school day (e.g., read aloud in morning meeting to set the stage for the science/social studies theme, read aloud during guided reading, read aloud of part of a chapter book before lunch and then finishing after lunch, and an afternoon read aloud focused on either math, social studies/science, an author study, a holiday, etc.).

"1st Grade Reading Lesson"

Shared reading happens whenever children read stories, poetry, songs, morning message, etc. as a group. Often, big books or print that has been written on easel chart paper makes it possible for all the children to see the print and to participate without feeling at all uncomfortable. Shared reading provides an opportunity to teach basic reading skills such as reading left-to-right with return sweep and from top of the page to the bottom, recognizing sight words, and one-to-one correspondence. Books that are repetitious, predictable, that use rhyme, and have a repeating pattern are particularly effective in shared reading. Often the teacher uses the shared reading book later in small guided reading groups to explicitly teach reading skills and strategies.

**"Maximizing the Effectiveness of Shared Reading
in the Primary Classroom, Grades K-2"**

Guided reading provides a chance for the teacher to meet with a small group of children to teach particular skills at children's instructional level. Teacher assessment of children's reading ability is very important as the instruction needs to focus on scaffolding children through skills that primary children cannot perform independently. The guided reading group usually has four components (Fountas & Pinnell, 1996):

- Introducing the text to the group
- Working with individuals in the groups as they read to themselves
- Selecting strategies to teach or items to discuss after reading
- Working with children on a follow-up activity

Guided reading groups should not remain fixed; as children learn a strategy or skill, groups can be re-constructed to meet their individual needs.

Independent reading is a time when children can relax and enjoy books of their own choice. There should be a variety of reading materials - books, magazines, song books, biographies, class-made books, sports books, etc. - at a wide range of reading abilities, encompassing many topics of interest. Browsing boxes are a great way to organize the materials by themes. These boxes can hold both narrative and informational books about a certain topic across various reading levels. One organizational suggestion is to choose a particular sticker with many copies, label the browsing box and put the sticker on the label, and then put one of  the matching stickers on each of the books that belongs in the browsing box. These browsing boxes may be organized into topics such as fall holidays, butterflies and caterpillars, US presidents, etc.

First grade children, who may be new to independent reading, usually spend 10-15 minutes at a time when they are starting out the school year. By third grade, children may want to spend 25-30 minutes a day in independent reading. During independent reading, teachers should also model the love of reading by enjoying a book. Often this time is used by teachers to meet with individual reading groups or to hold individual reading/writing conferences with children.

Reading and writing are closely linked. "During writing, the child constructs words (a building-up process) while composing and then writing text. During reading, a child takes words apart (a breaking-down process). Combining reading and writing activities allows the child to coordinate and use both processes" (Fountas & Pinnell, 1996, p. 165). In their writing, children take on the role of author, becoming more aware of how an author tells a story, while in their reading, they are exposed to the conventions of print that will inform their writing.

"1st Grade Writing Lesson"

Writing provides primary children with a vehicle for expressing their thoughts, using their imaginations, and displaying their newly acquired knowledge. First grade students use their sight word knowledge, invented (phonetic) spelling, and their emerging knowledge of basic punctuation and capitalization rules to create stories, poems, journal entries, etc. Children in second grade have more developed spelling and grammatical skills because of accumulated knowledge and practice. Third grade children, armed with more sophisticated skills in all areas of the mechanics of writing, attend to the meaning and language when writing stories, journal entries, reports and notes.

Shared writing – often occurring when creating language experience activity charts - is an opportunity for children to observe how oral language is transformed into print. The children talk as the teacher writes; this is a model of how written language is generated for a specific purpose. The charts that are created during shared writing can be used as resources for theme study, journal writing, and reference.

Interactive writing – often known as "sharing the pen" – is an activity where children and teacher cooperatively construct a poem, story, morning message or informational chart with both doing the actual writing. The teacher may have intentional, focused goals for the activity both in the content and mechanics areas. For instance, the interactive writing lesson may be a recipe that the class is going to be making, and it may also have as a goal how to write fractions and abbreviations.

Writing workshop is formal, guided writing instruction where the child constructs a writing piece of her own choosing and the teacher scaffolds the child in specific writing skills. Developed by Donald Graves (2003), the purpose of writing workshop gives primary children ownership of their writing ideas, and provides for teacher support in organizing ideas and in the mechanics of writing. Writing workshop usually begins with

a directed lesson, and then provides time for writing time, conferences, sharing time, revision, editing, and publishing.

The directed lesson comprises the first ten minutes of the writing time; the whole class is involved in the teacher-directed lesson that may cover choosing a topic, using vocabulary to develop rich language, writing mechanics, or organizing a paragraph. Writing time is when children gather their materials and begin to free-write, often beginning with a picture as a prompt. This can be a collaborative time where children share ideas or it can be a time where children have to concentrate and work quietly. Conferences can be between student and teacher, and between students. The teacher can circulate and offer guidance and feedback to individual children in the areas of ideas, organization, and mechanics. Peer conferencing can be set up so that children can help one another. Sharing time is a time when children can share a finished product, a work in progress, or part of a writing project. Children are taught to make constructive and positive comments that will help their peers. Revision of a piece of writing may include reorganizing the sequence of paragraphs,, adding or deleting information, or reorganizing sentences within paragraphs. Editing is one of the last steps in a writing workshop; the process begins when children use an editing checklist to check for misspellings, as well as mechanical and grammatical errors. The teacher can do the final edit with each child after direct instruction about how editing is done. Publishing happens when children present a final, polished piece or the class compiles an anthology of student products (Graves, 2003).

Independent writing can occur anytime during the school day; children can be encouraged to keep personal journals, write notes and cards to friends, create poetry and stories, and maintain a notebook of ideas for future writing projects. First-grade students often use a combination of writing and pictures to independently write, while second and third grade students have developed enough writing skills that they are often given writing assignments based on the ideas in their journals and notebooks.
First-grade students can generate rough drafts and can then use simple editing skills such as punctuation and capitalization rules. Second- and third-grade students having had greater exposure to words, demonstrate more accurate spelling and more refined English grammar usage. Often, the independent writing lesson begins with a choice of prompts such as "Describe the best day you can remember", or "Write an entry in Martin Luther King, Jr.'s journal on the day he gave the 'I Have a Dream' speech".

Creating an environment for literacy includes designing the classroom environment, setting up the daily schedule, and collecting and organizing literacy materials. It is important to use students' interests and abilities to provide literacy experiences most suitable for them. The classroom environment should provide students with a connection from oral language to print. Primary age students should see that print has a purpose to communicate information, whether it is a word wall, daily schedule or language experience activity chart.

Organizing the classroom is one way to use print – job charts, morning messages, classroom rules, daily schedules and material labels all are examples of organizational tools which teach students print usage. It is important that teachers look at their classroom with a critical eye to ascertain that all the print in the room is purposeful and not just for decoration. Daily use of *print in classroom activities and lessons* reinforces the usefulness of the environmental print which surrounds students in their daily lives. Language experience activity (LEA) charts document subject and concept knowledge and are cooperatively generated by students and teacher. The charts are displayed and used as references in reading, writing, mathematics, and content area study. Graphic organizers such as KWL charts, predictable charts, and Venn diagrams can also be posted for students to refer to. Word walls contain the high-frequency words that children use every day in their oral and written language. When a new word is learned and posted on the word wall it becomes a word that children are expected to spell correctly in their writing. Topic word walls can also be generated as children learn about new science, social studies, and mathematics topics or themes. For example, during the study of butterflies, the topic word wall could contain words such as *metamorphosis, molt, chrysalis.*

The *daily schedule* should include focused instruction, literacy integrated into content area lessons and activities, opportunities for small group and individual practice and application of new literacy skills, instruction individualized for student needs, and connected reading and writing activities. A literacy-rich environment provides daily whole group read alouds, shared reading, guided reading, independent reading, shared writing, interactive writing, writing workshop, and independent writing. Primary age students need to consistently interact with print throughout the day as they see the real-life purposes for reading and writing.

Whole group read alouds and activities are an excellent way to introduce new themes, concepts, vocabulary; to model and demonstrate a skill; and to later de-brief small group or individual learning. Whole group meetings provide an opportunity for shared and interactive writing, which is often tied to the read aloud and/or the schedule for the day. The primary age teacher needs to remember the importance of engaging and captivating the attention of the students as well as maintaining their focus on the activity.

Small group activities (literacy centers) can take many forms; this could be a time for small group skill instruction such as guided reading or a time to gather students who need focused instruction on a skill such as the cvc-silent e pattern in words. Small group is also the time that children work in independent learning centers on writing and journaling projects, independent reading, listening to books and CDs, and working with words (phonics). Many school districts schedule a 90-minute uninterrupted literacy block for the primary grades in which the read aloud time, guided reading, and literacy centers are held. A 10-to-15 minute debriefing session should conclude the literacy block so that students can review what they have learned.

Literacy events need to be planned daily and routinely; there should be several read alouds in varying length and formats throughout the day. Teachers need to choose books that are above children's independent reading level, that have more complex sentence structures and advanced vocabulary. Vocabulary instruction needs to be purposeful and well planned; intentionality is the key here as many children enter the primary grades lacking in background knowledge. Teachers need to plan for instructional time that focuses on high level vocabulary words which support deeper conceptual learning. Before, during, and after read alouds are times to build vocabulary which can then be revisited over subsequent weeks.

Moral Development

Primary age children are increasingly facile in understanding multiple perspectives and in reasoning about and reflecting upon rules of behavior, as well as what constitutes right and wrong. Thomas Lickona (1992) discusses the need for schools to address moral development of young children:

> Children learn morality by living it. They need to be in a community – to
interact, form relationships, work out problems, grow as a group, and learn directly, from their first-hand experience, lessons about fair play, cooperation, forgiveness, and respect for the worth and dignity of every individual. (p. 90)

Moral development begins in the classroom where children participate and interact with their peers and adults. Primary age children, around the age of six, begin to assume a set of moral rules of behavior that leads to the development of a "conscience". Their conscience is the small "voice" that monitors their behavior when they have to make decisions independently of adult guidance. By being part of a democratic classroom community, six- to eight-year olds develop respect for themselves and others, as well as a sense of responsibility for their actions, for their community and their world.

"Moral Development"

Respect is taught in an environment where respect is modeled in all situations. The adults help children to develop empathy for others by appealing to children's sense of fairness, and by modeling respect for others' rights to express their own ideas. Respect is also taught by demonstrating how a diverse group of people can work amicably and how differences can be resolved in socially appropriate ways. Responsibility is taught by providing decision-making opportunities and chances for children to be guided in making moral decisions.

Bibliotherapy is an effective way to read books portraying positive character traits and moral decision-making. Inviting visitors from other countries or another part of the country to allow children to compare and contrast cultural differences is an important strategy for teaching respect and tolerance for others. Collaborating with children in the formation and enforcement of classroom rules teaches primary age children the rights and responsibilities of citizens in a democratic society.

Summary

- As children mature through the age range, they become more adept at sustaining friendships by helping, cooperating, sharing, and finding ways to maintain and extend their play.

- Teachers can support children's development in self-regulation by helping them set goals, allowing them to self-evaluate, and to meaningfully praise every success. Role-playing and dramatization are strategies that allow children to problem-solve, come up with alternatives that demonstrate self-regulation, and learn the skill of negotiation.

- Children this age need to be active to both expend excess energy and to keep up energy levels. The classroom teacher needs to provide daily movement activities in addition to the structured activities in physical education.

- Six- to eight-year old children are entering Piaget's Concrete Operations Stage when children can begin to structure time and space as well as think logically. They still learn best through active participation and concrete experiences however, as children in this age range approach eight years old they have the ability to think abstractly as long as what they are thinking about has its roots in something that is familiar or relevant.

- Remaining focused on a task and ignoring extraneous, distracting stimuli is a skill that is refined as children grow and with experience. This skill allows children to concentrate to complete their work; difficulty paying attention and staying on task can impede a child's learning and school success.

- The National Council of Teachers of Mathematics (NCTM) has identified five areas of content understanding: numbers and operations, algebra, geometry, measurement, and data and probability, and five areas of process competencies: problem-solving, reasoning and proof, communications, connection, and representation.

- Science in the primary grades continues the inquiry-based learning that began in preschool and kindergarten. Inquiry-based learning involves children directly in asking questions, observing carefully while gathering and analyzing information, and ultimately proposing explanations that can be tested.

- The National Council for Social Studies (2010) has published curriculum standards which encompass ten themes: culture; time, continuity, and change; people, places, environments; individual development and identity; individuals, groups, institutions; power, authority, governance; production, distribution, consumption; science, technology and society; global connections; and civic ideals and practices.

- An important goal of the primary grades is to assist six- to eight-year olds in acquiring language and literacy skills that are used in meaningful and purposeful ways, connected to their everyday lives. Reading, writing, listening, speaking, and representing can be integrated into all the daily activities of the primary classroom.

- Moral development begins in the classroom where children participate and interact with their peers and adults. Primary age children, around the age of six, begin to assume a set of moral rules of behavior that leads to the development of a "conscience".

Key Terms

balanced literacy approach
executive function
inquiry-based learning
learned helplessness
mathematize
self-regulation

Suggested Readings

Adams, M.J. (1990). *Beginning to read: Thinking and learning about print.* Cambridge, MA: Massachusetts Institute of Technology Press.

Graves, D. (2003). *Writing: Teachers and children at work 20th anniversary edition.* Portsmouth, NH: Heinemann.

Hyson, M. (2008). *Enthusiastic and engaged learners: Approaches to learning in the early childhood classroom.* New York: Teachers College Press.

Pica, R. (2004). *Experiences in movement: Birth to age 8.* 3rd Ed. Clifton Park, NY: Delmar Learning.

Suggested Websites

International Association for the Child's Right to Play
www.ipausa.org

National Center for Family Literacy
www.famlit.org

National Council for Social Studies
   www.ncss.org

ScienceStart!
   www.sciencestart.com

Reflections

1. Observe reading and writing instruction in a first- or second-grade classroom. Do children seem motivated and engaged in reading and writing? Are teachers supporting children's learning in phonics, fluency, and comprehension? Are teachers addressing the individual literacy needs of children?

2. In a primary classroom, look at the science curriculum and teaching. Are science books, inquiry-based activities, and tools of inquiry available? Are time and resources being devoted to the study of science?

3. Investigate your community. What places and opportunities are available that might extend children's social studies learning? How could the community resources support children's understanding of geography, civics, and history?

4. Reflect on the obesity crisis in American children. In your opinion, what factors affect this alarming trend? What should be the role of teachers in addressing the issue of childhood obesity?

References

Bandura, A. (1997). *Self-efficacy: The exercise of control.* New York: Freeman.

Berk, L. E. (2016). *Infants and children* (8th ed.). Boston, MA: Allyn & Bacon.

Bickart, T. S., Jablon, J. R., & Dodge, D. T. (1999). *Building the primary classroom.* Washington, DC and Portsmouth, NH: Teaching Strategies and Heinemann.

Bodrova, E. & Leong, D. J. (2007). *Tools of the mind: The Vygotskian approach to early childhood education* (2nd ed.). Upper Saddle River, NJ: Pearson/Merrill Prentice Hall.

Bredekamp, S. (2011). *Effective practices in early childhood education: Building a foundation.* Upper Saddle River, NJ: Pearson Education.

Brown, S. A., Arnold, D. H., Dobbs, J., & Doctoroff, G. L., (2007). Parenting predictors of relational aggression among Puerto Rican and European American school-age children. *Early Childhood Research Quarterly, 22*(1), 147-159.

Centers for Disease Control (CDC). (2013). http://www.cdc.gov/nchs/fastats/overwt

Copple, C. & Bredekamp, S. (2009). *Developmentally appropriate practice in early childhood programs* (3rd Ed.). Washington, DC: National Association for the Education of Young Children.

Epstein, A. S. (2007). *The intentional teacher: Choosing the best strategies for young children.* Washington, DC: NAEYC.

Fountas, I. C. & Pinnell, G. S. (1996). *Guided reading: Good first teaching for all children.* Portsmouth, NJ: Heinemann.

Graves, D. (2003). *Writing: Teachers and children at work (20th Anniversary Edition).* Portsmouth, NJ: Heinemann.

Haywood, K. M., & Getchell, N. (2005). *Life span motor development* (4th ed.). Champaign, IL: Human Kinetics.

Hyson, M. (2008). *Enthusiastic and engaged learners: Approaches to learning in the early childhood classroom.* New York: Teachers College Press.

Kenny, D. A., West, T. V., Cillessen, A. H. N., Coie, J. D., Dodge, K. A., Hubbard, J. A., & Schwartz, D. (2007). Accuracy in judgments of aggressiveness. *Personality & Social Psychology Bulletin, 33*(9), 1225-1236.

Klomek, A. B., Sourander, A., Kumpulainen, K., Piha, J., Tamminen, T., Moilanen, I., Almqvist, F. & Gould, M. S., (2008). Childhood bullying as a risk for later depression and suicidal ideation among Finnish males. *Journal of Affective Disorders, 109*(1-2), 47-55.

Lickona, T. (1992). *Educating for character: How our schools can teach respect and responsibility.* New York: Bantam Books.

Mahone, E. M. & Silverman, W. (2008). ADHD and executive functions: Lessons learned from research. *Exceptional Parent 38*(8), 48-51.

Manross, M. A. (2000). *Learning to throw in physical education class: Part 3, Teaching Elementary Physical Education.* New York: Oxford University Press.

Morrison, G. S., (2012). *Early childhood education today.* Upper Saddle River, NJ: Pearson Education.

National Council for the Social Studies. 2008. www.socialstudies.org

National Council for the Social Studies. 2010. www.socialstudies.org/curriculumstandards

National Research Council (NRC). (2009). *Mathematics learning in early childhood: Paths toward excellence and equity.* Washington, DC: National Academies Press.

Pica, R. (2004). *Experiences in movement: Birth to age eight* (3rd ed.). Clifton Park, NY: Delmar Learning.

Seefeldt, C. & Barbour, N. (1998). *Early childhood education* (4th ed.). Upper Saddle River, NJ: Merrill Prentice Hall.

Snow, C. E., Burns, M. S., Griffin, P., (1998). *Preventing reading difficulties in young children.* Washington, DC: National Academy Press.

Tomlinson, H. B. (2009). In *Developmentally appropriate practice in early childhood programs* (3rd Ed.). Washington, DC: National Association for the Education of Young Children.

Chapter 11
Assessment and Diverse Learners

Understanding Assessment

Thinking Ahead

1. What is assessment? What are its purposes?
2. What are the many ways we gather assessment data on young children?
3. How is assessment data used?
4. What are some concerns about standardized testing in early childhood education?
5. What are the types and sources of individual differences among children?
6. What is cultural competence and what is its importance?
7. What are some strategies and supports for teaching children with special needs?

Thoughtful and focused assessment of children's learning and development is an essential element of early childhood education. Assessment is vital for teachers to plan, implement, and evaluate the effectiveness of educational experiences. If children are to be optimally served by early childhood programs, intentional teachers must know the purpose, process, and content of assessment; additionally, the intentional teacher must believe that assessment is embedded in every aspect of the child's daily routine. Utilizing assessment knowledgeably is essential to ensure children benefit from their early educational experiences; children progress in their learning more effectively if the teacher knows exactly where each child is in regards to learning goals.

"How Does Teacher Use of Student Assessment Data Change Instructional Practice?"

Assessment is defined as the ongoing practice of gathering evidence of children's learning and development and then organizing and interpreting the gathered data in order to make informed instructional decisions (McAfee, Leong & Bodrova, 2004). Developmentally appropriate assessment requires the use of multiple sources of evidence collected over time in various contexts. Evidence can be gathered from observations, children's work, individually administered assessments, family surveys, clinical interviews, etc.

Effective Assessment for Young Children

Developmentally appropriate assessment must take into consideration the age of the child as well as the linguistic and cultural contexts in which children live. Ongoing, purposeful assessment needs to be responsive to the individual differences of children. Developmentally appropriate and sound assessment for children birth through primary grades should encompass the following principles (Copple & Bredekamp, 2009, p. 22):

A. Assessment of young children's progress and achievements is ongoing, strategic, and purposeful. The results of assessment are used to inform the planning and implementing of experiences, to communicate with the child's family, and to evaluate and improve the teachers' and the program's effectiveness.

B. Assessment focuses on children's progress toward goals that are developmentally and educationally significant.

C. There is a system in place to collect, make sense of, and use the assessment information to guide what goes on in the classroom (formative assessment). Teachers use this information in planning curriculum and learning experiences and in moment-to-moment interactions with children – that is, teachers continually engage in assessment for the purpose of improving teaching and learning.

D. The methods of assessment are appropriate to the developmental status and experiences of young children, and they recognize individual variation in learners and allow children to demonstrate their competence in different ways. Methods appropriate to the classroom assessment of young children, therefore, include results of teachers' observations of children, clinical interviews, collections of children's work samples, and their performance on authentic activities.

E. Assessment looks not only at what children can do independently but also at what they can do with assistance from other children or adults. Therefore, teachers assess children as they participate in groups and other situations that are providing scaffolding.

F. In addition to this assessment by teachers, input from families as well as children's own evaluations of their work are part of the program's overall assessment strategy.

G. Assessments are tailored to a specific purpose and used only for the purpose for which they have been demonstrated to produce reliable, valid information.

H. Decisions that have a major impact on children, such as enrollment or placement, are never made on the basis of results from a single developmental assessment or screening instrument/device but are based on multiple sources of relevant information, including that obtained from observations of and interactions with children by teachers and parents (and specialists, as needed).

I. When a screening or other assessment identifies children who may have special learning or developmental needs, there is appropriate follow-up, evaluation, and, if indicated, referral. Diagnosis or labeling is never the result of a brief screening or one-time assessment. Families should be involved as important sources of information.

Sound and effective assessment of young children is often challenging due to many factors, development and context being two of the factors. Young children's development is uneven as evidenced by its inherent spurts and plateaus (McAfee et al., 2004), for example, a 2-year old who watches others intently, pointing and grunting for what he wants and then suddenly one day begins speaking in 3-word sentences. Children's development is not even across all developmental domains – a 3-year old may develop quickly in language but be unable to demonstrate self-regulation. Accurate assessment of young children requires an understanding of the inconsistency in children's development – the unevenness that makes a child appear to have mastered a skill one day and then having apparently "lost" the skill the next day.

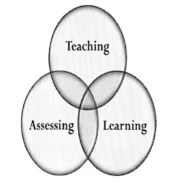

The context in which the assessment occurs is another factor that affects children's performance. Authentic assessment should take place in natural environments and with adults who are familiar with the child – the classroom in which the child has become comfortable and at ease, administered by the teacher with whom the child has developed a strong attachment. For very young children, assessment takes place in their own homes while children are playing, enjoying a book being read to them, or completing emerging self-help skills.

"Documenting Children's Learning"

Every Student Succeeds Act (ESSA) and Assessment

ESSA (2015) was intended to "end the obsession with testing in schools that began with its predecessor, No Child Left Behind" (AFT, 2016). Some provisions of ESSA include:

- Testing requirements are the same as under NCLB, but the sanctions and consequences are very different and hugely diminished.

- States are required to test students in reading or language arts and math annually in grades 3-8 and once in grades 10-12, and in science once in each of the following grade spans: 3-5, 6-9, and 10-12.

- Data is still required to be disaggregated by race, income, English language proficiency and other specified categories.

- States and districts can use funds to conduct audits of state and local assessment systems to eliminate unnecessary tests and improve assessments.

- Assessments will be used to help improve schools and inform instruction, not arbitrarily measure them.

- States will be responsible for establishing their own accountability systems that must be submitted to the U.S. Department of Education.

- The rigid system of AYP (the requirement that assessments be given to ensure that states increase student achievement in increments until all students in the state reach 100 percent proficiency) is gone.

- NCLB's prescriptive school closings, personnel requirements and punitive sanctions are gone. States, working with local stakeholders, have a great deal of latitude to provide targeted support and improvement as well as comprehensive support and improvement (AFT, 2016).

Despite the exclusion of 1st and 2nd grades in required formal assessment, preparing for children to pass the 3rd grade tests commences as early as kindergarten.

Purposes of Assessment

Before the teacher assesses children, he or she must determine the purpose for the assessment; once the purpose is determined, the teacher can then identify the most appropriate assessment tool, include the children who need to be assessed, determine who will administer the assessments, and how the assessment data will be used. There are five foundational purposes of assessment (National Research Council, 2008):

- Monitor children's development and learning
- Guide planning and decision making
- Evaluate programs
- Report and communicate with others, including families
- Identify children who might benefit from special services or supports

Through the consistent assessment of young children, the teacher can observe the development and learning that is distinctive for each child. That knowledge can be utilized in individualizing and differentiating instruction to meet the needs of the children. Developmentally appropriate practice insists that teachers meet each child where he or she is developmentally, culturally and linguistically, and to then plan a program that is tailored for that child.

"The Essential Role Of Observation And Documentation in Early Childhood"

Program evaluation collects data about the quality of the classroom and curriculum to determine if the objectives are being achieved. Program evaluation often includes data regarding the achievement of a group of children as they work toward meeting learning outcomes. Often, this type of assessment interests policy makers and stakeholders in order to determine the effectiveness and cost-worthiness of a program.

Accountability – "holding teachers, schools, or programs responsible for meeting a required level of performance" (McAfee et al., 2004, p.8) – is assessed to report what children know and are able to do in regards to state and national learning standards. The data provides information to parents, policy makers, funding agencies, and other stakeholders, holding schools accountable for educating all children.

Beginning at infancy, children are routinely screened for physical, cognitive, and emotional development. Many serious cognitive and physical disabilities are apparent at birth or soon after; as soon as delays or potential delays are suspected, further in-depth diagnostic testing can proceed. Early intervention holds many benefits and the earlier the child receives services, the greater the potential benefits of the intervention. Assessment for identification of special needs begins with a screening and then proceeds into diagnostic testing.

Types of Assessment

Understanding the different types of assessment clarifies for the teacher when and how each type of assessment should be administered and the uses for the collected data.

Informal assessment and formal assessment are the two categories of assessment. Informal assessments are assessments of child development and learning that are ongoing, conducted in many contexts, and are usually designed and carried out by the classroom teacher. They provide information for teachers to use in daily classroom decision-making. Informal assessment should follow a cycle that starts with observation (Wright, 2010, p.72):

1. Observing the behaviors and learning of children
2. Noting and documenting relevant observations
3. Examining evidence and reflecting on each child's needs and strengths
4. Organizing instruction to meet needs observed and documented in Step 2
5. Implementing the plan and providing needed instruction
6. Evaluating the effectiveness of the executed plan, and starting again

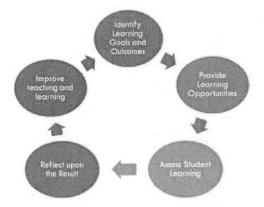

Formal assessment follows a pre-determined procedure, utilizing specifically designed instruments for assessment, producing a score. Formal assessment includes, but is not limited to, standardized tests.

Formative Assessment

Formative assessment is the series of strategies that teachers use to monitor children's progress as they master skills or information in lessons and activities. The data collected "along the way" in the cycle of teaching and learning informs the teacher of "next steps" in lesson planning and implementation. Formative assessment is embedded in daily classroom instruction and independent practice, and provides information that allows the teacher to make changes in the curriculum and to tailor the instruction to meet the individual child's needs. Examples of formative assessment include observational notes, anecdotal notes, checklists, time and event sampling, rating scales, work samples, interviews, portfolios, and rubrics.

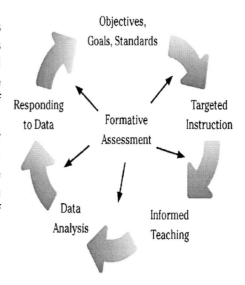

"Formative Assessment in the Classroom"

Another term that is often used interchangeably with formative assessment is **authentic assessment**; authentic assessment assesses children based on their own work products emanating from daily curricular activities. Authentic assessment includes **performance-based assessment** – data collected from children's demonstration of what they know and can demonstrate. Authentic, formative assessment provides the majority of the data an early childhood teacher uses in evaluating student learning and includes many tools:

1. **Observation** is one of the most important assessment tools in early childhood education. Systematic observation requires the observing teacher to focus on individual children as they work and play alone and in groups, as well as listening carefully to their conversations. Often, the teacher will begin an observation with a specific behavior they want to focus on in mind, but then flexibly change their observational focus when other behaviors emerge. Observation enables a teacher to evaluate children's behavior for decision-making purposes.

2. **Running records** (often called **note-taking/note-making**, and **narrative records**) is an observational tool that records in detail on a two-column recording sheet a sequence of events that the observer documents as they occur. The left column is where the observer records her unbiased detailed description. After the observation, the teacher reviews her notes and in the right

column makes comments, poses questions, and constructs inferences. Running records should include (Day, 2004): the date and time of the observation, the name(s) of the child (children) involved, the location of the observation, the context of the observation (whole group, small group, individual, etc.) exactly what the child (children) said and did. Running records assist the teacher in gaining valuable insight into a child's/children's behavior during an interval of time.

3. **Anecdotal records** are shorter descriptions of incidents involving one or more children, based on observations and written after the occurrence. The anecdotal record aids the teacher in understanding specific behaviors of a child or group of children; the purpose is to plan more effective teaching, change a routine, or modify the classroom environment.

4. **Checklists** are lists of sequential behaviors, skills or attitudes arranged in categories in each of the learning domains (e.g., the sequence of fine motor grasps an infant demonstrates). The teacher who is observing can use the checklist to verify whether a child displays a behavior or skill on the checklist. Some checklists are closed and require either a "yes" or "no" response to each item on the checklist. Open-ended checklists involve an explanation by the teacher judging the degree of mastery. Checklists work well with young children because they frame the assessment focus and direct teachers in the specific behaviors, skills, or attitudes that should be assessed.

5. **Rating scales** use numbers or categories that allow the observer to judge the degree of a characteristic that a child exhibits – for example, "usually – sometimes – seldom – never". They can be used to assess behaviors that are not as easily measured by other tools. For example, a child's ability to cooperate with his peers is assessed with more precision by using a rating scale instead of a checklist. Rating scales are easy to complete and can be done quickly and relatively effortlessly. Rating scales are also easy to develop and use because the descriptors can remain uniform – such as always, sometimes, rarely, and never – and the statements to be rated can change.

6. **Time sampling** involves focusing the observation on a child's particular behavior during uniform time periods. The observer determines the behavior to be observed ahead of time, how long the time interval will be, and how to record the frequency of occurrence. After the time sampling has been administered several times, the data are studied and then modifications are decided on to change the behavior.

7. **Event sampling** is used when a behavior most often occurs in a particular setting rather than during a particular time period. As a result of careful observation, the observer infers the context or situation in which the behavior is most likely to occur. The observer uses the *ABC* **observation system**; the A – the Antecedent – is the precursor, or catalyst to the B – Behavior, while the C is

the Consequence or result of the behavior. Event sampling allows the observer to look more deeply into children's behavior to see what conditions "set the behavior off" and what the result of the behavior is.

8. **Rubrics** are a descriptive rating scale with an ordinal sequence of qualities related to each rank on the scale; the rubric contains well-defined descriptions of each point on the scale (McAfee & Leong, 2007). Rubrics are very reliable because the guidelines for evaluation are explicit and clear; each level contains precise, measurable characteristics. Rubrics typically use a range of 3-5 levels – unsatisfactory, basic, developing, proficient, distinguished are typical level descriptors. Rubrics allow teachers to establish the criteria ahead of the assessment, clearly communicate the expectations to students so that students know what level of performance results in what grade, and allow children to partner with the teacher in evaluating their work.

9. **Interviews** that teachers conduct with young children can draw out a child's conceptual and skill knowledge, as well as his feelings and emotions. Interviews are especially appropriate for young children with emerging language skills that surpass their writing ability. Interviewing can stimulate children's problem-solving skills, ideas, and feelings (McAfee & Leong, 2007). The strategies in effective interviewing are based on Piaget's technique of asking predetermined, open-ended questions to understand children's thinking. Piaget allowed the interview to be built on children's responses, determining not only what the child understood, but also the thinking processes the child utilized in organizing the responses (Seefeldt, 2005).

Unstructured interviews are unplanned and can be conducted when children are playing. The questioning supports children in their thinking and aids them in extending their thinking. **Structured** interviews are planned by the teacher with the purpose of understanding the child's learning. These interviews are usually crafted around subject area content like mathematics and reading. **Diagnostic** interviews – unstructured and structured – allow the teacher to understand children's needs and then focus the help the child receives. Interviews can have performance-based response such as artwork and dramatic performance as well as verbal responses.

10. **Portfolios** are a method of assessment where student work samples and teacher observational data are compiled, stored, and interpreted. The portfolio can be a folder or a box containing student artifacts, work samples, anecdotal records, checklists, rating scales, etc. Some portfolios contain a child's best work and some house "works in progress"; it is up to the teacher's discretion exactly how to compile and optimally utilize the portfolio.

Kingore (2008) suggests the following when an early childhood educator wants to institute a system of portfolio assessment:

- Materials should be dated when selected for storage in the portfolio.
- Enrollment data about the child needs to be included (e.g., birthday, age, siblings, family structure, etc.)
- Work samples (artifacts) need to be included, organized by learning area:
  - Worksheets that have evaluative information in the content areas
  - Art samples and freely drawn illustrations
  - Writing samples
  - Video of child doing cognitive tasks
- Standardized measures including checklists need to be included
- Observations, anecdotal records, and teacher-made checklists need to be included
- Transcripts or videos of the child's creative storytelling need to be included
- Products, photos, and objects selected by the child need to be included

The student work artifacts should be linked to approved state learning standards and grounded in the instructional objectives of the early childhood curriculum (Doherty, 2004). The portfolio is a useful tool in parent conferences; it provides extensive information about their child's learning and accomplishments.

The advantages of portfolio assessment are that they provide evaluation of a child's development that is more informative than merely a letter grade, they include the child as a partner in the evaluation process, and they allow a wide range of ways the child can demonstrate mastery and growth. The disadvantages of portfolios are that they are time consuming to plan for, organize, and maintain; the evaluation process to assign grades is difficult.

11. **Audiotapes, videotapes,** and **photography** are useful tools to record activities during an observation. Audiotapes are useful in documenting children's language, while videotapes can record noteworthy events that can be analyzed at a later date. Photography captures a moment in a child's development that can be used for a documentation panel, portfolio artifact, and to discuss in a conference with a child.

Ultimately, the goal of formative assessment is to make the teacher better at her/his job (Tomlinson, 2008). Formative assessment provides insight to children's learning and development while instruction is going on. The early childhood teacher uses the formative assessment data to modify instructional plans and contexts, to re-teach the material, and to modify or enrich the activities for diverse learners.

Summative Assessment

Summative assessment is evaluation that occurs at the end of a teaching and learning cycle to substantiate mastery of skills and information. Summative assessment is planned to measure learning objectives and goals and to provide measures at different levels of cognition (Wright, 2010). The information gathered can be used for instructional planning, re-teaching of material, re-grouping of children, and for making placement decision. Summative assessment can be both teacher-made tests and standardized formal assessment. In early childhood education, summative assessment often occurs three times a year to first, set a "floor" of a child's benchmarked abilities and then to evaluate the child's progress throughout the school year.

Teacher-designed summative assessments usually are in the form of quizzes and tests; in early childhood education summative assessments can take the form of individual check-listing of benchmarked skills, writing and art samples, literacy running records, etc. Summative assessments provide information for teachers to write progress reports, to verify that instructional goals and objectives are being met, and to design parallel tasks which allow children to practice for standardized testing (Wright, 2010).

"Formative And Summative Assessment"

Standardized Testing

Standardized assessment is the assessment of a group of children using the same procedures and performing the same task under the same conditions (Bredekamp, 2011). **Standardized testing** is a part of this type of assessment; these tests must meet technical standards that ensure the tests have high levels of reliability and validity (AERA, APA, & NCM, 1999). **Reliability** is the extent to which test results are consistent over time. A test is reliable if it gets the same or similar results when used on different days and/or by different assessors. **Validity** is the degree to which a test measures what it claims to test. For instance, a test that is designed to measure only letter recognition, should not expect a child to produce the sound the letter represents.

"How Standardized Tests Are Created"

Standardized testing scoring falls into two categories: **criterion-referenced** and **norm-referenced**. **Criterion-referenced** tests provide information on specific knowledge or skills a student has mastered. The test measures particular skills or instructional objectives and does not compare test takers. The criterion for a passing grade is a pre-determined number of correct answers (cut score). **Norm-referenced** tests are assessments in which the test-taker's performance is compared with the people in a sample group (**norm group**) selected to represent the range of typical performances. The norm group should be representative of all children in the country and large enough so that when it is divided into age groups, there are still representative numbers of children in each norm group. The norm group should reflect both genders, all economic levels of families, all races and ethnicities, etc.

Testing companies norm a test by giving the test to large groups of children and comparing the scores. The resulting test scores, when plotted on a graph, show a pattern of scores that looks like a bell – named a **bell curve**, or **normal curve** – with most children scoring at the midrange and a few scoring at the high and low ends. The

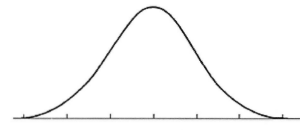

normal curve represents the **normal distribution** of test scores of people. The midpoint of the curve is the **mean,** dividing the curve into two symmetrical halves with half the scores above the mean and half below.

Types of standardized testing. Most standardized tests can be categorized as either screening, diagnostic, readiness, aptitude, or achievement tests.

Screening, also called **developmental screening** is a large-scale, brief assessment of a child's developmental status; screening is a first step in identifying, through tests, examinations, or other procedures children who may need further professional diagnostic evaluation and/or intervention. Screening is usually administered to all children in both preschool and kindergarten, and provides a broad profile of what children know and can do. High-stakes decision-making such as retention or a special education placement should never be made based on a developmental screening; screening is simply to identify children who need further evaluation (Meisels & Atkins-Burnett, 2005). The few children who do not pass the first screening are usually recommended for further diagnostic testing.

Diagnostic testing is the second stage of evaluation of the child to analyze the child's area of need or strengths and to determine the nature of the learning needs. Diagnostic testing data are usually gathered from multiple sources of information – observations, parent surveys and interviews, medical examinations, language evaluations, and standardized testing. The results of the assessments are compiled and an intervention plan is designed and tailored for the individual child's needs. For infants and toddlers, an Individualized Family Service Plan (IFSP) is the result of diagnostic testing; for children older than 36 months, an Individualized Educational Plan (IEP) is created to address the goals of learning. Diagnostic testing is normally administered by specialists – psychologists, speech pathologists, and special educators – who have particular training in standardized testing administration and interpretation.

Readiness testing. Most school districts require broad school readiness testing for entering kindergarten children – vision, hearing, emergent literacy skills, mathematics concepts, and language skills are all areas that are typically screened. Many of the academic readiness tests are merely tests of children's accumulated experiences, and do not reflect their true capabilities. The use of readiness testing to deny children entry to kindergarten is inappropriate (NAEYC, 1995), and in fact, constitutes unethical practice by blocking what children need most: the right and opportunity of an education.

"Tips for Testing For Kindergarten"

Aptitude tests. Aptitude is the potential to learn or develop proficiency in an area, if certain conditions exist, or if training is available (Wortham, 2008). Aptitude testing is supposed to measure children's potential for learning in the future, and attempts to predict future performance. Aptitude tests for young children remain controversial due to children's uneven development and the fact that these tests evaluate children regardless if they had the opportunity to learn the material.

Achievement tests. Achievement tests measure the skills or knowledge that a child has received as a result of instruction. These tests can assess general knowledge, or can be content-specific such as assessment of mathematics and literacy skills. The test elements are tied to standards-based curriculum; many of these tests are tied to state standards and are used for school accountability.

Standardized Assessment of Children with Special Needs

The primary goal of administering standardized assessments is early identification of possible learning delays and disabilities and subsequently, providing services that meet the needs of children and their families (Scarborough, et al., 2004). The benefits of early intervention are undeniable and it is the responsibility of early childhood professionals to identify young children with special needs and assist them and their families in accessing appropriate and targeted services (DEC, 2007).

The No Child Left Behind Act added accountability guidelines to IDEA/IDEIA; children receiving special education services must be included in the state assessments. School districts must include at least 95 percent of students with disabilities and include their disaggregated scores when reporting (US Department of Education, 2012).

In the area of Special Education, ESSA, supplanting NCLB requires:

- The same academic content and achievement standards for all students grades 3-12 except for the 1% of the Special Education population with the most significant cognitive disabilities who qualify for alternative assessment.

- All assessments must be developed using principles of Universal Design for Learning.

- Accommodations including computer-adaptive assessments, must be provided. States must establish ambitious long-term goals for all groups including Students with Disabilities. (CCSSO, 2016)

There is continued controversy between policy makers who feel this provision ensures high-quality education for children with disabilities and educators who feel that students with disabilities should not be expected to be evaluated on the same academic content as general education students.

The first step in the sequence of providing this appropriate intervention to support children's learning is *identification* of the children who may be at risk for a delay or

disability. The next step is *screening* to ascertain whether or not a referral for further assessment is warranted. The third step is *diagnostic assessment* that identifies the area of learning or developmental difficulty that must be addressed. At this point the child is often referred to an Instructional Support Team (Wright, 2010). Establishing the child's eligibility for services and constructing a *multidisciplinary team* is the fourth step in the process of identifying children. *Monitoring* the child is an ongoing practice.

"Assessment and Curriculum for Students with Disabilities"

Assessment should be based on multiple sources of information – no single test should be used as the basis for high-stakes decision-making. A variety of formal and informal assessment tools should be used; a battery of developmental assessments provides more information, and therefore, a more comprehensive assessment of the child. Neisworth and Bagnato (1988) define multidimensional assessment as "a comprehensive and integrated approach that employs multiple measures, derives data from multiple sources, surveys multiple domains and fulfills multiple purposes" (p. 24).

Establishing a partnership with families is important for all children being evaluated for delays and disabilities, however, it is most important when dealing with young children. Part C of the IDEA mandates that the family's goals for their birth to 36-month old child frame the early intervention process. Parents of three- to seven-year old children have a significant role in the design and evaluation of services provided to their children; they partner with the schools in developing IEP's.

Early childhood educators must understand the language and culture of the child. Early childhood special educators must be mindful when assessing children who are linguistically and culturally diverse, particularly when recommending the child for special education services. Screening and diagnostic assessment must be sensitive to cultural and linguistic differences that may lead to incorrect identification of learning deficits in children from various cultural and linguistic groups. Respect for and sensitivity to the home language, cultural values and beliefs of families are crucial to the success of the intervention the child receives.

Concerns about Standardized Testing in Early Childhood

Academic red-shirting is the decision made by many parents to delay their child's entrance to formal schooling. The result is that the range of ages between the youngest and the oldest child in the kindergarten class can be as much as two years. Parents make this momentous decision based on several factors. They believe that the extra year gives their child an academic advantage over their peers – a time that the child can become more cognitively and socially advanced. Often, parents fear the specter of push-down, developmentally inappropriate curriculum and regular assessment in the kindergarten and opt to keep their child in pre-school for an extra year. Nationally, approximately 6% of kindergarten age children are red-shirted every academic year however that percentage can soar to as much as 50% in more affluent suburban areas (NCES, 2016). Young boys are more likely to be academically red-shirted than young girls.

Research shows that red-shirted children have slightly higher reading scores at the end of first grade when compared to children who started kindergarten on time, and they actually lag in math behind the children who entered kindergarten on time (Morrison, 2012). However, any positive effect begins to subside by second grade and generally washes out before eighth grade (Marshall, 2003).

**"Parents, Educators Debate Merits of Redshirting
for Academic or Athletic Reasons"**

High-Stakes decision-making pertaining to school admission, grade retention, special education services, and summer school, is often made based on standardized test results. Despite the position of NAEYC that rejects standardized testing of children birth to eight, and despite early childhood educators' opposition, districts use standardized assessment data to assess children's development and for accountability of schools and teachers. Some argue that standardized assessment does not assess children's critical thinking skills, problem-solving, and creativity. It is also argued that standardized testing narrows the curriculum, encourages teachers to "teach to the test", and pushes out the deep, hands-on explorations that have been the hallmark of early childhood education. One of the most serious problems with using standardized testing to hold schools accountable is that the scores are often reported after the child has left the grade level in which they were assessed. This fact nullifies the intended purpose of using testing data to improve learning outcomes for individual children (Bredekamp, 2011).

The **effects on curriculum and instruction** are demonstrated in scheduling, the classroom environment, and the amount of time devoted to play. The kindergarten day has gotten longer with 80% of school districts now offering a full day program (Ackerman, Barnett, & Robin, 2005). The classroom set up has moved away from large blocks of time for center-based small group explorations to more whole-group instruction that often offers scripted phonics lessons and lengthy mathematics instruction (Wright, 2010). The loss of unstructured playtime in early childhood classrooms is evidenced by disappearing play kitchens and wooden building blocks (Elkind, 2007). Cognitive development suffers when children are not allowed time to interact with the people and items in their environment (Piaget, 1962). Social and emotional skills are stunted when children are not allowed time to interact and learn important social skills with their peers, and to pretend and use their powers of fantasy (Fein, 1981).

Assessment of Infants and Toddlers

A variety of tests have been designed that address the developmental domains of infants and toddlers. Children in this age range are often difficult to assess due to their short attention span, uneven developmental trajectory, lack of expressive language and brief periods of alertness when assessment can take place. For these reasons, the validity and reliability of infant and toddler assessments are uncertain and the administration and interpretation is problematic (Wortham, 2008). However, evaluations of infants and toddlers can provide valuable information.

The first assessment of the infant is usually the **APGAR** – an evaluation of the newborn's medical status. The APGAR is an observational rating scale that the delivering doctor administers one minute and five minutes after birth. The five dimensions are based on the letters in the assessment's originator's name – Dr. Virginia Apgar – who created the scale in 1952:

- **A**ppearance – skin color
- **P**ulse rate
- **G**rimace – irritability to stimulation
- **A**ctivity – flexing the arms and legs, muscle tone
- **R**espiration – effort of breathing and lustiness of the first cry

Each criterion receives a 0-2 score at both one minute and five minutes after birth. A total score of 7 to 10 indicates the infant is in good condition, a score of 4-6 may indicate a developmental difficulty, and a score of 3 and below is serious, suggesting a possible threat to the infant's survival (Wortham, 2008).

The **Neonatal Behavioral Assessment Scale (NBAS-III),** developed by Dr. T. Berry Brazelton and his colleagues in 1973 is used with infants from one day old to four weeks old. The screening focuses on the infant's behavior and responses in seven areas: reflexes, autonomic system, organizational status, regulation status, motor system, habituation, and social-interaction. There are seven additional items that can be used to assess the possibility of fetal alcohol syndrome or drug exposure (Brazelton & Nugent, 1995). This assessment can identify mild neurological impairment and, if administered in the presence of the parents, can assist parents in becoming more knowledgeable of their infant's cues and abilities.

Bayley Scales of Infant and Toddler Development Screening Test (Bayley III) is a quickly administered individual assessment of children from 1-42 months old. The purpose of the screening is to detect a possible developmental delay, which requires further evaluation. The Bayley Scale consists of three subscales: cognitive, language, and motor abilities. The cognitive subscale has 33 items in four categories: exploration, response to novelty, problem solving, and play tasks. The language subscale has 24 items in expressive language and another 24 in receptive language. The motor abilities subscale has 27 fine and 28 gross motor items.

Early Screening Inventory Revised (ESI-R) is a 20-minute screening assessment used to predict if a child is at risk for school failure. The test assesses visual-motor adaptive, language and cognition, and gross motor. The test is available in two forms: one for children between ages 36 and 54 months and one for children 55 to 72 months. There is also a parent questionnaire that is optional.

Ages and Stages Questionnaire (ASQ-III) is a developmental screening for children from 4 to 60 months old that is completed solely by parents either in an online format or in hard copy. There are 19 questionnaires each with 30 questions covering five major domains: communication, gross motor, fine motor, problem solving, and personal-social and it takes about 15 minutes to complete. The questionnaire changes for every two to six months of the child's growth. After the parents complete and submit the online questionnaire, they receive an analysis of their child's development and subsequently, they receive suggestions of activities they can offer their child. The purpose of the ASQ-III is to provide an early caution of a possible developmental delay so that early intervention can be provided.

Brigance Inventory of Early Development (IED-II) is a developmental inventory – a battery of assessment measures given after a screening indicates a child may be at risk for a developmental delay. The IED-II assesses children from birth to the developmental age of seven (Brigance & Glascoe, 2004). It measures physical development, language, academic/cognitive development in the areas of literacy and mathematics, daily living, and social-emotional development. If the full IED-II battery is administered the test administrator interviews the teacher and the parent and does a formal observation of the child outside of the testing context. Many school districts and state education departments use components of the Brigance for pre-school assessment and to monitor children receiving early intervention (Wright, 2010).

"CDE Baby Human to Feel 3 Temperament"

Children from birth to 3 years old, who are diagnosed with a developmental delay or have an identified disabling condition, usually qualify for early intervention (EI) services. An individualized family service plan (IFSP) provides guidance for the intervention services provided to the children who qualify for the services. The IFSP process brings together the child's family and the service providers as a team, which works together to promote the best interest of the child. These children enter EI services after initial developmental screening and subsequent diagnostic testing.

Diverse Learners

Accommodating diverse learners. The term "inclusion" is usually reserved for special education, representing a philosophy of education where children with special needs are included in the classroom with general education students. For the purposes of this chapter, we will use the term inclusive classroom in more general terms. Most early childhood classes today in the United States are inclusive based on the diversity of children's development and capabilities; ethnicities and races; genders; cultural backgrounds and home

languages; physical capabilities; and socioeconomic status. Children in early childhood programs mirror the diversity of the society as a whole. Continued documented and undocumented immigration from other countries coupled with varying birth rates within groups suggests that diversity will continue to increase (Cochran-Smith & Power, 2010). The early childhood professional is the person responsible for meeting the needs of every child in his or her classroom.

"Supporting Cultural and Linguistic Diversity in Early Childhood"

Recognizing the individuality of each child is just the beginning; the early childhood professional must understand child development, get to know each child individually, and be cognizant of the contexts in which children live and grow. They then use this knowledge to plan and modify the curriculum to help each individual child meet important learning goals (Bredekamp, 2011).

Gender differences result due to a combination of biological traits and gendered socialization practices. From the moment of birth, children receive parental and societal cues and overt messages about the expectations for males and females. For most children entering pre-school, their gender identity is becoming securely established. The gender differences that teachers are aware of are in the areas of social-emotional development and cognitive development.

In social and emotional development, there are vast gender differences; boys like to play in large groups and girls tend to develop more intimate friendships where they express their emotions much more than boys (Bredekamp, 2011). Young boys tend to be more physically aggressive and active, while most girls favor quieter activities.

In cognitive development, there seems to be little difference in overall intelligence, however, girls, on average reach developmental milestones such as expressive language earlier than boys (Bukatko & Daehler, 2003). Boys demonstrate a slim but consistent lead in visual-spatial ability – an academic skill necessary for engineering, drawing, and mathematics (Khairul & Azniah, 2004). Much of these differences may have to do with early experiences; girls have the opportunity to use expressive language while "playing school" – a common young female play scenario. Boys develop visual-spatial skills by building blocks and playing with Duplos and Legos.

"What Kindergarteners Taught Me About Gender"

It is important that early childhood professionals avoid gender stereotyping which limits children's exploration and development of their own unique identities. Morrison (2012, pp. 419-420) provides some excellent suggestions for avoiding gender stereotypes:

- Provide opportunities for all children to experience the activities, materials, toys, and emotions traditionally associated with both sexes.
- Become conscious of words that promote sexism. Use non-sexist terms such as *firefighter* and *mail carrier*.
- Determine what physical arrangements in the classroom promote or encourage gender-role stereotyping. All children should have equal access to all learning areas of the classroom; no area should be reserved exclusively for one sex.
- Examine your behavior to see whether you are encouraging gender stereotypes. Do you tell boys they should not play with dolls? Do you reward girls who are always passive, well behaved, and well mannered? Give all children a chance to respond to questions. Help all children become independent and do things for themselves.
- Encourage children to dress in ways that lead to full participation in all activities.

Differences in emotional and social development affect children's success in the classroom and in their daily lives outside of the classroom. Positive social skills – the ability to make friends, participate in play episodes, and to display empathy for other children when in distress (Beaty, 2013) – are important skills in which many young

children struggle. Children who have well developed social skills are generally more successful in school, in social situations and in relationships; children who lack these skills are more likely to fight, bully, or be withdrawn.

Much of children's emotional and social development has to do with their **temperament** – a person's general pattern of behavior, which includes typical activity level, attention span, and mood (Thomas & Chess, 1984). Out of interplay of temperament and environmental conditions, personality is born. Temperament is divided into nine characteristics: 1) rhythm and regularity of functions such as eating, sleeping, wakefulness; 2) level and degree of motor activity; 3) adaptability to environmental changes; 4) acceptance or rejection of new people and experiences; 5) sensitivity to environmental stimuli; 6) intensity of responses; 7) distractibility; 8) general mood (pleasant, irritable, engaging, unfriendly, etc.); and 9) attention span and persistence. The combinations of these nine characteristics produce unique personalities that can be categorized into 3 classifications: the easy child, the slow-to-warm-up child, and the difficult child (Thomas, Chess & Birch, 1970). For example, an easy child would have a positive mood, low to moderate intensity to reaction, and adaptability to new situations, while a difficult child might have a contentious mood much of the time, have tense reactions, and be slow to change to new situations (Morrison, 2012, p. 248).

The important understanding teachers must embrace is that basic personality is very difficult to change; teachers will have more success with each student if they understand the child's temperament and build positive relationships with them. Teachers will then need to adapt to each child's needs. These needs include their emotional and social needs as well as their approaches to learning.

"Understanding a Child's Temperament"

Approaches to learning are the "behaviors, tendencies or typical patterns that children use in learning situations" (Hyson, 2008, p. 10). These approaches to learning include persistence, curiosity, creativity, engagement, imagination, and initiative (NYSED, 2013). Each child brings to the classroom his/her own unique approach to learning. It is the early childhood educator's job to observe children carefully to understand the diversity of approaches to learning so as to use children's strengths to accommodate individual needs. For example, if a child enjoys listening to informational text about dinosaurs as opposed to narrative, at least half of the read alouds and browsing boxes should contain non-fiction literature about dinosaurs and paleontology that will engage that particular child.

Cultural and linguistic differences present a special challenge. Although the United States has been and continues to be a nation of immigrants, recent immigration patterns and irregular birth rates in particular groups have ushered in a new era of diversity. The 2010 Census figures (US Census Bureau, 2012) show that approximately 37% of the population is classified as Latino, Hispanic, African American/African, Asian, and 2 or more races. Projections are that before 2050, minorities will actually approach being the majority  (Hayes, 2008) of the American population. Many areas of the United States are already at or approaching this statistic – for example, the 2011 census figures for California show that 62% of the population is Latino, Hispanic, African American/ African, Asian and 2 or more races (US Census Bureau, 2012).

Culture is the explicit and implicit values, beliefs, and patterns of behavior passed down from generation to generation (NAEYC, 2009) that is comprised of customs, rituals, beliefs, values, religion, language, clothing, and food (Morrison, 2012). Children learn all these aspects of their culture as well as expectations for their behavior and assumption of roles from their cultural group. It is important that early childhood educators understand that culture shapes children's development and learning in the ways that they behave, solve problems, think, and communicate (Rogoff, 2003). Children are acculturated – taught the expected rules of behavior – from the cultural group's explicit teaching as well as modeling. Early childhood educators need to be aware that different experiences have different meaning for individual children based on their acculturation. For instance, some cultures feel that not establishing eye contact is a sign of respect while in other cultures it is sign of disrespect. Becoming informed about individual cultures is part of becoming a professional. It is beneficial to understand some key principles about the influence of culture on child development (Bredekamp, 2011, pp.169-170):

- *Everyone has a culture, and is a product of one or more cultural groups.* It requires that European American children teachers reject the tendency to see white, European American children as exhibiting *ordinary* behaviors, while thinking about children of other ethnic ancestries as exhibiting *cultural* behaviors (Day, 2006).
- *Culture is dynamic.* Culture is not a fixed, static entity. Because it is born of traditions and historical experiences, intervening events can affect and change cultural rules. Because culture is dynamic, teachers need to be careful not to make assumptions about students' and families' behaviors based on outdated information or even prior experience with members of a particular group.
- *Culture, language, ethnicity, and race are aspects of experience that influence people's beliefs and values.* Additional factors, including socioeconomic status, education, occupation, ability/disability, sexual orientation, personality, and events in the larger society, influence how people behave and how groups function (Lynch, 2004).
- *Differences within a cultural group may be as great as, or greater than, differences between cultural groups.* Assuming that children who share the same culture or language are alike is like assuming that all 3-year olds are alike. Although there are some similarities, there are many differences in their skills, abilities, and behaviors. Children from one cultural group are both alike and different from children of another. Therefore, it is vitally important not to stereotype individuals who are members of particular groups even while learning some of the common practices, values, or beliefs of those groups.

- *Culture is defined in terms of differences among groups and is complicated by issues of power and status.* When one group, such as European Americans, becomes the reference point against which other groups are compared, that group is the one with the most power and privilege in the society (Barrera, Corso, & Macpherson, 2003; Delpit, 2006).

Language is the primary vehicle for transmitting culture (Nieto, 2004); there is an inextricable link between language and culture. The "biggest child-specific demographic change in the United States over the next 20 years is predicted to be an increase in children whose home language is not English" (Copple & Bredekamp, 2009, p.2). It becomes apparent that all educators, beginning with early childhood educators, will work with linguistically and culturally diverse children and their families. With the increasing number of children who speak languages other than English at home and the increased  pressure for these children to be assessed in schools solely in English, educators are given the opportunity to support these children as they become bilingual. All of our children need to become fluent in English, yet not give up their home language (Tabors, 2008). This becomes a delicate balancing act as children need to explicitly develop both languages; but what often happens is that they sacrifice proficiency in one language for the other. The loss of home language can adversely affect children's long-term academic achievement and additionally, can seriously impact the communication at home and family relationships (Espinosa, 2007).

To be able to work most effectively with children from culturally and linguistically diverse contexts, it is most important to become culturally competent. **Cultural competence** is the ability to work respectfully and effectively in diverse settings. Some characteristics of cultural competence are (Bredekamp, 2011, Morrison, 2012):

- *Being aware of one's own cultural perspectives. Become knowledgeable about, proud of, and secure in your own culture.*
- *Recognizing that all children are unique.*
- *Appreciating and respecting individuals from other cultures and the contributions they have made.*
- *Acquainting yourself with and appreciating the cultural backgrounds of the children in your classroom.*
- *Believing that cross-cultural interactions should be viewed as opportunities for learning and understanding.*
- *Identifying and using cultural resources.*
- *Be willing to continue to try to understand other's perspectives.*

Embodying these cultural competencies serves to make successful educators for all children.

Teaching in a culturally and linguistically diverse world is a challenging yet exciting endeavor. Children from these two groups as well as those from low SES homes are the groups that are being underserved in schools and who need culturally competent, well-prepared teachers. There are several things that are effective early childhood teaching practices for culturally and linguistically diverse children: incorporating children's backgrounds into curriculum, using appropriate instructional materials and literature, and encouraging family and community involvement (Copple & Bredekamp, 2009)

Research shows that considering children's backgrounds when designing curriculum is positively correlated with positive learning outcomes (Tharp & Entz, 2003). Some of these principles of teaching culturally and linguistically diverse children include teachers and students working together on small group projects, connecting school learning to  children's lives, using problem-solving techniques, and incorporating literacy and language throughout the day and in all content areas (Tharp, Estrada, Dalton & Yamachuchi, 2000). The curriculum can be organized across all content areas – math, language arts, science, literacy, social studies, music, and art – in themes such as "All About Me" and "My Family" that allow children to study, honor, and respect the cultural and linguistic contexts in which they live and flourish.

Educators need to research and choose multicultural literature that offers a respectful and authentic portrayal of children and families in their everyday lives. These materials need to characterize cultural groups accurately and equitably, include several cultural groups and people of color, and avoid stereotyping of cultures, abilities and genders. Posters of children from the cultural groups, genders, and exceptionalities represented in the classroom should be displayed around the room. Dolls and other toys in the classroom should also be representative of all children in a diverse culture.

By learning about the families and communities in which children live, the culturally competent educator can become familiar with the beliefs and practices of these contexts. Inviting families and community members into the classroom to share their lives throughout the school year builds bridges of understanding and models for children's positive home-school connections. Many of the children will not speak English as their first language so it will be of utmost importance to become knowledgeable about teaching English Language Learners. Lessow-Hurley (2000) recommends that teachers of ELL's develop content around a theme, use routines to reinforce language, use hands-on activities and visual aids, pair ELL's with English speakers, allow non-verbal responses and don't insist on perfect English.

Differences in cognitive development and abilities pose challenges for the early childhood educator. Throughout a lifetime of teaching, the educator will work with students who have severe muscular, neurological, vision, or hearing disabilities that have been identified. The educator will also work with children who have disabilities that are less apparent such as learning disabilities, speech and language difficulties, mild developmental delays, and attention deficit disorder. Many times it will be the knowledgeable and perceptive early childhood educator who is the first to confirm that the child has a learning delay – a belief parents have presumed about their child.

As educators use their perception and knowledge to identify children with potential learning impediments, it is important to not "over-diagnose", misinterpreting normal development as being deficient. Young children are active, curious, impetuous and excitable. Often, when children are asked to sit still to accomplish inappropriate paper-pencil work for too long of periods of time, frustration results in behavior and emotional problems for the child. The well-educated, experienced early childhood educator provides developmentally appropriate educational programming, environments, and guidance that allows for exploration and hands-on experiences. It is important that young children are allowed to flourish in developmentally and individually appropriate settings so that identification of children with true special needs is more accurate.

Children who need a more challenging program are often the "forgotten" population among diverse learners. Young children enter programs with advanced language ability, many having had a wide range of experiences, often older than the other children, with a higher level of precociousness, or thought of as "gifted". Not all of these children are truly gifted, yet they need greater challenge to meet their more rapid cognitive maturation and positive approaches to learning. It is important that the early childhood educator knows these children individually, to tailor the program to their individual interests and learning styles, and provide a wide range of opportunities.

Differentiating instruction is the educational approach that calls for intentional and tactical planning to meet the needs of individual children by teaching to their needs, strengths, and interests. When the instruction is differentiated, there are multiple paths for children to achieve learning goals. First, the teacher must get to know each child and their strengths, needs, interests, and learning styles. The teacher must also know the curriculum he or she is teaching as well as both the curriculum the children may have already experienced and are going to be advancing into when they go to the next grade level. The teacher is now ready to differentiate the instruction in terms of the content, pedagogy, and product as well as the learning environment. Differentiation provides for classroom spaces that facilitate collaborative and individual learning, whole class meeting time, hands-on exploration, a combination of active and quiet learning, and a wide range of literature and materials. Differentiation of content focuses the instruction on each child's developmental level; for example, some kindergarten children will be working on letter recognition while others will be reading storybooks and need support in sight word recognition and fluency. The savvy teacher will incorporate multiple ways to teach – hands-on experiences, whole or half group read-aloud/think alouds, worthwhile computer programs, cooperative learning, etc. The products of learning that allow assessment of the learning will also be differentiated; for example, after studying about Arctic animals, one group of children may produce a labeled mural while another group may create a song or skit.

RTI is a tiered approach with the purpose of identifying students with learning needs early on and giving focused support to prevent school failure. This intervention model looks at all children; instead of waiting for children to fail, and before learning delays become learning disabilities, varying levels of instructional support are put in place. RTI is based on the belief that early, focused intervention is a child's best hope for academic success. The three-tiered approach includes:

- Implementing a research-based curriculum and instruction for all children which typically works for approximately 80% of the student population
- Approximately 15% of the remaining 20% are screened for learning delays, given focused small group instruction, and receive frequent ongoing progress monitoring. If this is not working for some children, they advance to Tier 3 intervention
- The remaining approximately 5% receive intensive, individual intervention

RTI's ultimate purpose is to help children reach Tier 1 standards by using research-based interventions, including explicit and direct instruction.

Inclusive special education or "inclusion" refers to the inclusion of children with special needs as much as possible in all areas of education and social life. Inclusive classrooms include all children and both the special educator and general education teacher are responsible for the learning of all the children in the classroom. The Division for Early Childhood (DEC) and the National Association for the Education of Young Children (NAEYC) have issued a joint statement on inclusion as education that:

> ...Embodies the values, policies, and practices that support the right of every infant and young child and his or her family, regardless of ability, to participate in a broad range of activities and contexts as full members of families, communities, and society. The desired results of inclusive experiences for children with and without disabilities and their families include a sense of belonging and membership, positive social relationships and friendships, and development and learning to reach their full potential. (DEC/NAEYC, 2009)

"Special Education – Support an Inclusive Classroom"

"Special Education Teaching: Teaching Students With Special Needs in Inclusive Classrooms"

The philosophy that frames the PL 94-142 amendments that provide inclusion for children with disabilities, is that all children learn and develop optimally in natural environments where there are typically developing peers. Inclusion benefits all children and their families. Children with disabilities have competent peers as models with whom they can interact, learning new communication and social skills. Children without disabilities have opportunities and exposure to develop positive attitudes towards others with diverse backgrounds and needs. Families of children with or without disabilities are given the opportunity to forge supportive, collaborative relationships and long-lasting friendships.

Universal Design for Learning (UDL) is built on the premise that all children need to be able to participate as fully as possible. Therefore, equipment, materials, and environments need to be serviceable for everyone. For instance, all children can use blocks, yet some variations on standard blocks make them usable by children with special needs (e.g., bristle blocks with Velcro strips to keep them on the table) and more interesting for all children. The principles of Universal Design (National Center on Universal Design for Learning, 2012) are:

- Multiple means of representation (the "what" of learning)
- Multiple means of action and expression (the "how" of learning)
- Multiple means of engagement (the "why" of learning)

Universal Design for Learning calls for thoughtful, far-sightedness in planning materials and environments, and may prevent the need to modify spaces at a later date.

Summary

- Assessment is vital for teachers to plan, implement, and evaluate the effectiveness of educational experiences.

- Developmentally appropriate assessment must take into consideration the age of the child as well as the linguistic and cultural contexts in which children live. Ongoing, purposeful assessment needs to be responsive to the individual differences of children.

- Authentic, formative assessment provides the majority of the data an early childhood teacher uses in evaluating student learning and includes many tools:
  - Examples of formative assessment include observational notes, anecdotal notes, checklists, time and event sampling, rating scales, work samples, interviews, portfolios, and rubrics.

- Summative assessment is evaluation that occurs at the end of a teaching and learning cycle to substantiate mastery of skills and information.

- Most early childhood classes today in the United States are inclusive based on the diversity of children's development and capabilities; ethnicities and races; genders; cultural backgrounds and home languages; physical capabilities; and socioeconomic status.

- Much of children's emotional and social development has to do with their temperament – a person's general pattern of behavior that includes typical activity level, attention span, and mood (Thomas & Chess, 1984).

- Culture is the explicit and implicit values, beliefs, and patterns of behavior passed down from generation to generation (NAEYC, 2009) that is comprised of customs, rituals, beliefs, values, religion, language, clothing, and food (Morrison, 2012).

- To be able to work most effectively with children from culturally and linguistically diverse contexts, it is most important to become culturally competent. **Cultural competence** is the ability to work respectfully and effectively in diverse settings

- Many times it will be the knowledgeable and perceptive early childhood educator who is the first to confirm that the child has a learning delay – a belief parents have presumed about their child.

- Children who need a more challenging program are often the "forgotten" population among diverse learners. Young children enter programs with advanced language ability, many having had a wide range of experiences, often older than the other children, with a higher level of precociousness, or thought of as "gifted".

- **Inclusive special education** or "inclusion" refers to the inclusion of children with special needs as much as possible in all areas of education and social life. Inclusive classrooms include all children and both the special educator and general education teacher are responsible for the learning of all the children in the classroom.

Key Terms

APGAR
authentic assessment
bell curve
criterion-referenced
cultural competence
Every Student Succeeds Act (ESSA)
formal assessment
formative assessment
informal assessment
mean
normal distribution
norm group
norm-referenced
performance-based assessment
reliability
RTI
standardized assessment
summative assessment
temperament
Universal Design for Learning (UDL)
validity

Suggested Readings

Hyson, M. (2008). *Enthusiastic and engaged learners: Approaches to learning in the early childhood classroom.* New York: Teachers College Press.
Jablon, J.R., Dombro, A. L. & Dichtelmiller, M. L. (2007). *The power of observation for birth through eight.* (2nd ed.). Washington, DC: Teaching Strategies and NAEYC.
Mc Afee, O. & Leong, D. (2007). *Assessing and guiding young children's development and learning.* (4th ed.). Boston: Pearson Allyn & Bacon.

Sandall, S. & Schwartz, I. (2008). *Building blocks for successful early childhood programs: Strategies for including all children.* (2nd ed.). Baltimore: Paul H. Brookes Publishing.

Suggested Websites

Council for Exceptional Children
www.cec.sped.org

Council for Learning Disabilities
www.cldinternational.org
National Center for Fair and Open Testing
www.fairtest.org/K-12

National Institute for Early Education Research (NIEER)
www.nieer.org/assessment

Reflections

1. Observe in an infant toddler setting. Ask the teacher how he or she assesses children's development. How is the data documented? Reflect on the challenges inherent in assessing this age group.

2. Interview a primary teacher about his or her thoughts on standardized testing. Has high-stakes testing impacted his or her teaching, and if so, how?

3. What are some of the ways you will encourage and support gifted and talented children?

4. Visit an inclusive early childhood classroom. How are the children with special needs, socially, emotionally, physically, and cognitively engaged in intentional ways? What are their associations with typical children?

5. Reflect on gender differences and the biological and experiential influences. Do you think the teacher should consider gender differences when working with young children? Treat all children the same?

References

Ackerman, D. J., Barnett, W. S., & Robin, K. B. (2005). *Making the most of kindergarten: Present trends and future issues in the provision of full-day programs.* New Brunswick, NJ: National Institute for Early Education Research.
AFT (American Federation of Teachers). (2016). Every student succeeds act: A new day in public education. www.aft.org/sites/default/files/**essa** faq.pdf

American Educational Research Association, American Psychology Association, & National Council on Measurement. (1999). *Standards for educational and psychological testing.* Washington, DC: AERA.

Barrera, I., Corso, R. M., & Macpherson, D. (2003). *Skilled dialogue: Strategies for responding to cultural diversity in early childhood.* Baltimore: Paul H. Brookes.

Beaty, J. (2013). *Observing the development of the young child* (8th ed.). Upper Saddle River, NJ: Pearson.

Brazelton, T. B. & Nugent, J. K. (1995). *The neonatal behavioral assessment scale* (3rd ed.). Port Chester, NY: Cambridge University Press.

Brigance , A. H. & Glascoe, F. P.(2004). *Brigance diagnostic inventory of early development* (2nd ed.). North Billerica, MA: Curriculum Associates.

Bukatko, D. & Daehler, M. W. (2003). *Child development: A thematic approach* (4th ed.). Boston: Houghton Mifflin.

CCSSO. (2016). www.ccsso.org/Documents/.../ESSA/ESSA_Key_Provisions_Implications_for_SWD.

Cochran-Smith, M. & Power, C. (2010). New Directions for Teacher Preparation. *Educational Leadership 67*(8), 6-13.

Copple, C. & Bredekamp, S. (2009). *Developmentally appropriate practice in early childhood programs* (3rd Ed.). Washington, DC: National Association for the Education of Young Children.

Day, C. B., (2004). *Essentials for child development associates working with young children* (rev.ed.). Washington, DC: Council for Professional Recognition.

Day, C. B., (2006). Every child is a cultural being. In J.R. Lally, P.L. Mangione, & D. Greenwald (Eds.), *Concepts for care: Essays on infant/toddler development and learning,* pp. 97-99. San Francisco: WestEd.

Delpit, L. (2006). *Other people's children: Cultural conflict in the classroom* (updated ed.). New York: New Press.

Division for Early Childhood. (2007). *Promoting positive outcomes for children with disabilities: Recommendations for curriculum, assessment, and program evaluation.* Missoula, MT: DEC.

Division for Early Childhood (DEC)/National Association for the Education of Young Children (NAEYC). (2009). *Early childhood inclusion: A joint position statement of the Division for Early Childhood (DEC) and the National Association for the Education of Young Children ((NAEYC).* Chapel Hill, NC: The University of North Carolina, FPG Child Development Institute.

Doherty, K. M. (2004). Assessment. *Education Week.* Retrieved March 30, 2013 from http://www.ed.week.org/context/topics/issuespage

Elkind, D. (2007). *The power of play: Doing what comes naturally.* Cambridge, MA: DeCapo Press.

Espinosa, L. (2007). English language learners as they enter school. In R. Pianta & K. Snow (Eds.), *School readiness, early learning, and the transition to school.* Baltimore: Paul H. Brookes.

Fein, G. (1981). Pretend play in childhood: An integrative review. *Child Development 52*(4). 1095-1118.

Hayes, B. (2008). Increasing the representation of underrepresented minority groups in US Colleges and Schools of Pharmacy. *American Journal of Pharmaceutical Education, 72*(1).

Hyson, M. (2008). *Enthusiastic and engaged learners: Approaches to learning in the early childhood classroom.* New York: Teachers College Press.

Keller, M. (2006, July 5). Academic redshirting is getting a mixed report card. *Los Angeles Times,* p. 83.

Khairul, A. S. & Azniah, I. (2004). The improvement of mental rotation through computer-based multimedia tutor. *Malaysian Online Journal of Instructional Technology, 1*(2).

Kingore, B. (2008). *Developing portfolios for authentic assessment, pre-k – 3: Guiding potential in young learners.* Thousand Oaks, CA: Corwin Press.

Lessow-Hurley, J. (2000). *The foundations of dual language instruction* (3rd ed.). New York: Longman.

Lynch, E. W. (2004). Developing cross-cultural competence. In E.W. Lynch & M.J Hanson (Eds.), *Developing cross-cultural competence: A guide for working with children and their families.* (3rd ed). Baltimore: Paul H. Brookes.

Marshall, H. (2003). Research in review. Opportunity deferred or opportunity taken? An updated look at delaying kindergarten entry. *Young Children, 58*(5), 84-93.

McAfee, O., Leong, D. J. & Bodrova, E. (2004). *Basics of assessment: A primer for early childhood educators.* Washington, DC: NAEYC.

McAfee, O. & Leong, D. (2007). *Assessing and guiding young children's development and learning* (4th ed.). Boston: Pearson Allyn & Bacon.

Meisels, S. & Atkins-Burnett, S. (2005). *Developmental screening in early childhood: A guide* (5th ed.). Washington, DC: NAEYC.

National Association for the Education of Young Children (NAEYC). (1995). School readiness: A position statement of the National Association for the Education of Young Children, revised. Washington, DC: NAEYC.

National Association for the Education of Young Children (NAEYC). (2009). *Developmentally appropriate practice in early childhood programs serving children from birth through age 8.* Position statement. Washington, DC: NAEYC.

National Center for Education Statistics (NCES). (2015). Available online at http://nces.ed.gov/programs.

National Center on Universal Design for Learning. (2012). www.udlcenter.org

National Research Council. (2008). *Early childhood assessment: Why, what, and how.* Washington, DC: National Academies Press.

Neisworth, J. T. & Bagnato, S. J. (1988). Assessment in early childhood special education: A typology of dependent measures. In S. I. Odom & M. B. Karnes (Eds.), *Early intervention for infants and children with handicaps: An empirical base* (pp. 23-51). Baltimore: Paul H. Brookes.

New York State Education Department (NYSED). (2013). www.nysed.gov/commoncore/

Nieto, S. (2004). *Affirming diversity: The sociopolitical context of multicultural education* (4th ed.). Boston: Allyn & Bacon.

Rogoff , B. (2003). *The cultural nature of human development.* New York: Oxford University Press.

Scarborough, A. A., Spiker, D., Mallik, S., Hebbeler, K. M., Bailey, D. B., & Simeonsson, R. J. (2004). A national look at children and families entering early intervention. *Exceptional Children, 70*(4), 469-483.

Seefeldt, C. (2005). *How to work with standards in the early childhood classroom.* New York: Teachers College Press.

Tharp, R. & Entz, S. (2003). From high chair to high school: Research-based principles for teaching complex thinking. *Young Children, 58*(5), 38-44.

Tharp, R. G., Estrada, P., Dalton, S., & Yamachuchi, I. A. (2000). *Teaching transformed: Achieving excellence, fairness, inclusion, and harmony.* Boulder, CO: Westview.

Thomas, A. & Chess, S. (1984). Genesis and evolution of behavioral disorders: From infancy to early adult life. *American Journal of Psychiatry, 141*(1), 1-9.

Thomas, A., Chess, S., & Birch, H. G. (1970). The origin of personality. *Scientific American, 223*, 102–107.

Tomlinson, C. A. (2008). Learning to love assessment. *Educational Leadership, 65*(4), 8-13.

US Census Bureau. (2012). http://www.census.gov

US Department of Education. (2012). http://www.ed.gov

Wortham, S. C. (2008). *Assessment in early childhood education* (5th ed.). Upper Saddle River, NJ: Pearson.

Wright, R. J. (2010). *Multifaceted assessment for early childhood education.* Thousand Oaks, CA: Sage.

Chapter 12
Guiding Children/Collaborating with Families/ Setting Up the Classroom/Putting It All Together

Thinking Ahead

1. How do early childhood educators use indirect guidance to build children's self-regulation skills?
2. How do early childhood educators use direct guidance to build children's self-regulation skills?
3. What are some of the strategies that can build positive relationships with families?
4. How can early childhood educators use their knowledge of family systems theory to build partnerships with families?
5. How do classroom design and materials, and daily scheduling foster the learning and self-regulation of young children?

 As early childhood educators, we have the pedagogical knowledge, content knowledge, nurturing capabilities, and dedication to young children and their families. We enter the field with a vision for young children – one in which we support children's development in all domains of learning. We want children to flourish cognitively and physically so we design challenging and engaging environments and curricula. Additionally, we want children to develop healthy self-esteem, respect for themselves and others, empathy, and strong **self-regulation** skills. Children require guidance to feel safe, secure and confident to explore, learn, and build relationships with others.

Guidance is not making a child "behave" or thinking of punishments for when they misbehave. It is not obsessively trying to get a child to do what we want them to do. Guidance is not reacting punitively to punish misbehavior. Guidance is helping children become autonomous, self-regulated, empathetic, contributing members of a particular culture as children and later, as adults.

"Understanding Challenging Behavior in Young Children"

Responsive and appropriate guidance requires a sensitive, knowledgeable educator who not only prepares the physical environment for education and nurture, but also constructs the interpersonal environment that sets the tone for children's development. Our responsiveness to children's needs, a firm knowledge of child development, a set of reasonable expectations for behavior, and strategies to guide children provides the framework to support children in the development of self-regulation.

Highly responsive early childhood educators are attuned to a child's development, needs, and strengths. They are able to communicate warmth, fairness, and firmness using good explanations along with guidance strategies (Baumrind, 1996). Warmth is communicated through interactions that show we genuinely care about the child. Fairness in guidance is shown through consistency in the creation and enforcement of guidelines. Firmness is displayed through vigilant monitoring and supervision of children and the use of guidance strategies that are developmentally, age, and culturally appropriate. Effective guidance requires basic mutual respect from educators, parents, and children.

Effective guidance also requires a "plan" after deep reflection about the kind of people we want our children to become. Early childhood educators develop a plan for effective interactions, appropriate expectations, supportive environments, engaging curricula, and responsive facilitation of children's self-regulation skills. The guidance plan that early childhood educators map out must be developmentally appropriate, taking into consideration 1) what we know about child development in general, 2) what we know about each child in the setting, and 3) what we know about the cultural values, customs, beliefs, and expectations of the child's family and community. For example, the guidance we give a two year old will be much different than for a five year old. Individual differences vary greatly in social, cognitive, and physical development. The interactions and guidance need to reflect the cultures of the children.

Effective Guidance

Effective guidance is everything that adults do, indirectly and directly, to motivate children to become self-regulated, self-directed, and contributing members of society. Much of our guidance of children is **indirect**; the planning of the environment (space, materials, and equipment), scheduling, purposeful transitions, engaging curricula, and establishing appropriate expectations are all components of indirect guidance. **Direct** guidance includes facilitating

prosocial behaviors, preventing problems by anticipating and re-directing particular behaviors, and using consequences to encourage or discourage particular behaviors (Hearron & Hildebrand, 2005).These are the verbal, physical, and affective procedures educators use to help the child become self-directed and able to function in society.

"School 'Misbehavior' and What to Do About It"

Indirect guidance. Organizing and arranging the environment is important in creating a caring community of learners and sending a set of messages to children (Tarr, 2001):

- You are safe here
- You can learn many things here
- You can play and work with other children
- You can work on many different projects
- You can make choices here
- When you finish your work in one area, you can go to a different spot and work there
- When you want to, you can work by yourself
- There is a space where all the children may gather

Room arrangement should foster independence and competence in each child, should support the purposes of a developmentally appropriate program, and promote acceptable behavior. An attractive and aesthetically pleasing environment as we see in programs such as Reggio Emilia demonstrates a respect for children's development, curiosity, competence, and resourcefulness. In Reggio Emilia, Italy, educators consider the environment that supports children's development to be the **third teacher** (Edwards, Gandini, Forman, 1998). The schools of Reggio Emilia emphasize children's need for beauty, simplicity, and challenge through their classroom design. Aesthetics is important in planning the environment; orderly, beautiful spaces convey respect for children and their learning and serve to support healthy self-esteem and feelings of competence (Marion, 2011). The room needs to be orderly, well arranged, and organized in order for children to feel comfortable in their workplace and predictable routine. Classrooms need to be set up with positive social interaction in mind; learning centers need to be thought out intentionally to foster collaborative work and play. There needs to be a space and time for children to make wise choices in their activities and use of materials. The space needs to encourage children's active learning and engagement with others as well as with materials and ideas.

"Bambini Creativi, Reggio Inspired Preschool-Kansas City"

The developmentally appropriate classroom should be organized into activity areas, personifying the principles of active learning, social constructivism and interaction, freedom to move and explore, with adult scaffolding. The activity areas should be designed to meet the needs of children as they explore the particular learning activity in each space; some of the spaces will be larger than others, some on hard surfaces and others on carpet, and some with an abundance of materials and others with few materials. Well-designed classrooms should contain small group activity areas, a large group meeting area, and private spaces.

There needs to be plenty of space to avert crowding; many times crowding can violate a child's personal space and initiate undue aggression (Marion, 2011) . Safety always has to be the first consideration in order to protect each child from harm. Careful placement of the center areas can prevent much of this inappropriate behavior; some activities such as block building require plenty of materials and space, while the book sharing corner is usually occupied by one to three children who quietly relax and share books. Children also need personal space – cubbies in which to store their belongings, their own labeled spot on the floor in which they feel secure when participating in a large group, and a place to find respite from the busy-ness and noise of the classroom.

Promoting independence is successfully accomplished when children can independently enter learning centers, access materials, and then proceed to explore and experiment. There should be abundant materials that are easily accessible by the children to promote self-regulation, autonomy and choice. There needs to be storage areas to house materials children should not have access to, toys and materials that you are temporarily rotating out of use, and thematic unit boxes. Consideration for floor surfaces has to be made when positioning centers; messy centers need to be placed on hard, cleanable surfaces and near a sink. Carpeting in the block area stifles much of the noise and offers a comfortable surface on which to sit.

Transitions are the times in a well-planned daily schedule when all of the children move from one location or activity to another. Transitions occur when:

- Children move from one center to another
- Children move into large group
- Children move from large group into centers
- Children move from the classroom to special classes, playground, or lunchroom
- Children arrive at and leave from school

"Transitions"

Transitions need to be as infrequent but as well-planned as the actual daily curriculum; if transitions are not thoroughly thought out, there can be stress on both the children and adults, and children can find a venue for acting out. This disruption can be averted to a large degree by eliminating all but the very necessary transitions and then, carefully planning the transitions that are necessary.

"Preschool Transition Songs"

One way that transitions can be eliminated is to plan large blocks of time in which children choose a center, spend time in the center and then go to a different center when they want to. This is preferable to the teacher ringing a bell every 15 minutes during a one-hour center time – in effect, creating four transitions. Some teachers include snack as one of the choices during centers time, eliminating two unnecessary transitions from centers to a table to eat and then from the table to another activity.

Once the early childhood educator carefully plans the daily schedule to minimize transitions, he or she can plan the transition so that it is calm and systematic. Intentional teachers think through every aspect of their teaching, including transitions. The teacher then needs to explain the transition, model the steps of the transition, and have the children practice until they learn it. Each transition could be accompanied by its own song, chant, poem, or game.

It is important to not make children wait for you, the educator. In the event children do have to wait for their turn or for the teacher to quickly pull together the lesson, provide an activity such as counting by 2's or looking at books. When children are engaged in centers, they need advanced warning of the impending transition so they can begin to close the activity they are working on and mentally prepare themselves for movement to the next activity. This will require cues that let the children know at what stage in the transition they should be – for example, "You have 5 minutes to clean up…you have 2 minutes and most of your blocks should be put away."

Indirect guidance is facilitated through a rich and intentional curriculum that is developmentally appropriate for the age and prior knowledge of each child. Effective teachers develop curriculum by observing and assessing children's abilities, needs, and interests, and then creating activities that support children's learning. These activities should be organized in an integrated curriculum that provides concrete experiences and active learning. Allowing student choice and providing for multiple learning styles engages children in meaningful learning; this positive engagement is indirect guidance in that children use their energies constructively in interesting work.

"Child Guidance & Classroom Management Preview"

Direct guidance includes the techniques that will anticipate, prevent, and re-direct problem behaviors; these strategies are used in combination with indirect guidance to provide a comprehensive, holistic plan. Explicit positive guidance strategies that focus on teaching and not punishment have the most long-lasting effect on young children. With the goal of guiding children, early childhood educators redirect children's behavior, explain limits, and teach more acceptable behaviors.

"Positive Behavior Support – the Pyramid Model"

Initially, adults spend a great deal of time helping children understand and respect boundaries. Early childhood educators must first develop reasonable and focused boundaries. The limits must be stated in simple, positive, and understandable terms and reviewed periodically. Limits should protect the child, the other adults and children in the group, and the learning environment. Some of the rules can be generated by the group however the educator must establish non-negotiable safety rules which are applied consistently and fairly.

Consistency in following through on enforcement of the boundaries takes a great deal of energy and time. Children will frequently test the boundaries and the adult's resolve to carry out the consequences when a child violates one of the boundaries. The consequences need to be logical (Dreikurs & Cassel, 1972) so that children can learn to control their behavior. **Consequences** need to be closely aligned with the behavior so that children can understand the relationship of behavior and after-effect. For example, if children are knocking over the block structures built by their friends, removing the offenders from the areas and making them clean up other areas of the room will not teach them how to respect others' work. It is more effectual to have children sign "block building contracts" before entering the center, explaining the importance of a signed contract, and then having an appropriate consequence such as cleaning the entire block corner if the contract is broken (Kaiser & Rasminsky, 2012).

"TeachingMinute: Consistency"

Inductive discipline is a conscience and empathy building type of discipline in which the adult makes the child aware of the feelings of the "other" by pointing out the effects of the child's misdeeds on the "other". The adult uses direct explanation – "He's crying because you hit him." The adult uses language that is appropriate for the child's level of understanding and firmly insists that the child listens and complies.

The success of induction lies in its capacity to motivate children in their growth of moral standards through the following ways (Berk, 2016, p.373):

- Induction gives children information about how to behave that they can use in future situations.

- By emphasizing the impact of the child's actions on others, induction encourages empathy and sympathetic concern, which motivate prosocial behavior.

- Giving children reasons for changing their behavior encourages them to adopt moral standards because those standards make sense.

- Children who consistently experience induction may form a *script* for the negative emotional consequences of haring others. The child causes harm, inductive message points out harm, the child feels empathy for the victim, and the child makes amends. The script deters future transgressions.

Often, the negative behaviors children display are to gain the teacher's attention regardless of the means children use. If the behavior is not threatening the safety of others or the environment, it is often appropriate to walk away and **ignore the behavior** the child is using to receive your attention. To be successful, teachers must purposefully give attention to children's positive behaviors and not the negatives ones. Teachers can identify a few negative behaviors that can be ignored and then intentionally praise children who are displaying the opposite behaviors that are being ignored.

Redirecting is the strategy of drawing a child's attention and behavior away from inappropriateness to a more desirable alternative (Bredekamp, 2011). When dealing with very young children such as toddlers, diverting and distracting (Marion, 2011) is most effective. The early childhood educator immediately distracts the child from the dangerous or prohibited behavior and then involves the child in another activity. Older children – preschoolers and kindergarten age children – can use substitution as a redirection strategy; a child learns how to do an activity in a safer, more appropriate way. For instance, when a child becomes frustrated to the point of aggressiveness against other children, the teacher can provide a punching doll or bag for the child to work off the tension in an acceptable way.

**"Consequences for Young Children at Home
and the Preschool Classroom"**

Positive feedback and encouragement is a powerful way to support children's prosocial behavior while giving attention to the acceptable behaviors you want all children to learn. It is important to validate children's positive behaviors with specific, supportive verbal and nonverbal feedback. Empty praise like "good job" should be replaced with substantive feedback such as "Erin, thank you for using your words to tell Ethan how he hurt your feelings." Often, positive feedback and encouragement come in nonverbal gestures such as a high-five or "thumbs up".

"TeachingMinute: Positive Reinforcements"

Active listening is another effective strategy that can be used when children have a behavior issue and need to communicate their questions and feelings. The teacher, without interrupting, judging, or offering immediate solutions, allows the child to "talk out" his feelings. Then the teacher may put into words the feelings of the child. For example, "Bobby, I could tell you became very angry and frustrated when the scissors you were using would not cut the paper and instead, tore the paper." The teacher can then use the data collected from their active listening to help the child work through the problem and reach a solution. "Bobby, why don't you try a different pair of scissors and try opening the scissor's 'jaws' much wider when you cut the paper?" By using active listening, you will gain deeper understanding into how children are thinking and feeling.

Teaching **conflict resolution** is an important job of the teacher; conflicts will inevitably occur and actually offer valuable opportunities to build stronger, more empathetic relationships. It is through conflict that the teacher can model and teach, instead of punishing children. In conflict resolution, it is important that all children in the conflict feel that they have had their voices heard and that in having to give something up,

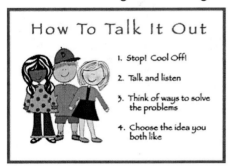

How To Talk It Out

1. Stop! Cool Off!
2. Talk and listen
3. Think of ways to solve the problems
4. Choose the idea you both like

they have also "won" something. The teacher has to actively listen to both sides and genuinely care about the feelings and needs of all the children involved. Carlsson-Page and Levin (1998) offer steps in teaching children conflict resolution:

- Identify the problem and define it as a shared problem
- Invite children to participate in fixing the problem
- Generate possible solutions as a group
- Examine each idea for its merits or drawbacks and then decide which ideas to try
- Work out ways of putting the plan into action
- Follow up and evaluate how well the plan worked

The important part of conflict resolution is for the teacher not to impose her solution, but instead to get children thinking about possible courses of action.

Teaching children strategies for self-regulation and problem-solving effectively gives children lifelong skills. Often, early childhood professionals first have to provide children with **emotional literacy** – the ability to identify, understand, and respond to emotions in oneself and others in a healthy manner (Joseph, Strain, & Ostrosky, 2006). Emotional literacy strategies include learning how to label feelings, strategizing acceptable expressions of emotions, using songs and books to reinforce feelings, scaffolding children's interactions to teach them the words they need, and making children aware of other's feelings and perspectives.

"Emotional Literacy"

Children need to learn social skills such as cooperation and constructive, acceptable interactions with peers and adults. Teachers need to help children build self-regulation by teaching them helpful behaviors such as how to listen when others talk without interrupting, how to join a play or work group, how to ask politely for something, and how to participate and contribute to a group. Daily lessons that teach, model, and provide children with time to practice these social skills can be incorporated in circle

time, centers, snack time, and transitions. After determining the skill that needs to be taught, teachers can utilize songs, finger plays, storybooks, DVD's, and flannel board lessons.

Interventions for challenging behaviors, though hopefully will be used more infrequently, must also be in a teacher's repertoire of skills. There will always be a few children who demonstrate persistent challenging behavior. Challenging behavior challenges the teacher's ability to guide the child and the child's ability to set internal limits for behavior. Challenging behavior can be defined as "behaviors that are dangerous, disruptive, or disgusting; cause injury to the child or others; damage the physical environment; interfere with learning; or cause the child to be isolated from peers" (Neilsen et al., 1999, p.6). In early childhood education this disruptive behavior will try the patience of even the most authoritative, nurturing professional. A teacher can become irritated, impatient, and frustrated with the challenging child.

Strain and Hemmeter (1999, p.19) provide guidelines for successfully dealing with a child's distressing behavior:

- Stop thinking about removing the child as the "real" answer to the problem.
- Stop blaming disturbing behaviors on uncontrollable, extraneous events such as "If only his parents cared more."
- Start celebrating what has been accomplished in comparison to where the situation began.
- Alter expectations about the effectiveness of the interventions. Don't expect that an intervention will result in challenging behavior being "fixed for good" or "never ever" occurring.

Early childhood educators are most effective in supporting the challenging child reach their potential to become self-regulated, well-adjusted, contributing members of society when the educator determines why the child is behaving a certain way. Recognizing that children's behavior conveys a message helps teachers assist the child in moving toward alternative, appropriate ways to interact with others instead of punishing the child.

Antecedent	Behavior	Consequence
The teacher places James' work folder on his desk in front of him.	James sweeps his folder and pencil onto the floor.	The classroom aide puts James in the time out corner. He Escapes doing his work.
At lunch, James sees that Martin has yogurt.	James bangs himself in the head with his fist at the lunch table.	Martin gives James his yogurt. He Acquires the desired object.

How does an early childhood educator learn what message is being transmitted through the challenging behavior? By careful and systematic observation and documentation of the child's behavior – a **functional behavior analysis** – using the A-B-C method (Neilsen et al., 1999):

- *A – Antecedent.* What condition or action precedes the behavior? By determining the triggers for the challenging behavior, the teacher can change the context to prevent the behavior. For example, if Thomas is hitting other children when the group is lining up for lunch, the teacher may want to give him a "job" such as line leader or "lunch box superintendent" in order to redirect his attention.

- *B – Behavior.* What is the behavior and what is its frequency? It is imperative that through systematic observation the observer describes the behavior and its frequency in detail. This is the only way an intervention will be successful. Possibly, the observer will find that Thomas has no trouble lining up for Physical Education class (which he looks forward to), yet lining up for lunch (a place where the noise and chaos bother him) and for art class (where his delay in fine motor skills triggers great frustration) sparks Thomas' acting out.

- *C – Consequence.* What does the child get, avoid, or change as a result of the behavior? Does Thomas get to feel a sense of power? Does he feel more empowered by intimidating others? Does he avoid going into these frustrating contexts by acting out and being held out of the lunchroom and art class?

When the antecedent-behavior-consequence pattern is documented, the professional can evaluate the purpose and meaning of the behavior. For example, Thomas' behavior may be to avoid going to the lunchroom or art class. He is using his behavior to gain attention and to wield his power in a situation or context in which he feels powerless. It is wise not to engage in a verbal or physical power struggle with the child, but instead to give him authentic choices over which he has some decision-making control. Thomas may be given the opportunity to eat in the classroom with the teacher and a few of his peers, if he shows self-control lining up and eating in the lunchroom for four days in a row.

Antecedent	Behavior	Consequence
• "X" is playing with shape sorter toy in living while sitting on the floor. Mother is braiding sister's hair on couch in living room	• "X" travels to mother and pulls mother's hair	• Mother stops braiding sister's hair and asks "Would "X" like to have their hair done too?" "X" sits on floor and mother begins braiding "X" hair

Implementing individual behavior plans is best facilitated when the teacher works with the parents and other professionals such as the school social worker, psychologist, therapists, etc. Behavior intervention plans work best if there is consistency between school and home; parents bring knowledge of the child's behavior outside of the school and of successful strategies they use with the child. The **behavior support plan** that is developed cooperatively by the professionals and parents should include three steps: making changes which prevent the inappropriate behavior, teaching the child a new skill, and then confirming the child demonstrates the new behavior. The team revisits the plan in subsequent meetings to ensure that the child's behavior is consistently improving.

Building Positive Relationships With and Among Children

Brain research tells us that consistent, securely attached, and nurturing relationships protect children from the risk of challenging behavior and help to build lifelong self-regulation skills. "The quality of children's early relationships with their teachers (is)...an important predictor of these children's future social relations with peers, their behavior problems, and school satisfaction and achievement" (Howes & Ritchie, 2002, p. 6). Teachers' positive connections with children provide a secure base for the child to confidently explore the world. This strong connection builds self-esteem, a sense of efficacy, empathy for others, and self-regulation. When the child's challenging behavior enters the relationship, it becomes difficult to maintain this important connection with the child. What is an educator to do?

It is important that early childhood educators reflect upon their own beliefs about and acceptance of certain behaviors. Educators need to examine their own value system regarding challenging behavior and its causes. Much of that value system is shaped by the professional's own upbringing and cultural group. Often, the way we were raised is the way we structure the behavior rules in our classrooms. For example, when the educator institutes a common strategy, such as "time out" and it turns out to not be successful in modifying the child's behavior, Pianta (1999) suggests the educator reflect deeply and try a fresh approach that may be outside her experience.

What is considered acceptable behavior in one family, cultural group, or community may be prohibited in another (Kaiser & Rasminsky, 2012). Teachers must help children to learn that certain contexts have different rules of behavior. Children must be able to "read their environments" to know which set of behavior rules they need to implement; teachers are important partners in building this skill.

Another strategy to foster positive relationships that support self-regulation is to **build a community of learners.** How children respect themselves, each other, and their environment is shaped considerably by the early childhood setting. The community of learners is built upon a framework of positive, consistent, and nurturing relationships among the adults and children. Developmentally appropriate practice (Copple & Bredekamp, 2009, pp. 16-17) provides educators with guidelines for creating a supportive community of learners:

- Each member of the community is valued
- Relationships are an important context through which children develop and learn
- Each member of the community respects and is accountable to the others to behave in a way that is conducive to the learning and well-being of all:
  1. Teachers help children develop responsibility and self-regulation
  2. Teachers are responsible at all times for all children under their supervision
  3. Teachers set clear and reasonable limits on children's behavior and apply those limits consistently
  4. Teachers listen to and acknowledge children's feelings and frustrations
  5. Teachers themselves demonstrate high levels of responsibility and self-regulation in their interactions
- Practitioners design and maintain the physical environment to protect the health and safety of the learning community members
- Practitioners ensure members of the community feel psychologically safe

In a caring community of learners children develop the skill of self-regulation of their behavior and own emotions. Teachers intentionally teach children social-emotional skills, create an environment that is conducive to learning self-regulation, and design individualized interventions for those children who unrelentingly demonstrate challenging behavior.

Building Partnerships with Families

Due in large part to the ecological theory of Urie Brofenbrenner (1979), which advocates the ongoing consideration of the child in his context as well as family systems theory (Christian, 2006) which supports the belief in the interconnectedness of family members, early childhood educators now view the child and family as inextricably linked. Support of families translates into direct support of the child in all their domains of development. Research shows that when families are actively involved with their children's education, children are more successful academically, emotionally, and socially (Hoover-Dempsey et al., 2005). The National Coalition for Parent Involvement in Education (NCPIE) (2006) outlines the influence of family involvement on children's academic success. Students with engaged parents are more likely to:

- Be promoted
- Earn higher grades
- Score higher on standardized tests
- Attend school regularly
- Get along better socially in school and other contexts
- Transition more readily to school
- Benefit from long-term effects such as completing high school, and advancing to postsecondary education

Many programs such as Head Start and Early Head Start make parental involvement and co-decision-making a priority.

"Involving Families"

Understanding family structure and the dynamics within each unique structure is an important part of working with young children. **Family systems theory** considers the interconnectedness of the individuals in the family. Each family member affects and is affected by the others in the family in predictable and recursive ways (Christian, 2006). Children learn the ways that their family expects them to behave and communicate. Teachers are more effective in guiding children if they understand how the family system operates for each child.

The common characteristics of family systems are rules, roles, and boundaries. Rules refer to the traditions and guidelines families use in their dealings with each other and with people outside their families. Roles are the responsibilities that each member of the family assumes. Boundaries refer to the family's values about autonomy and control, separateness and togetherness. Many children play out their family-assigned rules, roles, and boundaries in the classroom.

Building a partnership with parents. Developmentally appropriate practice too implores early childhood professionals to consider the contexts within which each child lives and develops. Parent involvement that is bilaterally constructed – parents voluntarily being present in children's school lives and professionals offering an "open door" policy – nurtures a partnership between home and school that honors and respects the insight about young children that both partners bring

to the relationship. Developmentally appropriate practice (Copple & Bredekamp, 2009, p. 23) provides the guidelines for building a partnership in which family members and educators work together as members of the learning community:

- In reciprocal relationships between practitioners and families, there is mutual respect, cooperation, shared responsibility, and negotiation of conflicts toward achievement of shared goals.
- Practitioners work in collaborative partnerships with families, establishing and maintaining regular, frequent two-way communication with them (with families who do not speak English, teachers should use the language of the home if they are able or try to enlist the help of bilingual volunteers).
- Family members are welcome in the setting, and there are multiple opportunities for family participation.
- Teachers acknowledge a family's choices and goals for the child and respond with sensitivity and respect to those preferences and concerns, but without abdicating the responsibility that early childhood practitioners have to support children's learning and development through developmentally appropriate practices.
- Teachers and the family share with each other their knowledge of the particular child and understanding of child development and learning as part of day-to-day communication and in planned conferences.
- Practitioners involve families as a source of information about the child (before program entry and on an ongoing basis) and engage them in the planning for their child.
- The program links families with a range of services, based on identified resources, priorities, and concerns.

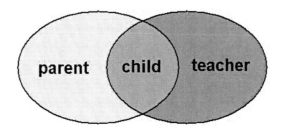

Family-centered programs recognize the importance of the family role in meeting their child's needs no matter what the needs are. Over the past few years, there has been a shift in view from that of the professionals as the "experts" who teach the parents how to support their child's development, to the present view that the parents are experts in their own right and the professional needs to respect and empower the family. This paradigm shift reflects the effect of early intervention and early childhood special education in which recommended practice includes family-based intervention services. In this practice, parents hold the majority of the responsibility for meeting the child's individual needs. In family-based intervention, families are partners in the assessment of the child's needs, designing the goals, developing the intervention plan, and carrying out the plan (Hearron & Hildebrand, 2005).

Developmentally appropriate practice's core considerations include knowledge of the individual child as well as the families and cultures in which those children live and flourish. Families know about their particular child in the present, the history of the child and the family since their birth, and the child's life outside of the classroom.

The importance of families is one of the basic tenets of the highly respected early childhood programs of Reggio Emilia, Italy. Parents are a vital component of the Reggio Emilia philosophy. Parents are viewed as partners, collaborators and advocates for their children. Teachers respect parents as each child's first teacher and involve parents in every aspect of the curriculum:

> A shared education sets in motion processes – neither easy nor short term – that promote a new culture of the teaching profession. The contribution of ideas, expectations, and abilities offered by families to the schools help the teachers to perceive the link with families as something that enriches rather than interferes, thereby affirming the primary values of collegiality and the integration of knowledge. Even with the best prepared teachers and in the richest situations, there are areas that can only be realized through sharing and interactive choices. (Spaggieri, 1998, p. 111)

Additionally, the early childhood educator will need the skills and cultural knowledge of families whose culture, language, ethnicity, and social background may diverge from their own.

One principle of exemplary early childhood practice is the establishment of relationships that demonstrate **cross-cultural competence** (Klein & Chen, 2001). Cross-cultural competence requires the educator to accept diverse cultures as they are and to not judge or construct stereotypes of the cultures from which their students come. The early childhood educator needs to locate resources from which he or she can learn about the families, their beliefs, customs, and expectations for their children. One must then listen to the families, understanding and respecting their point of view, yet maintaining the integrity of the classroom rules. For instance, children may be allowed to hit others at home as a way of standing up for their rights, however, they must learn to respect the school rule of "using your words". Keeping a positive, respectful dialogue that has the best interest of the child always as the goal, is possible when the professional has developed cross-cultural competence.

The changing face of the family. What is a family? At one point in American history this was a relatively easy question to answer – the nuclear family consisted of a mom, a dad, and their children. Modern families are as diverse in their structures as the individuals who make up the families. Often, we craft an image of "family" based on our experience and then judge any family structure that is not our "norm" as being deficient. However, throughout our professional lives we will work with children whose contexts are diverse, and it is our job to embrace all children and all families.

Single-parent families – those who are single because of both divorce and choice to have children while single – are the most common type of family diversity early childhood educators encounter. In 2015, 40% of American births were to single women and most single parents who have primary custody (82.2 %) are women (US Census Bureau, 2016). Many single parents are teenage parents who often come from culturally diverse backgrounds. Morrison (2012, pp. 464-465) suggests ways to involve single parents:

- Accommodate family schedules by arranging conferences and events at other times – perhaps early morning, noon, late afternoon, or early evening.
- Remember, single parents have a limited amount of time to spend on involvement with their children's school and with their children at home. When you talk with single-parent families, make sure that (a) the meeting starts on time, (b) you have a list of items to discuss, (c) you have sample materials available to illustrate all points, (d) you make specific suggestions relative to one-parent environments, and (e) the meeting ends on time. Plan for child care for every parent meeting or activity.

- Suggest some ways single parents can make time with their child meaningful.
- Get to know families' lifestyles and living conditions. All early childhood professionals need to keep in mind the condition of the home environment when they request that children bring certain items to school or carry out certain tasks at home.
- If the parent is a teenager, support them in their continuing development as adolescents and young adults; assist them in completing their education.
- Help develop support groups for single-parent families within your school, such as discussion groups and classes on parenting.
- Offer non-traditional opportunities for single parents to volunteer time or services.

More than 17% of single-parent homes have fathers as the head of the family (US Census Bureau, 2016). Additionally, about 50% of all US children will not live with their dads for all or part of their childhoods (Morrison, 2012). Early childhood educators must make a concerted effort to involve these fathers in their children's education. It is important that all parents are welcomed into the classroom, included in the curriculum, and provided with information for services and support that they and their children may benefit from.

Grandparents, now more than at any other time in our history, are parenting their grandchildren. Parents who are involved in drugs, incarcerated, physically and/or mentally ill, who have lost custody, who have died or abandoned their child, relinquish the child to the grandparents. Additionally, the economic recession has caused a "return to the family nest" where three generations – grandparents, parents, and children – live under the same roof. In both situations, the grandparents assume a great deal of responsibility for rearing the children. Early childhood educators can support grandparents in their new-found responsibility by helping them to connect with resources, offering parenting courses, holding parent information sessions to inform the grandparents about standard-based curriculum and how they can support the children academically as well as socially and emotionally.

Linguistically diverse parents face language and cultural barriers which impede their involvement in their children's education. Though they are dedicated to their children's academic success, they may not have minimal communication skills in order to gain information or convey it. Additionally, the family system of rules, roles, boundaries, parenting styles, and attitudes toward schooling may set up obstacles to home-school collaboration. The educational system may differ greatly from the one that the parents were taught in, resulting in misconceptions and a reluctance to participate in the school.

Gonzalez-Mena (1992) suggests that early childhood educators:

- Know what each parent wants for his or her child
- Become clear about their own values and goals
- Build relationships
- Become an effective cross-cultural communicator
- Use a problem-solving rather than power approach to conflicts
- Commit to education

Building reciprocal relationships and partnerships with parents, always putting the concerns for the child first, creates the most effective teaching practice. Both parents and teachers bring expertise to the table. Parents have a wealth of knowledge about the child's development and experiences outside of school. Parents are experts about the child's cultural and linguistic background. At the same time, the child profits from the more objective assessment of a child's strengths and needs that teachers contribute. Teachers have a grasp of what normal child development is and can use this knowledge as the benchmark for the individual child's growth. A reciprocal relationship in which information and decision-making is shared can develop when both parties have mutual respect, shared responsibility, and trust. This relationship building requires effective two-way communication.

Communication With and Involvement of Families

Effective reciprocal communication between parents and teachers requires a shared understanding of the child, an understanding of the goals each partner has for the child, and an agreed upon plan for accomplishing the goals. Positive communication flourishes in school environments that communicate a welcoming aura. Many parents enter the front door of their child's school burdened with negative feelings and anxiety about their own school experience. The warmth of the communication between teachers and parents is as important if not more, than the physical environment.

"Important Interactions – How To Communicate Effectively With Parents"

"Effective Strategies for Parent-Teacher Communication"

Assertive communication – telling parents the truth in a thoughtful and considerate manner – is the most effective way to communicate with families (Bredekamp, 2011). Often the situations in which the teacher needs to use assertive communication are those that are most challenging. The speaker tells the truth in a positive, caring way while the listener listens intently and responds to the clear, honest message being conveyed.

Communication with families can happen in multiple ways – informally, formally, through technology, and through meetings outside the school setting. Informal communication can take place at drop-off and pick-up times, through daily messages or notes that go back and forth from school to home, and in weekly newsletters blogs, and e-mails. Formal communication occurs during parent-teacher conferences; it is important that the teacher does not monopolize the conversation but instead listens to the parent as much as he or she talks to the parent. Technology provides vehicles of communication such as cell phones, e-mail, and text messaging. Home visits – regular visits by the teacher to the family's home – are required by some programs such as Head Start. Home visits are a wonderful way for teachers to establish a more casual and comfortable relationship with families. Often, the parent feels more comfortable meeting at a more neutral location such as a library or coffee shop. In this more casual setting both the parent and the teacher may feel more comfortable when confronting challenging issues.

Involving parents in school programs is an effective way to support children's success in school and to address the achievement gap between children of color and their more affluent, white peers (Swick et al., 2006). The more involved the family is in the child's education, the more likely that partnership will enhance the school environment as well as the individual child's learning.

Epstein, Sanders, Simon, Salina, Jansorn, and VanVoorhis (2002) developed a framework of family involvement that identifies six types of effective family school partnerships:

- Parent education – assistance with parenting and child-rearing skills, providing supportive home learning environments, and helping schools understand home cultures. This can be accomplished through adult education classes, workshops, and parent libraries and materials.
- Communication – schools communicate children's progress to families; families communicate about children's home lives to schools. Parents can be invited to performances, receive

informative newsletters, and be involved in the creation and evaluation of IFSP's and IEP's.

- Volunteering – involving families in the classrooms. Often, families are assigned to classrooms in which their children are not enrolled.
- Learning at home – provide curriculum materials and strategies. Books, curricular materials, classroom websites, reading packets, and tips for parents are all excellent resources.
- Decision-making – including parents in program decisions, committees, and parent organizations. Parents can provide input in fund-raising and event planning; hiring of staff; and curriculum development and textbook piloting.
- Collaborating with the community – coordinating services and resources for families, children and the school. Support groups, cultural events, dinners, and book fairs are all valuable opportunities to collaborate with the community.

Schools need to provide parent training and preparation for each of the six types of partnering. Preparation and coaching will enhance the parents' effectiveness and enrich a child's experience.

Setting Up the Classroom

The environment strongly influences how people act, feel, and learn. An environment that engenders a feeling of confidence and the possibility of success has to be intentionally planned – the design, materials, floor plan, and schedule all support children's learning and positive behavior. A well-planned classroom is safe, healthy, and meets the minimum state licensing requirements. The setting should reinforce positive classroom management; support the carrying out of program goals and objectives, and nurture children's learning and development.

"Teaching Tips: How to Set Up a Kindergarten Class"

Design. Well-designed classroom spaces have defined areas for exploration in a variety of activities. The organization of the physical space must take into consideration the types and numbers of activities; amount of space required for each activity; convenience of cleanup and storage; traffic flow; and the need for wall space. The allocation of activities in the room is dependent on the compatibility of the activities.

Active centers such as block-building need to be separated from quieter centers such as math work. Messy activities such as painting need to be near a clean-up sink and counter and away from materials that could be ruined by the paint and water.

"A Day in the Life of a Teacher"

The allotment of space for each activity needs to be thought through. Some centers such as gross motor require a larger amount of space, while other activities such as listening to books on CDs require very little space for the actual activity, but plenty of shelving for storing the materials. Some spaces must be used for multiple purposes – the tables can be used for meals and snacks as well as arts, crafts, and tabletop toys. Clear pathways are needed between activity areas, to the classroom door, and to the bathroom. Construction that is ongoing such as block building needs to be protected from being knocked over. Areas can be shielded by setting up low barriers such as bookshelves, rolling storage carts, and low furniture. Individual carpet squares can be used to delineate seating areas. Storage needs to be both low and high; low storage is for materials that children can easily access, while high closed storage is for materials that should be accessed only by adults and for the storage of children's materials that are not in use.

Materials. The well-stocked classroom provides enough materials and activities to stave off behavior problems, monotony, and difficulty sharing with others. Catron and Allen (2008) suggest a guideline of 50 per cent more play items and activities than the number of children in the classroom. For example, in a class of twenty children there should be at least thirty play items and materials available at any one time. Items can be combined to provide more complex units of play. Prescott (1984) advises that teachers create simple, complex and super units by combining materials. For example, a sand box with no equipment is a simple unit. Add digging utensils and it becomes a complex unit. By adding water as a third element, it becomes a super unit. Complex and super units will engage children and increase the number of activities that children can explore.

Our Class Schedule

7:55-8:30	announcements, journals, jump start our brain, break story and carpet time
8:30-9:45	workstations (language arts, science, social studies, independent reading)
9:45-10:05	recess
10:05-10:45	enrichment time
10:50-11:30	lunch
11:35-12:00	rest time
12:00-12:55	math
12:55-1:40	p.e.
1:40-2:15	calendar /math buckets
2:15-2:45	centers
2:45-3:10	snacks/playground
3:12	dismissal for kindergarten

Schedules. Well-designed schedules should be neither too rigid nor too "loose". One of the purposes of schedules is to promote a sense of security by enabling children to anticipate the order of activities in the daily routine. Balance is a key concept in creating a schedule based on these curricular aspects: indoor/outdoor, quiet/active, individual/small group/large group, large muscle/small muscle, and child-initiated/adult-initiated (NAEYC, 2005). Educators need to plan for transitions and routines such as meals and snacks, diapering, toileting, and napping. There should be large uninterrupted blocks of time for free play and inquiry-based learning so that children can become engrossed in what they are doing. Children should be provided with choices from a large variety of intentionally planned learning activities.

Infant Room

Infant rooms need to be planned around the infants' need to explore people and objects through their senses, while playing and learning. The infant's day at home and in childcare revolves around the activities of eating, diapering, playing, and sleeping. It is important to give consideration to the social and emotional needs of infants by providing a home-like, nurturing environment. Infants need the continuity between the home environment and the early childhood center environment.

"Infant Classrooms"

Play areas should provide infants with a variety of sensory experiences – textures to touch, interesting things to look at in an aesthetically pleasing space, and a mix of quiet and sounds that infants enjoy. Play areas should be cozy with comfortable furniture for the adults. The areas need to be the correct size for the number of babies; young infants need smaller areas in which to feel secure, while older infants need ample space to move around and play. Infants need to spend some time in the outdoors everyday if the weather permits. Older infants need to exercise their gross motor skills and coordination with push and pull toys, wagons, balls, climbers, steps, and other equipment.

The remainder of the **space** in the infant room is reserved for eating, diapering, and sleeping. The eating area needs to be close to a sink for hand and utensil washing and a kitchen preparation area that can be easily cleaned. Comfortable seating for the primary caregivers who bottle feed the young infants is a must. Older infants eat with the primary caregivers and their peers in small groups at low tables. Infants are usually diapered by their primary caregiver or familiar adult at a diapering center that is strategically located so that the adult can see the other children. All diapering supplies, including a sink separate from the meal preparation area, and extra clothing must be within easy reach of the diapering center. The sleeping area should be separate from play and eating areas; infants are only in their own cribs for the time they are sleeping. The sleeping area needs to be dimly lit and quiet, yet every child should be easily visible.

The **materials** that infants require for play and exploration need to be made of materials and the correct size that allows infants to grasp, manipulate and chew them – fabric balls, teethers, washable dolls and animals. Infants should be able to easily grasp board and cloth books which depict diverse people, families, activities, and objects. Safe household materials such as wooden spoons and measuring cups, objects that make noise such as squeeze toys, and toys that demonstrate cause and effect such as shape sorters and unbreakable mirrors are all good choices for infants. Play materials need to be well-organized and accessible on open shelving at children's eye level and within their reach.

	Activities	
Start time A.M.	Infants	Young Toddlers
8:00-8:45	Arrival, Daily Health check, Welcome children, Choice time, free play, story time, playing with puzzles, blocks, etc.	
8:15-9:00	Clean-up/toilet/wash up	Clean-up/toilet/wash up
9:00-9:30	1ˢᵗ nap/Bottle/morning cereal/ clean-up/wash up	Breakfast/ Clean-up/wash up
9:30-10:30	Free movement, games with blocks, balls, or reading books	Story time Read aloud
10:30-11:00	Music time, songs, dance, games. Project time (drawing, play dough …) Learning games with cards (colors, animals, alphabet…)	
11:00-12:00	Outside play-time If cold or raining-reading books, choice time, free playing	
12:00-12:30	Bottle/lunch/ clean-up/wash up	Lunch time Clean-up/toilet/wash up
12:30-2:30	2ⁿᵈ nap	Nap time
2:30-3:45	Calm music, games with toys, reading books.	
3:45-4:15	Afternoon snack Clean-up/toilet/wash up	
4:15-5:00	Outside play-time If cold or rain-reading books, story time, choice time, free playing, games with blocks, puzzles.	
5:00-5:45	Music /dancing time. Free playing, drawing, clean up time.	
6:00	Bye-Bye time! Pick up time. Talk with parents.	

In **scheduling** the infant's day, continuity of care by a primary caregiver or caregivers should be the guiding principle. The primary caregivers are able to read the infant's cues and so they are able to judge when the baby is uncomfortable, needs to be held and/or diapered, or is hungry. The schedule needs to include peaceful transition times both at the child's arrival and departure from the early education center. Feeding, diapering, and napping should all be on-demand according to the individual infant's needs. Caregivers provide responsive care in ways that are specific for each child using a pleasant, soothing voice and consistent eye contact. It is important that caregivers adjust to each individual child's sleep and eating schedules as well as food preferences. Infant caregivers spend a great deal of their day holding, stroking, and interacting with the

infants in their care in a warm, nurturing way. This trust-building is one of the most important gifts adults can give young children – the belief that the world is a secure, predictable place in which to explore and learn.

Toddler Room

Toddler rooms, like infant rooms, need to include spaces for eating, napping, toileting, and playing. Again, the play area needs to occupy the most space in the room; however, with toddlers, the activities can be housed in more specific areas such as the art center, dramatic play corner, block-building center, and quiet reading corner. "Toddlers need space to explore, experiment, discover, and move. This age child is constantly on the go and needs to have many opportunities to practice newly emerging skills" (Vartuli, 1987, p. 29).

"A Peek into the Toddler Classroom"

The space should be organized into interest areas including areas for small-group play, solitary play, dramatic play, and construction. The **play areas** should contain both large-motor areas and small-motor areas. The large-motor areas need plenty of **space** and all spaces should be designed with floor coverings that are appropriate for the activity that occurs there. There should be clear traffic patterns created by low room dividers, shelving and benches. The environment should contain space for whole groups, small groups, and for one or two children to have privacy. Outdoor space for toddlers should be separated from older children. The play equipment needs to be tailored to the size of the children so they do not need to be lifted onto or off the equipment.

"Toddler Room for 1-2 year olds – Buttercup Room"

The routines of everyday life such as eating, toileting, and dressing offer opportunities to help children learn about their world and to acquire important skills. The diapering/toileting, sleeping, and eating areas are separate, because of sanitation and to ensure restful areas. The eating area needs to be close to a sink for hand and utensil washing and a kitchen preparation area that can be easily cleaned. Toddlers eat in small groups with their caregivers at low tables. Just as with the infants, toddlers are usually diapered by their primary caregiver or familiar adult at a diapering center that is strategically located so that the adult can see the other children. All diapering supplies, including a sink separate from the meal preparation area, and extra clothing must be within easy reach of the diapering center. Caregivers work in concert with parents when children are ready for toilet learning. Toddlers can nap in the play area on cots that have an ample amount of space between them, using bedding that is not shared with other children. There should be low lights and soft music during naptime.

The large-motor area needs **materials** such as climbers, steps, and tunnels for climbing and maneuvering around. The small-motor areas should contain a variety of things that children can manipulate with their hands such as puzzles with knobs, shape sorters, beads to string, and interlocking construction toys such as Duplos. There should be plenty of containers in which children can sort and collect items. The block-building corner should contain a variety of blocks – wooden blocks, large cardboard blocks, smaller

tabletop blocks, etc. There should also be labeled storage areas so that blocks can be sorted and stored by the children. The block-building corner should be carpeted to cut down on noise with low barriers to prevent block structures form being knocked over. It is beneficial to have a large assortment of accessories such as people, animals, transportation toys, signs, etc. to extend the play. The dramatic play corner needs to be stocked with housekeeping items and play furniture such as a stove, sink, and refrigerator; dishes and pots; play food; table and chairs, dolls and doll beds; dress-up clothes; and items that can turn the dramatic play corner into a grocery store, pizza parlor, etc. The art area needs to contain materials for specific art projects such as paper, crayons, paints, etc. and aprons or smocks to protect children's clothing. Toddlers need sturdy picture books to explore and plenty of containers they can use to assist in clean-up. Music and movement activities include CDs and DVDs, puppets, and musical instruments.

Scheduling in the toddler room should be adapted to meet each child's individual needs within the group setting; there should be a relatively predictable sequence in the day with the flexibility to meet individual needs. Toddlers need large blocks of time in which they can repeat tasks until they have mastered them. Continuity of care continues to be a developmentally appropriate principle in the toddler room. Smooth transitions at the beginning and end of the day support an easy separation from parent and caregiver. Much of the day is spent in one-to-one interactions with the primary caregivers in an emotionally and physically supportive classroom. Toddlers begin to socialize and play together in small groups for short periods of time. Like infant care, toddlers are on their individual eating, sleeping, and toileting schedules which are respected and supported by the caregivers.

Preschool Room

The preschool room is very much like the toddler room in that the space is divided into specific activity centers. It is different in that there is no diapering area and there is a greater variety of activities and materials offered as choices. The 3-5 year old child's social growth is a priority and facilitated by teachers who help children establish positive, constructive relationships with others. The room design, materials and scheduling are the "third teacher" (Gandini, 1997) that foster collaborative learning. The classroom should reflect the diversity of the classroom and needs to involve the home culture and language of those in the classroom community.

"Preschool Classroom Tour"

Play areas are created so that both large-motor and small-motor activity choices can be offered to pre-school children. The room design should guarantee that the environment is safe, healthy, and encourages learning. The learning environment should be supportive of children's autonomy, active exploration of materials, and sustained collaboration with peers, adults, and activities. The design of the room needs to be flexible enough to welcome a number of formats – large and small groups, interest areas, and routines.

Materials for complex large-motor activities could include balance beams, bowling games, hopscotch, and trikes. The small-motor materials include more complex puzzles, peg boards, Duplos, Legos, bristle blocks, smaller beads to string, and counting manipulatives. The art area should be stocked with clay, play dough, crayons, markers, various types and sizes of paper, scissors, glue sticks and bottles, paints, and writing materials. A literacy center should contain picture books, student generated books, plastic numbers and letters, writing materials, letter and number stamps, and individual name cards with the children's names on them. A comfortable couch, bean bag chairs, and pillows can be added to create an inviting reading area. The block-

building corner can contain more complex materials and accessories. Often it is wise to locate this center next to the art center so that the decorations and artifacts for the block constructions can be created by children. The dramatic play area materials should reflect both more complex play of 3-5 year olds and the introduction of thematic units of instruction. Storage tubs can house props that transform this center into a veterinarian's office, pizza parlor, grocery store, travel center, beach, and so on. A discovery area with science-related materials invites children to manipulate and act upon the materials. A sensory center can contain a sand/water table with a variety of manipulatives and can be changed to accommodate the thematic unit that is being taught. Music and movement activities include CDs and DVDs, puppets, and musical instruments.

Scheduling should be organized to allow for periods of alternating active and quiet time, consistent times for meals and snacks, and rest time for all the children and nap time for younger children. The schedule should allow for large blocks of time (at least 60 minutes) in which children can become deeply engaged in an activity and be able to sustain complex play, construction, and creativity. There should be a balance of whole group instruction, small group collaborative inquiry, and individual exploration. The whole group times should be no more than 10-15 minutes at the beginning of the school year, extending to 15-30 minutes by the end of the school year. The majority of the group time is usually scheduled in the morning, with the afternoon reserved for individual and free exploration and play as well as rest/quiet time, and outdoor play.

Kindergarten and Primary Rooms

Children in primary education – 5-8 year olds – need a challenging learning environment with a standards-based curriculum that meets individual needs and is differentiated to match children's abilities and achievement levels. The physical layout of the classroom needs to support learning centers and peer interaction. Children usually sit at tables or desks which have been grouped together. Teachers provide a safe environment and age-appropriate supervision as children in this age range are given increasingly more autonomy and responsibility.

"Daily Routine in Second Grade Classes"

Learning areas are intentionally designed to support a variety of instructional formats including whole groups, small groups, individual quiet work, learning centers, free choice time, and one-on-one instructional time. A cozy, homelike atmosphere can be attained with comfortable furniture, pillows, rugs, and low, soft lighting. Centers need to be organized around the mastery of Common Core/State standards; for example, to meet the ELA standards there needs to be a Guided Reading table as well as independent reading and writing centers. Floor coverings should be appropriate for the activities that occur in each particular space. There should be spaces for  children to keep their work and personal items as well as storage area and display areas for children's work.

Materials should be varied and in large amounts to comfortably challenge children's learning. There should be plentiful materials that support literacy acquisition – sight words, magnetic letters and words, paper, pencils, crayons, markers, all kinds of books, art supplies, portable word walls, story chart paper, etc. The math center can contain manipulatives, games, computers, shapes, blocks, measurement tools, and so on. The science center should contain materials to teach physical science (levers, wheels, color

 mixing bags) as well as life science (plants, pets, seashells, magnifying glasses), and earth and space science (sand, soil, rocks, planet models). Materials for social studies instruction include globes, maps, books, travel brochures, magazines, and family pictures. Art supplies are more sophisticated – colored pencils, pastels, chalk, reproductions of famous artwork, photographs, and so on. Music and movement activities require CDs, DVDs, CD and DVD players, and musical instruments.

Scheduling should include periods of activity and movement balanced with quieter and more restful times. Learning takes place in a variety of formats – whole group, small group, centers, individually, and one-on-one with an adult. Snacks and water bottles are appropriate for children from 5-8 years old. There should be extended periods of time for children to be in learning centers or working in collaborative problem-solving activities. Kindergarten children (and first graders, in the opinion of many early childhood educators) should still have access to dramatic play and block-building. Schedules should be predictable and routine, yet there should be enough flexibility to allow children who are highly engaged in an activity to extend their time to satisfy their curiosity.

Technology

Developmentally appropriate practice allows for the thoughtful, intentional usage of technology in the early childhood classroom. Professional early childhood educators use technology such as computers, electronic tablets, and smart boards, not to replace children's interactions with authentic materials, but to expand the scope of tools children can use to research information, solve problems, refine new skills, and learn at their own

pace. The NAEYC in partnership with the Fred Rogers Center for Early Learning and Children's Media at Saint Vincent's College developed a position paper on the use of technology in early childhood education (2012). Its major recommendations are:

"Technology in Early Childhood Family Education Classrooms"

- Above all, the use of technology tools and interactive media should not harm children.
- Developmentally appropriate practices must guide decisions about whether and when to integrate technology and interactive media into early childhood programs.
- Professional judgment is required to determine if and when a specific use of technology or media is age appropriate, individually appropriate, and culturally and linguistically appropriate.
- Developmentally appropriate teaching practices must always guide the selection of any classroom materials, including technology and interactive media.
- Appropriate use of technology and media depends on the age, developmental level, needs, interests, linguistic background, and abilities of each child.
- Effective uses of technology and media are active, hands-on, engaging, and empowering; give the child control; provide adaptive scaffolds to ease the accomplishment of tasks; and are used as one of many options to support children's learning.
- Interactions with technology and media should be playful and support creativity, exploration, pretend play, active play, and outdoor activities.
- Technology tools can help educators make and strengthen home–school connections.

- Technology and media can enhance early childhood practice when integrated into the environment, curriculum, and daily routines.
- Assistive technology must be available as needed to provide equitable access for children with special needs.
- Technology tools can be effective for dual language learners by providing access to a family's home language and culture while supporting English language learning.
- Early childhood educators need training, professional development opportunities, and examples of successful practice to develop the technology and media knowledge, skills, and experience.
- Research is needed to better understand how young children use and learn with technology and interactive media and also to better understand any short- and long-term effects. (pp. 5-11)

The teacher's role in technology usage is to integrate technology into the total curriculum, create a positive classroom atmosphere, and choose appropriate software. Technology usage is seen by the early childhood educator as another opportunity for play and exploration. A child's communication and social skills can be enhanced through the use of technology. Software that supports the thematic unit can be chosen and the computer can be used as a learning center.

The NAEYC/Fred Rogers Center position on technology reminds us that:

> Educators should use professional judgment in evaluating and using technology and media, just as they would with any other learning tool or experience, and they must emphasize active engagement rather than passive, non-interactive uses. To achieve balance in their programs and classrooms, they should weigh the costs of technology, media, and other learning materials against their program's resources, and they also should weigh the use of digital and electronic materials against the use of natural and traditional materials and objects. (p. 12)

Teachers who focus on the needs of each child and the integration of curriculum will find developmentally appropriate, engaging, and intentional uses for technology in young children's learning.

Putting It All Together

Throughout this book, you have journeyed through the history, events, philosophy, and practice that make up early childhood education. Becoming a professional involves reflecting on all these aspects as well as on who you are becoming in the profession and where you want to travel throughout your career. Being an early childhood educator demands commitment to children and their families. In the *Standards for Early*

Childhood Professional Preparation, the NAEYC (2009) explains the following facets of becoming an early childhood professional:

- Identifying and involving oneself in the early childhood field
- Knowing about and upholding ethical standards and other professional guidelines
- Engaging in continuous, collaborative learning to inform practice
- Integrating knowledgeable, reflective, and critical perspectives on early education
- Engaging in informed advocacy for children and the profession.

Becoming a professional requires education in a specialized body of knowledge, knowledge of a specific, technical vocabulary that identifies one's membership in the profession, and the internalization of guiding principles that support decision-making. One of the touchstones of a profession is its **Code of Ethics** – a set of core values of a profession, providing guidance for what the professional should do when faced with an ethical dilemma. The *NAEYC Code of Ethical Conduct* (2005) provides the early childhood professional guidance in dealing with children, families, other professionals, and the wider community. The early childhood development and education field is constantly changing and expanding. It is incumbent on the professional to stay current with the latest research and practice; reading, participating in study groups, joining local and national associations, attending conferences, and conducting classroom-based research are all ways to engage in continuous, collaborative learning. Well-prepared professionals who work with children and families need to be reflective and critical as they analyze their own practice. Their goal needs to be continually refining their practice to sensitively and ethically meet the needs of children and families. Advocacy is working for a cause one believes in. Early childhood professionals have the obligation of becoming active advocates for children, their families, society, and the early childhood profession (NAEYC, 2009).

Congratulations on making a commitment to becoming a professional early childhood educator! Let this lifelong journey begin!

What lies behind us and what lies before us are tiny matters compared
to what lies within us
~Oliver Wendell Holmes

Summary

- Children require guidance to feel safe, secure and confident to explore, learn, and build relationships with others. Simply put, guidance is helping children become autonomous, self-regulated, empathetic, contributing members of a particular culture as children and later, as adults.

- The guidance plan that early childhood educators map out must be developmentally appropriate, taking into consideration 1) what we know about child development in general, 2) what we know about each child in the setting, and 3) what we know about the cultural values, customs, beliefs, and expectations of the child's family and community.

- Much of our guidance of children is indirect; the planning of the environment (space, materials, and equipment), scheduling, purposeful transitions, engaging curricula, and establishing appropriate expectations are all components of indirect guidance.

- Direct guidance includes facilitating prosocial behaviors, preventing problems by anticipating and re-directing particular behaviors, and using consequences to encourage or discourage particular behaviors (Hearron & Hildebrand, 2005).These are the verbal, physical, and affective procedures educators use to help the child become self-directed and able to function in society.

- Teaching children strategies for self-regulation and problem-solving effectively gives children lifelong skills.

- Research shows that when families are actively involved with their children's education, children are more successful academically, emotionally, and socially (Hoover-Dempsey et al., 2005).

- Understanding the family structure and the dynamics within each unique structure is an important part of working with young children. Teachers are more effective in guiding children if they understand how the family system operates for each child.

- Over the past few years, there has been a shift in view from that of the professionals as the "experts" who teach the parents how to support their child's development, to the present view that the parents are experts in their own right and the professional needs to respect and empower the family.

- A reciprocal relationship of parents and educators in which information and decision-making is shared can develop when both parties have mutual respect, shared responsibility, and trust. This relationship building requires effective two-way communication.

- A well-planned classroom is safe, healthy, and meets the minimum state licensing requirements. The setting should aid positive classroom management, support the carrying out of program goals and objectives, and nurture children's learning and development.

- Developmentally appropriate practice allows for the thoughtful, intentional usage of technology in the early childhood classroom. Professional early childhood educators use technology such as computers, electronic tablets, and smart boards, not to replace children's interactions with authentic materials, but to expand the scope of tools children can use to research information, solve problems, refine new skills, and learn at their own pace.

- One of the touchstones of a profession is its Code of Ethics – a set of core values of a profession, providing guidance for what the professional should do when faced with an ethical dilemma.

Key Terms

behavior support plan
Code of Ethic
conflict resolution
consequences
cross-cultural competence
direct guidance
emotional literacy
family systems theory
indirect guidance
inductive discipline
re-direction
self-regulation
third teacher
transition

Suggested Readings

Bruno, H. E. (2009). *Leading on purpose: Emotionally intelligent early childhood administration.* NYC: McGraw-Hill Companies.

Curtis, D. & Carter, M. (2003). *Designs for living and learning: Transforming early childhood environments.* St. Paul, MN: Redleaf Press.

Gonzalez-Mena, J. (2001). *Multicultural issues in child care* (3rd ed.). Mountain View, CA: Mayfield Publishing.

Kaiser, B. & Rasminsky, J.S. (2003). *Challenging behavior in young children: Understanding, preventing, and responding effectively.* Boston: Allyn and Bacon.

Paley, V. (1992). *You can't say you can't play.* Cambridge, MA: Harvard University Press.

Suggested Websites

Center for Effective Parenting
www.parenting-ed.org

National Black Child Development Institute (NBCDI)
www.nbcdi.org

National Latino Children's Institute (NLCI)
www.nlci.org

Spaces for Children – an architectural firm specializing in designing developmentally appropriate spaces for children's centers and schools.
www.spacesforchildren.com

Reflections

1. Why is it beneficial for an early childhood educator to understand some details about a child's neighborhood? How might a child's neighborhood affect his or her behavior?

2. Think about taking parents who are thinking of enrolling their toddler and preschool children in your early learning center, on a tour of the center. You point out the differences in the toddler and preschool rooms in terms of small group learning, individual learning centers, large group area, and private spaces. Explain to the parents why you have organized the classroom into the activity areas and explain what goes on in each area. Explain why the block corner is between the art and dramatic play centers.

3. Observe an early learning center in which children with disabilities are included. Investigate what changes in scheduling and room arrangement were made to accommodate those children. What other changes were made?

4. Interview a veteran early childhood educator. Ask if he or she has ever encountered an ethical dilemma and if so, how he or she handled it. Read the NAEYC Code of Ethics and decide how it could be used in resolving the ethical dilemma.

5. Research trends related to policies and services which impact young children and their families (e.g., Universal Health Care). Reflect on your own opinion on one of the issues. Decide what you can do to influence policy or advocate for this cause.

References

Baumrind, D. (1996). Parenting: The discipline controversy revisited. *Family Relations, 45*, 405-414.

Berk, L. E. (2016). *Infants and children* (8th ed.). Boston, MA: Allyn & Bacon.

Bredekamp, S. (2011). *Effective practices in early childhood education: Building a foundation.* Upper Saddle River, NJ: Pearson Education.

Bronfenbrenner, U. (1979). *The ecology of human development: Experiments by nature and design.* Cambridge, MA: Harvard University Press.

Carlsson-Page, N. & Levin, D. (1998). *Before push comes to shove: Building conflict resolution skills with children.* St. Paul, MN: Redleaf Press.

Catron, C. E. & Allen, J. (2008). *Early childhood curriculum: A creative-play model.* Upper Saddle River, NJ: Pearson Education.

Christian, L. G. (2006). Understanding families: Applying family systems theory to early childhood practice. *Young Children, 61*(1), 12-20.

Copple, C. & Bredekamp, S. (Eds.). (2009). *Developmentally appropriate practice in early childhood programs serving children from birth through age 8.* Washington, DC: NAEYC.

Dreikurs, R. & Cassel, P. (1972). *Discipline without tears.* New York: Hawthorn Books.

Edwards, C., Gandini, L., & Forman, G. (1998). *The hundred languages of children: The Reggio Emilia approach – Advanced reflections* (2nd ed.). Greenwich, CT: Ablex.

Epstein, J. L., Sanders, M. G., Simon, B., Salina, K., Jansorn, N., & VanVoorhis, F. (2002). *School, family, and community partnerships: Your handbook for action.* (2nd ed.). Thousand Oaks, CA: Corwin Press.

Gandini, L. (1997). The Reggio Emilia story: History and organization. In J. Hendrick (Ed.), *First steps toward teaching the Reggio way.* Upper Saddle River, NJ: Merrill/ Prentice Hall.

Gonzalez-Mena, J. (1992). Taking a culturally sensitive approach in infant-toddler programs. *Young Children, 1,* 8-9.

Hearron, P. F. & Hildebrand, V. (2005). *Guiding young children.* (7th ed.). Upper Saddle River, NJ: Pearson Education.

Howes, C. & Ritchie, S. (2002). *A matter of trust: Connecting teachers and learners in the early childhood classroom.* New York: Teachers College Press.

Joseph, G., Strain, P. S., & Ostrosky, M. M. (2006). *Fostering emotional literacy in young children: Labeling emotions.* Champaign, IL: Center on the Social and Emotional Foundations for Early Learning. Retrieved May 11, 2013, from http://www.vanderbilt.edu/csefel/briefs

Kaiser, B. & Rasminsky, J. S., (2012). *Challenging behavior in young children* (3rd ed.). Upper Saddle River, NJ: Pearson Education.

Klein, M. D. & Chen, D. (2001). *Working with children from culturally diverse backgrounds.* Albany, NY: Delmar.

Marion, M. (2011). *Guidance of young children* (8th ed.). Upper Saddle River, NJ: Pearson Education.

Morrison, G. S., (2012). *Early childhood education today.* Upper Saddle River, NJ: Pearson Education.

National Association for the Education of Young Children. (2005). *NAEYC early childhood program standards and accreditation criteria: The mark of quality in early childhood education.* Washington, DC: NAEYC.

National Association for the Education of Young Children. (2005). *Code of ethical conduct and statement of commitment.* Retrieved May 15, 2012, from http://naeyc.org/files/codeofethicalconduct

National Association for the Education of Young Children. (2009). *NAEYC Standards for Early Childhood Professional Preparation Programs.* Washington DC: NAEYC.

National Association for the Education of Young Children. (2012). Position paper on technology and early childhood. http://www.naeyc.org/content/technology-and-young-children

National Coalition for Parent Involvement in Education (NCPIE) (2006). *A new wave of evidence: The impact of school, family and community connections on student achievement.* Retrieved from http://www.ncpie.org/whatshappening/research

Neilsen, S. L., Olive, M. L., Donovan, A., & McEvoy, M. (1999). Challenging behaviors in your classroom? Don't react – Teach instead! In S. Sandall & M. Ostrosky (Eds.), *Practical ideas for addressing challenging behaviors,* (pp. 5-15). Denver, CO: Division for Early Childhood of the Council for Exceptional Children.

Pianta, R. C. (1999). *Enhancing relationships between children and teachers.* Washington, DC: American Psychological Association.

Prescott, E. (1984, Summer). When you think about spaces. *Beginnings,* pp. 3-5.

Spaggieri, S. (1998). The community-teacher partnership in the governance of schools: An interview with Lella Gandini. In C. Edwards, L. Gandini, & G. Forman (1998), *The hundred languages of children: The Reggio Emilia approach – Advanced reflections* (2nd ed.). Greenwich, CT: Ablex.

Strain, P. S. & Hemmeter, M. L. (1999). Keys to being successful when confronted with challenging behaviors. In S. Sandall & M. Ostrosky (Eds.), *Practical ideas for addressing challenging behaviors* (pp. 17-25). Denver, CO: Division for Early Childhood of the Council for Exceptional Children.

Swick, D. C., Head-Reeves, D., & Barbarin, O. (2006). Building relationships between diverse families and school personnel. In C. Franklin, M. B. Franklin, & P. Allen Meares (Eds.), *The school services sourcebook: A guide for school based Professionals,* (pp. 793-801). New York: Oxford University Press.

Tarr, P. (2001). Aesthetic codes in early childhood classrooms: What art educators can learn from Reggio Emilia. Retrieved April 29, 2013 from http://www.designshare.com

U.S. Census Bureau. (2016). *Custodial mothers and fathers and their child support.* Retrieved January 19, 2017, from http://www.census.gov/prod

Vartuli, S. (1987). Ideas: Teacher decisions that maximize learning and minimize disruptions in early childhood settings. *Dimensions, 15*(4), 28-31.

Chapter 13
Does Handwriting Really Matter?

Introduction

Virtually every early childhood classroom in America, regardless of public, private, religious based or secular continues to focus the teaching of writing, communication and organization of thoughts. We do this for two reasons – to produce globally competent individuals and to develop literate, thinking persons. We also do this because as educators we are well aware of the relationship between writing and reading. Writing helps one organize his/her thoughts. Writing is also, at least in early childhood classrooms, grounded in a foundation of conversational, phonological and general academic skills. (Committee, 2014) A quick look through history easily shows us the evolution of the writing process in today's schools. Writing began with pen and paper, graduated to typewriters, evolved to computers and finally has graduated into various computer programming systems that will type and organize our thoughts for us. What we seem to be forgetting is this fact: "Even in the age of technology, handwriting remains the primary tool of communication and knowledge assessment in the classroom … (and) … the demands for handwriting increase with age." (p1, hwt.com)

> A study published in 1992 revealed that "85% of all fine motor time in second, fourth and sixth grade classrooms were spent on paper and pencil activities." (hwt.com, p 1)

Current American kindergarteners spend upwards of 45% of their day learning, practicing and refining paper/pencil activities associated with handwriting. (Desai and Rege, p. 1) A study published in 1992 revealed that "85% of all fine motor time in second, fourth and sixth grade classrooms was spent on paper and pencil activities." (hwt.com, p 1) Further research shows us that as much as 35% of students struggle regularly with basic handwriting. These startling statistics makes proper handwriting instruction and integration all the more critical. Factor in time for snacks, lunch, bathroom breaks, transitions and special subject areas and today's early childhood educator is not left with an overwhelming amount of time to focus on core content.

What if there was a secret weapon, a fairly easy way to help increase our student achievement? There might be! First we need to answer a few questions.

1. Is it important for students to learn to read?

2. Is it important for students to know how to formulate and organize their thoughts?

3. Is it possible that Millennial students will spend more time than any generation before them engaged in computer related activities and communications?

4. Is it important for students to know how to write – as in compose – their thoughts?

5. Is it important for students to master basic fine motor skills for future life?

6. Does is matter if students can only accomplish the above via electronic methods of communication?

The answer to all of the questions posed above is a resounding "Yes".

Life without Longhand

No one, certainly not the author of this text, will argue the fact that we live in the 21st century where technology reigns supreme, social media is part of the daily routine and computer skills are essential for basic survival. Technology has made it almost effortless to talk, in real time, with a friend or relative halfway around the globe and, thus, has made the idea of a handwritten letter all but antiquated. The growth of online college courses and distance learning has all but caused the extinction of traditional, handwritten, hand scored tests and writing assignments. Students of all ages can manage homework, take practice quizzes, research topics and submit computer generated and processed work without ever touching actual paper and pencil. Parents can communicate with early childhood and elementary teachers without ever writing a single letter of the alphabet in longhand. The rapid rise of online financial services and online shopping has made the ideas of writing a check or actually composing a weekly grocery list unnecessary. So why exactly do early childhood educators need to be concerned with the slow death of longhand in American society? Just what would it mean for our overall society if our schools stopped teaching our children how to write?

Figure 1 Treasury Secretary Jacob Lew has faced criticism over the illegibility of his signature. (Puzzanghera, 2013)

Figure 2 Can you read this prescription? The lack of handwriting skill could put you in jeopardy. (n/a, 2010)

Research has been done on the effects 'losing longhand'. The resulting findings are both surprising and in some instances downright scary. For starters, reports indicate that "1 in 10 Americans is endangered by the poor handwriting of their physician." Estimates show that at least 7,000 people die each year as a result of their doctor's orders being illegible. (Caplan, p 1) Another 1.5 million patients are victims due to illegible handwriting and the annual cost of medical care each year (as a result of illegible handwriting) exceeds 3.5 billion dollars annually. (Alfano, p 1) Further, it is estimated that "$200,000,000 in time and money is lost each year" as a result of poor handwriting. (Starr, p 1) The lack of "longhand" results in such problems as packages being delivered to wrong addresses, important phone calls never being completed, critical mistakes in food service and other service industries, illegible handwriting on court and legal documents, and miscommunications between employee and employer. Additionally, it is widely hypothesized that the "demise of (penmanship) will diminish the power and accuracy of future historical research" as (Pressler, p 1) Handwritten letters, postcards, poems and other documents are also valued for sheer aesthetic purposes such as beauty, individualism and intimacy between the author and audience.

> "Approximately $95,000,000 in tax refunds remains unclaimed each year as a result of poor handwriting on IRS forms." (Starr, p 1)

Reviewing the Research

The benefits gleaned from successful, seamless integration of handwriting instruction are numerous. In early childhood environments handwriting can be correlated to the development of basic reading skills, spelling achievement and overall confidence. The Common Core State Standards (CCSS) have provisions that include standards for "legible manuscript writing" in kindergarten and first grade (Huneycutt, p 1). A study conducted by Sandler found that 75% of the "writing disorders identified in 9-to15-year-olds had links" to the development of skills such as "expressive language, rapid naming, attention span and memory." (Mar, et al, p 1) So the question remains, exactly what are the benefits for our students? And, what evidence can early childhood educators find to support the claim that handwriting instruction should be an integral part of early childhood education?

Karin James, Psychology Professor at Indiana University, conducted a research study to see if teaching children handwriting had an effect on the parts of their brains utilized for reading. Professor James' study focused on twelve four-and-five year olds which she divided into two subgroups. Over the course of four weeks, one group was given handwriting instruction and one group was not. Using functional MRI scans of the brain Dr. James attempted to map the brain activity of a group of children prior to and after the children were exposed to direct instruction on basic letters. Specifically, Professor James scanned the children's brains prior to instruction and again after instruction. The results were quite surprising. The scans of the students who received the handwriting instruction showed clear spikes in areas of the brain utilized for reading. (p1, Stokes)

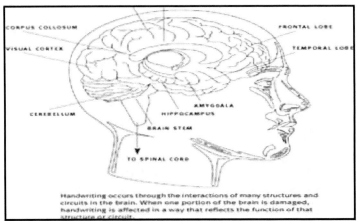

Figure 2: A diagram of the human brain highlights the critical areas necessary for the development of reading and writing.
(Seifer M. J., 2002)

Another study, conducted by Professor Steve Graham of Vanderbilt University, looked directly at the relationship between the acquisition of handwriting skills and the development of sentence construction and production. The study followed a group of first graders. Prior to the study the first graders where not receiving handwriting instruction. They could only construct and produce language at a rate of approximately 10 to 12 words per minute. As part of the study the students were given 15 minutes a day, three days a week of direct handwriting instruction. In a mere nine weeks, the Prince Georges county, Maryland first graders had "doubled their writing speed…increased their sentence construction skills … [and] were writing more complex thoughts and ideas." (Pressler, p 2)

This research has been replicated across the globe. Early childhood students in China learn to read through the teaching of individual characters. Chinese educators have long believed that the orthographic representations utilized when reading are also uniquely connected to each character a student learns to write. In their study Guan, Liu,

Chan, Yi and Perfetti attempted to show an effect of handwriting on reading and character recognition. (Guan, et al, p. 3) Once again, the results from this study supported the hypothesis that handwriting instruction is instrumental in developing reading skills in children. The researchers found that "when characters are taught (in conjunction with) handwriting, the characters….become represented in a higher quality form. This higher quality…allows for better (word) recognition at a later point." (Guan, et al, p. 6)

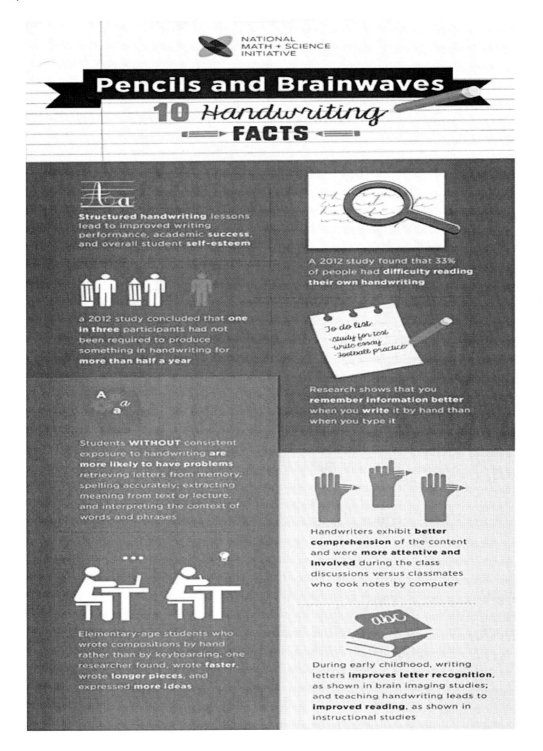

It is safe to say that the research associated with handwriting instruction is fairly conclusive. Teaching handwriting in our early childhood classrooms can result in a plethora of cognitive and physical benefits for our students. Further, the knowledge gleaned from that instruction as a child will serve to directly impact society as a whole when those children become the adults who are running our world.

The Keys to Proper Handwriting Instruction

How does an early childhood professional begin to integrate handwriting into his or her classroom? Especially when 75% of early childhood teachers surveyed report that they are not "adequately prepared to teach handwriting." (Starr, p 1) A national study conducted in 2007 revealed that "only 12 percent of current teachers" had received adequate training regarding handwriting pedagogy. (p2, hwt.com)

Figure 3 A preschool student engages in the kinesthetic learning activity of writing letters in shaving cream. (Geiger, 2013)

Figure 4 A little girl practices learning letters; first by making her letters with dough and then by forming the letters on a small chalkboard using a wet sponge. (King, 2010)

Handwriting instruction and assessment should be a natural and functional part of each student's day. The golden days of military style, drilled penmanship instruction are, thankfully, long gone. However, for our students to become successful, functioning adults we now know that explicit and integrated handwriting instruction need to become an integral part of the classroom. That requires today's teachers to at least have adequate handwriting themselves and to have some common standards for how and what to teach. A national study conducted in 2007 revealed that "only 12 percent of current teachers" had received adequate training regarding handwriting pedagogy. (p2, hwt.com) Much research confirms that handwriting instruction in the early childhood classroom has been neglected or totally abandoned due to four main reasons: emphasis and use of technology, lack of time, lack of teacher knowledge on the subject and lack of specific teacher training related to teaching handwriting. (Gwenyth et al. p 1) So who exactly is teaching our students how to write and what are they supposed to be teaching them?

Research in this field is wide yet conclusive; handwriting instruction whether manuscript or cursive should be an integral part of every early childhood students school day. As with any subject teachers must call upon their knowledge of *theory* (an orderly, integrated set of ideas that attempts to define or predict behavior) and *pedagogy* (the science and art of teaching) should be followed. Most experts agree that effective handwriting instruction must focus on three main components and follow a distinct sequence and focus on a single component at a time. Starr instructs teachers to begin with letter formation, then teach letter size and end by teaching letter spacing.

"....labored handwriting creates a drain on mental resources needed for higher –level aspects of writing, such as attention to content, elaboration of details and organization of idea." (p1, Spear-Swerling)

First, ECE teachers should monitor for execution, legibility and speed. *Letter formation* focuses on form and slant of the handwriting. Regardless of the style of handwriting (we will discuss the most common forms of handwriting instruction later in the text) all children should be instructed on how to properly grip their pencil, how to effectively position their paper, what correct posture looks like and exactly where to begin and end each letter.

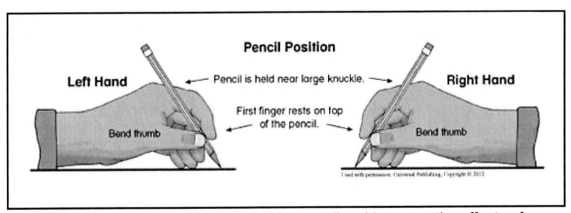

Figure 5: The correct way to hold a pencil and increase the effects of handwriting instruction.
(Back to School Basics #4 for Handwriting Instruction, 2012)

As a child progresses with fine motor and writing skills she will demonstrate a range of grasps and grips with whatever writing utensil they are employing. An average child can successfully grasp a pencil, crayon or pen by the age of 12 months old. Teachers will observe a host of incorrect grasps and grips as their students progress to mastery of writing skills. An observant and knowledgeable teacher will employ strategies such as popping bubble wrap, teaching and reciting finger plays, sorting coins, dropping coins into piggy bank slots, using peg boards, pinching clothespins open and shut or tearing pieces of construction paper. All of these activities help to strengthen the fine motor skills and develop the hand-eye coordination needed to achieve a correct, efficient pencil grasp.

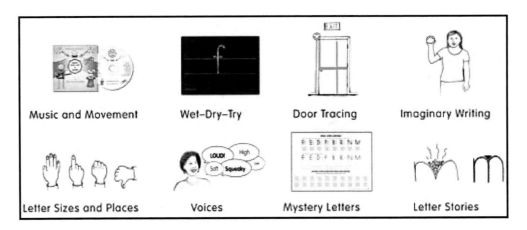

Summary of Inefficient Grasp Patterns in Handwriting Development

Fisted grasp	The pencil is held in a fisted hand with the point of the pencil on the fifth finger side on the hand. This is typical of very young children.
Pronated grasp	The pencil is held diagonally within the hand with the tips of the thumb and index finger on the pencil. This is typical of children ages 2 to 3.
Five finger grasp	The pencil is held with the tips of all five fingers. The movement when writing is primarily on the fifth finger side of the hand.
Thumb tuck grasp	The pencil is held in a tripod or Quadripod grasp but with the thumb tucked under the index finger.
Finger wrap or inter digital brace grasp	The index and third fingers wrap around the pencil. The thumb web space is completely closed.
Flexed wrist or hooked wrist	The pencil can be held in a variety of grasps with the wrist flexed or bent. This is more typically seen with left-hand writers but is also present in some right-hand writers.

The *palmar grasp* is usually displayed during the toddler years. The pencil is normally laid in the hand and the writing is mostly done with the elbow facing outward. The *tripod grasp* is usually the next to appear. A student who is utilizing the tripod grasp will hold the pencil using only the tip of the thumb and index finger while resting the pencil against the side of one of the remaining fingers; essentially forming a circle around the pencil. The *dynamic tripod grasp* is recognized and accepted as the most correct grasp for handwriting. In the dynamic tripod grasp the student holds the pencil between the index finger and thumb; the pencil rests gently on the middle finger. Some students may exhibit a *quadripod grasp*. In this style of holding a pencil the student will rest the pencil against the side of the fourth finer while simultaneously holding the pencil in the tips of the thumb, index and third fingers. With both the dynamic tripod grasp and the quadripod grasp the students thumb and index fingers will form a circle. (Wise, 2014) (Heidi Schwellnus, 2013)

⊞ HANDWRITING GRIPS ⊞

CORRECT

1. The pencil rests on the first joint of the middle finger with the thumb and index fingers holding the pencil in place.

2. Same as Figure 1, except the fingers are closer to the pencil point.

3. Same as Figure 1, except the pencil is held perpendicular to the table.

INCORRECT

4. Thumb and index finger holding pencil, with index finger overlapping the thumb.

5. Pencil held by tips of fingers, thumb on one side, middle and index fingers on the other.

6. Thumb wraps around pencil with index and middle fingers pressing pencil to ring finger.

7. Pencil is held between the index and middle fingers, pressing pencil to the thumb.

8. Index, middle and ring finger tips hold one side of the pencil, the thumb holds the other.

9. Thumb on one side, index and middle fingers on the other, all pressing the pencil to ring finger.

10. Index finger holds pencil to middle finger with the thumb overlapping the index finger.

11. The thumb holds the pencil along the first joints of the rest of the fingers.

12. The pencil is grasped in the fist, and held up against the thumb.

It is at this point in handwriting instruction that teachers should also begin letter: sound recognition and correspondence. This includes making students aware of the headline, the baseline and the midline. This also includes beginning a discussion on the concepts of angles, left, right, top, bottom, pull and slant. The proper paper position is a 45° angle aimed towards the dominant hand.

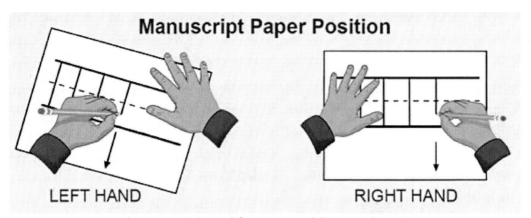

Image retrieved from www.blog.upub.net

One last issue of concern before teaching handwriting is the correct posture for handwriting. Ideally, the student should be positioned in such a way that he has unrestricted vision for writing, keeps the paper in one place and keep his body balanced. For this to occur, the student should be seated at his desk and have both feet firm and flat on the floor below the desk. To achieve this posture the desk should be slightly sloped and the student's arms should rest on top of the desk at a perfect 90 degree angle. (Fact Sheet: The Importance of Posture for Handwriting, 2013)

Figure 6: The diagram to the right shows the correct seating and posture for optimum development of handwriting skills in children. (Wasylyk)

Letter size (also called letter proportion) focuses on the uniformity of similar letters. For example, short or small letters such as a, c, e, i, m, n, o, r, s, u, v, w, x and z should uniformly be half the size of tall letters like b, d, f, h, k, l, t and descender letters such as g, j, p, q, and y. Additionally, students should be taught that capital letters are formed to the same height as ascender letters. This technique is commonly referred to as the *Carnine Order*, or the order that the alphabet is most effectively taught. (Unknown, 2014) This is the first step to proper handwriting instruction. Like teaching any new concept making sure that you have properly built a student's prior knowledge and have developed a firm foundation for learning is critical.

Letter spacing deals with proper spacing between letters as well as between words. Letter spacing is a critical skill necessary for one to develop legible, comprehendible handwriting of any form. The spacing between letters should be uniform. The spacing between words and punctuation should also be uniform. For some students this skill comes slowly and with great difficulty due to lack of fine motor development or lack of spatial reasoning. Teachers can assist the development of this skill by sharing 'tricks' with their students such as leave a pencil point between each letter and a pencil width between each word.

Research abounds regarding best practice in handwriting pedagogy. Universally, handwriting instruction should be a natural, inclusive part of every early childhood student's day. Handwriting instruction, regardless of the specific form of script being taught, should be taught for approximately 10-15 minutes per day and be firmly connected to the content being taught for that classroom. Additionally, all handwriting instruction should focus on instruction for consistent formation of letters, continuous pencil strokes and correct habits. Much like anything else in life undesired handwriting habits in early childhood become lifelong habits that are hard, if not impossible, to correct in adulthood.

Louise Spear-Swerling suggests (p 3)

1. Teach similarly formed letters together. For example o, c, a, d, g all begin with a common handwriting stroke. Teach the stroke first then apply the stroke to the formation of common letters.

2. Separate reversible letters such a b and d, g and q.

3. Focus on the overall pattern of letter production at first instead of perfection regarding execution, speed, legibility. Those essential skills can monitored for later

4. Teach similarly formed letters together. For example o, c, a, d, g all begin with a common handwriting stroke. Teach the stroke first then apply the stroke to the formation of common letters.

5. Separate reversible letters such a b and d, g and q.

Execution includes correct and consistent pencil hold. It also relates to how a student creates a letter. Is it formed (i.e. – written with one consistent stroke of the pencil) or drawn (i.e. – written using several separate strokes where the pencil leaves the paper)? Research shows us that formed letters lead to higher rates of speed, comprehension and performance. *Legibility* includes the overall readability of the letters but also the overall spacing in the writing sample. *Speed*, simply put, is defined as how efficiently is the student able to handwrite information that is also legible and comprehendible for the reader. (Spear-Swerling, p 2)

Stage 1 - Imitation
The child watches as the teacher writes and then imitates the teacher.

Stage 2 - Copying
The child looks at the completed model of a letter, word, or sentence and copies it to match the model.

Stage 3 - Independent Writing
The child writes unassisted, without a demonstration or a model.

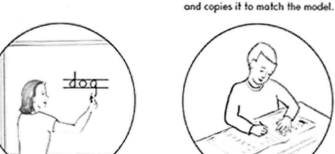

Figure 7: A pictorial timeline shows the steps to teaching a child the correct methods for handwriting. (HWT)

Types and Forms of Handwriting

Zaner-Bloser (Zaner Method of Arm Movement)

Charles Paxton Zaner and Elmer Ward Bloser published the *Zaner Method of Arm Movement* in 1904. The text was designed to teach children in elementary schools across the country to perfect the methods developed at the Zanerian College of Penmanship. At the time, the Zaner-Bloser based their handwriting instruction on psychological research that showed early childhood students could complete manual tasks more easily if allowed to utilize their primitive, large motor skills. (https://www.zaner-bloser.com/history) Zaner-Bloser manuscript consists of all 26 letters of the alphabet (upper case and lower case, including numerals) written in the same straight, upright style that historically matches most of the storybooks, textbooks, etc. that are utilized in a traditional early childhood classroom. One drawback of employing this handwriting method in the classroom is the lack of consistency and translation ability between the manuscript and cursive styles. The manuscript version of Zaner – Bloser, traditionally based on a circle-stick print, offers little carry over for the student learning the cursive version of the script. (Thurber, p. 1) For the typical child to write the word 'wake' in Zaner-Bloser manuscript she would have to make 51 separate print strokes. The same word can be dictated in 31 strokes if a cursive style is utilized. (Thurber, p. 3)

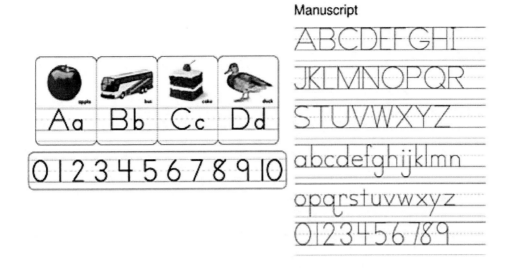

Manuscript

D'Nealian

In the mid 1970's Donald Neal Thurber developed the D'Nealian Method of Handwriting. His method employs slanted letters to teach handwriting based on the belief that this will lead to a smoother transition from print to cursive writing. (http://www.schoolhousefonts.com/methods.htm) In the D'Nealian Method students are taught the lower case letters first with emphasis placed on size, shape, slant and spacing. Noted early childhood theorist Maria Montessori commented in the early 1900's "Yet it does not seem natural that to write the letters of the alphabet, which are all rounded, it should begin with straight lines and acute angles." (Thurber, p. 2) Thus, the D'Nealian Method is employed in most Montessori based early childhood programs.

Peterson Directed

The *Peterson Directed Handwriting Method* was created in 1908 by Dr. P.O. Peterson. The Peterson Directed Method uses direct instruction techniques to teach students movement, sequencing and rythmicity. Using what they call a "We Write to Read" method students develop handwriting that is fluid, legible and reflexive. (Benson, p 5) Reading, writing and handwriting are linked together in all aspects of the classroom.

Cursive Desk Strip, 1.75 inches x 16 inches

Image retrieved from *http://shop.peterson-handwriting.com/category.sc?categoryId=13*

Handwriting without Tears

Handwriting Without Tears1 (HWT) is another method of instruction currently utilized in classrooms across the country. Developed by Jan Z. Olsen in the late 1900's and includes employs a defined "multisensory approach by modeling letter formations, using verbal descriptions of the strokes, finger tracing (and) drawing letters in the air" (Gwenyth et al, p 2) Groups of letters are taught together using researched early childhood teaching methods such as modeling, imitation, copying, and tactile experiences while following a logical progression from easier to more complex. Teachers who utilize HWT must subscribe to and implement the program according to three main principles:

1. Utilization of materials that are "intuitive, engaging and developmentally progressive",

2. Instruction that is engaging to children through singing, dancing, talking, movement and other hands on experiences,

3. Practice provides for and supports the extension of teacher knowledge and training. (Gwenyth et al, p 2)

Analyzing Handwriting Progress

As with every aspect of the teaching and learning process assessment of handwriting progress is a necessary evil. Early childhood students can experience difficulty with letter formation due to motor learning and execution, visual motor control, kinesthetic sensitivity, expressive language, phonological awareness, lack of emotional development or simple lack of motivation. (Bonney, p 1) (Boney, 1992) To properly instruct our students we, the teachers, must first know where to begin. Analyzing handwriting samples can help us achieve this task. Further, the time spent analyzing handwriting samples can help us to more easily identify a student who needs more intensive interventions such as occupational therapy and can help the student possibly avoid future academic failure. On a daily basis, identification of handwriting difficulties can help prevent teachers from unintentionally grading work wrong. It can also help teachers work offensively to prevent the lower self-esteem and motivation issues that often accompany such difficulties.

Regardless of the assessment tool we choose to implement in our early childhood classrooms each of us will be assessing for handwriting consistency. *Handwriting consistency* can be defined as the level of qualitative handwriting performance that persists over time. Alston and Taylor present 6 factors that contribute to incorrect handwriting and letter formation. These include letter reversals, variable slant, poor alignment, irregular spacing and inconsistent size and height of letters. (Desai and Rege, p. 1)

Although handwriting instruction is often not considered a major academic skill the assessment available to early childhood educators carry the same reliability, validity and consistency rates as a typical criterion and norm referenced instruments. This text highlights two of the most prominently utilized assessments. It should go without saying that any teacher, regardless of student ability, should practice portfolio assessment for each student. This method of assessment can work in perfect tandem with most data gleaned from a standardized tool. Another benefit of portfolio assessment is the large variety of assessment methods that can be utilized and then incorporated in to the student portfolio. Teachers assessing handwriting can utilize observation (with anecdotal records), complete product analysis using handwriting rubrics, allowing for student self-assessment of writing samples and peer review conferences. (Unknown, 2014)

The Beery-Buktenica Visual-motor Integration Test (VMI) was developed by Beery in 1997. The tool generally tests a student's abilities related to eye-hand coordination, copying of letters, visual closure and form constancy. The VMI includes 15 different, geometric shapes which become progressively more difficult as the assessment progresses. The student is asked to replicate each of the shapes; normally three per page. (Daly et al, p. 2)

Stages of Children's Handwriting Development (Low, 2014)

Stage	Description	Samples
1-1 Scribble stage	Starting point may be any place on the page	
1-2 Pictures	Pictures stand for words or phrases	
1-3 Writing scribble (approximation)	Left to right progression (progressively downward)	
1-4 Symbolic/mock letters	Can be personal or conventional	
1-5 Strings of conventional letters	Left to right – upper and lower case mixed	
1-6 Adding sound/letter relationships	Strings of letters to sounds	ICDUKTT
1-7 Groups of letters	Grouping sounds to resemble words	I SE D CAT

The Scale of Children's Readiness In PrinTing (SCRIPT) was developed by Weil and Cunningham in 1994. The test is a letter form copying research method that analyzes a student's ability to copy all 26 lower case letters and 8 upper case letters (A, K, M, N, V, W, Y and Z). The SCRIPT traditionally employs a horizontal page layout that frames two rows with three equally sized boxes in each. The first row of blocks generally contains the letterform to be copied and the bottom row of blocks in designated for the reproduction of the letter. (Daly et al. p. 2)

Criteria for Scoring the Scale of Children's Readiness In PrinTing (SCRIPT)

1. The letter is quickly and easily recognized as itself and no other symbol using the "peek hole" method; no gross errors in proportion are present. Case (upper or lower) is correct.

2. The letter has no missing parts and no extra parts. This includes the need to have the "stick" on a lowercase n.

3. No lines extend beyond the intersection by more than 2 mm.

4. Baselines and toplines must be parallel to the horizontal boundary lines of the blank stimulus box within 3 mm. Toplines and bottom boundary lines are not used for the letters a, b, d, q, g, r, and p, and the bottom of u.

5. Upstrokes and downstrokes must be parallel to the vertical boundaries within 3 mm. The capital letter M and the dots on i and j are not included in this criterion. The side points of z, s, x, k, e, and c must fall within a 3-mm space of each other, which is perpendicular to the horizontal boundaries.

6. Letter forms must be closed correctly, with no more than a 2-mm gap. For k, this means that the intersection of the two angled lines can be no more than 2 mm apart.

7. Curved lines must be curved, and straight lines must be able to fit within a 2-mm space. These criteria include any extension lines that may be present.

8. Angles must be present.

9. There is no rotation of more than 45∞ in any part of the letter: No reversals are present.

10. Each side of the horizontal line in t and f must be within 2-mm length of the other: The bottom portion of the vertical line of the t must be at least 2 mm longer than the top side.

11. Oblique lines cannot be perpendicular to the outer boundary lines (e.g., v, w, y).

Note. Each letter must pass each criterion to be awarded 1 point. Failure on any one criterion results in a score of 0 for that letter (Marr et al., 2001).

Summary

There seems to be consensus in the research that American children are not learning the art of handwriting. The lack of mastery of such a simple skill can carry over to reading, writing, science, math and even social skills. As a society lack of handwriting skill accounts for millions of dollars lost each year and countless life altering human errors. Regardless of the teaching method employed – Zaner Bloser Handwriting, D'Nealian Handwriting, The Peterson Directed Instruction, Handwriting Without Tears or any other researched method – explicit instruction in the formation of letters needs to remain an integral part of the early childhood curriculum. Further, those new to the early

"Two generations ago, 95% of people in America used handwriting. Today, most use keyboarding. Yet the skills of handwriting remain important. They are memory, focus, prediction, attention, sequencing, estimation, patience and creativity." (Huneycutt, p 1)

childhood profession should themselves receive explicit instruction in how to both execute and instruct proper handwriting.

References

Alfano, P. (2007, October 16). *Prescription For Trouble*. Retrieved February 14, 2015, from Reading Eagle: http://www2.readingeagle.com/article.aspx?id=64041

Back to School Basics #4 for Handwriting Instruction. (2012, August 09). Retrieved November 19, 2014, from Universal Publishing: http://blog.upub.net/writing-is-learning-blog/bid/205129/Back-to-School-Basics-4-for-Handwriting-Instruction

Boney, M.-A. (1992). Understanding and Assessing Handwriting Difficulty: Perspectives from the Literature. *The Australian Occupational Therapy Journal*, 9.

Caplan, J. (2007, January 15). Cause of Death: Sloppy Doctors. *Time*, p. 2.

Cermak, D. M. (2002). Consistency of Handwriting in Elementary Students. *American Journal of Occupational Therapy*, 7.

Christopher J. Daly, G. T. (2003). Relationship Between Visual-Motor Integration and Handwriting Skills of Children in Kindergarten: A Modified Replication Study. *The American Journal of Occupational Therapy*, 4.

Committee, W. S. (2014, November 10). *NCTE Beliefs about the teaching of Writing*. Retrieved February 19, 2015, from National Council of Teachers of English: http://www.ncte.org/positions/statements/writingbeliefs

Connie Qun Guan, Y. L. (2011). Writing Strengthens Orthography and Alphabetic-Coding Strengthens. *Journal of Educational Psychology*, 14.

Deardorff, J. (2014, October 10). *Chicago Tribune*. Retrieved November 15, 2014, from www.chicagotribune.com: www.chicagotribune.com Fact Sheet: The Importance of Posture for Handwriting. (2013, December). Sydney, Australia: University of Sydney.

Geiger, A. (2013, August 15). *Teach kids to write the alphabet – set up stations at the kitchen table!* Retrieved January 04, 2015, from The Measured Mom: http://www.themeasuredmom.com/teach-kids-to-write-the-alphabet-set-up-stations-at-the-kitchen-table/

Gentry, R. (2014). How Writing Instruction is Changing Schools. *Psych Today*, 2.

Gwenyth Robers, A. F.-F. (2014). An examination of the effectiveness of Handwriting Without Tears® instruction. *The Canadian Journal of Occupational Therapy*, 14. *Handwriting Posture*. Your Therapy Source.

Heidi Schwellnus, H. C. (2013). Writing Forces Associated With Four Pencil Grasp Patterns in Grade 4 Children. *American Journal of Occupational Therapy*, 218-227.

Huneycutt, T. (2013, September 25). *Pencils and Brainwaves: An Analysis on Handwriting and Memory*. Retrieved January 14, 2015, from National Math + Science Initiative: http://www.nms.org/Blog/TabId/58/PostId/179/pencils-and-brainwaves-an-analysis-on-handwriting-and-memory.aspx

Jeryl D. Benson, M. A. (2013). A Comparison of the Handwriting without Tears Program and Peterson Directed Handwriting Program on Handwriting Performance in Typically Developing First Grade Students. *Journal of Occupational Therapy, School and Early Intervention*, 12.

King, K. B. (2010, October 21). *Handwriting Without Tears*. Retrieved January 04, 2015, from Homeschooling in Paradise: http://homeschoolinginparadise.blogspot.com/2010/10/handwriting-without-tears.html

Klemm, W. (2014). Why Writing by Hand Could Make Your Smarter. *Psych Today*, 3.

Low, P. (2014, April 11). *Kindergarten Handwriting Rubric #8155*. Retrieved March 01, 2015, from Cheryl Hoffman Handwriting: http://www.crystalhoffman.com/kindergarten-handwritng-rubric

Morato, K. L.-A. (2008). The Effectiveness of Sensory Based Approaches. *JBI Library of Systematic Reviews*, 12. n/a. (2010, April 14). *Pharmacy Times*. Retrieved March 05, 2015, from http://www.pharmacytimes.com/publications/issue/2010/April2010/CanYouReadThe seRxs-0410

Puzzanghera, J. (2013, June 19). *Treasury secretary improves his penmanship for currency signature*. Retrieved December 28, 2014, from Los Angeles Times: http://articles.latimes.com/2013/jun/19/business/la-fi-mo-lew-signature-treasury-currency-20130619

Rege, A. S. (2005). Correlation between Developmental Test of Visual Motor Integration (VMI) and Handwriting in Cerebral Palsy Children. *Indiana Journal of Occupational Therapy*, 6.

Roberts, G. I., Derkach-Ferguson, A. F., Siever, J. E., & Rose, M. S. (2014, April 01). An examination of the effectiveness of Handwriting Without Tears® instruction. *ReadPeriodicals*.

Seifer, M. J. (2002). *The Tell Tale Hand: How Writing Reveals the Damaged Brain*. The Dana Foundation.

Seifer, M. J. (2014). *The Telltale Hand: How Writing Reveals the Damaged Brain*. n/a: The Dana Foundation.

Thurber, D. N. (1995, March 02). *D'Nealian Handwriting vs. Circle-Print Stick*. Retrieved February 05, 2015, from ERIC: https://archive.org/stream/ERIC_ED381911/ERIC_ED381911_djvu.txt

Unknown. (2014). *Handwriting in the South Australia Curriculum*. Retrieved March 02, 2015, from A Handwriting Program: https://www.sa.gov.au/__data/assets/pdf_file/0014/22127/HandwritingProgram.pdf

Walker, S. (2011, August 23). *The Science of Learning Blog*. Retrieved January 02, 2015, from http://www.scilearn.com/blog/teaching-handwriting-skills

Wasylyk, T. Handwriting. *Second Edition Handwriting Book C*. Universal Publishing, Waymart, PA.

Windsor, D. M.-M. (2001). Handwriting Readiness: Locatives and Visuomotor Skills in the Kindergarten Year. *Early Childhood Research and Practice*, 16.

Wise, R. (2014, September 03). *How to Help Your Child with Handwriting and Pencil Grip*. Retrieved January 10, 2015, from Education and Behavior: http://www.educationandbehavior.com/teaching-proper-pencil-grip-to-develop-or-improve-handwriting/

Chapter 14
Standardized Testing

Does Standardized Testing Work?

"Standardized testing has swelled and mutated, like a creature in one of those old horror movies, to the point that it now threatens to swallow our schools whole." This statement, echoed by many entrenched in the world of early childhood education, originates with Alfie Kohn. (Kohn, 2000) Kohn, a longtime advocate against the overuse of standardized testing, has a valid argument. Most valid research conducted over the last 50 years speaks against the use of standardized testing for the early childhood population. (Kohn, 2000) In 1998, Richard Rothstein (a noted educational economist) stated "Measurement of student achievement is complex – too complex for the social science of methods presently available." (P. Harris, 2012) Yet, in the United States we continue to evaluate our students and our teachers using exactly these methods.

"We are raising today's children in sterile, risk-averse and highly structured environments. In so doing, we are...

...cultivating a generation of children who can follow the rules in organized sports games, sit for hours in front of screens and mark bubbles on standardized tests"

- Darell Hammond

(Hammond, 2014)

Now more than ever students in America are destined to face the inevitability that is standardized testing. In fact, 48 states adopted and began implementing Common Core State Standards and the PARCC Assessment in 2015. Research shows that U.S.

students are now tested at a rate never before seen in American history. Why? Secretary of Education Arne Duncan has even gone on record regarding the very tests that his department endorses saying "State assessments in Mathematics and English often fail to capture the Full spectrum of what students know and can do." (Evans, 2013)

A plethora of research, some of which is presented in this chapter, speaks to the discontinuation of reliance on such testing. As this chapter is published the directives from standardized testing, long kept in the elementary and high schools, has somehow encroached upon our precious early childhood. What do early childhood educators do? How do we handle the onslaught of the testing movement? To answer that question one must examine the history of the standardized test movement and give serious credence to both the supporters of the movement and the detractors.

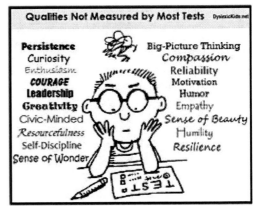

(Malespina, 2013)

What is a Standardized Test?

By definition a *standardized test* is any test or evaluation that is administered, scored and interpreted to a predetermined standard. Traditionally, standardized testing instruments are developed and prepared by a test publisher and normed to represent a particular group. (Morrow, 2012) Often the terms test and assessment are used interchangeably in the discourse of education. The technical definition of an *assessment* is "a group of formal and informal practices that yield specific information about a particular child's development." (Darragh, 2010) For the purposes of this chapter we will use the term "test" to reference the standardized, high stakes forms of evaluation that we utilize in the United States.

Two major forms of standardized tests exist and are currently are in use in our schools. An *aptitude test* attempts to predict a student's future educational success. (Popham, Standardized Testing Fails the Exam, 2015) This form of test seeks to represent a student's capacity to perform a certain task. Examples of aptitude tests include the Wechsler Intelligence Scale for Children V (WISC V) and the classic Stanford Binet Intelligence Test. An *achievement test* attempts to compare a student's performance to either a designated standard or to that of a similar population. (Popham, 1999) Examples of an achievement tests include the Iowa Test of Basic Skills (ITBS) and the California Achievement Test (CAT) both of which are widely administered across the United States.

Almost universally standardized tests do not make any effort to assess a student's *native intellectual ability*; that is the natural, inborn intelligence that has remained unaffected by a child's culture and educational opportunities. (Steele, 1997) Instead the current crop of standardized tests used in this country routinely test for academic prowess in math, English, reading, writing and even social skills. The results of these tests are then used to determine the success or failure of a school, a teacher, a district, a state or a student.

The last several decades have seen the emergence of the term high stakes assessment. A *high stakes assessment* is a standardized test whose results are utilized to make major decisions regarding education. (Morrow, 2012) Evan Secretary Duncan has stated that "educators know there is…more to a sound education than picking the right answer on a multiple-choice question." (Evans, 2013) So what precipitated this current fixation on the need to over assess our early childhood students and their teachers? To understand that one needs to understand the history behind the testing movement and follow the timeline to 2015.

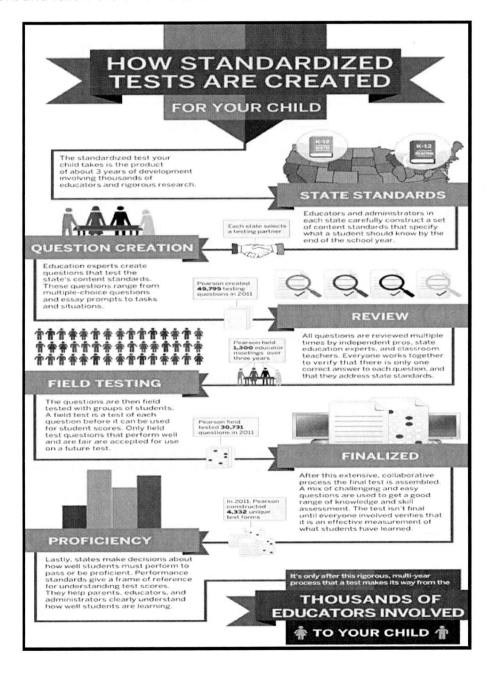

A Brief History of the Standardized Test Movement

To trace the history of testing in the United States one must travel back in history to 1892 when the Committee of Ten was appointed at a meeting of National Educational Association of Saratoga. (National Educational Association of the United States, 1894) The Committee stated that although the needs of secondary school students differed, with some college bound and some who were not, all students complete an "academic curriculum based almost entirely on a college preparatory format." (Armstrong, 2006) It was this report that catapulted the United States on its current pathway to standardized test overload.

Alfred Binet introduced the world to standardized testing in 1903. Binet was a French psychologist who spent much of his academic career attempting to measure human abilities in reasoning, mental processes and logic. To accomplish this task Binet developed a sophisticated array of techniques that included pictures, hands-on and portable materials, paper, pencils and written passages. (Editors of Encyclopeadia Britannica, 2013) The thirty questions posed to students related to everyday life experiences. It was Binet's main goal to be able to assess the *mental age*, the mental sophistication of an individual, of a child based on their test performance as opposed to *chronological age*, the actual, physical age of a person. (L.S.A. University of Michigan) Prior to the creation of Binet's standardized test children were deemed intelligent based on a review of their visual physical features. The belief of the time was that an outward, visible, physical abnormality was also representative of mental capabilities. (Collins, 1999) With Binet's work fully realized the world now had an objective, reliable, valid measure of intelligence and, therefore, could begin to compare the aptitude of one to another.

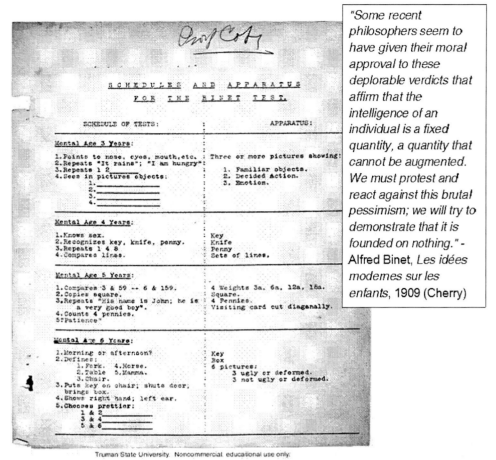

"Some recent philosophers seem to have given their moral approval to these deplorable verdicts that affirm that the intelligence of an individual is a fixed quantity, a quantity that cannot be augmented. We must protest and react against this brutal pessimism; we will try to demonstrate that it is founded on nothing." - Alfred Binet, *Les idées modernes sur les enfants*, 1909 (Cherry)

A sample Binet test, c. 1921. This example is indicative of Alfred Binet's earliest attempts to assess and quantify intelligence for the masses.
(Unknown, Race and Intelligence: 'The Bell Curve' 20 Years Later, 2014)

Approximately 20 years later, in 1926, the Scholastic Aptitude Test (S.A.T.) was created. Originally, the S.A.T. was "promoted as a tool to create a classless, Jeffersonian-style meritocracy." (Balf, 2014) Creators argued that the test measured natural intelligence, much like the WW1 Army I.Q. test had done, and therefore could provide much needed knowledge about a student's potential success. Ironically, the S.A.T. was created to provide society with a report about "what a student was capable of learning (rather) than in what he had already learned." (Gladwell, 2001)

The year 1938 saw the creation of the first ever standardized test tutoring service when Kaplan Co. opened its doors. Stanley H. Kaplan began operating a tutoring service for students out of his parents Brooklyn, New York basement. (Gladwell, 2001) Mr. Kaplan purported that a student could be trained or taught to pass a test; in this case, the S.A.T.s. As his business grew he expanded throughout the country and his Kaplan Test Prep system became the norm. The "teaching to the test" movement was effectively born in the United States.

If we time travel to 1955 we will meet Rudolf Flesch, author of the *Why Johnny Can't Read*. In *Why Johnny Can't Read* Mr. Flesch argued that elementary teachers relied too heavily on the use of *basal readers* (a series of stories and books that contain limited vocabulary and are taught in a predetermined sequence to develop specific skills associated with reading) and gave harsh criticism on the way that reading and literacy was taught in American classrooms. (Armstrong, 2006) Mr. Flesch argued that due to heavy reliance on basal readers U.S. students advanced at a much slower rate than their European counterparts. Thanks in part to Mr. Flesch, America became embroiled in a debate over the effectiveness of our schools that continues to this day. (Armstrong, 2006)

The U.S. Elementary and Secondary Education Act (ESEA) became law in 1965. Since that time, standardizes tests have been solely utilized to evaluate and assess our schools. The *ESEA Act* is considered to be the "first major infusion of federal funds into local schools (that) required educators to produce test-based evidence" that education dollars were being spent correctly. (Popham, Standardized Testing Fails the Exam, 2015)

Figure 1: The Classic Dick and Jane books of the early to mid 1900's are illustrative of early basal reader series in America. (O'Donnell, 1956)

The standardized testing movement was further rocketed to the forefront in the discourse of public education in 1981. It was then that former President Ronald Reagan convened the *National Commission on Excellence in Education* to determine the overall quality of teaching that was occurring in American public schools. (Armstrong, 2006) It took 18 months to create and publish the 36 page document that was written by a blue-ribbon panel of educators. (Graham, 2013) In the resulting report, *"A Nation at Risk"* (ANAR) declared that "regardless of race or class or economic status, are entitled to a fair chance and to the tools for developing their individual powers of mind and spirit to the utmost". (Armstrong, 2006) Secretary of State Terrell Bell presented the Commission findings; overall U.S. schools were performing at a mediocre level and needed to be redirected. Overall, the report generated as a result of A Nation at Risk resulted in a call for more of everything in education. (Ansary, 2007) Translated the report calls for more science, math, humanities, social studies, creativity and higher order thinking. Additionally, ANAR called for an increase in the length of the average school year, an increase in the length of the average school day and heavier reliance on homework for practicing skills. (Ansary, 2007)

Former President George W. Bush signs the No Child Left Behind Act on January 8, 2002, surrounded by school children and supporters of the bill, including Senators Edward M. Kennedy (D-MA) and John Boehner (R-OH). *Image retrieved from* *http://standardizedtests.procon.org/*

Fast forward to 1991 and the administration of President George W. Bush and we are introduced to the controversial *No Child Left Behind (NCLB)*. NCLB was considered a corner stone of President Bush's administrative policy. It reauthorized spending from the ESEA of 1965 to help American schools to increase standards, allow school choice for students and parents, allow greater flexibility for the use of government education monies and to increase overall accountability standards for all states, school districts and schools. "(U.S. Department of Education, 2002)

Unique to NCLB was its focus on our youngest children. As a provision of the ESEA, President George Bush signed to new programs aimed at improving early childhood education into law on January 08, 2002. The *Early Reading First* program was created with the mission to "prepare young children to enter kindergarten with the necessary language, cognitive, and early reading skills for learning success." (Programs: Early Reading First, 2014) Reading First was signed into law in 2002. The grant funded program provided approved states with the funds necessary to "establish scientifically based reading programs for students enrolled in kindergarten through grade three." (Programs: Reading First, 2014)

Today the United States operates under "Race to the Top". Signed into law by President Barack Obama, Race to the Top (RTT) has proven to be a powerhouse in the early childhood education game. Since its inception in 2009 RTT has invested over $780 billion dollars in the American education system. That money, mostly funded through the American Recovery and Reinvestment Act, has been directed towards school reform and staff trainings. An additional $361 million was awarded to the Partnership for Assessment for Readiness for College and Careers (PARCC) for the creation of a national assessment to align with the new national standards. (Onosko, V 19) Under RTT the new primary goal of American education has evolved to create a generation of students who "read, compute, and possess other workplace skills to better serve the nation's economy." (Onosko, V 19) To achieve this goal RTT proposes increasing evaluation of teachers (relative to their student's assessment scores). In schools that show little or no progress one of several options will be considered: replace administrators and teachers in the poorly performing schools, morph the public schools into charter or private schools or close the schools entirely. (Ravitch, 2010)

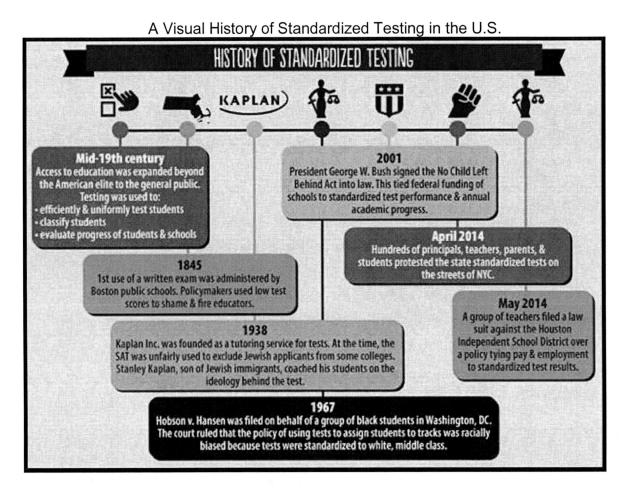

Common Core State Standards in Today's ECE Classrooms

Common Core State Standards were a result of former Governor Janet Napolitano who, in 2007, served as the chair of the National Governor's Association (NGA). (Bidwell, 2014) In tandem with the Council of Chief State School Officers (CCSSO), the NGA led the development of the first incarnation of Common Core. The original standards were first released to the public in September 2009 and formally presented less than a year later in June 2010. By June 2012 forty-six states, the District of Columbia, and several other U.S. territories had officially adopted Common Core. (Development, 2012)

What exactly are Common Core State Standards? In a nutshell, *Common Core State Standards (CCSS)* are a set of internationally benchmarked, K–12 academic standards for mathematics, English language arts and literacy designed to foster college and career readiness for American children. The standards were planned, developed and designed with the intent that "teachers from any part of the country can share ideas and (if students) move across state lines, they will have a smooth academic transition." (Golod, 2014) CCSS are grade specific standards and provide explicit direction regarding classroom content. CCSS do not include pedagogical directives. Critics who oppose the implementation of CCSS have argued that CCSS is a state funded, government led initiative. In fact, the ESEA prohibits the federal government from interfering in or directing state, public school curriculum. (Golod, Common Core: Myths and Facts, 2014) The Partnership for Assessment of Readiness for College and Careers (PARCC), operating with on a $170 million budget, with input from 26 states, has worked to develop an assessment tool to successfully align and measure the standards set forth by the CCSS document. (Andrew Porter, 2001)

The standards were based on many decades of research on student learning, best practice and assessment. CCSS authors consulted organizations such as Standards by Success, the American Diploma Project, American College Testing, the College Board exam and the Texas Higher Education Coordinating Board and the National Council of Teachers of Mathematics. Much of the research and development for CCSS was funded by the Bill and Melinda Gates Foundation. It is reported, as of publication of this chapter that the Gates Foundation has invested over $200 million dollars to the CCSS machine. (Strauss, 2014)

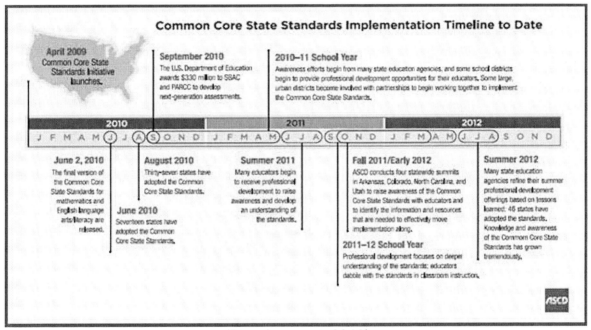

(Development, 2012)

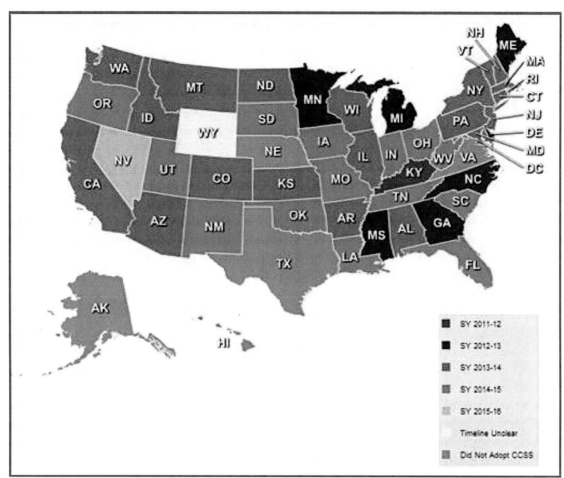

Figure 3: The map above depicts the timeline, by state, for Common Core State Standards implementation in the United States. To view a video presenting further explanation of Common Core State Standards click on the map above.

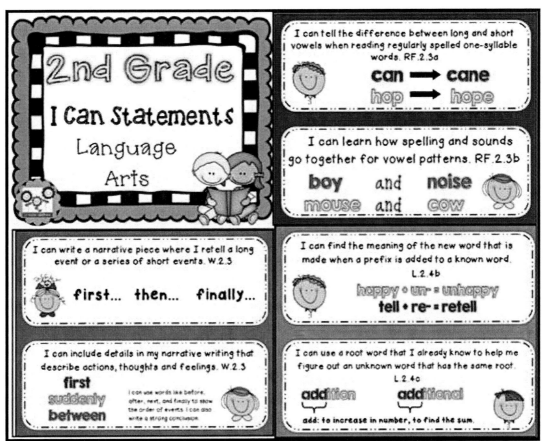

Figure 4: One characteristic of Common Core is the emphasis on Reading and Literacy. By ----, 70% of student reading must come from informational text. The image above is an example of a classroom poster, "2nd Grade I Can Statements", that is currently in use in classrooms throughout the country.

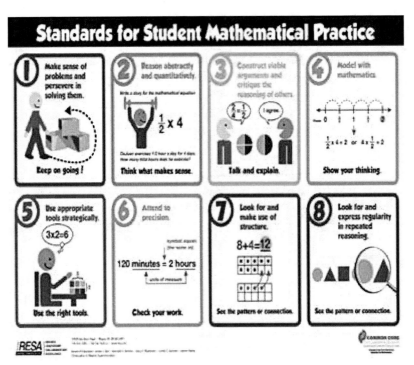

Figure 4: Much like the ELA standards, the Mathematical Practice standards for CCSS are focused on the content rather than the pedagogy. Above is an example of a student directed publication (For classroom use) to help students and parents better understand the expectations for the Math portion of Common Core.

Defining Intelligence

Much research has been done regarding the most effective definition of the term intelligence. Overall we can think of intelligence as being the basis of how a person executes efficient, accurate information processing. We know that intelligence is *adaptive* (it can be used flexibly across all situations and circumstances), is dependent on *prior knowledge* (the sum total of a student's previous experiences, interactions, activities both in and outside of the school environment) and is relative to culture. (Ormrod, Boston)

In general intelligence (IQ) is considered one of the most stable psychological attributes across the human lifespan. (Bergin, 2015) Some think of intelligence as the mere ability to perform on a given assessment; not applicable outside of the immediate setting. Linda Gottfredson compares the concept of intelligence to the concept of heat. She says "neither heat nor intelligence can be directly seen, touched or held. We nonetheless notice differences in both." (Gottfredson, Of what value is intelligence?, 2008) Other researchers have classified intelligence as a character trait. Normally character is thought of as a non-cognitive trait and intelligence is viewed as a cognitive trait. In fact, there is much support for the idea that a person's character is indeed connected to intelligence. (DeYoung, 2011) Stephan L. Jackson defines intelligence as the "property of the mind that encompasses many related abilities, such as the capacity to reason, to plan, to solve problems, to think abstractly, to comprehend ideas, to use language and to learn." (Jackson, 2008) This definition provides a broad, easily applied definition to the term that most anyone can understand.

Charles Spearman was the first to apply a psychometric, statistical approach to determine intelligence. (Richard H. Williams, 2003) Spearman proposed that intelligence consists of two parts: general factors and specific factors. Spearman called this the "*g factor*" (general factor). Spearman believed that "any cognitive performance (was) a function of two "factors" – the general ability common to most cognitive performances and an ability specific to a given test." (Richard H. Williams, 2003) General factors include aspects such as a person's pervasive reasoning ability. Specific factors are less broad and speak to the abilities needed for the completion of specific, individual tasks. (Ormrod, Boston) In short, Spearman proposed that all aspects of intelligence, to some extent, correlate with one another.

Others followed Spearman in an attempt to define intelligence. A statement published in a 1994 edition of Readers Digest began its definition of intelligence as "a very general mental capability that, among other things, involves the ability to reason, plan, solve problems, think abstractly, comprehend complex ideas, learn quickly and learn from experience." (Gottfredson, 1997) This definition was created, signed and supported by 52 unrelated, professors and experts in the field of education. Interestingly, this definition consisted of 24 separate statements on intelligence that, when taken in totality, comprise one of the most comprehensive definitions of the term in history. (Jackson, 2008) Like Spearman's definition of intelligence this definition emphasizes intelligence as an ability to solve problems in a variety of ways and purports that specific abilities related to intelligence are all interconnected.

For the purposes of this text we will define intelligence in the following manner: *Intelligence* is a complex and diverse orchestration of genetic predispositions and inherent personality traits that is dependent upon a multitude of environmental influences as it attempts to measure the intangible factors related to accuracy, speed and efficiency of one's ability to comprehend and problem solve. This definition takes into account all previous definitions of the term. It also attempts to present a definition of the term that can be widely applied in early childhood classrooms and by early childhood educators.

Types and Forms of Standardized Tests

The multitude of species and phylum that make up the current face of standardized testing is often misunderstood. What are the tests looking for? What kind of information will we glean about our students? In truth only a handful of actual differences exist within the standardized test world. According to the United States Congress, Office of Technology a *standardized test* is defined as a test that utilizes standardized procedures "for administration and scoring in order to assure that the results from different people are comparable." (Bond, 1996)

Currently, the *National Assessment of Educational Progress* (NAEP) is the largest and most widely utilized standardized test and nationally representative test. As of 2014 NAEP tests student learning in a number of diverse areas including math, reading and writing, science, the social sciences, the arts and technology. (Dogan, 2014) While NAEP is not traditionally administered in early childhood the test is administered nationally to monitors student achievement at key points in grades 4, 8 and 12. (Fields, 2014) NAEP utilizes a standardized test booklet and testing procedure throughout the country to ensure reliability and validity of test results. Additionally, NAEP does not yield individual student scores rather it provides "subject-matter achievement, instructional experiences, and school environment for populations of students (e.g., all fourth-graders) and groups within those populations (e.g., female students, Hispanic students)." (Gorman, 2010)

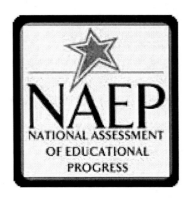

By clicking on the photo link to the left you can view sample math, science and social studies questions from the most recent 2015 NAEP.

Tests can be either criterion or norm referenced and utilize either summative or formative assessment techniques. *Norm referenced tests* are traditionally formatted to measure a students' performance to a group of his or her peers. (Morrow, 2012) Using a *standard bell curve* (the assignment of scores based on frequency of distribution) a student's score will be interpreted and the question "how does this student compare cognitively to peers of the same intellectual or developmental age?" will be answered. (Logsdon, 2014) We use the term 'bell curve' in response to the general curvature of shaper that is created when scored are plotted on a standard graph. As educators we refer to a curve as having a *normal distribution* when the height of the curve is concentrated in the center of the 'bell' and the sides evenly decrease on either side. (Russell)

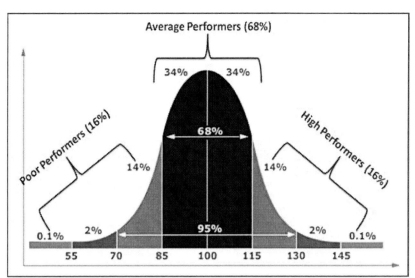

Figure 3: Above an image of what is considered a standard bell curve. The tallest portion of the diagram (the "bell") is indicative of the most people having an average score. The extreme ends of the diagram (2%) indicate those with extremes highs or lows regarding performance. (Vilet, 2014)

Criterion referenced tests are tests designed with the specific purpose of measuring student performance against a preset or predetermined standard (or criteria). Unlike a norm referenced test a student can effectively "pass" a criterion referenced test by meeting or exceeding the predetermined standards and criteria. Criterion referenced tests are the most widely utilized form of standardized test in the United States today. (Hidden curriculum, 2014)

Both standardized and criterion referenced tests can yield valuable information for educators and parents. Most standardized tests yield a score, or set of scores, that correlate with each other across a wide range of cognitive abilities such as intelligence, tests, vocabulary tests, analogies and proficiency exams. (Bergin, 2015) In addition to a traditional score most standardized tests give us information related to a student's grade equivalency, percentile rank and general intelligence quotient. *Grade equivalency* scores (G.E. scores) utilize a formula to translate the raw score generated from the standardized test instrument into a grade level score. *Percentile rank* compares the student's performance to those of all others who took the same test. (Morrow, 2012) Neither G.E. of percentile rank actually provides a measure of the student's true intelligence. For that we have to consider the definition of the term itself and examine how it can be measured.

Formative assessment is traditionally thought of as an ordinary, integral part of the classroom experience. Teachers administer tests and quizzes, assign writing prompts, ask questions, hold discussions, assess performances and grade projects all in an effort to gauge a students' progress and to direct future classroom instruction. (Lepi, 2014) Another way to think of a formative assessment is to think of it as a "pit stop" on a road trip; you are checking your route as you travel along instead of waiting until you get to the final stop. On the contrary, a *summative assessment* usually results in a final grade (i.e. – the assignment has a point value) and is administered at the end of an instructional period. Teachers use summative assessment to determine the level to which a student has mastered the content. This can take the form a final exam, a culminating project, a performance recital, a chapter test or final writing piece. (Lepi, 2014) Incorporating the travel scenario, with a summative assessment you won't check the progress of your route until you actually arrive at the end destination.

Regardless of the method of assessment utilized it is critically important that any classroom assessment is as authentic as possible. *Authentic assessment* is assessment that attempts to observe children in their normal routine without disrupting the learning process. (Knestrick, 2013) The main benefit of authentic assessment is that teachers can readily incorporate learning readiness, cultural sensitivity, learning disabilities and prior knowledge into the assessment process. (Rice, 2014) This can take the form of photographs, anecdotal records, teacher narratives, developmental checklists, journal writing samples, videotapes and portfolio assessments. Most early childhood educators find that they employ authentic assessment on a daily basis in their classrooms. The resulting information about a child allows for future planning and facilitation of learning activities and provides teachers with a holistic and accurate picture of a child's developmental path. (Rice, 2014)

Table 1. Traditional vs. Authentic Assessment Methods

Traditional Assessment	Authentic Assessment
Generally relies on forced-choice, written measures	Promotes integration of various written and performance measures
Relies on proxy measures of student learning to represent target skills	Relies on direct measures of target skills
Encourages memorization of correct answers	Encourages divergent thinking in generating possible answers
Goal is to measure acquisition of knowledge	Goal is to enhance development of meaningful skills
Curriculum directs assessment	Assessment directs curriculum
Emphasis on developing a body of knowledge	Emphasis on ensuring proficiency at real-world tasks
Promotes "what" knowledge	Promotes "how" knowledge
Provides a one-time snapshot of student understanding	Provides an examination of learning over time
Emphasizes competition	Emphasizes cooperation
Targets simplistic skills or tasks in a concrete, singular fashion	Prepares students for ambiguities and exceptions that are found in realistic problem settings
Priority on summative outcomes or product	Priority on the learning sequence or process

(Lombardi, 2008)

Additionally, teachers must ensure that any assessment tool they incorporate into the early childhood classroom is both reliable and valid. *Reliability* speaks the extent to which results are consistent and reproducible across the population. *Validity* speaks the extent to which a test measures what it is supposed to measure. (Ann S. Epstein, 2004) Many different aspects of validity have been identified – content validity, face validity, developmental validity, curricular validity and predictive validity. *Content validity* measures the relationship between the test questions and the content the test intended to assess. Basically, if a test has content validity one can administer the assessment with the knowledge that the test is actually measuring the content intended. (Shuttleworth, 2009) *Face validity* attempts to identify the relationship between the test and the purpose for administering the test. (McLeod, 2013) *Developmental validity* is defined as the ability of an item to be read, correctly and understood appropriately responded too by a child of the targeted test age. A test administered in an average kindergarten class should be written, developed, formatted and constructed for that audience. (Michael E. Woolley, 2004) *Curricular validity* measures the extent to which the content of the assessment matches the curricular and/or program goals it is intended to test. (Phillips, 1987) Regardless of the test chosen, the early childhood educator should feel confident that the test directly relates to and measures the curriculum of the classroom or program. *Predictive validity* speaks to an assessments ability to predict a student's future achievements. (Shuttleworth, 2009) The younger a child is the more difficult it will be to discern valid scores on any assessment. Research informs us that it is quite "difficult to assess children's cognitive abilities accurately before age 6". (Ann S. Epstein, 2004) Children may not always grasp the importance of assessment and their performance can often be influenced by emotional, motivational and physical conditions. It is because of this information that the issues of reliability and validity become so prominent the discussion of standardized testing.

> "Research demonstrates that no more than 25% of early academic or cognitive performance is predicted from information obtained from preschool or kindergarten tests." (Ann S. Epstein, 2004)

The Pros and Cons of Standardized Testing
(Standardized Tests ProCon.org, 2014)

Pros of Standardized Testing	Cons of Standardized Testing
Standardized tests are reliable and valid.	Teachers teach to the test.
Teaching to the test focuses learning on essential content and skills and eliminates time-wasting activities.	Valuable instructional time is used to administer the tests.
Common standards help ensure consistency among schools and regions.	States traditionally have set their own standards of "proficiency".
Testing generates much useful information for parents, teachers and school officials.	Delays in scoring and reporting prohibit teachers from utilizing the results in a timely manner.
The increased standards associated with testing are better preparing our students for college success.	Tests are inherently biased.
Someone must be held accountable for student learning and standardized tests do that.	Standardized tests fail to measure critical thinking, creativity and imagination.

Utilization of Standardized Assessment Results

Regardless of the form of standardized testing it is important that the data generated is used for the correct reasons. An early childhood educator can gain much rich, irreplaceable knowledge from the proper use of standardized test results. Research supports the fact that standardized assessments "systematically measure skills such as literacy and mathematics." (Ann S. Epstein, 2004) Further, standardized assessments allow us to assess our students in an efficient, valid, reliable manner. In general, most schools utilize standardized test data to determine how well a teacher and/or program is meeting the goals for the students. This isn't a bad use for test data. It is important to evaluate teachers, teaching pedagogy and curricular materials on a regular basis. The data gleaned from such a process can be directly used to identify what programs are lacking, what additional training needs exist for staff, where instruction and grouping can be tweaked and what materials to keep or restock. The second way assessment data can be utilized is to help identify students who are in need of specialized services. These students may need special education services or gifted/talented services.

Summary

The reality of education in America is that standardized testing does and will continue to exist. As educators we must evaluate our students, our programs, ourselves on a regular basis. It is in the best interest of the students we are charged with protecting and preparing that early childhood educators make it their task to be informed on all aspects of the assessment process. Whether in the form of No Child Left Behind, the current version of Common Core State Standards or another as of now unknown act it seems that we will always hold our teachers and their students accountable for achieving ever unobtainable proficiency levels. For the early childhood educator in the 21st century this means a shift in thinking; our training, our preparation, our teaching strategies, our knowledge of psychology and especially of student and program assessment.

References

Andrew Porter, J. M. (2001, April). Common Core Standards: The New U.S. Intended Curriculum. *Educational Researcher*, pp. 103-116.

Ann S. Epstein, L. J.-P. (2004, July). *Preschool assessment: A guide to developing a balanced approach*. Retrieved March 01, 2015, from National Institute for Early Education Research: www.nieer.org

Ansary, T. (2007, March 09). *Education at risk: Fallout from a flawed report*. Retrieved March 05, 2015, from edutopia: http://www.edutopia.org/landmark-education-report-nation-risk

Armstrong, T. (2006). Academic Achievement Discourse. *ASCD*.

Balf, T. (2014, March 06). *The Story Behind the SAT Overhaul*. Retrieved February 24, 2015, from The New York Times Magazine: http://www.nytimes.com/2014/03/09/magazine/the-story-behind-the-sat-overhaul.html?_r=0

Bergin, C. C. (2015). *Child and adolescent development in your classroom.* Australia: Cengage Learning.

Bidwell, A. (2014, February 27). *The History of Common Core State Standards.* Retrieved February 16, 2015, from U.S. News & World Report: http://www.usnews.com/news/special-reports/articles/2014/02/27/the-history-of-common-core-state-standards

Bond, L. A. (1996). Norm-and-criterion-referenced testing. *Practical Assessment, Research and Evaluation*, 1-4.

Cherry, K. (n.d.). *Alfred Binet Biography.* Retrieved March 01, 2015, from AboutEducation: http://psychology.about.com/od/profilesal/p/alfred-binet.htm

Collins, A. F. (1999). The enduring appeal of physiognomy: Physical appearance as a sign of temperament, character, and intelligence. *History of psychology*, 251-276.

Darragh, J. C. (2010). *Introduction to early childhood education: Equity and inclusion.* Boston: Pearson.

Development, A. o. (2012). Fulfilling the Promise of the Common Core State Standards: Moving from Adoption to Implementation to Sustainability. Alexandria, Virginia, United States.

DeYoung, C. G. (2011). Intelligence and personality. In R. J. Sternberg, *The Cambridge handbook of intelligence* (pp. 711-737). New York: Cambridge University Press.

Dogan, L. H. (2014). *National Assessment of Educational Progress (NAEP).* Retrieved April 01, 2015, from Encyclopedia of Quality of Life and Well-Being Research: http://link.springer.com/referenceworkentry/10.1007/978-94-007-0753-5_1899

Editors of Encyclopeadia Britannica. (2013, September 26). *Alfred Binet: French Psychologist.* Retrieved December 28, 2014, from Encyclopeadia Britannica: http://www.britannica.com/EBchecked/topic/65636/Alfred-Binet

Evans, J. (2013, November 04). *Problems with Standardized Testing.* Retrieved February 01, 2015, from Education.com: http://www.education.com/reference/article/Ref_Test_Problems_Seven/

Fields, R. (2014). *Towards The National Assessment of Educational Progress (NAEP) as an Indicator of Academic Preparedness for College and Job Training.* Washington, D.C.: National Governing Board.

Gladwell, M. (2001, December 17). *Examined Life: What Stanley H. Kaplan taught us about the S.A.T.'s.* Retrieved February 28, 2015, from The New Yorker: http://www.newyorker.com/magazine/2001/12/17/examined-life

Golod, A. (2014, March 04). *Common Core: Myths and Facts.* Retrieved February 16, 2015, from U.S. News and World Report: http://www.usnews.com/news/special-reports/a-guide-to-common-core/articles/2014/03/04

Gorman, S. (2010, August 03). *NAEP Overview.* Retrieved April 01, 2015, from National Center for Education Statistics: http://nces.ed.gov/nationsreportcard/about/

Gottfredson, L. S. (1997). *Mainstream Science on Intelligence: An Editorial with 52 Signatories, History and Bibliography.* Retrieved April 01, 2015, from University of Delaware: http://www.udel.edu/educ/gottfredson/reprints/1997mainstream.pdf

Gottfredson, L. S. (2008). *Of what value is intelligence?* Retrieved April 01, 2015, from University of Delaware: http://www.udel.edu/educ/gottfredson/reprints/2008WISC.pdf

Graham, E. (2013, April 25). *'A nation at risk' turns 30: Where did it take us?* Retrieved March 05, 2015, from neatoday: http://www.neatoday.org/2013/04/25/a-nation-at-risk-turns-30-where-did-it-take-us-2/

Hammond, D. (2014, April 05). *Are standardized tests necessary for college acceptance?* Retrieved March 02, 2015, from Live Declared: https://livedeclared.wordpress.com/2014/04/15/are-standardized-tests-necessary-for-college-acceptance/

Hidden curriculum. (2014, August 26). Retrieved February 03, 2015, from Education glossary: http:edglossary.org/hidden-curriculum

Jackson, S. L. (2008). *The FaQ: The Principles for Overcoming Adversity and Dealing Effectively with Life's Issues.* U.S.: LuLu.com.

Knestrick, J. (2013, July 10). *Early childhood assessment: 9 keys to effective practice.* Retrieved March 01, 2015, from Teach.Learn.Grow. The education blog: http:www.nwea.org/blog/2013/early-childhood-assessment-9-keys-to-effective-practice

Kohn, A. (2000, September 27). *Standardized Testing and It's Victims.* Retrieved December 22, 2014, from Education Week: http://www.alfiekohn.org/article/standardized-testing-victims/

L.S.A. University of Michigan. (n.d.). *Role of Intelligence Testing in Society: Alfred Binet.* Retrieved December 28, 2014, from U.M. Department of Psychology: http://sitemaker.umich.edu/356.loh/alfred_binet

Lepi, K. (2014, February 13). *The key differences between summative and formative assessments.* Retrieved February 03, 2015, from Edudemic: http://www.edudemic.com/summative-and-formative-assessments/

Logsdon, A. (2014, December 16). *Norm referenced tests – What are norm referenced tests?* Retrieved February 03, 2015, from AboutHealth: http://learningdisabilities.about.com/od/mo/g/normreferenced.htm

Lombardi, M. M. (2008, January). *Making the Grade: The Role of Assessment in Authentic Learning.* Retrieved April 01, 2015, from EduCause: http://net.educause.edu/ir/library/pdf/eli3019.pdf

Malespina, E. (2013, April 22). *My Thoughts on Standardized Testing.* Retrieved March 01, 2015, from http://www.elissamalespina.com/thoughts-on-technology---blog/my-thoughts-on-standardized-testing

McLeod, S. A. (2013). *What is validity?* Retrieved March 15, 2015, from Simply Psychology: http://www.simplypsychology.org/validity.html

Michael E. Woolley, G. L. (2004). Cognitive Pretesting and the Developmental Validity of Child Self-Report Instruments: Theory and Applications. *Research on Social Work Practice*, pp. 191-200.

Morrow, L. M. (2012). *Literacy development in the early years: Helping children read and write.* Boston: Pearson.

National Educational Association of the United States, C. o. (1894). *The Report of the Committee of Ten on Secondary School Studies.* New York: American Book Company.

O'Donnell, M. (1956). *The New Alice and Jerry Books Basic Readers, Reading Foundation Series: Here and There.* New York: Row, Peterson and Company.

Onosko, J. (V 19, N 2). Race to the top leaves children and future citizens behind: the devastating effects of centralization, standardization, and high stakes accountability. *Democracy and education*, pp. 1-11.

Ormrod, T. M. (Boston). *Child development and education.* 2013: Pearson.

P. Harris, J. H. (2012). Standardized tests do not effectively measure student achievement. *At Issue: Standardized testing*, 33-45.

Phillips, W. A. (1987, December). Sensitivity of Item Difficulties to Curricular Validity. *Journal of Educational Measurement*, pp. 357-370.

Popham, W. J. (2015, March 23). *Standardized Testing Fails the Exam.* Retrieved March 01, 2015, from What Works in Education: George Lucas Educational Foundation: http://www.edutopia.org/standardized-testing-evaluation-reform

Popham, W. J. (1999). Why Standardized Tests Don't Measure Educational Quality. *ASCD*, 8-15.

Programs: Early Reading First. (2014, June 12). Retrieved December 30, 2014, from U.S. Department of Education: http://www2.ed.gov/programs/earlyreading/index.html

Programs: Reading First. (2014, May 05). Retrieved December 30, 2014, from U.S. Department of Education: http://www2.ed.gov/programs/readingfirst/index.html

R. (n.d.). Charles Spearman: British behavioral scientist.

Ravitch, D. (2010, August 01). *Obama's Race to the Top will not improve education.* Retrieved March 05, 2015, from Huffington Post: http://www.huffingtonpost.com/diane-ravitch/obamas-race-to-the-top-wi_b_666598.html

Rice, M. R. (2014, November 05). *What can we learn from children's play? Using authentic assessment in the early childhood classroom.* Retrieved February 03, 2015, from Virginia Department of Education's Training & Technical Assistance Center: http://www.ttacnews.vcu.edu/2014/11/what-can-we-learn-from-childrens-play-using-authentic-assessment-in-the-early-childhood-classroom

Richard H. Williams, D. W. (2003, March 12). Charles Spearman: British Behavioral Scientist. *Human Nature Review*, pp. 114-118.

Russell, D. (n.d.). *Bell Curve, Normal Distribution Defined.* Retrieved April 01, 2015, from About Education: http://math.about.com/od/glossaryofterms/g/Bell-Curve-Normal-Distribution-Defined.htm

Shuttleworth, M. (2009, November 08). *Types of Validity.* Retrieved March 15, 2015, from Explorable.com: https://explorable.com/types-of-validity

Standardized Tests ProCon.org. (2014, July 03). Retrieved January 03, 2015, from Procon.org: http://standardizedtests.procon.org/

Steele, C. M. (1997). A threat in the air: How stereotypes shape intellectual identity and performance. *American Psychological Association*, 613-629.

Strauss, V. (2014, January 18). *Everything you need to know about Common Core.* Retrieved February 14, 2015, from The Washington Post: http://www.washingtonpost.com/blogs/answer-sheet/wp/2014/01/18/everything-you-need-to-know-about-common-core-ravitch/

U.S. Department of Education. (2002). *THE NO CHILD LEFT BEHIND ACT OF 2001.* Washington, D.C.: U.S. Department of Education.

Unknown. (n.d.). *History.* Retrieved February 24, 2015, from Kaplan: http://www.kaplan.com/about-kaplan/history/

Unknown. (2014, November 03). *Race and Intelligence: 'The Bell Curve' 20 Years Later.* Retrieved March 11, 2015, from Haunted files at A/P/A: http://www.nyu-apastudies.org/hauntedfiles/tag/intelligence-testing-2/

Vilet, J. (2014, April 08). Ding! Dong! The Wicked Bell Curve is Dead!